A Seventeenth-Century
Letter-Book

A Seventeenth-Century Letter-Book

A Facsimile Edition of Folger MS. V.a. 321

with Transcript, Annotation, and Commentary
by
A. R. Braunmuller

Newark: University of Delaware Press
London and Toronto: Associated University Presses

Associated University Presses, Inc.
440 Forsgate Drive
Cranbury, N.J. 08512

Associated University Presses Ltd
25 Sicilian Avenue
London WC1A 2QH, England

Associated University Presses
2133 Royal Windsor Drive
Unit 1
Mississauga, Ontario
Canada L5J 1K5

Library of Congress Cataloging in Publication Data

Folger Shakespeare Library. Manuscript. V.a. 321.
  A seventeenth-century letter-book.

  Bibliography: p.
  Includes index.
  1. English letters—Early modern, 1500–1700—
Manuscripts—Facsimiles.   2. Manuscripts, English—
Facsimiles.   3. Authors, English—Early modern,
1500–1700—Correspondence.   4. Great Britain—
History—Elizabeth, 1558–1603—Sources.   5. Great
Britain—History—James I, 1603–1625—Sources.
I. Braunmuller, A. R., 1945–   . II. Title.
III. Title: 17th-century letter-book.
PR1344.F64   1983   826'.3'08   81-50652
ISBN 0-87413-201-0

Printed in the United States of America

*The editor dedicates his work
to E.S.B. and the memory of A.R.B.*

Contents

Preface

Today, a private individual's written records tend to be carefully separated by function. Financial records (commercial and personal), diary or journal, copies of business letters, copies or notes of personal letters, memoranda of engagements, and so forth all exist independently, often in books, files, or other physical compartments devoted to a single class of material. In the sixteenth and early seventeenth centuries, however, the scarcity and cost of paper and the novelty of the act of writing made such a separation unlikely in theory and virtually unexampled in practice. Instead of separating these written records, the writer tended to combine them into a single document or series of related documents, according to ideas of order very different from those which govern comparable modern collections. Consequently, large and overlapping groups of written records survive that have been called commonplace books, miscellanies, and letter-books. The first two categories are hardest to distinguish, and the taxonomy is perhaps not very helpful; A. G. Rigg describes commonplace books as "collections of miscellaneous material assembled simply for the interest and amusement of the compiler" (*A Glastonbury Miscellany of the Fifteenth Century* [Oxford: At the University Press, 1968], p. 24). While the miscellany continued as a very general compilation, the commonplace book gradually developed into a grouping of useful snippets that the collector might eventually incorporate into private letters or speeches; sometimes the compiler arranged his commonplace book by subject, like a thesaurus or anthology or florilegium.

Strictly defined, a letter-book would probably contain copies of the writer's own letters and perhaps the originals (or copies) of responses to them. The best-known sixteenth-century example belonged to Edmund Spenser's friend Gabriel Harvey, but it mingles letters with draft poetry and prose, lecture notes, and the like. Even the so-called letters in this document may in fact have been embryonic essays rather than private communications between two individuals. A less sophisticated letter-book like the one kept by John Conybeare (from the period 1579–94) includes copies of his personal correspondence, copies of letters written for his illiterate neighbors, academic exercises, sporadic lists of Latin adages, and much else. Conybeare was a rural schoolmaster, but an urban letter-writer would be apt (on the evidence) to add several other kinds of material to his letter-book. He might note major political,

9

military, or diplomatic events, often in narrative form; he would copy out famous letters or similar documents by famous letter-writers (for example, Burghley's advice to his son, or Sidney's letter on the uses of foreign travel). These famous letters were preserved not just as examples of art or morality, but as potential aids in writing one's own letters. The letter-book thus became a formulary, and sometimes included model letters for various occasions (condolence or congratulation, for instance) and examples of common legal documents (warrants, commissions, and so on). The collection could then serve as a guide should the compiler ever need to compose (or draft for someone else) such a letter or need to recognize a bona fide legal document (forgeries were common).

The fact that the Folger letter-book contains copies and not original documents in the identifiable handwriting of the supposed writers deserves a preliminary explanation. The practice of drafting personal letters as well as official or business communications was much more common in the Elizabethan period than it is now; even educated writers tended to dictate letters to a professional scribe or secretary. Speech, for so long the dominant medium, gave way slowly before the written symbol. Copies were also made for the sender's information, or even by a third party who had some indirect interest in the sender, the addressee, or the subject of the letter. Finally, the form that was soon to be recognized as the essay owes a great deal to the letter (see M. B. Hansche, "The Formative Period of English Familiar Letter-writers and Their Contribution to the English Essay," Ph.D. diss., University of Pennsylvania, 1902). Thus, many documents that appear to be letters may never have been sent as a private communication between two individuals; they may well have been designed either for printed publication or for manuscript circulation and recopying into letter-books like Folger MS. V.a. 321.

In offering this edition of a valuable and fascinating manuscript, I feel very deeply not only the debts recorded in my acknowledgments, but also the responsibility for presenting an accurate text, usefully annotated. For the errors that undoubtedly remain in the transcript, the reader has my apologies and a true copy in the manuscript facsimile.

Acknowledgments

Many individuals and organizations have helped me in preparing this edition. At the Folger Shakespeare Library, the director, O. B. Hardison, Jr., originally suggested that I investigate the manuscript, and the Library graciously permitted it to be reproduced. Many present and former Folger staff members assisted me; I learned much from Megan Lloyd, Sandy Powers, Lily Stone, Laetitia Yeandle, Giles Dawson, and Richard Schoeck. Paul Kristeller and Richard Proudfoot, two visiting Folger scholars, offered crucial hints and objections when I was struggling to learn about the manuscript's composition and origins. At the British Library (or British Museum, as it was called for most of the time I worked on this project), the staffs of the North Library and the Students' Room of the Department of Manuscripts were diligent, helpful, and very understanding. The staff of the Public Record Office, London, patiently taught me to use that splendid treasury. The staff and collections of the Huntington Library have proved a constant blessing.

In tracing the manuscript's history and collateral relatives, I received help from: William McIntyre and J. S. English, respectively clerk of the council and librarian, Gainsborough, Lincolnshire; C. P. C. Johnson, assistant archivist of the Lincolnshire Records Office; Eileen Simpson of the Cheshire Record Office; Annette M. Kennett, city archivist of Chester; Shelagh Bond, hon. archivist, St. George's Chapel, Windsor Castle; the registrar of the Charterhouse; J. Coburn, deputy head archivist, Greater London Record Office; Dudley Massey of Pickering and Chatto, Ltd.

Individuals who answered my often ill-informed questions include G. P. V. Akrigg, Steven L. Bates, William J. Bouwsma, Elizabeth Read Foster, G. K. Hunter, the late Joel Hurstfield, C. H. Josten, William Keach, Carol Lanham, Richard Lanham, Pierre Lefranc, Gail Kern Paster, and C. E. Wright. Robert Dent read and improved many parts of the edition, and J. A. Leo Lemay provided both practical and spiritual support. Theodora Poloynis helped check the edition, and Edith Lufkin typed portions of the transcript. Throughout the time I worked on the manuscript, Leonard Barkan, Lee Bliss, and the late Richard S. Sylvester remained true friends and thoughtful critics.

I should also like to thank the National Endowment for the Humanities, the Folger Shakespeare Library, and the Research Committee of the Academic Senate of the University of California, Los Angeles, for their generous financial support.

A Seventeenth-Century
Letter-Book

1

The Manuscript

The manuscript has ninety-five folios with the following watermarks: a pot with the initials AV (Heawood 3561); golden fleece (Briquet 2291; Heawood 481); fleur-de-lis (Heawood 1721A; cf. 1768) and two popular sixteenth-century French watermarks belonging to the large classes of grapes and of pillars that have not been further identified.[1] Folios 1–31 and 77–95 have been cropped and are of approximately the same size (14.0 by 20.4 cm); folios 32–76 are slightly smaller (13.8 by 19.6 cm) and do not appear to have been cropped. Most of the folios have been mounted. Of the ninety-five folios, seventeen sides are blank (ff. 68v, 69r-v, 70v, 71–76, and 89v); two scribes have written on the remaining 173 pages. One scribe (hand A) has written, in both secretary and italic hands, all but part of ff. 65r and 67r and 65v, 67v–68r, 70r, and 95v; these folios are the work of a second scribe (hand B) and are entirely in the secretary hand except for part of f. 70r (in italic), which cannot be confidently assigned to either scribe, but probably represents hand B's italic script.

Evidence provided by the pot watermark indicates that some of the manuscript, at least, can date from little earlier than ca. 1600. Three occurrences of what appears to be paper with the same watermark may be mentioned: Folger MS. V.b. 187, an abstract of judicial examinations connected with Essex's rebellion, dated 18 March 1601; an apparently uncropped sheet (40.4 by 30.4 cm) in the Folger watermark collection containing a document dated 6 June 1600; the paper in some copies of Sir Clement Edmondes, *Observations vpon . . . Caesars Commentaries* (1600; STC 7488) entered for publication on 7 February 1600.[2] The handwriting, the manuscript's physical makeup, and internal evidence of the documents themselves also indicate the last years of the sixteenth century and/or the first thirteen or fourteen years of the seventeenth as the likeliest period of the manuscript's writing.[3] The Folger Library rebound the manuscript in 1949; prior to that time it was bound in marbled boards of eighteenth-century origin. All leaves but four (ff. 59, 60, 86, and 87, which form, respectively, two half sheets) have been mounted and the original stubs destroyed.

COLLATION, ORDER OF COMPOSITION, EARLIER BINDING AND ARRANGEMENT

Through earlier loss of important evidence, a full collation for the manuscript is now impossible; matters of both the manuscript's physical makeup and
its chronology of composition are complex enough to make a gathering-by-
gathering discussion the most concise. The general structure of MS. V.a. 321
seems to have been quarto foldings in gatherings of twenty: several such complete or nearly complete gatherings still exist, and the remaining evidence (with
the exception of the highly anomalous fifth gathering, quarto in eight and
almost entirely blank) can be reconciled with an original organization of this
sort.

The first "gathering" is not really a gathering at all, because the first six folios
were disjunct when the manuscript arrived at the Folger; these leaves may
belong with what is called the second gathering below, though that now has a
convincing integrity of its own. These first six leaves had their present order
when written, however, because the text runs without a break through the
group and because an ink flourish at the end of line 3 on f. 4r continues in the
margin of f. 5r (near "libertie," line 3) and most of the e that ends "yeelde" (f.
4r, line 6) may be seen in the margin of f. 5r opposite "Th'erle." The AV pot
watermark indicates that ff. 1 and 6 were originally conjugate, as were 2 and 5.
(The watermarks are clearly "twins.") The evidence of the flourish and e that
run over the edge of f. 4r indicates that ff. 3 and 4 were probably conjugate as
well. This evidence may suggest an original quarto gathering in eight with a
title page and/or wrapper discarded at some stage, perhaps during some form
of stabbing or sewing. The text does not connect f. 6v with f. 7r, which begins
the second gathering.

After f. 8 in the second gathering, an incomplete quarto fold (a stub and
three leaves) has been inserted not into the gathering proper, but into its "side."
Thus the collation at this point seems to be: 8:29, stub:11, 9:10, 12:28; it then
runs regularly (with a single cancel) to f. 31, which is conjugate with a stub
before f. 7. Although no disturbance of the text can be seen in this area, the
scribe does seem to be organizing his material chronologically. It may be that
he found, before completing this gathering, that he had omitted Cecil's speech
(now ff. 9v–11r) between Howard's letter and Ashton's defense. Or, of course,
Cecil's text may only later have come into the scribe's hands. By canceling the
half sheet that originally completed the fold and included the present ff. 12 and
28, the scribe could insert a quarto fold of three leaves (ff. 9, 10, 11) that would
have enough space for Cecil's speech as well as allowing him space to recopy
the conclusion of Howard's letter and the first side of Ashton's defense (now
ff. 9r and 11v, respectively) from the canceled half sheet. He would thereby
maintain his order as well as cause the least disruption to the gathering's latter
end; he would have remaining a blank leaf (without watermark, part of the
inserted AV pot sheet) and a half sheet (also without watermark, part of the

present ff. 12 and 28 sheet that shows the golden fleece watermark) consisting of a blank leaf and a canceled leaf with the end of Howard's letter and the beginning of Ashton's defense.

This hypothesis explains the present watermarks' evidence, which, ignoring the inserted quarto fold, places an evidently complete AV pot fold beside a half sheet of paper with a complete golden fleece watermark. Two further assumptions must be made: (1) the scribe discovered his error, or received new material, after (a) he finished writing the present gathering (at least to f. 30) and / or (b) the gathering had been joined together in some way that made this insertion more feasible than the introduction of an entire new fold into the gathering; (2) the scribe's paper stock mixed AV pot with golden fleece marks fairly randomly. Assumption (2) is quite probable: two sheets of fleur-de-lis paper appear in this gathering, though one might have expected the insert to be an intrusion of golden fleece into a pattern of AV pots. The first assumption, especially (a), may seem less likely, but my hypothesis saves the scribe work (presumably his own goal) and avoids introducing four blank sides, perhaps interrupting another item already written, late in the gathering. Moreover, while the scribe might easily judge the length required for Cecil's speech, he might not be sure of finding new material exactly suited to the two leaves that would appear between the present ff. 28 and 29 were he to insert the new fold "properly" into the gathering. He seems to have had some trouble in this area as well, since f. 13 is a stubbed leaf, probably part of the sheet containing ff. 14 and 27. Either plan leaves the scribe with the same amount of loose paper, but it may be that economy mattered less than consistent (i.e., chronological) organization at this point. The present f. 31, without watermark, is conjugate with a stub formerly before f. 7 and shows no obvious relation with other sheets or leaves in the gathering.

In many respects, the third and fourth gatherings are bibliographically the most consistent in the manuscript. Both are quarto foldings in twenty, both have pages of markedly smaller size than those in the rest of the manuscript, and the handwriting, though mostly hand A, also includes several examples of secretary hand B. Differences in size and speed distinguish hand A's appearance here from elsewhere in the manuscript.

These gatherings have been in their present position for some time, and their leaves have been smaller than others in the manuscript for some time as well. Folio 31v has discoloration around its margins that outlines the area f. 32 covers when the leaves are turned; similarly, f. 77r shows discoloration around the area covered by f. 76 (part of the fifth gathering, which has the smaller page size and several other features of the third and fourth gatherings). In no other place in the manuscript can similar discoloration be seen; thus it may be that during much of its dirt-collecting existence (i.e., at least prior to binding in the eighteenth century or after that binding had begun to deteriorate), the manuscript had substantially its present order. Moreover, the sheets making up these gatherings seem to have been smaller than their fellows for some time as well, and this difference may not be attributed solely to cropping for the binder's purposes, since many of the edges, especially the lower ones, are very uneven.

Finally, the most recent of the datable material appears in these pages as well as all but two of the second scribe's contributions. The first scribe writes larger and (it would appear) more hastily, with a broader pen more prone to blotting in these gatherings, than in those before or after. This observation suggests that the two large portions of the text (gatherings one, two, five, and six vs. three and four) were written at different times with different equipment, though largely by the same scribe. Possibly gatherings three and four may be later (say, three or four years) than the other gatherings. Some of the variation in the appearance of these gatherings as compared with the remainder may also be due to differences of paper: all the paper with the grape watermark and all but four sheets with the golden fleece mark appear in these two gatherings, while they contain no pots, no fleurs-de-lis, and no pillars.

The curious fifth gathering, having paper with a watermark that appears nowhere else in the manuscript and consisting entirely of blank leaves except for a single side written by the second scribe (B), has been mentioned above. On the evidence of paper discoloration, it has had its present position for quite a while, but it seems hard to believe that its present position represents anything like its place in the order of writing. One would like to think that the manuscript had passed conclusively from the hands of scribe A to those of scribe B; unfortunately, since B's work on one occasion appears sandwiched between items written by A, this pretty hope requires the further hypothesis that B dropped back to fill in blank areas before striking off on his own (rather unsatisfactorily, if the unfinished item in this gathering means anything).

The sixth gathering returns to the quarto-in-twenty pattern seen in the third and fourth gatherings. Although f. 83 is conjugate with a stub before f. 90, textual links with ff. 82 and 84 make any movement unlikely; certainty is impossible because f. 89v is blank, perhaps to mark a division in the material.

Evidence of earlier binding and arrangement of the manuscript is intriguing but inconclusive. Folio 49, for example, is in poor condition and much less well preserved than those around it. Since it is conjugate with a stub formerly before f. 32 and the text breaks between ff. 31 and 32, f. 49 could once have been elsewhere in the manuscript. The eruption of blanks and of hand B in ff. 69–76 forms the fifth gathering and may have been inserted in an earlier system that moved directly from the present third and fourth gatherings to the present sixth gathering. The single unfinished document in these folios is also, arguably, the latest in the manuscript. The paper discoloration already mentioned shows, however, that the manuscript here has had its present order for some time.

Scribe A rarely divides one item from another when two or more appear on the same side; when he does, he tends to use a single line drawn across the page. On some folios showing hand B, however, a curious narrow-lozenge design, perhaps superimposed on a single line, divides items. Possibly it was meant to call attention to hand B's work in the midst of A's. It is possible that scribe B filled in blank spaces in A's work and then began on his own (i.e., with the present f. 70). This hypothesis assumes that a later binding has interrupted an originally continuous movement from the present f. 68 to f. 77. It does not explain why A should have left gaps on ff. 65, 67, and 68 and then used all, or nearly all, the space to f. 95r, leaving B to fill in the gaps, write on f. 95v and, presumably, then begin on the present fifth gathering. The absence of textual links among most gatherings theoretically permits a great deal of movement, but no rearrangement plausibly explains the scribes' intertwined contributions while simultaneously restoring a chronological order or an obvious organization of some other sort (e.g., by subject matter or type of document).

Finally, some stab marks suggest that certain gatherings, most clearly three and four, were joined in that fashion before being sewn. Some punctuation marks at the gutter edge of the verso leaves in the fourth gathering appear beneath the last letter in a given line (e.g., the comma under "vniust" at f. 57v, line 98). This situation implies that the sheets were fastened together in some way before the scribe wrote on them. On ff. 55, 57, and 59, such punctuation beneath the line occurs beside a stab mark. Whoever prepared the paper for writing often followed the common practice of creasing the loose sheets to form at least the inner text margin; such folds are especially clear on the rectos of many folios.

HANDWRITING AND DATE

Hand A is a very clear, professional or near-professional secretary hand; most scriveners and lawyers of the period could probably write very like it when not in a hurry. The fact that Thomas Kyd, whose father was a scrivener and who may himself have been trained for that profession, and Mr. Serjeant Yelverton both write a hand quite like A indicates how neutral and unindividualized it is.[4] Certain unusual features exist: the capital *A*, the absence of either "epsilon" or "*r*-type" *es*, for example. Hand A's italic is very fine, almost equaling in quality if not in size the work of a professional calligrapher such as Peter Bales. Generally, though, hand A is too common, in a sense too perfect, to help very much with identification. Hand B, contributing very little to the manuscript, has many more distinctive features, though it, too, remains unidentified. B suggests the work of a writer well educated, but not professionally concerned with writing per se; perhaps the often shaky ascenders and the frequent mendings, partial erasures, and corrections indicate an older writer. One is tempted to hypothesize that the writer of B commissioned a professional (A) to copy items, and that the owner of B sometimes intervened. Such speculation has little value when neither hand can be identified. At present, the judgment of Giles Dawson and Laetitia Yeandle on item 59 may describe, slightly qualified, the entire manuscript:

At first sight this hand might seem to have been written about the time of the original letter [1587]. But the restrained and controlled ascenders and descenders, though they are occasionally found much earlier, are more characteristic of the first decades of the seventeenth century.[5]

Evidence examined below in the discussion of possible compilers might indicate compilation before 1614.

MODERN HISTORY, PROVENANCE, PUBLICATION OF EXTRACTS

The first modern mention of MS. V.a. 321 occurred in several articles written by Bertram Dobell for *The Athenaeum*, vol. 74, pt. 1 (23 and 30 March, 6 and 13 April, 1901). Chatto and Pickering, London booksellers, published soon afterward "A List of Old and Rare Books, Illuminated Manuscripts, and Specimens of Old and Modern Bindings . . . offered For Sale in New York, by Thomas Chatto" that includes item 304, "Elizabethan Dramatists, &c.—A Volume of Manuscript, containing Transcripts of Signed letters by Ben Jonson . . . 1580–1610. Small 4°, *a neatly written contemporary MS. . . .*" (pp. 49–50). Despite some inaccuracies in the description, the identity of this volume with the Folger manuscript is assured by the penciled notations on the fly-leaf, in the new owner's hand, "W. A. White   Nov 16 1901" and "of Chatto, in N.Y." After a very terse entry in H. C. Bartlett's first catalogue of the White collection,[6] the manuscript disappears until listed by Dr. A. S. W. Rosenbach in 1941.[7] Edwin Wolf has described the way in which the Folger acquired the manuscript through the generosity of Arthur Houghton and Rosenbach himself.[8] Aside from White's note and several notes (both typewritten and handwritten) of the manuscript's contents by Giles Dawson, only one other evidently modern mark has been made in the manuscript: a short ink description of the document as concerning Essex and being "temp Q. Elizabeth," written in a nineteenth-century hand, probably by Thomas Chatto.[9]

Dobell's articles, concentrating on Chapman and Jonson, offer the largest body of transcripts previously available; E. K. Chambers's references in *The Elizabethan Stage* derive from Dobell's inaccurate and partial selection. C. H. Herford and P. Simpson examined the Jonson items when White owned the manuscript; their results appear in their edition of Jonson's work. Some use has been made of the manuscript in connection with *Eastward Ho!*, and S. G. Culliford reprints most of the Strachey material in his biography.[10] Single items and references appear in other scholarly works on Chapman and Jonson.[11]

2

This Edition

IDENTIFICATION OF ITEMS

The vast majority of the documents copied in MS. V.a. 321 are letters, some so brief that three appear on the same folio side. Since many of these letters lack any note of the date, sender, or addressee and since other documents offer even less information for easy reference, it has seemed best simply to number the items in sequence through the manuscript. Occasionally, editorial judgments have been made on what constitutes a separate item; the most common problem arises when one letter seems to "enclose" (i.e., be meant to accompany) another or when the text moves repeatedly between direct and indirect discourse. When referring to separate items, I have sometimes categorized them (e.g., "letter," "petition," "warrant") in order to suggest their evidential value. The reader must remember, however, that any reference such as "letter, 58" or "petition, 66" does not imply that the first item is the fifty-eighth letter or the second the sixty-sixth petition. All documents are numbered in a single sequence (1 to 140); identification beyond the item's number is explanatory and does not indicate a place in any other series. Above the transcript of each item, enclosed within square brackets, is the number of that item and its original date, if known or explicit within the text itself. Inferred dates have been made as specific as possible, and this aim of exactitude has forced such cumbersome and perhaps inelegant designations as "after 4 May 1605; ca. mid-1605(?)." At the head of some items, the phrase "see Commentary" also appears, referring the reader to the section that follows the entire transcript and offers evidence for the date and other details that require explanation.

ANNOTATION

Editorial additions to the text-transcription consist of two kinds: those described as "annotations" and those collected in the Commentary. In the annotation section, identified by a line number and a lemma in a font opposite its original, are brief entries on special paleographic signs, difficult readings, proper names, places, dates, and significant details of public and private events mentioned in the text. In cases of possible confusion (e.g., when two complete items appear on the same page), the line numbers and lemmata have been preceded by the bracketed number of the item referred to. More discursive commentary on selected items, as well as detailed evidence for suggested dates, senders, addressees, and so on, appears in the Commentary.

Throughout the editorial apparatus, proper names appear in the form adopted by the *Dictionary of National Biography,* or if not there recorded, in their most common modern form. English books printed before 1700 are cited by date of publication and the appropriate entry number or numbers from the short-title catalogues by Pollard and Redgrave and Wing, cited as "STC" and "Wing," respectively. Place of publication for all books mentioned is London unless otherwise noted. In citing early printed materials, I have followed the spelling (except long *s*), but not the typography of the originals; manuscript sources are transcribed on the principles established for this edition. Unless otherwise indicated, classical authors are cited from the appropriate Loeb edition. The King James translation of the Bible is cited unless otherwise noted.

TRANSCRIPTIONAL PRINCIPLES

The hands of the manuscript are generally easy to read. In deciding upon principles of transcription, the editor has had to compromise among the various sorts that different groups of readers might find most satisfactory. Since this edition is intended to serve the needs of students of paleography as well as of various linguistic conventions, a completely modernized text (the other extreme from a type facsimile) would be inappropriate. The following conventions are not entirely consistent with one another, but the editor hopes to have walked the narrow path between destroying the individuality of the hands and producing a type transcription that is as difficult to read as the facsimile of the original.

In general, the writers of MS. V.a. 321 use (or misuse) few of the common medieval conventions developed for writing Latin. For convenience, most raised letters have been lowered and all but the commonest abbreviations expanded. Abbreviations and their expanded forms appear in a table below and will not be mentioned in the annotations of separate items. Several symbols require special remark. The writers use the symbol (a raised *r*-like sign) to indicate omission of a vowel before a terminal (and occasionally medial) *r*. Many times a perfectly conventional usage will appear: o^r and yor for "our" and "your," respectively; other times, however, one finds hono^r and favo^r, although when the writer chooses to spell the words in full they usually appear as "honor" and "favour," respectively. Consequently, the editor has taken the liberty of expanding the raised *r* as either "ur" or "r," as the conventional full spellings of the manuscript indicate the writer's preference. In such cases as "La:" (for "Lady" or "Ladie"), where the manuscript's writers make no clear choice between several possible full spellings, the modern one has been used for the expansion. The cursive downward loop ($\boldsymbol{\ell}$) at the ends of words or syllables has been transcribed as "es" rather than simply "s" since the writers frequently employ the more standard letter for a terminal s ($\boldsymbol{\sigma}$). The tittle over a letter indicating omission of a nasal has been silently expanded.

Other signs expanded without note include: the crossed p for "per," "par," or "pro"; the crossed s for "ser"; the variety of a tittle formed by continuing the last stroke of a terminal letter in a word or syllable upwards and backwards to indicate several different contractions; the extreme contraction represented by the tittle in such a word as "l$\overline{\text{re}}$s" for "letteres"; the suspended a for "au."

The long s has been reduced to the modern form, but u/v and i/j have not been normalized. Capitalization and punctuation have been reproduced as accurately as possible. Capitals are often especially doubtful, since only difference in size, requiring editorial judgment, distinguished between the lower and upper case forms of many letters. Initial $f\!f$- has been transcribed as F-. The writers usually mark their standard abbreviations with some punctuation (e.g., M.^{r} or Matie), and their mark has been retained for unexpanded abbreviations; in those cases lacking any such punctuation, none has been added. The symbol that resembles a modern question mark tipped slightly to one side, used by the writers to signal both interrogation and exclamation, has been transcribed by "?" alone. Variations in the margins have not been echoed in the transcript, though slight attempts to indicate spacing on the page have been made. A few items appear entirely in italic script, and many of the "signatures" (full names or initials) to letters otherwise written in the secretary hand also are in italic. The first of these uses of italic has not been signaled in the transcript. All other obvious choices of italic (e.g., place names, signatures, or phrases in foreign languages) have been transcribed as italic. Various forms of the ampersand and abbreviations for *et cetera* have been reduced to "&" and "&c.," respectively. Material inserted above or below the line of text has been enclosed within plus signs (+ +) and deleted material when it can be read, or ellipses when it cannot, within broken brackets (⟨ ⟩).

Abbreviations Expanded without Special Note

Sign	*Transcription*
Capt $\backsim$	Captain
-con $\supset$	-cion
compl	complainant, complainants
Eng $^{)}$	England
$\boldsymbol{\ell}$	-es
Esq	Esquier
favo^{r}	favour
gent	gentleman
hono^{r}	honor

ho:	honor, honors, honored, honorable
La:	Lady, Ladyship
l$\bar{r}$e, l$\bar{r}$es	lettere, letteres
Ld, Lo	Lord, Lords, Lordshippe
L^{ppe}, L^{ppes}, Lo^{p}	Lordshippe, Lordshippes, Lordshippe
Matie, Maties	Maiestie, Maiesties
o^{r}	our
-m^{t}	-ment
∮	-pro-, -par-, -per-
S^{r}	Sir
suppl	suppliant
-ω-	-uer-
yor	your

Unexpanded Abbreviations

D^{r}	for	Doctor	transcribed as	Dr.
M^{r}		Master		Mr.
M^{rs}		Mistress(e)		Mrs.
w^{ch}		which		wch
wth		with		wth
y^{t}		that		yt

Abbreviations and Short-Title List

abbrev.	abbreviation
Add.	Additional MSS, British Library, London
APC	*Acts of the Privy Council*, ed. J. R. Dasent (1890–1907); volumes cited by years calendared
Birch, *Mem. Eliz.*	Thomas Birch, *Memoirs of the Reign of Queen Elizabeth*, 2 vols. (London: Millar, 1754)
B.L.	British Library, London

Cal SP Dom
    Ireland
    Scotland
    Ven
	Calendar of State Papers, Domestic series, Irish series, Scottish series, Venetian series, respectively; individual volumes distinguished by the year(s) calendared

Chamberlain, *Letters*	N. E. McClure, ed., *The Letters of John Chamberlain*, American Philosophical Society Memoirs, vol. 12, parts 1 and 2, 2 vols. (Philadelphia: American Philosophical Society, 1939)
Chambers, *Eliz. Stage*	E. K. Chambers, *The Elizabethan Stage*, 4 vols. (Oxford: Clarendon Press, 1923)

Chapman, *Poems*	P. B. Bartlett, ed., *The Poems of George Chapman* (New York: Modern Language Association, 1941)
Cheyney, *Hist. England*	Philip Cheyney, *A History of England: From the Defeat of the Armada to the Death of Elizabeth,* 2 vols. (1926; Reprint. New York: Peter Smith, 1948)
Collins, *Letters*	Arthur Collins, comp., *Letters and Memorials of State* . . . 2 vols. (London: Osborne, 1746)
Complete Peerage	G[eorge] E[dward] C[okayne], *The Complete Peerage,* rev. ed. V. Gibbs, et al., 13 vols. (London: St. Catherine Press, 1910–59)
conj.	conjecture
Cot.	Cotton MSS, British Library, London
Culliford, *William Strachey*	S. G. Culliford, *William Strachey, 1572–1621* (Charlottesville, Va.: University Press of Virginia, 1965)
DNB	*Dictionary of National Biography*
Eger.	Egerton MSS, British Library, London
Harl.	Harleian MSS, British Library, London
Harl. Soc. Pub.	Publications of the Harleian Society, London
Herford and Simpson	C. H. Herford and P. and E. Simpson, eds., *Ben Jonson,* 11 vols. (Oxford: Clarendon Press, 1925–54)
HMC	Historical Manuscripts Commission, Reports. Individual volumes distinguished by the name of the manuscripts' owner and volume number within the report (e.g., *HMC Salisbury,* 14)
OED	*Oxford English Dictionary*
orig.	originally
poss.	possibly
Poulton, *John Dowland*	Diana Poulton, *John Dowland* (London: Faber, 1972)
PRO	Public Record Office, London. For abbreviations of classes of documents, see *A Guide to the Contents of the PRO,* 2 vols. (London: HMSO, 1963)
Proc. Parliament 1610	E. R. Foster, ed., *Proceedings in Parliament, 1610,* 2 vols. (New Haven, Conn.: Yale University Press, 1966)
punc.	punctuation
qy.	query
S.R.	Edward Arber, ed., *A Transcript of the Register*

                              of the Company of Stationers of London, 1554–1640, 5 vols. (London: Privately printed, 1875–77)

STC   A. W. Pollard and G. R. Redgrave, *A Short-Title Catalogue of Books Printed in England . . . 1475–1640* (London: Bibliographical Society, 1926); W. A. Jackson, F. S. Ferguson, and Katharine F. Pantzer, 2d rev. ed., vol. 2 (London: Bibliographical Society, 1976)

Wing   Donald Wing, *Short-Title Catalogue of Books Printed in England . . . 1641–1700*, 3 vols. (New York: Index Society, 1945–51); rev. ed., vol. 1 (New York: Modern Language Association, 1972)

3

Contents of the Manuscript

GENERAL NOTE OF CONTENTS AND ORGANIZATION

Folger MS. V.a. 321 contains unique or very rare copies of letters and other documents from the period 1582 to ca. 1614. Identifiable authors range from Queen Elizabeth, Robert Cecil, Francis Bacon, and the poets Chapman and Jonson to Peter Ferryman, William Strachey, N. Coote, and Marie Candish. Documents other than letters include invitations to dinner, partial and complete transcripts of Privy Council warrants, petitions for jobs, for justice, and for money, and a copy of a House of Commons petition of right.

Insofar as the manuscript's assignment of authorship may be checked, it is accurate. The Folger version of a letter signed "Ben: Iohnson," for instance, and Jonson's holograph at Hatfield differ in slight but substantive ways that led Herford and Simpson to state that the Folger version represents a draft of the letter that eventually reached Cecil.[12] The petition of right, 23 May 1610, follows very closely the official version in the House of Commons *Journal*. Some items in this manuscript repeat accurately the text, date, and/or ascribed authorship of other copies, either in manuscript or print. On internal evidence, the manuscript also shows great authority: Chapman responds in characteristically arrogant fashion to the troubles surrounding his plays on the duc de Biron. If he wrote about these and other difficulties, he would certainly have written letters like those the copyist assigns him. Students of such diverse individuals as William Strachey, an early traveler to Virginia, and the musician John Dowland have accepted completely the items relating to their subjects, and no technical evidence exists to cast doubt on the manuscript's authenticity.[13]

The manuscript opens with material devoted to the earl of Essex, arranged in approximately chronological order. With two exceptions—an undated document of "advice to a son" and a letter by Chidiock Tichbourne, one of the Babington conspirators—the manuscript then groups a number of late Elizabethan and very early Jacobean items together. Most of these have a general public interest (e.g., the earl of Southampton's pardon, or the account of Sir Francis Vere's and the earl of Northumberland's "duel"), but two petitions, one by Marie Candish, the other anonymous, and a grant of a reversion to William Huxley, prefigure the lack of either subject or chronological organization, which extends from f. 20 to f. 43. This section has no obvious organizing principle except, perhaps, the compiler's interest in the diverse and generally little-known individuals involved. Among other items, this part of the manuscript includes several letters to Peter Ferryman, the bulk of the letters that may recount George Chapman's courtship of a widow, and a number of documents that would interest many citizens (the Oath of Association, for example, and several diplomatic items).

With a few exceptions, the manuscript then continues with definitely Jacobean material to its conclusion. The arrangement in this half seems roughly chronological; anachronistic intrusions may result from the times at which the compiler received older materials. This hypothesis can explain the "public" documents, such as the account of the *Revenge* or Burghley's letter of advice to Cecil, but again smaller items—a family squabble among the Sidleys or an anonymous letter to the countess of Warwick—pose less easily dispatched puzzles. In this latter portion appear blocks of material devoted to Ferryman's admission to the Charterhouse and Chapman's attempts to gain compensation for various literary productions. Here, too, occur materials concerning the Burghs of Gainsborough and a family related by marriage, the Brookes (a branch of the Cobham family).

A brief discussion of several individual items will indicate the manuscript's diversity and illustrate the complexities surrounding its origin, purpose, and history. One curious document has already been mentioned. "Certein Principles or Instructions: From a greate man of this Land to his best beloved Sonne" follows the initial letters, speeches, and other documents devoted to the earl of Essex. It may be a "stray," irrelevant to what precedes and follows it, or it may be an attack, most probably post-mortem, on Essex, or it may be a contribution to the period's voluminous anti-Cecil literature. Later in the manuscript we find a translation, restarted and completed after a false beginning, of a letter allegedly sent by Genoa to Venice during the religious crisis of 1605–6. Contemporaries considered the letter a Jesuit forgery and modern scholars agree; it may imply Roman Catholic sympathies on the compiler's part. A third oddity is "Advertisementes of a Loyall Subiect . . .," which represents a superior text of a document formerly known in another version, now among the Fortescue papers in the Bodleian Library. J. D. Mackie, the document's discoverer, thought Henry Howard, first earl of Northampton, the likeliest author.[14]

Although far from certain, some connection between Howard and each of these three documents may be hypothesized. A man of strong but concealed Catholic sympathies, Howard early followed Essex and sought James's favor before his accession. On principle, the more diverse the items linked with a single individual, the more likely that individual's involvement in the manuscript's compilation. Still, Howard's connections with all but one of these three documents are very debatable; moreover, his intimacy with Jonson and especially with Chapman (the latter an apparent sine qua non for the compiler) is most unlikely. In semiofficial contexts (e.g., a dedicatory sonnet to him in Chapman's *Iliad* translation) or official proceedings (e.g., his objection to *Sejanus* or Chapman's appeal to him as Lord Privy Seal), the earl may be linked with the poets, but hardly as a friend or very significant patron.[15]

To survey all the possible connections that appear in the manuscript would return this introduction to the manuscript's own chaotic state. Three large groups of material deserve further mention, however, since they seem most likely to bear upon questions of compilation, purpose, and origin. The three groups include the two most famous in the manuscript—the letters by Jonson and Chapman—and a third, smaller block devoted to the Burgh family. A fourth large series, concerning Peter Ferryman, will be examined later.

JONSON, CHAPMAN, AND BURGH MATERIALS

With the exception of letters concerning Ferryman's application to the Charterhouse, Jonson's contribution deals with his imprisonment following official censorship of *Eastward Ho!* These materials have been well canvased by students of Jonson and of the play. Detailed treatment appears in the Commentary. It is worth noting, however, that Jonson's letters are much less personal than many of Chapman's letters; they may have entered the manuscript only through association with the elder poet.

Letters and documents relating to George Chapman fall into two main categories: his literary activities and their attendant disappointments and difficulties and his "courtship" of a widow. The first group spans the period between *Eastward Ho!* (1605) and Chapman's futile attempt to collect the reward Prince Henry promised for the Homeric translations (ca. 1613–14). In between, Chapman defends *The Conspiracie and Tragedie of Charles, Duke of Byron* (1608) and argues about his reward for *The Memorable Maske of . . . the Middle Temple, and Lyncolns Inne* (1613). A few other documents concern legal difficulties not directly connected with his writing. Both the literary material and the other scattered items require close scrutiny more appropriate to the Commentary. The second group (the "widow letters") may be most succinctly examined here. These letters excited Bertram Dobell's interest, mainly because few biographical materials for Chapman have survived.[16] Certainly, the letters provide more puzzles and lead to more speculation than any other set of documents in the manuscript.

Although many letters seem to concern the progress of such an affair and many items appear to be letters exchanged between the two principals, the identification of Chapman as the suitor rests on one letter, item 50. Addressed to the widow by an unnamed third party, this letter explicitly mentions "the Motion lately made betwixt you and my Frend Mr Chapman" and several times refers to the suitor's brother. Inferentially, these remarks can be attached to George Chapman, poet and translator, on two bases: he is the only individual of that surname in the manuscript, and he had an elder brother, wealthier than he and intermittently concerned with his welfare.[17]

On the assumption that only one courtship involving a widow is likely to appear in the manuscript,[18] a number of letters may be grouped together, viz., items 34–41, 46–50, 112, 113, and, perhaps, 134. The course of love traced in these letters is far from smooth, despite the efforts of friends to aid and to mend. Another suitor, "Androwes," apparently failed (letter, 112, ll. 4–6), but Chapman himself (if it be he) delayed matters six weeks at the very start, to his subsequent regret (letter, 113, ll. 7–10). Chapman seems frequently to have taken offense at his treatment and then had to remedy matters through various subterfuges (see, for example, letters, 46–50, and Commentary).

The lady of the piece remains even more shadowy than her suitor. Hypotheses concerning her identity naturally involve the manuscript's origin and the purpose of its compilation. Letter 112 has the subscript, "To my Sweete Love Fayre Mistresse .B."; this letter, though immediately followed by one addressed to the "Sweete wydowe," does not refer to the lady's marital status. The writer does, however, mention her "Childers children" (l. 24) and speaks of his love exceeding "the kyndest comforte yt ever you had, muche more then yet you have ever conceyved" (ll. 28–29), thus making the link with the other widow letters likely.

By this series of hypotheses, then, it is possible to say—tentatively—that George Chapman courted, unsuccessfully, a widow whose first, or more probably, last name began with the letter B. To go further enters very speculative realms. Two widows with an appropriate surname appear in the manuscript— Elizabeth Burgh Brooke, widowed by her husband's execution in 1603, and her mother, Frances, Lady Burgh, whose husband, the fifth baron, died in the Irish wars, 1597. Facts and coherent inferences upon which to base a choice between these two candidates do not exist or do not advance the argument very far. For example, consider their ages: Lady Burgh died fifty years after her husband, and her four daughters married between the years 1599 and 1620, but the dates of her own birth and marriage are unknown.[19] Similarly, while we know Elizabeth Burgh married George Brooke in 1599, the dates of her birth and death are not known. Although the suitor often addresses the widow as "Lady," he sometimes does not, and given the familiarity of even Elizabethan courtship, one cannot rest too much confidence in such titular distinctions. On the basis of propinquity to datable items, the two largest groups of letters might be placed around 1600,[20] but three years' margin on either side would be a negligible and likely error; thus, both women would have been widowed in the period that surrounding material vaguely indicates. Thomas Burgh's death left his widow and children with little financial support, and after 1597 the *Calendar of State Papers Domestic* and *Acts of the Privy Council* record her attempts, partly successful, to provide for the family. Given the period's litigiousness, such remarks as "You sewe to a Lord, and I to a Sainct" (letter, 39, ll. 11–12) or "wishing . . . prosperous successe to your sewtes in lawe" (letter, 41, ll. 39–41) may be quite insignificant; on the other hand, they could link the widow letters with Lady Burgh. On balance, Lady Burgh is perhaps the more probable "lady," since she was a grandmother by 1600 (cf. "Childers children") and the letters imply a more mature affair, financial and social in its aims and discords, as well as amorous.

The manuscript contains three items certainly connected with the Burghs of Gainsborough. Thomas Burgh had a moderately distinguished career as soldier and occasional diplomat, cut short after a briefly successful campaign in Ireland. Burgh received the Knighthood of the Garter in 1593 and thus appears, as a lord "of liuely hope" in George Peele's *Honour of the Garter* (1593; STC 19539); Peele further characterizes him as "brought vp in learning and in Armes,/Patrone of Musicke and of Chiualrie" (C4r-v). Burgh also appears momentarily in Peele's *Polyhymnia* (1590; STC 19546). Evidence for Peele's specific compliment may be seen in the dedications of Holborne's *The Cittharn Schoole* and Churchyard's edition of *G. di Grassi his true Arte of Defence*, to Thomas Burgh. At his death, he left behind his widow, Frances, four daughters, and a single son, Robert, then aged three. Financial demands associated with Burgh's military and diplomatic missions forced the sale of his Lincolnshire estates, and even before his death the family had been in difficulty. The years following 1597 and especially after Robert's death in February 1602 brought numerous petitions for help, first to Elizabeth and then to James. After the sixth baron's death, the heirs sought to retain the title in a petition included here. The other two items clearly associated with the Burghs are a letter from Thomas to his daughter Elizabeth and a letter from Elizabeth to Cecil pleading for George Brooke's life. Although Elizabeth Burgh Brooke was Cecil's sister-in-law, he could do nothing to save a man condemned for treason. Several other items appear to be continued appeals from Elizabeth on behalf of her children. In view of the manuscript's collection of documents favorable to both Essex and Cecil, it may be significant that the Salisbury manuscripts show that Burgh had friendly relations with both men, though he seems to have owed more to Cecil.

These Burgh materials have a value beyond the tentative hints they offer concerning Chapman's "courtship," for the compiler's interest in the family exceeds a normal curiosity about public affairs. For example, Vere or even Sidney appears much more frequently than Burgh in contemporary military collections, and anyone interested in the 1603 "Bye" or "Main" plots against James would focus his attention on Ralegh or Cobham or Watson rather than on George Brooke. Even the inheritance issue lacks sufficient complexity or general human interest to draw a genealogist's or an observer's eye. Consequently, one might hypothesize some more intimate connection between the compiler and the Burgh family, or an identity of interests, accomplishments, or history with the family's. Although no family connection has been established, one Captain Nicholas Burghe (or Birch) copied, sometime between 1623 and 1634, about 200 lines of Chapman's otherwise unrecorded poem, "An Invec-

tive . . . against Mr. Ben: Johnson" (now Bodleian Ashmole MS. 38, ff. 16–
18).[21]

THE COMPILER

Some of the items in the manuscript need no specific explanation: they
would be of general interest (Drake's letter, for example, or most of the Essex
material); others, however, require information so detailed and obscure as to
be inexplicable but for the chance survival of particular records. Why, for
instance, should the compiler be interested in William Huxley's attempts to
gain a sinecure or in Mr. Harrington's financial embarrassment? Perhaps the
compiler kept track of old school friends. The most promising sources of
identification are items that fall between these extremes, especially large groups
of documents having (hypothetically) a personal interest but at the same time
enough accidental qualities to allow us some insight into the general qualities of
the compiler's mind—his political sympathies, for instance, or his education or
his close friends. From such hints, one may "triangulate" a hypothetical compiler who might then metamorphose into a known historical figure.

Peter Ferryman qualifies as the compiler under many, but by no means all,
such tests. For example, many names—Roydon, Coote, Harrington, even
Chapman—have some connection with the Inns of Court or of Chancery.
Since the admissions registers and most associated documents of the Inns of
Chancery have disappeared, the modern student can only guess from sub-
sidiary documents the connection of some individuals with these inns. On the
other hand, it seems plausible that through a popular amalgamation of the two
types of inn or through an individual's pardonable fraud, many people might
be described or describe themselves as Inns of Court men when in sober fact
they had attended the less exclusive Inns of Chancery. Ferryman claims an Inns
of Court education, but he does not appear in the registers;[22] though Chapman
associated professionally and privately with members of both the Inns of
Chancery and of Court, his name does not appear in the surviving documents.
Men from the Inns figure prominently in turn-of-the-century literary and
political activities, in the Virginia Company, and in the mild hoaxes and sensa-
tions perhaps inaccurately associated with the "Mermaid Club." Jonson writes
Bond (both were members of Coryate's celebrated list of celebrants at the
Mermaid) in supporting Ferryman; William Strachey of the Virginia expedition
appeals to "your olde frend Mr Royden" when explaining his inability to help
an imprisoned Ferryman. Strachey also held a part share in the theatrical company that produced many of Jonson's and Chapman's plays.[23] And so, on and
on, half-links, slender connections, near-misses asking for a simple hypothesis—all wind their subtle way through the manuscript.

A fair complaint against Ferryman as compiler is, paradoxically, the presence
of his name. Ordinarily (and understandably) in similar Elizabethan compila-

tions, the name of the collector rarely appears, for he has little need to record his own actions, no need to sign his name to a copy of a letter *he* sent. Thus, for example, Chapman and Jonson knew very well that they had written letters to various patrons and powerful courtiers; they might want copies for reference (or keep corrected drafts),[24] but they would recognize their own work. The argument against signed file copies runs *a fortiori* in the cases of documents of less importance than an appeal from prison. For instance, whoever lent Mr. Sares a lute (see letter 78) might wish to remember that he had called in the loan, but he would hardly sign his name to the copy. When Elizabethans kept copies of letters sent to them, however, they often did write (or have rewritten) their own names as addressees, though mistaking the copy's significance would presumably be as unlikely as forgetting what the individual himself had written.[25] With this final observation, it becomes possible to explain all the occurrences of Ferryman's name: he appears as addressee; he appears in third person references; he appears in copies of official documents submitted by him or on his behalf. Still, the possibility remains that the compiler's name appears nowhere in the manuscript.

An elusive figure, Ferryman has connections with many individuals represented in this volume. By a slight margin, more private papers, or items of restricted personal interest, relate to him than to any other person mentioned in MS. V.a. 321.[26] This predominance partly justifies the Folger Manuscript Catalogue's speculation that Ferryman compiled the volume. Evidence other than sheer bulk exists; for instance, the latest material dates from around the time Ferryman entered the Charterhouse ("3.1614"),[27] suggesting that his withdrawal and the compilation's end might be connected.

Ferryman, "a gentleman by birth and education" according to his own description, has long been known as a participant in the ugly attempt to blackmail Lady Essex with letters forged by the famous "calligraphist," Peter Bales.[28] Never indicted, Ferryman apparently aided Lady Essex by bringing Bales to her and getting a helpful statement from him.[29] Acquainted, probably, with Chapman, Ferryman also knew William Strachey, Ben Jonson, Matthew Roydon, and John Davies of Hereford.[30] Much more information appears in this manuscript, however, for Charterhouse's rules required that Ferryman establish a history of military or governmental connections as well as piety. Thus, he recounts his service under Sidney and then Walsingham (perhaps as a spy),[31] documents a trip to Jerusalem, and enlists Jonson's help with some of the great men serving as governors of the new "hospital."[32] Once admitted to Charterhouse, Ferryman disappears until the record of his death, 28 September 1642.[33] Long before retiring from the world, however, he seems to have followed various powerful men into court intrigue, stumbling more than once.

Ferryman, then, is a good candidate as chief compiler, not merely because many documents of little interest to anyone else appear in the manuscript, but because his own career, his search for governmental employ, and his known political interests make him likely to have been interested in many other items. Thus, his concern with the Essex affair accounts for that material; his Dutch service (perhaps even under Thomas Burgh)[34] might interest him in that family and military matters generally; the Jonson–Strachey connection would permit an entry into the theatrical world. Pretensions to culture, to be expected in a man claiming attendance at the Inner Temple, might lead Ferryman beyond Jonson to Anthony Holborne and John Dowland, also represented here. Strachey mentions Roydon's friendship for Ferryman, strengthening the likelihood that Ferryman knew another of Roydon's good friends, George Chapman.[35]

The material tentatively associated with Henry Howard does not point to Ferryman; no connection between them has been found. Moreover, anything less than wholehearted support of Essex (cf. the blackmail scandal), at least before 1600, would not fit him for intimacy with Howard. Still, Ferryman did enter Charterhouse, and Howard was entirely spiteful enough (and powerful enough) to prevent it had he wished. "Advertisementes of a Loyall Subiect," tentatively linked with Howard, is quite rare and very tantalizing. If it is Howard's, then the compiler must either have been close to him in some capacity or have had other very effective political associations.

Unfortunately, no sample of Ferryman's handwriting has been found, though one may have existed in the eighteenth century.[36] It would probably be unusual for a man of his accomplishments and apparent background to have so clear and regular a hand as hand A, though he might once have studied with Bales or Davies of Hereford, both exceptional writing-masters. Ferryman might possibly have been wealthy enough to employ a professional (as Danyell did Bales), but his imprisonment for debt, recorded in this manuscript, and his appeal for charity hardly suggest it.

Despite the strong case that can be made for Ferryman's responsibility, the debatable presence of Henry Howard (or, more probably, an associate) is not the only challenge. Even if one postulates an intimacy with Chapman great enough to explain the presence of the widow letters (assuming they relate to the poet), it remains hard to believe that mere and unproven military service with Thomas Burgh would lead Ferryman to collect documents relating to Robert Burgh's succession or Elizabeth Burgh Brooke's troubles after her husband's arrest. Granting that most active individuals would collect copies of Drake's letter to Foxe, or the description of the *Revenge*, or Southampton's pardon, or Vere's altercation with Northumberland, what could interest Ferryman in the "little people" of the manuscript—Marie Candish or William Huxley, for example?[37] Ranging further, one finds the material concerning Holborne and Dowland, for instance, of perhaps marginal interest to Ferryman. While Peter Ferryman remains the best candidate as compiler, the manuscript's heterogeneity stands as a constant obstacle to tidy categorization. The apparent randomness of many items, the manuscript's general lack of perceptible organization, the intricate yet inconclusive sets of friendships probably do have a single explanation—or perhaps two, if one remembers the manuscript's two hands—but lost, or unretrieved, documents, unthought-of hypotheses, and simple ignorance prevent this explanation's discovery. One can only delight in the valuable individual documents and admit puzzlement before the manuscript's great variety.

4

Notes

1. See Edward Heawood, *Watermarks, Mainly of the 17th and 18th Centuries,* Monumenta chartae papyraceae historiam illustrantia, vol. 1 (Hilversum, Netherlands: Paper Publications Society, 1950) and C. M. Briquet, *Les Filigranes . . . A Facsimile of the 1907 Edition,* ed. Allan Stevenson, 4 vols. (Amsterdam: Paper Publications Society, 1968). Since many similar but not quite identical watermarks exist, these references to Heawood and Briquet should be regarded only as guides. According to Kent van den Berg in "An Elizabethan Allegory of Time by William Smith," *English Literary Renaissance* 6 (1976): 40–59, the pot watermark with initials AV also occurs in a manuscript now held in the Osborn collection, Yale University; van den Berg also notes that the watermark is illustrated in Philip Gaskell, *A New Introduction to Bibliography* (Oxford: Clarendon Press, 1972), p. 71, fig. 40, incorrectly captioned as dating from 1660.

2. Published by Peter Short, who was also responsible for Holborne's *The Cittharn Schoole* (see item 31 and Commentary); I have been unable to trace this paper in any other of Short's books.

3. See, for example, the discussion of the second gathering (pp. 16–17) and of Peter Ferryman's career (pp. 32–34).

4. See Arthur Freeman, *Thomas Kyd: Facts and Problems* (Oxford: Clarendon Press, 1967), pp. 2–3 and 12.

5. Giles Dawson and Laetitia Kennedy-Skipton [Yeandle], *Elizabethan Handwriting 1500–1650: A Manual* (New York: Norton, 1966), p. 96.

6. H. C. Bartlett, comp., *Hand-List of Early English Books . . . Collected by W. A. White* (New York: Privately printed, 1914); p. 50 lists MS. V.a. 321.

7. A. S. W. Rosenbach, "English Poetry to 1700," Catalogue 45 (Philadelphia: Privately printed, 1941), reprinted in *The Collected Catalogues of A. S. W. Rosenbach,* 10 vols. (New York: Arno, 1967), vol. 7. MS. V.a. 321 is item 183 ("a Commonplace Book").

8. Edwin Wolf, *Rosenbach* (New York: World, 1960), p. 504.

9. Private communication from Dudley Massey of Pickering and Chatto, Booksellers, London. The firm's records for the indicated period no longer exist.

10. C. G. Petter's edition of *Eastward Ho!* (London: Benn, 1973) reprints items 124–33, loosely modernized, and they appear as Appendix 2 in R. W. Van Fossen's fine Revels edition of the play (Manchester: At the University Press, 1979). S. G. Culliford, *William Strachey, 1572–1621* (Charlottesville, Va.: University Press of Virginia, 1965) reprints items 51, 86, and 90.

11. The most notable use of a single item occurs in Mark Eccles, "Chapman's Early Years," *Studies in Philology* 43 (1946): 176–93. Excerpts from MS. V.a. 321 appear in Charlotte Spivack, *George Chapman,* Twayne's English Authors Series, vol. 60 (New York: Twayne, 1967), pp. 17–29.

12. C. H. Herford and P. and E. Simpson, eds., *Ben Jonson,* 11 vols. (Oxford: Clarendon Press, 1925–54) 1:190; for a collation of the Hatfield and Folger versions, see 1:194–96.

13. See Culliford, *William Strachey* and Diana Poulton, *John Dowland* (London: Faber, 1972).

14. See J. D. Mackie, " 'A Loyall Subiectes Advertisement' as to the Unpopularity of James I.'s

Government in England, 1603–4," *Scottish Historical Review* 23 (1925): 1–17; for a detailed analysis of these documents, see the appropriate commentary (items 10 and 102, respectively).

15. For details of Jonson's relations with Howard, see Herford and Simpson, 1:36–38 and 9:587–91.

16. See Dobell's articles cited above (p. 20).

17. For details of this brother, Thomas Chapman, see C. J. Sisson and Robert Butman, "George Chapman, 1612–1622: Some New Facts," *Modern Language Review* 46 (1951): 185–90 and Albert H. Tricomi, "Two Letters Concerning George Chapman," *Modern Language Review* 75 (1980): 241–48.

18. Although other widows appear, see, e.g., items 32 and 114.

19. One might propose 1560–65 for her birth, but without much hope of accuracy; she married Burgh before the Yorkshire Visitation of 1584. Certain dates derive from *Complete Peerage*, R. E. G. Cole, *History of . . . Doddington* (Lincoln, England: J. Williamson, 1897), and personal research in Gainsborough and Lincoln. Letters to Katherine Burgh from her husband have been printed in Bertram Schofield, ed., *The Knyvett Letters 1620–1644*, Norfolk Record Society Publications, vol. 20 (1949); they add some incidental facts concerning the Burgh family in the seventeenth century, and the notes cite further information from the Gawdy papers (e.g., BL MS. Eger. 2716 and 2722).

20. Cf. the very debatable attribution of item 38 to 29 February 1599/1600.

21. George Chapman, *The Poems of George Chapman*, ed. P. B. Bartlett (New York: Modern Language Association, 1941), pp. 476ff. Information beyond that offered by Bartlett may be found in E. H. Fellowes, *The Military Knights of Windsor 1352–1944* (Windsor, England: Dean and Canons of St. George's Chapel, 1944), pp. xliii and 35, and in C. H. Joston, *Elias Ashmole 1614–1692*, 5 vols. (Oxford: At the University Press, 1966), 3:812. Burghe's will, preserved at Windsor Chapel, sheds no light on this manuscript; his handwriting (in Ashmole MS. 1131, ff. 221–22) resembles none in the Folger manuscript.

22. See petition 91. The published admissions registers do not mention Ferryman, and Culliford says "there is no mention of him among the records of the Inner Temple" (*William Strachey*, p. 94).

23. See Culliford, *William Strachey*, pp. 53–54, for Strachey's share in the Blackfriars children's company.

24. This parenthetical phrase alludes to two specific instances: one of Jonson's letters (128, mentioned above) and one of Chapman's petitions (138) that show signs of authorial revision, rather than a copyist's correction or error.

Exceptions to the general observation that file copies sent by an individual rarely had his signature naturally exist. One example is described by Conyers Read in "A Letter from Robert, Earl of Leicester, To a Lady," *Huntington Library Bulletin*, no. 9 (1936): 15–23. This document, described by Read as "probably . . . Leicester's copy of an original he dispatched," has the initials "R. L." as a signature and appears to be in Leicester's own hand. Read observes, "the highly confidential character of this particular epistle may explain why Leicester preferred to do his own transcribing" (p. 15).

25. For a typical example, see the Hoby letters in Bodleian Add. MS. D. 109. I should add, of course, that many documents clearly related to Chapman, for instance, have no signature or other attribution. One very curious (and anonymous) letter, item 76, does not "fit" Ferryman or, so far as I know, any other putative compiler.

26. See items 44, 51, 91–95, and 116. This calculation excludes the widow letters; they would give Chapman pride of place, if they relate to him.

27. This date appears in the Charterhouse Brothers' Book; see Commentary on item 91.

28. For the investigation of Bales and others and details of the blackmail, see John Hawarde, *Les Reportes del Cases in Camera Stellata*, ed. W. P. Baildon (London, 1894), pp. 119–23 and 396–409; the fullest biography of Peter Bales appears in *Biographia Britannica*, ed. Andrew Kippis, 2d ed., (London, 1771), vol. 1. Bales was arrested during Essex's rebellion (see Folger MS. V.a. 164, f. 130v), and the earl mentioned him at the subsequent trial (see William Cobbett et al., comp.,

Complete Collection of State Trials, 33 vols. [London, 1809], 1:1343). Bales claimed to have been a "servant" to Lord Keeper Puckering (see Harl. MS. 675, f. 9v), and his son later asserted that Peter Bales had been tutor to Prince Henry (see *Dictionary of National Biography*, s.v. "Bales"). Thomas Nashe refers to "Peter Bales *Brachigraphy*" in *Summer's Last Will and Testament* (see R. B. McKerrow, ed., *The Works of Thomas Nashe*, 5 vols. [London: Bullen, 1905], 3:252; cf. 3:318 and note). Ralph Rabbard's "To the indifferent Reader" in George Ripley's *The Compovnd of Alchymy* (1591; STC 21057), M4v, implies that Bales acted as bookseller for that work. In view of Thomas Lodge's possible appearance in item 21, it may also be noted that he wrote a prefatory poem for Bales's *The Writing Schoolemaster* (1590; STC 1312).

29. For details of Ferryman's involvement in recovering the Essex letters, see PRO SP 12/279/124 (statement by G. Lisle, secretary to Lady Essex) and PRO SP 12/281/34 and SP 12/282/3 (two versions of Bales's statement, in his own hand).

30. See Culliford, *William Strachey*, pp. 94–96 and items 51, 93, and 94; Roydon, called Ferryman's "olde frend" in letter 51, appears with Ferryman, Richard Martin, Chapman, and Bales in John Davies, *Scourge of Folly* (1611?; STC 6341), pp. 201, 200, 44–45, and 104, respectively.

31. See petition, 91; letter 27 implies spying activities, but cannot be certainly linked with Ferryman.

32. See items 95, 93, and 94, respectively.

33. Charterhouse Brothers' Book, private communication from the Registrar.

34. Thomas Burgh and Sidney certainly knew one another (see Emanuel van Meteren, *A Trve Discovrse . . . of the Svcceeding Governovrs in the Netherlands* [1602; STC 17846], pp. 85–86), and Thomas's younger brother, Sir John Burgh, governor of Doesburg, commanded various companies in which both Sidney and Essex served (for a short biography of Sir John, see Anthony Esler, *The Aspiring Mind of the Elizabethan Younger Generation* [Durham, N.C.: Duke University Press, 1966], pp. 208–14). Perhaps Jonson and Ferryman met in the wars.

35. See letter 51. Chapman served as one of the judges in a celebrated writing contest won by Bales in 1595 (see Harl. MS. 675 and note 30, above). For Chapman's friendship with Roydon, see Chapman, *Poems*, pp. 19, 49–50, and 422.

36. William Oldys, the writer of Bales's entry in *Biographia Britannica*, mentions a letter (1589) from Ferryman to Thomas Randolph and cites "MS. collections of Nat. Boothe, Esq., late of Grays-Inn" (a reference repeated in the *Dictionary of National Biography*, s.v. "Bales"). This document does not appear in a sale catalogue, *A Catalogue of the Libraries of that Learned Antiquarian Nathaniel Boothe, Esq. and Others . . .* (T. Osborne, 12 January 1747; Bodleian shelfmark 2593e2), listing Boothe's collection, and I have not found it in the major British collections. The "original" may in any case have been a copy. John Davies might have copied MS. V.a. 321 at Ferryman's request, but the samples of his best hands in *The Writing Schoolemaster, or The Anatomie of Faire Writing* (1663; Wing D390) do not resemble either hand in this manuscript.

37. Still, Ferryman apparently knew at least one of the manuscript's very minor figures, Robert Sidley (see items 103, 104, and 116).

5
Bibliography

This bibliography is divided into manuscript and printed references. It excludes manuscripts calendared in and cited from the Historical Manuscripts Commission's Reports, and it excludes common reference works such as the *Oxford English Dictionary* and the *Dictionary of National Biography*. The conventions of citation are the same as those used in the Commentary and Annotations. For English books printed up to 1640, *Short-Title Catalogue* numbers are given; for those printed between 1641 and 1700, Wing numbers are provided. George Chapman's Homeric translations are entered under the translator's name.

MANUSCRIPTS

Bodleian Library, Oxford
  Additional D. 109
  Ashmole 38, 1131
British Library, London
  Additional 4130, 25247, 33051, 34599, 48119
  Harleian 35, 167, 675, 677, 3638
Folger Library, Washington, D.C.
  V.a. 164, V.a. 321, V.a. 402
  V.b. 187, V.b. 214
  X.c. 11
  X.d. 212
Huntington Library, San Marino, California
  HM 102
Public Record Office, London
  C 25/65
  SO 3/2, 3/3
  SP 12/147/87, 12/173/87, 12/246/98, 12/279/124, 12/281/34, 12/282/3, 12/283a/78
  SP 14/66/28–29

PRINTED SOURCES

Ahmed I, Sultan. *Letters from the Great Turke . . . vnto the . . . Pope and to Rodolphus. . . .* London: 1606; STC 207.

Arber, Edward, ed. *A Transcript of the Registers of the Company of Stationers of London, 1554–1640.* 5 vols. London: Privately printed, 1875–77.

Bacon, Francis. *A Declaration of the Practices & Treasons Attempted and Committed by Robert Late Earle of Essex*. London: 1601; STC 1133.

———. *Life and Letters of Francis Bacon*. Edited by James Spedding. Vols. 8–14 of *The Works of Francis Bacon*. Edited by James Spedding, R. L. Ellis, and D. D. Heath. 14 vols. London: Longman, 1857–74.

———. *Resvscitatio ... Several ... Works ... of ... Francis Bacon ... Third Edition*. London: 1671; Wing B321.

Baildon, W. P., ed. *The Records of the Honorable Society of Lincoln's Inn. The Black Books ...* 4 vols. London: Lincoln's Inn, 1897–1902.

Bald, R. C. *John Donne: A Life*. Oxford: At the University Press, 1970.

Bales, Peter. *The Writing Schoolemaster. London: 1590; STC 1312*.

Bartlett, H. C., comp. *Hand-List of Early English Books ... Collected by W. A. White*. New York: Privately printed, 1914.

Batho, G. R., ed. *Household Papers of Henry Percy, Ninth Earl of Northumberland (1564–1632)*. Camden Society Publications, 3d ser., vol. 93 (1962).

Bigg-Wither, Reginald F. *Materials for a History of the Wither Family*. Winchester, England: Warren, 1907.

Birch, Thomas. *Memoirs of the Reign of Queen Elizabeth*. 2 vols. London: Millar, 1754.

Bouwsma, W. J. *Venice and the Defence of Republican Liberty*. Berkeley and Los Angeles: University of California Press, 1968.

Breton, Nicholas. *The Vncasing of Machivils Instructions to his Sonne . . .* London: 1613; STC 17170 and 3704.3.

Brettle, R. E. "Eastward Ho, 1605; By Chapman, Jonson, and Marston; Bibliography and Circumstances of Production." *Library* 9 (1928–29): 287–302.

Briquet, C. M. *Les Filigranes. Dictionnaire Historique des Marques du Papier*. A Facsimile of the 1907 Edition, edited by Allan Stevenson, 4 vols. Amsterdam: Paper Publications Society, 1968.

Brown, William Haig. *Charterhouse, Past and Present*. Godalming, England: Stedman, 1879.

Cecil, William. *Certaine Precepts, or Directions for the Well Ordering and Carriage of a Mans Life*. London: 1617; STC 4897.

Chamberlain, John. *The Letters of John Chamberlain*. Edited by N. E. McClure. American Philosophical Society Memoirs, vol. 12, parts 1 and 2. 2 vols. Philadelphia: American Philosophical Society, 1939.

Chambers, E. K. *The Elizabethan Stage*. 4 vols. Oxford: Clarendon Press, 1923.

Chapman, George. *Chapman's Homer*. Edited by Allardyce Nicoll. Bollingen Series, vol. 41, 2 vols. 1956. Reprint. Princeton, N.J.: Princeton University Press, 1967.

———. *The Conspiracie, and Tragedie of Charles Duke of Byron, Marshall of France*. London: 1608; STC 4968.

———. *Homers Odysses*. London: 1615; STC 13637.

———. *Homer Prince of Poets ... twelve bookes of his Iliads. . . .* London: 1609?; STC 13633.

———. *The Iliads of Homer, Prince of Poets*. London: 1611?; STC 13634.

———. *The Memorable Maske of ... the Middle Temple, and Lyncolns Inne*. London: 1613; STC 4981 and 4982.

———. *Plays and Poems of George Chapman: The Tragedies.* Edited by T. M. Parrott. London: Routledge, 1910.

———. *The Poems of George Chapman.* Edited by P. B. Bartlett. New York: Modern Language Association, 1941.

———, et al. *Eastward Ho!* Edited by G. C. Petter. London: Benn, 1973.

———, et al. *Eastward Ho.* Edited by R. W. Van Fossen. Manchester: At the University Press, 1979.

Cheyney, Philip. *A History of England: From the Defeat of the Armada to the Death of Elizabeth.* 2 vols. 1926. Reprint. New York: Peter Smith, 1948.

Clay, C. T. "A Document Relating to the Collection in Yorkshire of a Subsidy under the Act of 1601." *Yorkshire Archaeological Journal* 33 (1936–38): 309–13.

Cobbett, William, et al., eds. *Complete Collection of State Trials.* 33 vols. London: Hansard, 1809–26.

C[okayne], G[eorge] E[dward]. *The Complete Peerage,* revised and edited by V. Gibbs et al. 13 vols. London: St. Catherine Press, 1910–59.

Cole, R. E. G. *History of the Manor and Township of Doddington.* Lincoln, England: J. Williamson, 1897.

Collins, Arthur. *The Peerage of England. A Supplement.* 2 vols. London: W. Innys, 1750.

———, comp. *Letters and Memorials of State in the Reigns of Queen Mary, Queen Elizabeth, King James, King Charles the First, Part of the Reign of King Charles the Second, and Oliver's Usurpation,* 2 vols. London: Osborne, 1746.

Cooper, C. H. *Annals of Cambridge.* 5 vols. Cambridge, England: Warwick, 1842–53.

Coppinger, W. A. *County of Suffolk.* 5 vols. London: Sotheram, 1905.

Corbett, J. S. *Drake and the Tudor Navy.* Rev. ed. 2 vols. London: Longmans, 1899.

Culliford, S. G. *William Strachey, 1572–1621.* Charlottesville, Va.: University Press of Virginia, 1965.

Dalrymple, Sir David, Lord Hailes. *The Secret Correspondence of Sir Robert Cecil with James VI, King of Scotland.* Edinburgh: A. Millar, 1766.

Davies, G. S. *Charterhouse in London.* London: J. Murray, 1921.

Davies, John. *The Scourge of Folly.* London: 1611?; STC 6341.

———. *The Writing Schoolemaster, or The Anatomie of Faire Writing.* London: 1663; Wing D390.

Davis, Herbert, and Gardner, Helen, eds. *Elizabethan and Jacobean Studies Presented to Frank Percy Wilson.* Oxford: Clarendon Press, 1959.

Dawson, Giles, and Kennedy-Skipton [Yeandle], Laetitia. *Elizabethan Handwriting 1500–1650: A Manual.* New York: Norton, 1966.

Dekker, Thomas, and Webster, John. *North-ward Hoe.* London: 1607; STC 6539.

Dobell, Bertram. "Newly Discovered Documents of the Elizabethan and Jacobean Periods." *The Athenaeum* 74, part 1 (1901): 369–70, 403–4, 433–34, 465–67.

Dowling, Margaret. "Sir John Hayward's Troubles over *His* [sic] *Life of Henry IV.*" *Library* 11 (1930–31): 212–24.

Eccles, Mark. "Chapman's Early Years." *Studies in Philology* 43 (1946): 176–93.

Edmondes, Sir Clement. *Observations vpon the Five First Bookes of Caesars Commentaries.* London: 1600; STC 7488.

Ellis, Sir Henry, ed. *Visitation of the County of Huntingdon, 1613.* Camden Society Publications, vol. 43 (1849).

Elton, G. R., ed. *The Tudor Constitution: Documents and Commentary.* Cambridge: At the University Press, 1965.

Esler, Anthony. *The Aspiring Mind of the Elizabethan Younger Generation.* Durham, N.C.: Duke University Press, 1966.

Evelyn, John. *Numismata: A Discourse of Medals, Antient and Modern.* London: 1697; Wing E3505.

Fellowes, E. H. *The Military Knights of Windsor 1352–1944.* Historical Monographs Relating to St. George's Chapel, Windsor Castle, vol. 4. Windsor, England: Dean and Canons of St. George's Chapel, 1944.

Ferguson, Donald. "Captain Benjamin Wood's Expedition of 1596." *Geographical Journal* 21 (1903): 330–34.

Foster, E. R., ed. *Proceedings in Parliament, 1610.* 2 vols. New Haven, Conn.: Yale University Press, 1966.

Freeman, Arthur. *Thomas Kyd: Facts and Problems.* Oxford: Clarendon Press, 1967.

Gabel, John. "The Original Version of Chapman's *Tragedy of Byron.*" *Journal of English and Germanic Philology* 63 (1964): 433–40.

Gardiner, S. R. *What Gunpowder Plot Was.* London: Longmans, 1897.

Gaskell, Philip. *A New Introduction to Bibliography.* Oxford: Clarendon Press, 1972.

Gawdy, Philip. *Letters of Philip Gawdy.* Edited by I. H. Jeayes. London: J. B. Nichols and Sons, 1906.

Goldberg, S. L. "Sir John Hayward, 'Politic Historian.'" *Review of English Studies,* n.s. 6 (1955): 233–44.

Grassi, Giacomo di. *G. di Grassi his True Arte of Defence.* Edited by Thomas Churchyard. London: 1594; STC 12190.

Greepe, Thomas. *The True and Perfecte Newes of the Woorthy and Valiant Exploytes, Performed and Doone by that Valiant Knight Syr Francis Drake.* London: 1587; STC 12343.

Greg, W. W. *The Collected Papers of Sir Walter Greg.* Edited by J. C. Maxwell. Oxford: Clarendon Press, 1966.

Grimestone, Edward, trans. *A True Historie of the Memorable Siege of Ostend.* London: 1604; STC 18895.

Hakluyt, Richard. *The Principal Navigations. . . .* 12 vols. Glasgow: MacLehose, 1903–5.

Hall, A. C. S., comp. *Guide to the Reports of the Historical Manuscripts Commission, 1911–1957.* 3 vols. London: Her Majesty's Stationery Office, 1966.

Hall, G. D. G. "Impositions and the Courts, 1554–1606." *Law Quarterly Review* 69 (1953): 200–218.

Hansche, M. B. "The Formative Period of English Familiar Letter-writers and Their Contribution to the English Essay." Ph. D. diss., University of Pennsylvania, 1902.

Harrison, Stephen. *The Archs of Triumph.* London: 1604; STC 12863.

Hardie, Colin G., ed. *Vitae Vergilianae antiquae.* Oxford: Clarendon Press, 1954.

Haugaard, William P. *Elizabeth and the English Reformation.* Cambridge: At the University Press, 1968.

Hawarde, John. *Les Reportes del Cases in Camera Stellata*. Edited by W. P. Baildon. London: Privately printed, 1894.

Hayward, John. *The first part of the life and raigne of King Henrie IIII*. London: 1599; STC 12995.

Heawood, Edward. *Watermarks, Mainly of the 17th and 18th Centuries*, Monumenta chartae papyraceae historiam illustrantia, vol. 1. Hilversum, Netherlands: Paper Publications Society, 1950.

Henslowe, Philip. *Henslowe's Diary*. Edited by R. A. Foakes and R. T. Rickert. Cambridge, England: At the University Press, 1961.

Holborne, Anthony. *The Cittharn Schoole*. London: 1597; STC 13562.

―――. *Pauans, Galliards, Almains and other Short Aeirs*. London: 1599; STC 13563.

[Huntingdon] *Victoria History of the County of Huntingdon*. Edited by William Page and Granville Proby, assisted by H. E. Norris. 3 vols. London: St. Catherine Press, 1926–36.

Ingeldew, J. E. "The Date of Composition of Chapman's *Caesar and Pompey*." *Review of English Studies*, n.s. 12 (1961): 144–59.

Jeffery, Brian. "Anthony Holborne." *Musica Disciplina* 22 (1968): 129–206.

Jones, Marion, and Wickham, Glynne. "The Stage Furnishings of George Chapman's *The Tragedy of Charles, Duke of Biron*." *Theatre Notebook* 16 (1961–62): 113–17.

Jonson, Ben. *Ben Jonson*. Edited by C. H. Herford and P. and E. Simpson. 11 vols. Oxford: Clarendon Press, 1925–54.

―――. *Complete Masques of Ben Jonson*. Edited by Stephen Orgel. New Haven, Conn.: Yale University Press, 1971.

―――. *Sejanus*. Edited by Jonas Barish. New Haven, Conn.: Yale University Press, 1971.

Joston, C. H. *Elias Ashmole 1614–1692*. 5 vols. Oxford: At the University Press, 1966.

Jusserand, J. J. "Ambassador La Boderie and the 'Compositeur' of the Byron Plays." *Modern Language Review* 6 (1911): 203–5.

Kippis, Andrew, ed. *Biographia Britannica*. 2d ed. Vol. 1. London: C. Bathurst, 1771.

Kiralfy, A. R. A., comp. *A Source Book of English Law*. London: Sweet and Maxwell, 1957.

Langston, Beach. "Essex and the Art of Dying." *Huntington Library Quarterly* 13 (1949–50): 109–29.

Latham, Agnes M. C. "Sir Walter Ralegh's *Instructions to his Son*." In *Elizabethan and Jacobean Studies Presented to Frank Percy Wilson*, edited by Herbert Davis and Helen Gardner. Oxford: Clarendon Press, 1959.

Lefranc, Pierre. *Sir Walter Ralegh, écrivain, l'oeuvre et les idées*. Paris: Colin, 1968.

Lipsius, Justus. *Iusti Lipsi Epistolarum Selectarum Centuria Prima*. London: 1586; STC 15697.

―――. *Iusti Lipsi Epistolarum Selectarum Centuria Secunda*. London: 1590; STC 15698.

Lodge, Edmund. *Illustrations of British History*. 3 vols. London: Nicol, 1791.

Lodge, Thomas. *A Fig for Momus*. London: 1595; STC 16658.

―――. *A Treatise of the Plague*. London: 1603; STC 16676.

M., T. *The True Narration of the Entertainment of his Royall Maiestie*. . . . London: 1603; STC 17153 and 14433.

Mackie, J. D. " 'A Loyall Subiectes Advertisement' as to the Unpopularity of James I.'s Government in England, 1603–4." *Scottish Historical Review* 23 (1925): 1–17.

McKerrow, R. B., ed. *A Dictionary of Printers and Booksellers in England, Scotland, and Ireland and of Foreign Printers of English Books 1557–1640*. London: Bibliographical Society, 1910.

McManaway, J. G. "Elizabeth, Essex, and James." In *Elizabethan and Jacobean Studies Presented to Frank Percy Wilson*, edited by Herbert Davis and Helen Gardner. Oxford: Clarendon Press, 1959.

Markham, Clements R. *The Fighting Veres*. London: Sampson and Low, 1888.

Marsh, Bower, and Crisp, Frederick Arthur, eds. *Alumni Carthusiani: A Record of the Foundation Scholars of Charterhouse, 1614–1872*. London: Privately printed, 1913.

Meteren, Emanuel van. *A Trve Discovrse Historicall of the Svcceeding Governovrs in the Netherlands*. London: 1602; STC 17846.

Morley, Thomas. *A Plaine and Easie Introdvction to Practicall Mvsicke*. London: 1597; STC 18133.

Morris, John. "The Martyrdom of William Harrington." *The Month* 20 (1874): 411–23.

Mozley, J. F. *John Foxe and His Book*. London: Society for Promoting Christian Knowledge, 1940.

Munk, William, comp. *The Royal College of Physicians*. 2d rev. ed. 3 vols. London: Royal College of Physicians, 1878.

Nashe, Thomas. *The Works of Thomas Nashe*. Edited by R. B. McKerrow. 5 vols. London: Bullen, 1905.

Neale, J. E. *Elizabeth I and Her Parliaments, 1584–1601*. London: Cape, 1957.

Nef, John U. *The Rise of the British Coal Industry*. 2 vols. London: Routledge, 1932.

Nichols, John. *The Progresses, Processions, and Magnificent Festivities, of King James the First, his Royal Consort, Family and Court*. 4 vols. London: J. B. Nichols, 1828.

———. *The Progresses and Public Processions of Queen Elizabeth*. 2d ed. 3 vols. London: J. Nichols, 1823.

Orbison, Tucker. "The Case for the Attribution of a Chapman Letter." *Studies in Philology* 72 (1975): 72–84.

Osborne, Thomas. *A Catalogue of the Libraries of that Learned Antiquarian Nathaniel Boothe, Esq. and Others*. . . . London: T. Osborne, 1747.

Overall, W. H., and Overall, H. C., eds. *An Analytical Index to the Series of Records Known as the Remembrancia*. London: E. J. Francis, 1878.

Paul V, Pope. *A Declaration of the Variance betweene the Pope, and the Segniory of Venice*. London: 1606; STC 19482.

Peele, George. *The Honour of the Garter*. London: 1593; STC 19539.

Pollard, A. W., and Redgrave, G. R. *A Short-Title Catalogue of Books Printed in England . . . 1475–1640*. London: Bibliographical Society, 1926.

———. *A Short-Title Catalogue of Books Printed in England . . . 1475–1640*. 2d ed. Revised by W. A. Jackson, F. S. Ferguson, and Katharine Pantzer, vol. 2. London: Bibliographical Society, 1976.

Pollen, J. H. *Mary Queen of Scots and the Babington Plot*. Scottish Historical Society Publications, 3d ser., vol. 3. Edinburgh, 1922.

Poulton, Diana. *John Dowland*. London: Faber, 1972.

Purchas, Samuel. *Hakluytus Posthumus or Purchas his Pilgrimes*, 20 vols. Glasgow: J. MacLehose, 1905–7.

Ralegh, Sir Walter. *A Report of the Trvth of the fight about the Iles of Açores.* . . . London: 1591; STC 20651.

Read, Conyers. "A Letter from Robert, Earl of Leicester, to a Lady." *Huntington Library Bulletin*, no. 9 (1936): 15–23.

Rice, G. P. *The Public Speaking of Queen Elizabeth*. New York: Columbia University Press, 1951.

Rigg, A. G. *A Glastonbury Miscellany of the Fifteenth Century*. Oxford: At the University Press, 1968.

Ripley, George. *The Compovnd of Alchymy*. London: 1591; STC 21057.

Rosenbach, A. S. W. *English Poetry to 1700*. Catalogue 45. Philadelphia: Privately printed, 1941.

Rutton, W. L. *Three Branches of the Family of Wentworth*. London: Privately printed, 1891.

Rye, Walter, ed. *Visitations of Norfolk, 1563, 1589, and 1613*. Harleian Society Publications, vol. 32 (1891).

Sarpi, Paolo. *The History of the Quarrels of Pope Paul .V. with the State of Venice.* . . . London: 1626; STC 21766.

———. *Istoria dell' Interdetto e altri scritti editi e inediti*. Edited by M. D. Busnelli and G. Gambarin. Bari, Italy: G. Laterza, 1940.

Schofield, Bertram, ed. *The Knyvett Letters 1620–1644*. Norfolk Record Society Publications, vol. 20 (1949).

Scrinia Sacra; Secrets of Empire in Letters of Illustrious Persons. A Supplement of the Cabala. London: 1654; Wing S2110.

Shrewsbury, J. F. D. *A History of Bubonic Plague in the British Isles*. Cambridge, England: At the University Press, 1970.

Sisson, C. J. *Lost Plays of Shakespeare's Age*. Cambridge, England: At the University Press, 1936.

———, and Butman, Robert. "George Chapman 1612–1622: Some New Facts." *Modern Language Review* 46 (1951): 185–90.

Smith, A. Hassell. *County and Court: Government and Politics in Norfolk, 1558–1603*. Oxford: Clarendon Press, 1974.

Smith, G. C. Moore. "Matthew Roydon." *Modern Language Review* 9 (1914): 97–98.

Smith, George Adam. *Historical Geography of the Holy Land*. 25th rev. ed. London: Hodder and Staughton, 1931.

Somers, John, et al., comp. *A Collection of Scarce and Valuable Tracts on the most Interesting and Entertaining Subjects*. 4 vols. London: F. Cogan, 1748.

Speed, John. *The History of Great Britaine*. London: 1611; STC 23045.

Spivack, Charlotte. *George Chapman*. Twayne's English Authors Series, vol. 60. New York: Twayne, 1967.

Strype, John. *Annals of the Reformation*. 4 vols. Oxford: Clarendon Press, 1824.

———. *The Life and Acts of John Whitgift*. 4 vols. Oxford: Clarendon Press, 1822.

Sugden, E. H. *A Topographical Dictionary to the Works of Shakespeare and His Fellow Dramatists*. Manchester: At the University Press, 1925.

Sutcliffe, Matthew. *The Practice, Proceedings, And Laws of armes.* London: 1593; STC 23468.

Tenison, E. M. *Elizabethan England.* 12 vols. Royal Leamington Spa, England: Privately printed, 1930–60.

Tricomi, Albert H. "Two Letters Concerning George Chapman." *Modern Language Review* 75 (1980): 241–48.

Troup, Frances B. "Some Biographical Notes on Dr. Matthew Sutcliffe, Dean of Exeter, 1588–1629." *Transactions of the Devonshire Association for the Advancement of Science, Literature and Art* 23 (1891): 171–196.

Teixeira, Pedro. *The Travels of Pedro Teixeira.* Edited by Donald Ferguson. Hakluyt Society Publications, ser. 2, vol. 9 (1902).

Ustick, W. Lee. "Advice to a Son: A Type of Seventeenth Century Conduct Book." *Studies in Philology* 29 (1932): 409–41.

Van den Berg, Kent. "An Elizabethan Allegory of Time by William Smith." *English Literary Renaissance* 6 (1976): 40–59.

Vere, Sir Francis. *The Commentaries of Sr. Francis Vere.* Cambridge, 1657; Wing V240.

Vlieger, Abraham de. *Historical and Genealogical Record of the Coote Family.* Lausanne, Switz.: Bridel, 1900.

Waller, J. G. "The Lords of Cobham (Part II)." *Archaeologia Cantiana* 12 (1878): 113–66.

Ward, J. M. "A Dowland Miscellany." *Journal of the Lute Society of America* 10 (1977): 5–153.

Watson, A. G. *The Library of Sir Simonds D'Ewes.* London: British Museum, 1966.

Whitelocke, Sir James. *Liber Familicus.* Edited by J. Bruce. Camden Society Publications, vol. 70 (1858).

Williams, Sir Roger. *A Briefe Discourse of Warre.* London: 1590; STC 25732–25733.

Wilson, Elkin Calhoun. *Prince Henry and English Literature.* Ithaca, N.Y.: Cornell University Press, 1946.

Wing, Donald. *Short-Title Catalogue of Books Printed in England . . . 1641–1700.* 3 vols. New York: Index Society, 1945–51. Rev. ed. vol. 1. New York: Modern Language Association, 1972.

Wingfield, Mervyn Edward, Lord Powerscourt. *Muniments of the Ancient Saxon Family of Wingfield.* London: Mitchell and Hughes, 1894.

Winwood, Ralph. *Memorials of Affairs of State in the Reigns of Q. Elizabeth and K. James I.* 3 vols. London: T. Ward, 1725.

Wood, A. C. *A History of the Levant Company.* London: Oxford University Press, 1935.

Wright, Cyril Ernest. *Fontes Harleiani.* London: British Museum, 1972.

Wright, Louis, ed. *Advice to a Son.* Ithaca, N.Y.: Cornell University Press, for the Folger Library, 1962.

6
Analytical Table of
Contents

7
Facsimile Text and Transcriptions

[1   15 July (?) 1598   see Commentary]

The Lord keepers letter to the   1
Earle of Essex
My verie good lord, It is often seen that a stander by
seeth more, then he that playes the game; and for the
most part, everie man in his owne cause standeth in   5
his owne light, and seeth not so cleere as he shoold. your
lordship hathe dealt in other mens causes, and in great
and weightie affayres wth great wysdome and Iudgment;
nowe your owne is in hand, you are not to contempne –
or refuse the advice of any that love you, how simple   10
soever, in this order I rancke my self, of those that
love you none more simple, and none that loveth you wth
more true and honest affection, wch shall pleade my
excuse, yf you shall either mislike or misconster my wordes
or meaninge. But in your lordshipes honorable wisdome, I   15
neither doubt nor suspect the one or the other. I will
not presume to advise you, but will shoote my bolt and
tell you what I thinke: the begynnyng and long continu =
ing of this vnseasonable discontentment you have seene
and proved, by wch you may ayme at the ende, yf you hold   20
still this course, wch hitherto you fynde to be worsse and
worsse: and the longer you goe, the further out of the way.
there is little hope or likelihoode that the ende will be better
You are not yet so farre gone, but you may returne; the
return is safe, the progresse is daungerous and desperate,   25
In this course you holde, if you had enimyes; you doe yt
for them wch they coulde never doe for them selues; youre
frendes you leave to open skorne and contempt, you forsake
your self, overthrowe your fortunes, and ruynate your honor

The lord keepers letter to the
Earle of Essex

My verie good lord, It is often seen that a stander by
seeth more, then he that playes the game; and for the
most part, everie man in his owne cause standeth in
his owne light, and seeth not so cleare as he should. yo'
lordship hath dealt in other mens causes, and in great
and weightie affayres wth great wysdome and Judgment;
nowe yo' owne is in hand, you ar not to contempne
or refuse the advise of any that love you, how simple
soever, in this order I ranke my self. of those that
love you none more simple, and none that loveth you wth
more true and honest affection, wch shall pleade my
excuse, if you shall either mislike or misconster my wordes
or meaninge. But in yor lordships honorable wysdome, I
neither doubt nor suspect the one or the other. I will
not presume to advise you, but will shoote my bolt and
tell you what I thinke: the begynnyng and long contyn-
ing of this unreasonable discontentment you have seene
and proved, by wch you may ayme at the ends, yf you
still this course, wch hitherto you fynde to be woorse and
woorse: and the longer you goe, the further out of the way
there is little hope or likelihoode that the ende will be better
You are not yet so farre gone, but you may returne; the
returne is safe, the progresse is daungerous and desparate
In this course you holde, if you had ynnyng; you doe
for them wch they coude never doe for them selves; your
frendes you leave to open scorne and contempt, you forsake
yor self, overthrowe yor fortunes, and ruynate yor honor

and ostentation, you give that comfort and corage to the
forraine enimye, as greater they can not have: for what
can be more or welcom newes vnto them, then to heare y[t]
her Ma[tie], and the realme are maymed of so worthie a
member, who hath so often, and so valyauntlie quayled
and daunted them; you forsake your countrie when it
hath most neede of your counsell and helpe; Lastlie,
you fayle in your indissoluble dutie w[ch] you owe vnto yo[r]
most gratious soveraigne; A dutie not imposed vpon you
by nature and policie onlie, but by religious and sacred
bonde: wherein the divine Ma[tie] of almightie god hath
by the rule of Christianitie obliged you. ffor the
flower first, your constant resolution may perhapp
move you to esteeme them as light; but being well
weighed, they are not light, nor lightlie to be regarded
ffor the two last, it may be that the clearnes of yo[r]
inward conscience may seeme to content yo[r] selfe: but
this is not jnough, these duties stand not onlie in contem
placion or inward meditacion: they can not be perfor=
med but by externall actions; and where y[t] faylethe
the substance faylethe: This being yo[r] private state
and condition, what is to be done, what is the remedie
my good Lorde, j lacke wysdome and judgment to
advise you, but j will never lacke an honest true harte
to wishe you well, nor being warranted by a good con=
science, will feare to speake what j thinke; j have
begonne plainlie, be not offended iff j proceede so:
Bene cedit qui cedit tempore: and Seneca sayth,

and reputation, you give that comforte and corage to the
forrayne enimye, as greater they can not have: for what
can be more + pleasing + or welcom newes vnto them, then to heare yt
her Maiestie and the realme are maymed of so worthie a
member, who hathe so often, and so valyauntlie quayled
and daunted them; you forsake youre countrie when it   35
hathe most neede of your counsell and helpe; lastlie,
you fayle in your indissoluble dutie wch you owe vnto your
most ʒratious soueraigne; A dutie not imposed vpon you
by nature and policie onlie, but by religious and sacred
bondes: wherein the divine Maiestie of almightie god hathe   40
by the rule of Christianitie obliged you./ For the
Fower first, youre constant resolution may perhapes
move you to esteeme them as light; but being well
weighed, they are not light, nor lightlie to be regarded
For the two last, it may be that the clearnes of your   45
inwarde conscience may seeme to content your self: but
this is not Inough, these duties stand not onlie in contem =
placion or inward meditacion: they can not be perfor =
med but by externall actions; and where yt fayleth
the substance fayleth:/ This beinge your private state   50
and condition, what is to be done, what is the remedie
my good lorde, I lacke wysdome and Iudgment to
advise you, but I will never lacke an honest true harte
to wishe you well, nor being warranted by a good con =
science, will feare to speake what I thinke; I haue   55
begonne plainlie, be not offended if I proceede so:
Bene cedit qui cedit tempore: and Seneca sayth,

Lex si nocentem punit, cedendum est iusticiæ, si innocentem, – –
cedendum est fortunæ. The medicine and remedie is not
to contend and stryve: but humblie to submytt & yeelde;   60
you have gyven cause, and yet take a scandall vnto you;
then all that you can doe is to little to make satisfaction.
Is cause of scandall gyven vnto you, yet policie, dutie,
and religion, enforce you to yeild and submytt your self
to youre soueraigne, betwene whom and you there can be   65
no proportion of dutie, when god requires it as a prin =
cipall dutie and service to hym self, and when it is
evident that great good may ensue of it, to your frendes,
your self, your countrie, and your soveraigne; and extreeme
harme to the contrarie. There can be no dishonor nor   70
hurt to yeelde, but in not doinge, or in not yeeldinge, –
dishonor and Impietie; The difficultie in you my good
lord, is to conquer your self: wch is the height of true valor
and fortitude, whervnto all your honors actions have –
ever tended: doe it in this, and god will be pleased,   75
her maiestie (I doubt not) well satisfied, and your Countrie
will take good, and youre frendes comforte by it, and
your self, I mention you last, for I knowe that of all
these you esteeme your self least, shall receyve honor,
and your enimyes (if you have any) shall be disapointed   80
of their bitter sweete hope. / I have delyvered what
I thinke plainlie and simplie, and leave you to deter =
myne accordinge to youre wisdome; if I have erred,
it is *Error amoris,* not *Amor erroris*: conster and

Lex, si nocentem punit, cedendum est iusticiæ, si innocentem, ~~
cedendum est fortunæ. The medicine and remedie is not
to contend and stryve: but humblie to submytt & yeeld;
yow have gyven cause, and yet take a skandall vnto yow;
then all that yow can doe is to little to make satisfaction.
If cause of skandall gyven vnto yow, yet pollicie, dutie,
and religion, enforces yow to yeeld and submytt yo.r self
to yower soveraigne, betwene whom and yow there can be
no proportion of dutie, when god requireth it as a prin=
cipall dutie and service to hym self, and when it is
evident that great good may arise of it, to yo.r frende,
yo.r self, yo.r countrie, and yo.r soveraigne; and extreme
harme to the contrarie. There can be no dishonor nor
hurt to yeeld, but in not doinge, or in not yeeldinge, ~
dishonor and iniurie; The difficultie in yow my good
lord, is to conquer yo.r self: w.ch is the height of true valor
and fortitude; whereunto all yo.r honor'd actions have ~
ever tended: doe it in this, and god will be pleased,
her ma.tie (I doubt not) well satisfied, yo.r Countrie
will take good, and yower frendes comforte by it, and
yo.r self. I mention yow last, for I knowe that of all
these yow esteeme yo.r self least, shall reioyce honor,
and yo.r enimyes (iff yow have any) shall be disapointed
of their bitter sweete hope. I have delyvered what
I thinke plainlie and symplie, and leave yow to deter=
myne accordinge to yower wisdome; iff I have erred,
it is Error amoris, not Amor erroris: correct and

accept it I beseeche you as I meane, not an advise, but
an opinion, to be allowed or cancelled at yo[r] pleasure,
iff I might have convenientlie conferred wth yo[r] selfe
in personne, I wolde not have troubled you wth so
many idle blotts, what soever you judge off this my
opinion, yet be assured my desyre is to further all
yo[r] good meanes that may tend to yo[r] good, and so
wishing you all honorable happines, I rest yo[r] most
woddie and faithfull (though unable) poore frend

Thomas Egerton,

The Erle off Essex his answer
to the Lord keeper :

My verie good Lord, Though ther is not that man
this day lyvinge, whom I wolde sooner make a Judge
off any question that dyd concerne me then yo[r]
selfe: yet you must gyve me leave to tell you, that in
some causes I must appeale from all earthlie Judges,
and iff in any, then surely in this: when the highest
Judge on earth, hathe imposed upon me the heaviest
punnyshment, w[th]out tryall, or hearinge. Sithence
then I must either answere yo[r] Lordshipp argumente,
or forsake myne owne iust defence, I will force my
akinge head to do me servise one hower : I must
first deny my discouragement, w[ch] was forced to be an

accept it I beseche you as I meane, not an advise, but   85
an opinion, to be allowed or cancelled at your pleasure:
if I might haue convenientlie conferred wth your self
in personne, I wolde not have trobled you wth so –
many Idle blottes, what soever you Iudge of this my
opinion, yet be assured my desyer is to further all   90
your good meanes that may tend to your good, and so
wishing you all honorable happines, I rest your most
readie and faithefull (thoughe vnable) poore frend

Thomas Egerton

[2   18 July (?) 1598   see Commentary]

Th'erle of Essex his aunswer   1
to the lord keeper:/

My verie good lord, Though there is not that man
this day lyvinge, whom I wolde sooner make a Iudge
of any ⟨thing⟩ question that dyd concerne me then youre   5
self: yet you must gyve me leave to tell you, that in
some cawses I must appeale from all earthlie Iudges,
and if in any, then surely in this: when the highest
Iudge on earth, hathe imposed vpon me the heaviest
punyshement, wthout tryall, or hearinge./ Sithence   10
then I must either answere youre lordshipes argumentes,
or forsake myne owne iust defence, I will force my
aking head to do me service one hower:/ I must
first deny my discoragement, wch was forced to be an

humorous discontentment: and in that it was vnseasonable   15
or is too longe contynuynge, youre lordshippe should rather
Condole wth me, then expostulate; Naturall seasons are
expected here belowe, but violent and vnseasonable – –
stormes come from above; There is no tempest to the
passionate indignation of a prince, nor yet at any tyme   20
so vnseasonable as when it lighteth on those yt might
expect an harvest of there carefull and painfull labours,
he that is once wounded must feele smart tyll his –
hurt be cured, or the part sencelesse be cutt of: I ex =
pect not her Maiesties hart being obdurate: and be wthout   25
sence I can not, being made of fleshe and blood. But
then you say I may ayme at the ende, I doe more then
ayme, for I see an ende of all my fortunes, and have
sett an ende to all my desyers. In this course doe I
any thing for myne enimyes? when I was present I founde   30
them absolute, and therfore I had rather they shoulde
tryvmph alone, then have me attendant on their Chariottes:
Or doe I leave my Frendes, when I was a Courtier I
coulde yeelde no fruyte of my love to them, Nowe I am an
hermytt, they shall feare no envie for there love to me;   35
Or doe I forsake my self bycause I doe enioye my
self; Or doe I overthrowe my Fortune, bycause I buyld
not my fortune of paper walles, wch everie puffe of
wynde bloweth downe; Or doe I Ruynate myne honor,
bycause I leave following the pursuyte, or wearinge   40
the false marke of the shadowe of honor; Doe I
gyve corage or comfort to the forraigne enimyes, bycause

clamorous discontentment: and in that it was unseasonable
or is too longe contynnynge, youre lordshippe should rather
condole wth me, then expostulate; Naturall seasons are
expected here belowe, but violent and unseasonable ~ ~
stormes come from above; There is no tempest to the
passionate indignation of a prince, nor yet at any tyme
so unseasonable as when it lighteth on those y^t might
expect an harvest of theire carefull and painfull labours,
He that is once woonded must feele smart tyll his ~
wound be cured, or the part senselesse be cutt off; if I re=
port not her Matie hart being obdurate; and be wthout
sense I cannot, being made of fleshe and blood. But
then you say I may ayme at this ende, I doe more then
ayme, for I see an ende of all my fortunes, and have
sett an ende to all my desyres. In this course doe I
any thing for myne enimyes? when I was present I founde
them absolute, and therefore I had rather they shoulde
triumphe alone, then have me attendant on theire charriotts
Or doe I leave my freinde, when I was a Courtier I
coulde yeelde no fruyts of my love to them, nowe I am an
hermytt, they shall feare no envie for theire love to me;
Or doe I forsake my selfe, bycause I doe enioye my
selfe; Or doe I overthrowe my fortune, bycause I buyld
not my fortune of paper walls, wth everie puffe of
wynde bloweth downe; Or doe I inyniate myne honour,
bycause I leave following the pursuyte, or wearinge
the false marke of the shadowe of honour; Doe I
gyve corage or comfort to the forraigne enimyes, bycause

I reserve my self to encounter them, or because I keepe
my heart from basenes, thoughe I can not keepe my
fortune from declyninge; no, no, I gyve every off theese
considerations his deue right, and the more I weighe,
the more I fynde my self justified from offendings in
any one off them; As for the two last objections,
that I forsake my contrey when it hathe most neede
off me, and fayle in that indissoluble dutye which I
owe to my soveraigne; I answere, that if my contrey
had at this tyme nede off my publique service, her
ma.tie that governs it, wolde not have dryven me to a
private lyfe; I am tyed to my contrey by two bonds,
one publique, to discharge carefully, faithfully, and
industriouslie, that trust that is committed unto me,
and thother private, to sacrifice for it my lyfe and
carcase which hathe bene norished in it; from the first
I am freed, being dismissed or misliked by her ma.tie;
Off the other, nothings can free me but death; and
therfore, no occasion off performance shall offer it self,
but I will meete it half way. The indissoluble
dutie which I owe to her ma.tie, is onlie the dutie off
alleageance, which neither will, nor can fayle in me. The
dutie off attendance is no indissoluble dutie; I owe
her ma.tie the office: dutie: off an Earle Marshall off
England; I have bene content to doe her the service
off a Clarke, but I can never serve her as a villain
or a slave; But yet you say I must gyve way to tyme;

I reserue my self to encounter them, or bycause I keepe
my hart from basenes, though I can not keepe my
fortune from declynynge; no, no, I gyve every of these   45
considerations his dewe right, and the more I weigh,
the more I fynde my self Iustified from offendinge in
any one of them; As for the two last obiections,
that I forsake my countrey when it hathe most neede
of me, and fayle in that indissoluble dutye wch I   50
owe to my soveraigne; I answere, that if my Countrey
had at this tyme nede of my publique service, her
Maiestie that governs it, wolde not have dryven me to a
private lyfe; I am tyde to my countrey by two bondes,
one publique, to discharge carefully, faithfully, and – –   55
industriouslie, that trust that is commytted vnto me,
and thother pryvate, to sacrifice for it my lyfe and
Carase wch hathe bene norished in it; From the first
I am freed, being dismyssed or misliked by her Maiestie;
Of the other, nothinge can free me but death; and   60
therfore, no occasion of performance shall offer it self,
but I will meete it half way. The indissoluble
dewtie wch I owe to her Maiestie, is onlie the dutie of
alleageaunce, wch neither will, nor can fayle in me. The
dutie of attendaunce is no indissoluble dutie; I owe   65
her Maiestie the office: dutie: of an Earle Marshall of
England; I haue bene content to doe her the service
of a Clarke, but I can never serve her as a villain
or a slave; But yet you say I must gyve way to tyme,

So I doe, for nowe I see the storme come, I haue put   70
my self into harbor; Seneca sayeth, we must gyve –
way to fortune, I knowe that fortune is bothe blinde and
stronge, and therfore I goe as farre out of the way –
as I can; you say, the remedie is not to stryve, I
neither stryve, nor seeke for remedie; But I must yeelde   75
and submytt: I can never yeeld my self to be guyltie, or
this imposition lately layde vpun me to be iust: I owe
so muche to the author of truthe, as I can never yeeld
truthe to be falshood, or falshood to be truthe. / have
I gyven cause you aske, and ⟨y⟩ take a scandall: no, I   80
gave no cause to take vp so muche as *Phymbria: Phyne =*
as: his complaintes: for I dyd *Totum telum corpore recipere,*
I pacientlie beare and senciblie feele all that I then –
receyved when the Scandall was gyven me, nay, when
the vylest of all indignities was done vnto me; Dothe –   85
religion enforce me to sewe? dothe god require it? is it
impietie not to doe it? why? can not princes Erre?
and can not subiectes receyve wronge? is an earthlie –
power, an authoritie infinyte? Pardon me, pardon me,
my lorde, I can never subscribe to these principles: let   90
Salomons foole laugh when he is striken, let those
that meane to make their proffytt of Princes faltes,
shewe to have no sence of Princes Iniuries: let them
acknowledge an infinite absolutenes in earth, that doe
not beleue an infinite absolutenes in heaven. / as for   95

So I doe, for nowe I see the storme come, I have put
my selfe into harbro5; Seneca sayeth, we must give
way to fortune, I knowe that fortune is both blinde and
stronge, and therfore I goe as farre out off the way
as I can; you say, the remedie is not to stryve, I
neither stryve, nor seeke for remedie. But I must yeeld
and submytt: I can never yeeld my selfe to be guyltie, or
this imposition lately layde upon me to be iust: I owe
so muche to the author off truthe, as I can never yeeld
truthe to be falshood, or falshood to be truthe. Have
I given cause you aske, and I take a scandall: no, I
gave no cause to take up so muche as _Phymbria: Phyne-
as:_ his complainte: for I dyd _Totum telum corpore recipere,_
I pacientlie beare and sencablie feele all that I then
receyved upon the scandall was given me, nay, when
the vylest off all indignities was done unto me; Dothe
religion enforce me to sewe? dothe god require it? is it
impietie not to doe it? why? can not princes erre?
and can not subiects receyve wronge? is an earthlie
power, an authoritie infinyte? Pardon me, pardon me,
my lordes, I can never subscribe to thes principles: let
Salomons foole laughe when he is strikon, let those
that meane to make their proffett off Princes faltes,
shewe to have no sense off Princes iniuries: let them
acknowledge an infinite absolutenes in earthe, that doe
not beleve an infinite absolutenes in heaven. As for

me, I haue receyved wronge and I feele it, my cause is
good and I knowe it, and whatsoever come, all the
powers on earth can never showe more strength or
constancye in oppressinge, then I can showe in suffe-
ringe, whatsoever shall or can be imposed on me. /
Yor lordshippe in the beginninge off yor letter, makes
yor self a looker on, and me a player off myne owne
game, so you may see more then I: But you must
geve me leave to tell you in thende off myne: That
thence you but se, and I doe suffer; I must needs
feele more then you; I must crave yor lordshippes
pardonet, to geve hym leave that hath a crabbed
fortune, to use a crabbed stile. / But whatsoever
my stile is, there is no hart more humble, nor more
affected towardes you, then that off yor lordshippes
poore frend. /

             Essex:

    Articles whereupon Therle off Essex
    was accused in the Starre chamber.
    .29. November. 1599 ./.

·1· First, for dilapidations, spendinges, and wrongfull
    using her Ma[hie] treasure committed unto hym. /

·2· Secondlie, for tarying in England a monneth after
    his directions in goinge into Ireland. /.

me, I haue receyved wrong and I feele it, my cause is
good and I knowe it, and whatsoever come, all the –
powers on earth can never shewe more strength or –
constancye in oppressinge, then I can shewe in suffe =
ringe, whatsoever shall or can be imposed on me. /   100
Your lordshippe in the beginnynge of your letter, makes
your self a looker on, and me a player of myne owne
game, so you may see more then I: But you must –
gyve me leave to tell you in thende of myne: That
sithence you but see, and I doe suffer; I must needes   105
feele more then you; I must crave your lordshippes
pacyence, to gyve hym leave that hathe a crabbed
fortune, to vse a crabbed stile. / But whatsoever
my stile is, there is no hart more humble, nor more
affected towardes you, then that of your lordshippes   110
poore Frend. /

                                        Essex:

[3   29 November 1599   see Commentary]

                 Articles wherevpon Therle of Essex   1
                 was accused in the Starre chamber.
                      .29. November. 1599. /.
.1.   First, for dilapentions, spendinge, and wrongfull
       vsing her Maiestie treasure commytted vnto hym. /   5
.2.   Secondlie, for tarying in England .2. Monnethes after
       his directions in goinge into Ireland. /.

.3.   Thirdlie, for not followinge Th'erle of Tyrone
       her Maiestie enimye at his first arryvall. /

.4.   Fourthlie, for talkinge wth Tyrone, wthout libertie   10
       of her Maiestie and Counsell. /.

.5.   Fiftlie, for Commytting the Armye to Th'erle
       of Wormewood yt was commytted to himself. /.

.6.   Sixtlie, for gyving vp the Swoorde of Iustice to
       the deputies handes wthout lycence. /.   15

.7.   Lastlie, for leavinge his charge, and commynge into
       England, beinge forbydden and Commaunded the
       contrarie. /.

3. Thirdlie, for not followinge the Erle of Tyrone her Ma.tie enimye at his first overthrall./

4. ffowrthlie, for talkinge w.th the Erle, w.thout libertie of her Ma.tie and Counsell./

5. ffiftlie, for Comittinge the Armye to the Erle of wormewood that was comitted to himselfe./

6. Sixtlie, for gyuing vp the sworde of Justice to the Deputies hande w.thout lycence./

7. Lastlie, for leavinge his charge, and comynge into England, beinge forbydden and Commaunded the contrarie./

My dutifull affection to yo[r] Ma[tie] alwayes so overwayned
all other worldlie respecte, that seeking in all p[ar]ticuler
to manifest my trueth, I have maymed my estate
in generall.:/

As I dare in the Zeale of my thoughtes compare w[th]
the greatest that ever vowed youre faithfull allegeaunce,
so is there not the meanest that passe not out stript
me, I will not say in recompence, but in some p[ro]portions
estate of service, those w[hi]le my faith wrastlethe
w[th] my fortune, the one raynneth to beare the
other downe.

Though I have no hope to repayre the ruynes of my
overthrowt, yet I can not but p[re]sume, that youre Ma[tie]
will suffer me to preserve them from blowinge vpp. and
what youth and forward beliefe have vndermyned in
myne estate: p[ro]vydence by a retyred lyfe may vnderlay
for w[th] discontynuance from Courte, there shall be added
(iff any thinge may be added) nowaies of loyaltie; nor
so solitarie shall be my course, as it shall seeme to
p[ro]ceede of discontentment, but of necessitie. And in
all actions bothe w[th] my lyfe and lyving so forwardes,
as though some may have outronne me in fortune, now shall
in dutie. /

Next my allegeaunce to yo[r] Ma[tie] (w[ch] shall be held most
sacred and inviolable) the respecte of myne honor calling
chiefe interest; wth that I may preserve in woonted state

[4   mid-1598–before 5 June 1600 (?)   see Commentary]

            Th'erle of Essex his letter to   1
                her Maiestie: /
My duetifull affection to your Maiestie alwayes so overaymed
all other worldlie respectes, that seeking in all perticuler
to manifest my truthe, I have maymed my estate – –   5
in generall. /
As I dare in the Zeale of my thoughtes compare wth
the greatest that ever vowed youre faithfull alleageance,
so is there not the meanest that hathe not outstript
me, I will not say in recompence, but in some gratious   10
estate of service, Thus while my faith wrestleth
wth my fortune, the one wynneth breath to beare the
other downe. /
Though I have no hope to repayre the ruynes of my
oversight, yet I can not but presume, that youre Maiestie   15
will suffer me to preserue them from blowinge vp. and
what youthe and forward beliefe haue vndermyned in
myne estate: provydence by a retyred lyfe may vnderlay.
In wch discontynuance from Courte, there shall be added
(if any thinge may be added) encrease of loyaltie; nor   20
so solitarie shall be my course, as it shall seeme to –
proceede of discontentment, but of necessitie. And in
all actions bothe wth my lyfe and lyving so forwarde,
as though some may haue outronne me in fortune, none shall
in dutie. /   25
Next my alleageance to your Maiestie (wch shall be held most
sacred and inviolable) the respectes of myne honor challenge
chiefe interest; wch that I may preserue in woonted state

for your service, is reason to drawe me to stay my self –
slyppinge, from fallinge./.   30
That of late (by what secrett or venemous blowes I
knowe not) my faithe hathe receyved some woundes; your
Maiesties wonted grace wthdrawne assures me, but truthe &
my patience in this case are one wth me, and tyme in
youre princely thoughtes may weare it out for me./ Let   35
heaven be Iudge, I will leave you wth as greate a – –
lothnesse, even as that I were to loose what I love
best; but your favoure faylinge, in wch I haue placed –
all my hopes, and my self lesse graced after seaven yeeres,
then when I had served but seaven dayes; may be occasion   40
to excuse, if there were no other reason./
These thinges pressed out of a distressed mynde, & offred
in all humilitie: I hope it shall not be offensyve, if I
chuse in this wearysome course, rather to be retyred, then
tyred./   45
If any of envie take advantage of absence, seekinge by
Cunnynge to drawe me into suspition of discontentment,
my confydence is setled in your never erringe Iudgment, yt
if he come wth Esawes handes and Iacobs voyce, youre
highnes will censure it but a rowgh malice, vnder smooth – –   50
simplicitie./
It is true, that griefe can not speake, and these griefes haue
made me to wryte, least yt when I leave you, I shoulde so
forsake my self, as to leave this vnsayde./
To youre graces acceptance I commend it, and wth all – –   55
humble and reverend thoughtes that may be, rest ever readie
to be commaunded to dye at youre feete./.

for yo[r] service, is reason to drawe me to stay my self ~
slyppinge, from fallinge. /

That off late (by what secrett or venemous blowes I
knowe not) my father hathe receyved some wounded; yo[r]
ma[jesties] wonted grace w[i]thdrawne assures me, but truly
my patience in this case are one w[i]th me, and tyme in
yo[ur] princely thoughtes may weare it out for me. / Let
reason be Judge, I will leave you w[i]th as greate a ~
losse w[i]sh, then as that I were to loose what I love
best; but yo[r] favoure faylinge, in w[hi]ch I have placed ~
all my hopes, and my self lesse graced after seaven yeares,
then when I had served but seaven dayes: may be occasion
to exprese, iff there were no other reason. /

These thinge pressed out off a distressed mynde, & offred
in all humilitie: I hope it shall not be offensybe, iff I
chuse in this wearysome course, rather to be retyred, then
tyred. /

Iff any off entire take advantage off absence, seekinge by
Emmynge to drawe me into suspition off discontentment,
my confydence is settled in yo[r] never erringe Judgment, &
iff he come w[i]th Esawes hande and Jacobs voyce, yo[ur]
highnes will censure it but a wronge malice, under smooth ~
simplicitie. /

It is true, that griefe can not speake, and these griefes have
made me to wryte, least that when I leave you, I should so
forsake my self, as to leave this unsayde. /

To yo[ur] graced acceptance I commend it, and w[i]th all ~
humble and reverend thoughtes that may be, rest ever readie
to be commaunded to dye at yo[ur] feete. /

Earlie did I hope this morninge to have had myne eyes
blest w[th] yo[ur] Ma[ties] beautie, But seings the sunne dept
into a clowde, and meeting w[th] spirites that did presage by
the wheeles off their Charriott some thunder in the ayre,
I must complayne and expresse my feares to that hie
Ma[tie] and devine oracle, from whence I receyved a
doubtfull answer: vnto whose power I must sacrifice
again the teares and prayers off the afflicted, y[t] must
dispaire in tyme, iff it be to soone to importune heaven,
w[hen] we feele the miseries off hell; or that wordes
directed to yo[r] sacred wisdome should be out off season
delyvered for my vnfortunate Brother, whom all men have
libertie to defame, as iff his offences were capitall, and
he so base descended a creature, that his love, his lyfe,
his servise to yo[r] Ma[tie] and the state, had deserved no
absolution after so hard punyshment; or so much as
to answer in yo[ur] faire presence, who woold bouche safe
more Justice and favo[r] then he can expect off partiall
Judges or those combyned ennemyes, y[t] labour vpon false
groundes to buylde his ruyne, vrginge his falte as
crymynall to yo[r] devine honor; Thinkinges it a heaven
to blaspheme heaven: when their own particuler malice
and coveybles have practised onlie to gluett them selves
in their privat revenge, not regarding yo[r] servise or
losse so much as their ambitious endes, to rise by his
overthrowe. And I have reason to apprehend, that

[5   late February (?) 1600   see Commentary]

The Ladie Rich to her Maiestie   1

Earlie did I hope this morninge to have had myne eyes
blest wth youre Maiesties beautie, But seinge the Sunne depart
into a clowde, and meeting wth spirittes that did presage by
the wheeles of their Chariottes some Thunder in the Ayre,   5
I must complayne and expresse my feares to that high
Maiestie and devine Oracle, from whence I receyved a –
doubtfull answer: vnto whose power I must sacrifice
again the teares and prayers of the afflicted, yt must
dispaire in tyme, if it be to soone to importune heaven,   10
when we feele the miseries of hell; or that wordes –
directed to your sacred wisdome should be out of season
delyuered for my vnfortunate Brother, whom all men haue
libertie to defame, as if his offences were Capitall, and
he so base deiected a creature, that his love, his lyfe,   15
his service to your Maiestie and the state, had deserved no
absolution after so hard punyshment; or so muche as
to answer in youre faire presence, who wolde vouchsafe
more Iustice and favour, then he can expect of partiall
Iudges or those combyned enimyes, yt Laboure vpon false   20
groundes to buylde his ruyne, vrginge his faltes as –
cryminall to your devine honor; Thinkinge it a heaven
to blaspheme heaven: when their own perticuler Malice
and counsayles haue practised onlie to glutt them selues
in their private revenge, not regarding your service or   25
losse so muche as their ambitious ende, to ryse by his
overthrowe./ And I haue reason to apprehend, that

if your fayre handes doe not checke the course of their –
vnbrideled hate, their last course will be his last breath,
since the evyll instrumentes (that by their office & cunnynge)   30
they provyde for the feast, have sufficient poyson in their hartes
to infect the service they will seeme shall be easie to disgest
till it be tasted; and then it will prove but a preparation
for greater mischiefe concealed by such craftie workmen
as will not onlie pull <u>downe</u> all the obstacles of their –   35
greatnesse, but when they are in their full strength, like the
Gyantes make warre against heaven./ But your Maiesties gratious
conclusion in gyvinge a hope of the voyder is all ye comfort
I haue, wch if you hasten not before he take a full surfeite
of disgraces, they will say the spottes they have cast against   40
hym are too fowle to be <u>taken</u> away; and so his blemished
reputation must disable hym for ever serving again his
sacred goddesse: whose excellent beautie and perfection will
never suffer those fayre eyes to turn so farre from compass =
ion, but that at the least, if he may not return to the   45
happinesse of his former service, to lyve at the feete of
his admyred mistresse: yet he may sytt down to a private
lyfe, wthout the Imputacion of infamye, that his posteritie
may not repent their fathers were borne of so hard a –
destenye; two of them perishing by being imployed in one   50
Countrie, where they wolde haue done you loyall service
to the sheddinge of their last bloodde: if they had not bene
wounded to the death by them and their factions that care
not on whose neckes they vniustlie buylde the walles of their

iff yo{r} fayre hande doe not checke the course off their
vnbridoled gate, their last course will be his last breath,
since the obyll instrumentes (that by their office & cunnynge)
they provyde for the feast, have sufficient poyson in their hartes
to infect the services they will serve, shall be easie to digest
till it be tasted; and then it will prove but a preparation
for greater mischiefe concealed by suche craftie workmen
as will not onlie pull downe all the obstacles off their
greatnesse, but when they are in their full strengthe, like the
Gyantes make warre against heaven. But yo{r} Ma{tie} gratious
conclusion in gyvinge a hope off the wonder is all y{e} comfort
I have, vff iff you hasten not before he take a full surfeite
off disgraces, they will say the spottes they have cast against
him are too fowle to be taken away; and so his blemisshed
reputation must disable him for ever servinge again his
sacred goddesse: whose excellent beantie and perfection will
never suffer those fayre eyes to turn so farre from compassion, but that at the least, iff he may not return to the
happinesse off his former service, to lyve at the feete off
his admyred mistresse: yet he may sytt downe to a privat
lyfe, wthout the imputacion off infamye, that his posteritie
may not repent their fathers were borne off so hard a
destonye; two off them perisshing by being imployed in one
comtrie, where they would have done you loyall service
to the shedding off their last bloode: iff they had not bene
wounded to the death by them and their factions that care
not on whose necke they builde be the walles off their

owne fortunes: w[hi]ch I feare will growe more dangerouslye
stinge then it is discovered, iff god do not hinder the workes
as the Tower off Babell, and confounde their Tongues that
understand one another too well./ And lastlie, since out
off yo[u]r Ma[jes]ties owne princely nature and unstayned vertue,
theire must needes appeare, that mercye is not farre from
such beautie, I most humblie besech you to make it
youre owne woorke, and not to suffer those that lye in
ambush to take advantage, thinking (so soone as they
discover a relenting and compassion in youre worthie
mynde) to take the honor upon them as meanes off our
salvation; not out off charitie, but pryde: that all must
be attributed to them, and youre sacred clemencye abusd
by forcinge us to go throughe purgatorie to heaven;
But let yo[u]r Ma[jes]ties devine power be no more eclypsed then
youre Beautie, w[hi]ch hathe shyned throughe the woorlde;
and imitate the highest in not distroyinge those that
trust onlie in youre mercie: w[hi]ch w[i]th humble request I
presume to kyss yo[u]r sacred hands, owinge the
obedience and endles love off :/

Yo[u]r Ma[jes]ties most dutifull
and loyall servant

own fortunes: wch I feare will growe more daungerouslye   55
high then it is discovered, if god do not hinder the workes
as the Tower of Babell, and confounde their Tounges that
vnderstand one another too well./ And lastlie, since out
of your Maiesties owne princely nature and vnstayned vertue,
their must needes appeare, that mercye is not farre from   60
suche beautie, I most humblie beseche you to make it
youre owne worke, and not to suffer those that lye in
ambush to take advantage, thinking (so soone as they
discover a relenting and compassion in youre worthie
mynde) to take the honor vpon them as meanes of our   65
salvation; not out of charitie, but pryde? that all must
be attributed to them, and youre sacred clemencye abused
by forcinge vs to go through purgatorie to heaven;
But let your Maiesties devine power be no more eclypsed then
youre Beautie, wch hathe shyned through the worlde;   70
and Imitate the highest in not distroyinge those that
trust onlie in youre mercie: wth wch humble request I
presume to kysse your sacred handes, vowinge the –
obedience and endles love of ./

                 Your Maiesties most duetifull   75
                 and loyall Servant

[6   3 December 1599   see Commentary]

Frauncis Bacon his letter to my   1
lord henrie howarde:/.
My verie good lorde. There be verie fewe besydes youre
self, to whom I wolde performe this respect: For I
contemne *mendacia famæ* as it walkes amonge inferiours, though   5
I neglect it not as it may haue entraunce to some eare. For
your Lordshippes love grounded vpon good opinion I esteeme it
highlie, bycause I haue tasted of the fruytes of it, and we
bothe haue tasted of the better water in my accompte to knytt
myndes together. There is shaped a tale in a lewde forge yt   10
beateth a pace at this tyme, that I shoulde delyver my opinion
to the Queene, in my lord of Essex his case: First, that
it was Premunire, and nowe last, that it was highe treason;
and this opinion to be in opposition and encounter of the lord
Chiefe Iustices opinion, and the Attarney generall. My lorde,   15
I thanke god my witt serveth me not to delyver any opinion
wch my stomack serveth me not to maintaine, and the same
conscience of dutie guydinge and fortefyinge me. But the
vntruthe of this fable God and my Soveraigne can witnesse,
and there I leave it, knowinge no other remedie against lyes,   20
then others haue done against Libells. The Roote of it
no doubt is some light headded envie at my accesses to her
Maiestie, wch being begonne and contynued since my childehoode,
so long as her Maiestie shall thinke me worthie of them, I
scorn those that shall thinke the contrarie. And another   25
thing is the aspersion of this tale and the envie therof
vpon some greater man in respect of my nearnes. And
therfore my lord: I humblie pray you aunswer for me to
any personn that you thinke worthie youre owne replie &

8

Fraunces Bacon his letter to my
lord Henrie Howarde :/.

My verie good lorde. There be verie fewe besydes your
selfe, to whom I wolde performe this respect: ffor I
contemne mendacia famae as it walkes amongst inferiours, though
I neglect it not as it may have entrance to some eares. ffor
your Lordshippe love grounded vpon good opinion I esteeme it
highlie, bycause I have tasted of the fruytes of it, and we
bothe have tasted of the better water in my accompte to knytt
myndes together. There is shaped a tale in a lewde forge, that
beateth a pace at this tyme, that I should delyver my opinion
to the Queene, in my lord of Essex his case: ffirst, that
it was Premunire, and nowe last, that it was highe treason;
and this opinion to be in opposition and encounter of the lord
chiefe Justices opinion, and the Attorney generall. My lords,
I thanke god my witt serveth me not to delyver any opinion
wch my stomack serveth me not to maintaine, and that same
conscience of dutie guydinge and fortefyinge me. But the
untruthe of this fable God and my Soveraigne can witnesse,
and there I leave it, knowinge no other remedie against lyes,
then others have done against Libells. The roote of it
no doubt is some light headded envie at my accesse to her
Ma, wch being begonne and contynued since my Childehoode,
so long as her Ma shall thinke me worthie of them, I
scorne those that shall thinke the contrarie. And another
thing is the aspersion of this tale and the envie thereof
vpon some greater man in respect of my warines. And
therfore my lord: I humblie pray you answer for me to
any persone that you thinke worthie youre owne replie

my defence. ffor my Lo: of Essex, I am not servile to
hym, having regard to my superior Dutie, I have bene
much bounde to hym, and on the other syde I doe protest
before god I have spent more thoughte about his welldoing
then ever I dyd about myne owne. I pray god you his
freinde be in the right. Nulla remedia tam faciunt dolorem quam
quæ sunt salutaria. ffor my parte I have deserved better
then to have my name objected to envie, and my lyfe to a
ruffians violence, but I have the pritie coate of a
good conscience, I am sure that comfort and benefits
quit my Lo: more then all. So having writt to yor
Lo: in freedome, I desyre exceedinglye to be preserved
in youre Lops good opinion and love, and so betake you to
gods goodnes. /

My lordes answere to Mr Bacon. /

I might be thought unworthie good Mr Bacon: of that
good conceyte you have of me, iff I dyd not sympathize
with so sensitive a mynde in this smarte of wrongfull imputacon
of unthankfullnes; you were the fyrst that gave me
notice I protest at Richmond of that rumor; though
within two dayes after I heard more then I wold of it,
But as you suffer more then you deserve, so can I not
beleve what the giddie malice of the worlde hath layd
upon you. The travaile of that worthie gent in youre
behalf when you stood for a place of credyt, the delight
wch he hath ever taken in youre companie, his griefe that
he could not scale up thaffayres of his lyvely fruytes,
advise, and offices, proporcionable to an infinite desyre, his

my defence. For my Lord of Essex, I am not servile to   30
hym, having regard to my superiour dutie, I haue bene
muche bounde to hym, and on thother syde I doe protest
before god I haue spent more thoughtes about his welldoing
then ever I dyd about myne owne. I pray god you his
freindes be in the right *Nulla remedia tam faciunt dolorem quam*   35
quæ sunt salutaria. For my parte I haue deserved better
then to haue my name obiected to envie, and my lyfe to a
Ruffians violence, but I haue the privie Coate of a
good Conscience, I am sure those courses and brutes –
hurt my Lord more then all. So having writt to your   40
Lordshippe in freedome, I desyre exceedinglye to be preserved
in youre Lordshipes good opinion and love, and so leave you to
godes goodnes./.

[7   shortly after 3 December 1599   see Commentary]

My lordes aunswere to Mr Bacon./.   1
I might be thought vnworthie good Mr Bacon: of that
good conceyte you haue of me, if I dyd not Simpathize
wth so sensitive a mynde in this smarte of wrongfull imputacion
of vnthankfullnes; you were the fyrst that gave me –   5
notice I protest at Richmond of that rumour; though –
wth in two dayes after I heard more then I wolde of it,
But as you suffer more then you deserue, so can I not – –
beleve what the gyddie malice of the worlde hath layd
vpon you. The travaile of that worthie gentleman in youre   10
behalf when you stood for a place of credytt, the delight
wch he hathe ever taken in youre companie, his griefe that
he coulde not seale vp th'assurance of his lyvely fruytes,
effectes, and offices, proporcionable to an infinite desyre, his

studie by my knowledge to engage youre love by the best − −   15
meanes he coulde devise, are forcible perswasions and instances
to make me Iudge, that a gentleman so well borne, a wise gentleman
so well levelled, a gentleman so highlie valued, by one of his
vertue? worth? and qualitie? will rather hunt after all occasions
of expressing thankfullnes (so farre as dutie dothe permytt)   20
then either omytt oportunitie or increase indignation. No man
alive out of the thoughtes of Iudgment, the groundes of
knowledg, and lessons of experience, is better able to distin =
quishe betweene publique and private offices, and to direct a
measure of keeping measure in discharge of bothe. To wch   25
I will referre you to the fyndinge out of the golden Nomber.
and in myne owne perticuler opinion esteeme of you as I haue
ever done, and youre rare partes deserue, and so farre as my
voice hathe creditt iustifie youre creditt, accordinge to the warrant of youre profession, and the scope of my best wishes   30
in all degrees towardes you. / / My creditt is so weake in −
workinge any strong effectes of frendship where I wolde doe
most, as to speake of blossomes wthout givinge taste of fruites
were Idlenes: But if you will give credite to my wordes,
it is not long since I gave testimonie of my good affection   35
in the eare of one that neither wantes desire nor meanes to
doe for you./ Thus wishinge to youre creditt yt allowance
of respect and reverence, wch youre wise and honest
dothe deserue, and resting readie to relieve all myndes (so
farre as my abilitie and meanes will stretche) that groane   40
vnder the burden of vndeserved wronges: I commend −
you to Goddes protection, and my self to the best vse
that you will make of me./ In haste from my Lodginge./

studie by my knowledge to engage yonr love by the best
meanes he coulde devise, aws forcible perswasions and instances
to make me iudge, that a gent so well borne, a wise gent
so well beloved, a gent so littlie valued, by one off his
vertue, worth, and qualities, will rather gnat after all occasions
off expressing thankfullnes (so farre as duttie dothe permytt)
then either omytt oportunitie or increase indignation. No man
alive out off the thoughtes off iudgment, the groundes off
knowledge, and lessons off experience, is better able to distin=
guishe betweene publique and privbate offices, and to direct a
measure off keeping measure in discharge off both. To this
I will referre you to the fyndinge out off the golden Nomber.
and in myne owne particuler opinion esteeme off you as I have
ever done, and yonr vast parttes deserve, and so farre as my
voice gathe creditt iustifie yonr creditt, accordinge to the war
rant off yonr profession, and the scope off my best wishes
in all degrees towardes you. / My creditt is so weake in
workinges any stronge effecte off frendship where I wolde do
most, as to speake off blossoms whout givinge taste off fruit
were folenes: But iff you will give credite to my wordes,
it is not long since I gave testimonie off my good affection
in the vast off one that neither wante desire nor meanes to
doe for you. / Thus wisshinge to yonr creditt & allowance
off respect and reverence, wh yonr wise and honest
dothe deserve, and restinge readie to relieve all myndes (so
farre as my abilitie and meanes will stretche) that groane
under the burden off undeserved wronges: I commend
you to Goddes protection, and my selff to the best use
that you will make off me. / In haste from my Lodginge. /

The Speache of Mr Secretarie in the
Starrechamber, in the Monethe of februarij.
1601. Anno Regina. 43.

I have many tymes spoken in this place, yet did I never speake
vpon greater cause of griefe in some degree, nor stirred vp w{th}
greater ioye and comforte in another, in regarde that our iust
god hath so miraculously preserued my gracious Queene from
the bloodie hand of hir most treacherous & popular Trayto{r}
Essex: who for the space of theise .8. yeares, hath greedely
thirsted to be King of England, and to haue sette hir or hir
sacred person in the place of confusion w{th} Richard the .2.
And for the better effecting his purpose theise were the
meanes he had: wytt he wanted none, Power & Authoritie
that was geuen to him, fauoure he had in abundant measure,
And himselfe was one of the priuie Counsell.

The steppes w{ch} by degrees he followed
were theise:

first, his plott w{th} Tyrone y{e} Archetraytor was wrought
by letters sent by Blunt his chiefe counsellor in all those
actions, w{th} whom there was a secret conspiracie w{th} Tyrone
of their desyred subuersion of the estate of England: and
that the traytor Essex his comynge into England, was to
no other ende, but hoping after a Momethes stay w{th} the
Queene to attribute some of his deceytfull and flatteringe
practises w{th} hir highnes, and so to haue in his returne
most a wretched Tyrone w{th} .4000. men, who should also
w{th} his power of Irishe rebells haue inuaded this Realme
of England.

The second steppe, he spent his substance, promised pre-

[8   after 13 February 1601–before 19 February 1601   see Commentary]

The Speach of Mr Secretarie in the   1
Starrchamber, in the Moneth of februarij.
.1601. Anno Regina. 43.
I haue many tymes spoken in this place, Yet did I never speake
vpon greater cause of griefe in one degree, nor stirred vp wth   5
greater Ioye and comforte in another, in regarde that our iust
god hath so miraculously preserued my gratious Queene from
the bloodie hand of yt most trecherous & popular Traytor
Essex: who for the space of these.6. Yeeres, hath greedely
thirsted to be King of England, and to haue lefte her   10
sacred person in the place of Confusion wth *Richard the*.2·.
And for the better effecting his purpose these were the
meanes he had: Wytt he wanted none, Power & Authoritie
that was geven to hym, favoure he had in abundant measure,
And himself was one of the privie Counsell./   15
        The steppes wch by degrees he followed
                were these:/
First, his plott wth Tyrone yt Archtraytor was wrought
by letters sent by. Blunt his cheife counsellor in all these
actions, wherin there was a 'secret conspiracie wth Tyrone   20
of their desyred subuersion of the estate of England: and
that the traytor Essex his commynge into England, was to
no other ende, but hoping after a Monnethes stay wth the
Queene to atchive some of his deceytfull and flatteringe
practises wth her highnes, and so to haue in his returne   25
mett & receyved Tyrone wth.8000. men, who should also
wth his power of Irishe rebells haue invaded this Realme
of England./.
The second steppe, he spent his substaunce, promised pre =

fermentes, and gave advauncement to soldiers to winne their   30
generall love to hym./.
The third stepp was his great shewe of Religion to the
Ministerie, in whose sight no man more Zealous then hee./.
The .4. stepp argued and approved his affection to popish
priestes and their schismaticall errors, of whose condition   35
he vpheld more unde⟨r⟩ his pretence & colour of intelligence
for the good of the state, then all the Counsell of England
besydes, for his favour to them was ever great, and his
mercie to them was never wantinge, and to win them
the more he proposed to suppresse this religion, and   40
promysed to maintein poperie, & gyve libertie of conscience./
The .5. stepp, to carie the hartes of the Cominaltie, was
manifested by + his + great affabilitie & curtesie: for his ambitious
reachinge desyer was to be popular, but at length he blinded
hymself in his owne follie, when he sent Temple his   45
chiefe Secretarie into London on Satterday being the .7.
of Februarij .1600. to move assistaunce & procure prepa =
ration of strength amongst his frendes to this his divelish
enterprice for the accomplishment of his hartes desyre./.
The .6. stepp, before his commynge out of Ireland, that   50
popular traytor Essex greatlie envying the Authoritie
that was gyven some men by the Counsell here in
England, who executed the same in Ireland, in regarde
his vnsatiable desyre to the Crowne of England
was no way to be quenched but by the suppressing of   55
suche as he dyd dispayre ever to wyn to be combyned
wth hym in his trecherie, they not making for his purpose
depryved them from the Power of their Commaundes
fearinge yt else they wolde see to farre into his villanie wth
Egles eyes./.   60

furmente, and gave advancemente to souldiers to winne their
generall love to him. /

The third steppe was his great shew of Religion to the
Ministerie, in respect whereof no man more zealous then he. /

The 4. steppe argued and approved his affection to popish
priests and their schismaticall vicours, of whose condicion
he wolde move under his pretence & colour of intelligence
for the good of the state, then all the Counsell of Engl:
besydes, for his favor to them was ever great, and his
mercie to them was never wantinge, and to win them
the more he purposed to suppresse this religion, and
promysed to maintein poperie, & gyve libertie of conscience. /

The 5. steppe, to raise the hartes of the Dommaltie, was
manifested by his great affabilitie & curtesie: for his ambitious
reachinge desyer was to be populars, but at length he blinde
himselfe in his owne follie, when he sent Cuffe his
chiefe Secretarie into London on Saterday being the 7.
of Februarij 1600. to move assistance & provoke prepa=
ration of strength amongst his frendes to this his divelish
enterprise for the accomplishment of his hartes desyre. /

The 6. steppe, before his comminge out of Ireland, that
populars travels & his greathe enioynge the Authoritie
that was gyven some men by the Counsell here in
England, who executed the same in Ireland, in regardes
his unsatiable desyre to the Crowne of England
was no way to be quenched but by the suppressinge of
suche as he dyd dispayre ever to wyn to be combyned
with him in his heresie, they not making for his purpose
deprived them from the Power of their Commaunded
saieinge & else they wolde soe to farre into his villanie with
Engl. obs. /

Blunt in his confession to the Counsell acknowledged to be
reconciled to the Pope in Ireland, and for discharge of
his conscience (as he said) revealed many of their ~
treyborous actions, as at their arraignment will be more
manifest.

As for the traytor Davis that hath longe tyme bene a proud
knave and of Base condition, who was by this popular
traytor Essex advanced to keepe the Lord Keeper,
the Chiefe Justice of England, and others of the counsell
at his comandement, and himselfe to keepe the great
Seale of England, and was this villanous traytor
Davis now, or can it be thought possible he had bene
before of that Religion professed by Essex and ——
assistant to maintain trewe religion as they counter-
fayted in profession, who no sooner was comitted to prison,
but openly and audariously called for a priest to absolve him.
And was this all, no not by much: for amongst the rest,
that seditious booke of Henry the 4: by his owne practice
being dedicated to himselfe by the woordes of Celsitudine
tua &c: was he kept 14 dayes in his trayterous bosome,
and then acquainted the Lo: great Canterbury therwith to
colour his Macchebilian meaning therein, as wishing the same
might be supprest.

What was his pretence in this his last diabolicall treason
did he not as he was pricked forward in his trayterous ~
rebellion, doatinge upon the affection of the people to him,
who out in base speeches that he was in feare to be murthered
in his bed by Cobham, Rawley, & Cicill:

To stirre up her Mates subiectes the rather to follow him,
and having drawne the most partes of them into this nett of

Blunt in his confession to the Counsell acknowledged to be
reconciled to the Pope in Ireland, and for discharge of
his conscience (as he said) revealed many of these –
traytorous actions, as at their arraignment will be more
manifest./.   65
As for yt traytor Davis yt hathe longe tyme bene a prowde
knave and of Base condition, who was by this popular
traytor Essex advaunced to keepe the Lord Keeper,
the chiefe Iustice of England, and others of ye counsell
at his commaundement, and himself to keepe the greate   70
Seale of England, and was this villanous traytor
Davis now, or can it be thought possible he had bene
before of yt Religion professed by Essex and ⟨. . . .⟩
assistaunt to maintain trewe religion as they counter =
feyted in profession, who no soner was commytted to prison,   75
but openly and audaciously called for a priest to absolue him./
And was this all, no not by muche? for amongst ye rest,
yt seditious booke of *Henry* the .4: by his owne practice
being dedicated to hymself by the wordes of *Celsitudine*
tuæ &c: wch he kept .14. dayes in his trecherous bosome,   80
and then acquainted the Lord grace + of + Canterbury therwth to
colour his Machevilian meaning therin, as wishing ye same
might be supprest./.
What was his pretence in this his last Diabolicall treason,
did he not as he was pricked forward in his trayterous –   85
rebellion, doatinge vpon the affection of the people to him,
gyve out in base speeches yt he was in feare to be Murthered
in his bed by *Cobham*, *Rawley*, & *Cicill*:
To stirr vp her Maiesties subiectes the rather to follow him,
& having drawne ye most parte of them into his nett of   90

rebellion, to haue gyven the spoyle of the Cittie to swag =
gering mates his complices. / .
What should I say, is it possible yt he whom her Maiestie
hathe so tenderly brought vp vnder the shadowe of her
owne winges, yt her highnes graced wth so many princely   95
advauncementes, as first, at .22· yeeres of age to make him
Mr of the horsse, president of her Maiesties Counsell,
Earle Marshall of England, and lastly gave him
300. thowsand poundes, I say can it be possible to any
Christian harte, yt this man should become suche a Monster   100
as this his vnnaturall & savage kynde of rebellions
haue laide open to the worlde, hathe not this Archre =
bell Essex had such audatious adherentes yt wolde not
tremble to lay violent handes vpon her Maiesties sacred person,
to impryson her Maiesties Counsell, threatening the   105
Murthering of them, and scornefully to byd cast the
great seale of England (wch is the Key of this
land) out at windowe, to kyll her Maiesties Iudges in
their seate of Iustice, to enterprize the takinge of the
Tower of London, and so to haue againe delyuered the   110
traytores therin to the vtter subversion of this Kingdome;
Well, I am amazed at the remembraunce hereof: but
the dew and reverent regarde I haue of her Maiesties care
to all her loving subiectes and vassalles whereof I am
one: hathe made me say so muche; Wch had I not bene   115
prest to speake vppon so suddain advysement, I wolde
haue drawne my wyttes together for delyuerie hereof in
some better method. / . /

rebellion, to have vpon the spoyle of the Cittie to stagg-
gering matter of complices.

What should I say, is it possible that he whom her Ma[tie]
hathe so tenderly brought vp vnder the shadowe of her
owne wings, & her highnes graced with so many princely
advancements, as first, at 22 yeres of age to make him
M[r] of the horsse, president of her Ma[ties] Counsell,
& erle Marshall of England, and lastly gave him
300 thousand poundes, I say can it be possible to any
Christian harte, that this man should become suche a Monster
as this his vnnaturall & savage kynde of rebellions
have layde open to the worldes, hathe not this wretche-
ble Essex had suche audatious adherents that wolde not
tremble to lay violent handes vpon her Ma[ties] sacred person,
to imprison her Ma[ties] Counsell, threatning the
murthering of them, and scornefully to bydd cast the
great seale of England (w[ch] is the Key of this
land) out at windowe, to kyll her Ma[ties] Judges in
their seates of Justice, to enterprize the takinge of the
Tower of London, and so to have againe delyvered the
trayto[r] therein to the vtter subversion of this kingdome;
Well, I am amazed at the remembrance hereof: but
the dew and reverent regarde I have of her Ma[ties] care
to all her loving subiects and vassalls wherewith I am
one, hathe made me say so muche; yet had I not bene
prest to speake vpon so suddain advisement, I wolde
have drawne my wyttes together for delyvery hereof in
some better method

Doctor Assheton his owne letter concerninge
my Lorde off Essex :|

Bycause some are offended wth mee, and mistake the
Articles whereunto I sett my hand at the Counsell table,
being required so to doe by the Lordes off her Maties
Counsell, I will briefly & truelie reporte ye proceeding,
and to what seemes I have subscribed.|

Being sent from my Lord Constable off the Tower to the
Counsell sitting at whitehall the afternoone off the day
my Lord dyed, After divers questions propounded and
answered, it was required off mee two severall tymes to
preach at Paules the Sunday following the sermon yt Dr
Barlow preached. whereupon twyes upon my knees I
humblie besought their Lorpps to pardon mee.| At the
later tyme, one off the Lordes said to mee, you shall speake
nothing but truthe, take, read this paper: gyving me this
wch in the ende off the booke is called my Lo: Confession,
written & subscribed wth the two Drs hande. whereon
when I had read it I spoke to this effect, My Lo: the
substance off this is true. what said hee, will you give
yor hand to this: yea said I, iff you doe require it, Now
the meaninge to wch I have & could subscribe is this.|

Art: 1. The late Earle off Essex thanked god most hartely, that
he had given hym a deeper insight into his offences, being
sorie he had so stood upon his justification at his arraignement
for he was since become another man.| The sence.| His Lo:
was sorie he had justified his purpose off takinge from aboute
her Matie suche as he thought bad instrumentes, and his privat
enimyes, by his owne meanes & strength.| Secondly: his going
into London after the manner he did, and the cariage off the
matter yt day, for now his Lop: sawe, yt wch a good conscience

[9   shortly after 25 March 1601   see Commentary]

Docter Asheton his owne letter concerninge   1
my Lorde of Essex :/
Bycause some are offended wth mee, and mistake the
Articles whervnto I set my hand at the Counsell table,
being required so to doe by the Lordes of her Maiesties privie   5
Counsell, I will briefly & trulie reporte ye proceeding,
and to what sence I haue subscribed./.
Being sent from my Lord Constable of the Tower to the
Counsell sytting at whitehall the afternoone of the day
my lord dyed, After divers questions propounded and   10
answered, it was required of mee two severall tymes to
Preach at Poules the Sunday following the sermon yt Dr.
Barlow preached. Wherevpon twyce vpon my knees I
humblie besought their Lordshipes to pardon mee./ At the
later tyme, one of the Lordes said to mee, You shall speake   15
nothing but truthe, take, read this paper: gyving me this
wch in the ende of the booke is called my Lords Confession,
wrytten & subscribed wth the two Drs. handes. To whom
when I had read it I spake to this effect, My Lord the
substance of this is true. What said hee, will you give   20
your hand to this: yea said I, yf you doe require it, Now
the meaninge to wch I haue & could subscribe is this./.

: 1·   The late Earle of Essex thanked god most hartely, That
he had given hym a deeper insight into his offence, being
sorie he had so stood vpon his Iustification at his arraignement, 25
for he was since yt become another man./ *The sence.*/ his Lordshippe
was sorie he had Iustified his purpose of takinge from aboute
her Maiestie suche as he thought bad instrumentes, and his private
enimyes, by his owne meanes & strength./. *Secondly:* his going
into london after the manner he dyd, and the cariage of the   30
matter yt day, for now his Lordshippe sawe, yt wth a good conscience

in dutie to god & his prince he might not doe it./. *Thirdly.*/
that he had carried himself after a braver & gallanter fashion
at his arraignement then beseemed his cause./.

·2· he thanked god yt his course was so prevented, for if his proiect   35
     had taken effecte, God knowes (saith hee) what harme it had
     wrought in the Realme./. *sence.*/ his lordshippe now by proofe seeing
     neither himself so followed, nor his enimyes so forsaken as hee
     expected: and wthall considering yt many of his companie
     were discontented wth the present establyshed religion, fewe   40
     of knowledge and feeling in the true religion, and that her Maiestie
     wolde not haue indured longe to be ⟨overuled⟩ over ruled in so greate
     matters, so nigh her owne person; his Lordshippe now in sorrowe &
     repentaunce saide, weighinge + the + vncerteintie of these eventes, and how
     vnprosperous he had bene in the begynnynge, God knowes &c   45
     leavinge ⟨as⟩ it as an vncertain matter knowne onlie to god, & not
     vnlikely to haue bene the cause of muche bludshed in the land,
     if not of greater evylls./.

·3· he humblie thanked her Maiestie, yt he should dye in so private
     manner, least the acclamation of the people might haue bene   50
     a temptation vnto him, to wch he added : That all popularitie
     & trust in man was vaine, the experience whereof himself had
     felt./ Yf any thinke I haue testified yt my Lord made a
     request to dye privately he is deceyved & dothe me wronge./
     I disclayme yt vtterly, and hope in god I shall never say it,   55
     vntill I certainly knowe it to be a truthe, wch yet I professe I
     doe not: Onlie this I perceyved, yt his lordshippe made accompt of
     lyfe a longer tyme then it fell out to bee: and as it seemed to
     me once or twyse, was not altogether wthout hope of endinge
     his dayes in a naturall death: Wch thing I professe I   60
     vnfeynedly desyred of almightie god it might haue pleased
     his goodnes by her Maiestie to haue graunted; yt beinge a good

in dutie to god & his prince he might not doe it. / Thirdly
that he had carried / himselfe after a braver & gallanter fashion
at his arraignement then beseemed his cause. /

2. He thanked god y his course was so prevented, for iff his project
had taken effecte, God knoweth (saith hee) what harme it had
wrought in the Realme. / hence. / his Lo: now by proofe seeing
neither himselfe so followed, now his enimyes so forsaken as hee
expected: and withall considering y many off his companie
were discontented wth the present established religion, fewe
off knowledge and feeling in the true religion, and that her maiestie
wolde not have indured longe to be other ruled in so great
matters, so nigh her owne person; his Lo: now in sorrowe &
repentance saide, weighing the uncertainties off these eventes, and how
unprosperous he had bene in the beginnynges, God knoweth yet
leavinge it as an uncertain matter knowne onlie to god, & not
unlikely to have bene the cause off much bludshed in the land,
iff not off greater evills. /

3. He humblie thanked her maiestie y he should dye in so private
manner, least the acclamation off the people might have bene
a temptation unto him, to wch he added: That all popularitie
& trust in man was vaine, wch experience wherof himselfe had
felt. / Iff any thinke y I have testified y my lo: made a
request to dye privately he is deceyved & doeth me wronge. /
I disclayme yt utterly, and hope in god I shall never say it,
untill I certainly know it to be a trueth, wch yet I professe I
doe not: Onlie this I perceyved, y his Lo: made accompt off
lyfe a longer tyme then it fell out to bee: and as it seemed to
me once or twyse, was not altogether without hope off endinge
his dayes in a naturall death: wch thing I professe I
unfaynedly desired off almightie god it might have pleased
his goodnes by her maiestie to have graunted; y beinge a good

Christian (as no doubt but he was from the verie hartroote)
he might not have dyed a violent death in an evill cause. /
But this is that which I acknowledge, ye when his Lo[rdship] understoode
it was appointed he should dye privately, in christian humilitie
& obedience to the will of god (and his ordinance on earth) hee
approoved it, resolving ye to be best for him weh it pleased god
to appoint unto him by ordinarie meanes. And upon this
consideration as I allwayes understoode it, his Lo[rdship] added the
reason ye followeth: least the acclamation of the people ret[urning]
weynisting the doores, & if they perceyved any outward things
falling into his sences to drawe away his mynde from that he
ought then to be thinkings upon, to put them in mynde, and he
woold wrall them self. / And this his Lo[rdship] might say, and
yet not made any request to dye privately in the Towre-yard
for suche was his custome, not there onlie but often afore
duringe my atteadance, proceeding from a religious and godly
mynde, to make the best use unto his owne soule, of whatso
croce & judgment yt befell him, for the quiet & contentment
of his owne mynde. / And as it is in the article followinge, /

. 4 .   He thanked god the worlde showed him out, (for now said his
Lo[rdship] I shall more willingly forsake the worlde) when he sawe
the will of god manifested in this behalf, and yet I fullie
perswade my self, he never made any request to god yt the
worlde might showre him out: even so it was in this case
for ought I knowe, when he heard it was so appointed for him
to dye privately, submytting hymself to the will of god and
his lieutenant here on earth, hee approoved it, and gave a
reason thereof, knowinge out of the scriptures: yt all thinge
fall out to gods childern for the best /.

. 5 .   He publickly in his prayer & protestation as also privately,
approobated the detestation of his offence: and specyally in the

christian (as no doubt but he was from the verie hartroote)
he might not haue dyed a violent death in an evill cause./.
But this is that wch I acknowledge, yt when his Lordshippe vnderstoode   65
it was appointed he should dye privately, in christian humilitie
& obedience to the will of god and his ordinaunce on earth hee
approved it; resolving yt to be best for him wch it pleased god
to appoint vnto hym by ordinarie meanes. And vpon this –
consideration as I alwayes vnderstoode it, his Lordshippe added the   70
reason yt followeth: least the acclamation of the people &c:/
requesting the doctores yt if they perceyved any outward thinge
falling into his sences to drawe away his mynde from that he
ought then to be thinkinge vpon, to put hym in mynde, and he
wolde recall hym self./. And this his Lordshippe might say, and   75
yet not make any request to dye privately in the Towre-yard.
For suche was his custome, not there onlie but often afore – –
duringe my attendance, proceeding from a religious and godly
mynde, to make the best vse vnto his owne sowle, of everie
crosse & Iudgment yt befell hym, for the quiet & contentment   80
of his owne mynde./ And as it is in the article followinge,/

·4·   he thanked god the worlde spewed him out, (for now said his
      Lordshippe I shall more willingly forsake the worlde) when he sawe
      the will of god manifested in this behalf; and yet I fullie
      perswade my self, he never made any request to god yt the   85
      worlde might spewe hym out: even so it was in this case
      for ought I knowe; when he heard it was so appointed for him
      to dye privately, submyttinge hymself to the will of god and
      his lieutenaunt here on earth, hee approved it, and gave a
      reason therof, knowinge out of the scriptures: yt all thinges   90
      fall out to godes children for the best./.

·5·   he publickly in his prayer & protestation as also privately,
      aggravated the detestation of his offence: and specyally in the

hearinge of them yt were present at the execution, he exagge =
rated it wth .4. Epithites, desyring god to forgive his –   95
Great: his *Bloodie:* his *Cryinge:* his *Infectious sinne;* whiche
woorde Infectious hee 'privately had explayned to vs, that it
was a leprosie wch had infected farre & nere./.
These wordes are said to aggravate my lords offence, & therfor
everie one should be content to take them at the shortest meaninge,   100
and not to ratch them to the furthest./ And sure it is, a
true penitent soule confessing to god, and specyally ready to goe
vnto his Maiestie, will loade it self sufficiently, as every truly
humbled chrystian knoweth; therfore men ought rather to –
subtracte then to adde any thinge vnto them; For my owne part   105
I vnderstand them thus: *Great:* bycause it was a great attempt
vnwarantable by godes worde, of great & vncertaine consequence:
rashly attempted wthout consultation wth godes worde, against his
Lordshippes promysse to god of patient induringe the crosse in yt his
affliction, against his dutie to her Maiestie, and the present peace   110
of the land; *Bloodie,* not bycause hee intended to imbrue his
sworde in her Maiesties bloude, against wch his last wordes are a
sufficient testimonie: nor yet by the sworde to shed the bloude
of his enimyes, but bycause in the action some were slayne,
hymself was ready to dye, and others he feared should follow   115
after hym./ *Infectious,* because the multitude yt followed hym
were of diverse conditions and countries, and some of them farre
dwellers from the citie./.

To these pointes vpon th' aforesaid oration, and in the manner
mentioned, being required at the Counsell table by the Lordes of   120
her Maiesties privie Counsell then sitting to give my hand, I gave it
as I thought my self in duety bounde to the governoures of the
land vnder her highnes, not then knowinge what vse they wolde
make of it, vnderstanding all thinges as I haue expressed./

hearinge of them y were present at the execution, & so aggra-
vated it with .4. Epithites, desyring god to forgive his ~
Great: his Bloodie: his Cryinge: his Infectious sinne; whiche
woordes Infections hee (privately) had explayned to me, that it
was a leprosie which had infected farre & nere./

These woordes are said to aggravate my Lo: offence, & therefore
therein one should be content to take them at the shortest meaninge,
and not to racke them to the furthest./ And sure it is, a
true penitent soule confessing to god, and specyally ready to goe
unto his Ma[tie], will loade it self sufficiently, as every truly
humbled christian knowech; therefore men ought rather to
subtracte then to adde any thinges unto them; ffor my owne part
I understand them thus: Great: because it was a great attempt
unwarrantable by gods woorde, off great & uncertaine consequence;
rashly attempted without consultation with gods worde, against his
L[P] promise to god off patient induringe the crosse in y his
affliction, against his duty to her Ma[tie], and the present peace
off the Land; Bloodie, not because hee intended to imbrue his
woordes in her Ma[ties] blondes, against which his last woordes are a
sufficient testimonie: nor yet by the swoorde to shed the blonde
off his enimyes, but because in the action some were slayne,
himself was ready to dye, and others he feared should follow
after him./ Infectious, because the multitude y followed him
were off diverse conditions and cuntries, and some off them farre
dwellers from the citie./

To these pointe upon the aforesaid oration, and in the manner
mentioned, being required at the Counsell table by the Lorde off
her Ma[ties] privie Counsell then sitting to give my hand, I gave it
as I thought my self in duety bounde to the governoures off the
land under her Highnes, not then knowinge what use they would
make off it, understanding all thinges as I have expressed./

To nor yf any shall take exception as to vntrothes,
I beseeche them to pardon me, for I can not say so, and I
ought and desyre so to deale, as I dare answere the god of
truthe the just Judge, and my owne conscience (a witnesse
yt cannot be corrupted) at the last day of Judgement. If
I could truly say and avouche any of these thinges to be vntrue,
I had rather a thousand tymes acknowledge my folly and
rashnes in being overshot in a sodaine subscription of wch
I never once dreamed afore it was put into my hand, then
Joyne wth any in layinge the least wrongfull imputation vpon
my good Lord, vnto whom I will ever accompt my selfe most
bounden, for his Lo: honorable affection towardes me. /

Abdie Assheton

To wch ⟨I say⟩ yf any shall take exception as to vntruthes,   125
I beseche them to pardon me, for I can not say so, and I
ought and desyer so to deale, as I dare answere the god of
truthe the iust iudge, and my owne conscience (a witnesse
yt cannot be corrupted) at the last day of Iudgment./ If
I could truly say and avouche any of these thinges to be vntrue,   130
I had rather a thousand tymes acknowledge my folly and
rashnes in being overshot in a sodaine subscription of wch
I never once dreamed afore it was put into my hand, then
Ioyne wth any in layinge the least wrongfull imputation vpon
my good Lord, vnto whom I will ever accompt my self most   135
bounden, for his Lordshippes honorable affection towardes me./.

Abdie Assheton

f. 14r

[10   before 25 October 1600   see Commentary]

Certein Principles, or Instructions: 1
From a greate man of this Land
to his best beloved Sonne . /.
Love no man but thy self: or if any man, for thy self.
Trust no man, so shalt thou not be deceyved.   5
Be ritch in promysses to all, though in performance to fewe:
Make no dyfference betwene an honest servant, & a dishonest,
but make them bothe serue thy turn ./.
Above all thinges make not thy servant too ritch, for then
thou shalt want hym: Let him neither sincke nor swym ./   10
Yf any man be grieved, give hym good wordes, but be not
moved ⟨to⟩ wth compassion./
Thankfullnes, take for a vertue not beseeminge a great man,
for it is as muche as an Obligation of debt. /
Dissemble wth everie man, but be not seene to dissemble,   15
wyn the service of many vnto you, it is no matter
for there hartes./
Though thou get nothing, Yet be still in the Princes eare;
if thou can: it wilbe a Revenewe vnto you./
What soever thyne adversarie say, how right soever it bee,   20
oppose it bycause he sayd it ./
You must be as carefull to breake his faction, as to
strengthen your owne: to breake it, devide it./
Wth the head of the contrarie faction, neither haue frendship,
nor seeme to haue enmytie: Whatsoever you doe   25
against hym, pretend the Princes good, and the
Common wealth: By this slye course, you
shall soone cutt his throate. /.
Those that depend vpon hym, crosse them in their suytes:
disgrace them wth lookes, kyndle emulation betweene them;   30

Certain Principles, or Instructions:
from a greate man off this Land
to his best beloved sonne .

Love no man but thy selfe: or iff any man, for thy selfe.
Trust no man, so shalt thou not be deceyved.
Be ritch in promisses to all, though in performance to fewe:
   make no dyfference betwene an honest servant, & a dishonest,
   but make them bothe serve thy turne .
Above all thinge make not thy servant too ritch, for then
   thou shalt want him: Let him neither sincke nor swymme .
Iff any man be grieved, give him good wordes, but be not
   moved to vse compassion .
Thankfullnes, take for a vertue not beseeminge a greate man,
   for it is as muche as an Obligation or debt .
Dissemble with everie man, but be not seene to dissemble,
   Wynn the service off many vnto you, it is no matter
   for theyr hartes .
Thoughe thou get nothing, yet be still in the Princes eare;
   iff then cam: it wille a dishonour vnto you .
What soever thyne adversarie say, how right soever it bee,
   oppose it because he sayd it .
You must be as carefull to breake his faction, as to
   strengthen yor owne: to breake it, devide it .
With the head off the contrarie faction, neither have friendship,
   nor seeme to have enmytie: Whatsoever you doe
   against him, pretend the Princes good, and the
   Comon wealth :   By this slyt comest you
   shall soone owtt his secrets .
Those that depend vpon him, wynne them in theyr suytes:
   disgrace them wth lookes, bredle emulation betweene them;

If they be of the same profession, breeds discontentment to
share the knott of them a sunder, discover the plotts of
their chiefe artes, and either by ennobling them or
gracing them, quite them: When thou hast loppped
the braunches one after another, watch thy tyme to
strike at the roote.

If any man will have Justice at this hand, let hym buy
it: Geve not the Common wealth for naught.
But take no bribes thy selfe by any meanes, let that
be done by some honest man.

The officers of the Crowne: of the Wardes: of the
Lawe: and of the Churche: will bringe in a
reasonable harvest.

Be not over fond of vertue, it hath hurt many worthie
& famous men (of her doatinges lovers) and broken their
neckes: onlie caine an opinion of it.

But above all thinges be not too Religious, at the rocke many
men have made Shipwrackes: If it will serve thy
turne bowe up the Protestant for the Puritane, and
the Puritane for the Papist. This Arte hath
bene verie gainfull being rightly used.

In tyme of action, gather vnto thee men of the swoordes:
Use them as Phisitions when you neede them: give
them their fee but when you vse them.

The Preachers, heare them: It is a good thinge, or custome,
and it is tyme well spent: Make profitt of
their divition.

Yf they be of the same profession, b⟨. .⟩de discontentment to
    shake the knott of them a sunder, discover the plottes of
    their chiefe ⟨purp⟩ actores, and either by crusshing them or
    graceing them, quite hym: When thou haste lopped
    the braunches one after another, watch the tyme to   35
    strike at the Roote. /.
Yf any man will haue Iustice at thie hand, let hym buy
    it: Serve not the Common wealth for naught./
    But take no bribes thy self by any meanes, let that
    be done by some trustie man . /.   40
The Offices of the Crowne: of the Wardes: of the
    Lawe: and of the Churche: will bringe in a
    reasonable harvest./.
Be not over fond of vertue, it hathe hurt many worthie
    & famous men (of her doatinge lovers) and broken their   45
    neckes: onlie carie an opinion of it./.
But above all thinges be not too Religious, at the Rocke many
    men haue made shipwracke: Yf it will serue thy
    turn beare wth the Protestant for the Puritane, and
    the Puritane for the Papist: This Arte hathe   50
    bene verie gainfull being rightly vsed./.
In tyme of action, gather vnto thee men of the swoorde:
    Vse them as Phisitions when you neede them: give
    them their fee but when you vse them./.
The Preachers, heare them: It is a good thinge, or custome: 55
    and it is tyme well spent: Make profitt of
    their division./.

The Scholers, let them haue in their colledges to breath
   and live, & no more? Vse them as wardes as yet
   in their nonage: Imploye none of them: The greatest   60
   Clerkes are not the wysest men: Amongst
   all their lectures, their is wanting the lecture
   of discretion./.
The Merchantes, handle them as spunges, they ⟨. .⟩ are
   Full, Wringe them: To be able to doe this,   65
   there are many Artes required./.
Yff any man be verie valyaunt and forward, suppresse
   hym: These tymes may not beare a stirring spiritt.
A bodie crazed wth the gowte, it is daungerous to have
   it cured wth a quicke silver'd spiritt./   70

Subditorum minimæ virtutes, Regibus formidolosæ:/
The least vertues of subiectes, are terrible to princes./.

The Schooles, let them pant in their colledges to bleate
and bite, & no more. Use them as wardes as yet
in their nonage: imploye none of them: The greatest
Clerks are not the wysest men: Amongst
all their lectures, their is wanting the lecture
of discretion. |

The Merchante, handle them as spongs, they are, and
fill, wringe them: To be able to do this,
there are many Artes required. |

If any man be valiant and forward, imploye
them: These tymes may not beare a stirring spirit.
A bodie ragged with the gowte, it is dangerous to have
it cured with a quick silvered spirit. |

Subditorum minima virtutes, Regibus formidolosa : |

The least vertues of subiects, are terrible to princes. |

To the kinge most excellent Maᵗⁱᵉ.

Vouchsafe great kinge (and most gratious Maᵗⁱᵉ) to receyve the complaint, the most greevous complaint, off a poore gentlewoman exceedingly distrest, yea ready to sterve for lacke off Justice. The wofull petition (most Royall kinge) off Marie Cavendish a widdowe, daughter off the Lord Wentworth, off the age off fower score yeares and vpward. vᶻ 64. children and grandchildren, wᶜʰ have no reliefe but from God and my selfe. This Scedule annexed will shew yoᵉ Maᵗⁱᵉ my greevous oppressions, yea greevous indeede in respect off myne age: and that I, lyving in a christian kingdome and ready for my grave, must leave thys worlde and go to heaven to complaine me there, before the Tribunall seat off God, for lacke off Justice here on earthe. / Onlie my hope, and all the hope I can have in this worlde, is from yoᵉ Maᵗⁱᵉ my Soveraigne Lord: whom god hathe sent off his infinite goodnes to pitie the poore, to redresse our wronges and manifolde Iniuries, and yᵉˡᵉ to have administration off Justice. / yoᵉ Maᵗⁱᵉ sytte in the seate off God: In the name off God, I aske this Justice: not from any other, but even from yoᵉ selfe most noble kinge: wᶜʰ this poore countrie hath longe tyme lacked: but god hathe nowe gyven vs fresh hopes again by yoᵉ excellent Maᵗⁱᵉ. / (refer not my cause (most noble kinge) except yᵉ greate will be vnawares yoᵉ selfe; for we are off this opinion in england (and not wᵗʰout cause as many men thinke) that no great Magistrate in this countrie, will controll the Actes or deedes off another: but off course will commytt all such as complaine, except yoᵉ Maᵗⁱᵉ please to protect vs; Read Royall king (but read it quickly) this Scedule annexed, and let her not dye (she is ready to dye wᵗʰ her extreeme age, before she have Justice: I am ready for my grave, as my grave is for me, and desyre but Justice in right off their wronges I must leave behinde me. / Reade then, o read, most gratious kinge: and grannt vs but Justice, wᶜʰ wee have bene to to longe delayed. And during this small remainder off my lyfe, my aged yeares shall evermore pray for yoᵉ graces long lyfe, and most happie raigne. /

[11   *c.* mid-1603–1604   see Commentary]

To the Kinges most excellent Maiestie/.   1
Vouchsafe great Kinge (and most gratious Maiestie) to receyve the
complaint, the most greevous complaint, of a poore gentlewoman
exceedingly distressed, yea ready to sterve for lacke of Iustice:
The wofull peticion (most Royall Kinge) of Marie Candish a   5
Widdow, daughter of the Lord Wentworth, of the age of fower
score yeeres and vpward: wth .64. children and grandchildren, wch
haue no reliefe but from God and my self. This Scedule anex =
ed will shew your Maiestie my greevous oppressions, yea greevous indeede
in respect of myne age: and that I lyving in a Christian kingdome   10
and ready for my grave, must leave the worlde and go to heaven to
complain me their. before the Tribunall Seat of God, for lacke
of Iustice here on earth./ Onlie my hope, and all the hope I
can haue in this worlde, is from your Maiestie my Soveraigne Lorde:
Whom god hathe sent of his infinite goodnes to pitie the poore,   15
to redresse our wronges and manifolde Iniuries, and gyve vs true
administration of Iustice./ Your Maiestie syttes in the seate of God: In
the name of God, I aske this Iustice: not from any other, but even
from your self most noble kinge: wch this poore countrie hath longe
tyme lacked: but god hathe nowe gyven vs freshe hopes again by   20
your excellent Maiestie / Refer not my cause (most noble kinge) except
your grace will be Vmpeere your self; for we are of this opinion in
england (and not wthout cause as many men thinkes) that no
great Magistrate in this countrie, will controll the Actes or –
deedes of another: but of course will commytt all suche as complain,   25
except your Maiestie please to protect vs; Read Royall king (but
read it quickly) this Scedule anexed, and let her not dye
yt is ready to dye wth her extreeme age, before she haue Iustice:
I am ready for my grave, as my grave is for me, and desyer but
Iustice in right of their wronges I must leave behinde me./ Reade   30
then, o read, most gratious kinge: and graunt vs but Iustice,
whereof we haue bene to to longe delayed. And during this
small remainder of my lyfe, my aged yeeres shall evermore
pray for your graces long lyfe, and most happie raigne./.

[12   19 September 1586]

A lettere written by Chidiock Tichborne to   1
his wyfe, the night before he suffred. /
The most loving wife alive I commend me to thee, and desier god
to blesse the wth all happines. Pray for thy dead husband, and
be of good comforte, for I hope in Iesus Christe this morninge to   5
see the face of my Redeemer, in the most ioyfull Throne of his
glorious Kingdome. / Commend me to all my frendes & desier them to
pray for me, and in all charitie to pardon me if I haue offended
them. Commend me to my .6. sisters, poore desolate Soules: advise
them to serue god, for wthout hym, their is no goodnes to be expected.   10
Were it possible (Deare wyfe) my little sister *Bab*: (the darlinge of my
care) might be bred by thee, it were happie for her, & god wolde rewarde
thee. But I haue done the (poore soule) to muche wronge, I must nedes
confesse it, to hasten my death, & impaire thy estate by my dissolute –
negligence: thou having hereby to little for thy self, yt I should adde   15
a further charge vnto thee. Sweete wyfe forgive me, yt haue by these
meanes so impoverished thy fortunes: Patience and Pardon good wyfe
I crave, make of these our necessities a vertue, & lay no further burthen
on my necke, then is laid already. / Their be certein debtes wch I owe,
and because I knowe not the order of the lawe, wch hathe taken all from   20
me as forfeyted by the course of this my offence to her Maiestie, I cannot
advise the what to doe herein, but if there fall out wherewthall: let
them be discharged sweete wyfe for godes sake: I will not that you
troble your self wth the performance hereof (myne owne harte) but make
it knowne to my Vnckles, and desyer them for the honor of god to do their   25
best in it. Nowe (deare hart) what is lefte me to bestowe on thee, a
small Ioyntare (god knowes) a small recompence for thy deservinge:
these legacies following to be thine owne: God of his infinite goodnes
& mercie, give the alwayes his grace to remain his true & most faithfull
servaunt, yt through the merittes of his bitter and blessed passion, thou – 30
maiest become an inheritrix of his kingdome wth the blessed weomen in
heaven. Iesus give thee of his feare, and to his glorie all ye benefittes
of this transitorie lyfe. The holy ghost comforte thee wth all necessa
ries for the wealth of thy soule in the worlde to come: where vntill
it shall please almightie god I meete the. Farewell Lovinge wyfe,   35
Farewell the dearest to me in all the earth: Farewell for ever
in this worlde: Farewell. /.   By the hand & the harte of thy
                                              most loving husband:/.
                                              Chidiock Tichborne./

A lettr written by Chidiock Tichborne to
his wyfe, the night before he suffered.

To the most loving wiffe alive I commend me to thee, and desier god
to blesse thee w(i)th all happines. Pray for thy dead husband, and
be of good comforte, for I hope in Jesus Christe this morninge to
see the face of my Redeemer, in the most ioyfull Throne of his
glorious kingdome. Commend me to all my frends, & desier them to
pray for me, and in all charitie to pardon me if I have offended
them. Comend me to my .6. sisters, poore desolate soules: advise
them to serve god, for w(i)thout him, ther is no goodnes to be expected.
were it possible (deare wyfe) my little sister Bab: (the darlinge of my
care) might be bred by thee, it were happie for her, & god wolde rewarde
thee. But I have done the (poore soule) so much wronge, I must nedle
confesse it, to hasten my death, & impaire thy estate by my dissolute
negligence: thou havinge hereby so little for thy selfe, that I should adde
a further charge unto thee. Sweete wyfe forgive me, & have by least
meanes so impoverished thy fortunes: Patience and Pardon good wyfe
I crave, make of these our necessities a vertue, & lay no further burthen
on my necke, then is laid already. There be certein dettes w(hich) I owe,
and because I knowe not the order of the lawe, w(hich) hath taken all from
me as forfeyted by the compse of this my offence to her Ma(jesti)e I cannot
advise thee what to doe herein, but if there fall out wherewithall: let
them be discharged sweete wyfe for godes sake. I will not that you
trouble yo(u)r selfe w(i)th the performance hereof (myne owne harte) but make
it knowne to my Kuncles, and desier them for the hono(u)r of god to do their
best in it. Now (deare hart) what is lefte me to bestowe on thee, a
small ioyntare (god knowes) a small recompence for thy deservinge:
these legacies followinge to be thine owne: God of his infinite goodnes
& mercie, give thee alwayes his grace to remain his true & most faithfull
servaunt, & through thy merrite of his bitter and blessed passion, thou
maiest become an inheritire of his kingdome w(i)th the blessed women in
heaven. Jesus give thee of his feare, and to his glorie all & chuse the
of this transitorie life. The holy ghost comfort thee w(i)th all necessaries
tive for the wealth of thy soule in the worlde to come: whereuntill
it shall please almighty god I meete thee. farewell loving wyfe,
farewell the dearest to me in all the earth: farewell for short
in this worlde: farewell.

By the hand & the harte of thy
most loving husband.

Chidiock Tichborne.

To our Right trustie & right welbeloved, The
Nobilitie and Peares of our Realme of England,
And to our right trustie & welbeloved, our Counsellor
of Estate, assembled at Whitehall.

Although we are now resolved (aswell in regarde of ye great
& honest affection borne unto us by the Earle of Southt: as in
respect of his good partes enabling him for the service of us & the
state) to extend our grace & favor towardes him, whom his greate
also the late Queene of England (Notwstanding his fault towarde
her) was moved to exempt from the stroke of Justice, Nevertheless,
because we wolde be lothe in such a case as this (wherein the
Peares of or Realme have proceeded according to the honorable
formes usd in like cases) to take any such course as may
not stand wth our owne greatnes & the gravitie fitt to be observed
in such matters: We have thought meete to give you notice of
or pleasure (though the same be to be executed by our owne Regall
powers) wch is onlie this: because the place is tonesome and
dolorows to him (to whose bodie & mynde we wolde give present
comfort, intending unto him much further grace & favor) we
have written unto or Lieutenant of the Tower, to deliver him
out of prison presently, to any such place as he shall chuse
in or neare or Citie of London: There to carrie himselfe in such
quiet & honest sorte as we know he will thinke meete in his
owne discretion, untyll the bodie of or state now assembled shall
come unto us, at wch tyme we are pleased he shall also
come to our presence, for as it is on us that his only hopes
depend, so we will referre those workes of further favor untill
the tyme he beholdes our owne eyes, wherof as we know the
comfort will be great unto him, so it will be contentment to
us to have oportunitie to declare our estimation of him in any thing
herunto belonging. Wherein ye shall be doubtfull, we have now
by or letters directed our servant the Lo: of Kynlos to give you
satisfaction, who bothe before his comynge in partes, and now by
these our letters sent after him is best instructed therein. we

f. 16v

[13   5 April 1603   see Commentary]

To our Right trustie & right welbeloved, The   1
Nobilitie and Peares of our Realme of England,
And to our right trustie & welbeloved, our Counsellores
of Estate, assembled at Whitehall ./.
Although we are now resolved (aswell in regarde of ye great   5
& honest affection born vnto vs by the Earle of Southampton as in
respect of his good partes enablinge him for the service of vs & the
state) to extend our grace & favour towardes him, whom we perceyve
also the late Queene our Sister (Notwthstanding his falt towardes
her) was moved to exempt from the stroke of Iustice, Neverthelesse,   10
bycause we wolde be lothe in suche a case as this (wherein the
Peares of our Realme haue proceeded according to the honorable
formes vsed in like cases) to take any suche courses as may –
not stand wth our owne greatnes & the gravitie fytt to be observed
in suche matters: We haue thought meete to gyve you notice of   15
our pleasure (though the same be to be executed by our owne Royall
power) wch is onlie this: bycause the place is vnholsome and
dolorous to him (to whose bodie & mynde we wolde give present
comfort, intending vnto him muche further grace & favour) we
haue wrytten vnto our Lieftenaunt of the Tower, to delyver him   20
out of prison presently, to any suche place as he shall chuse
in or neare our citie of London: Their to carrie him self in such
quiet & honest forme as we know he will thinke meete in his
owne discretion, vntyll the bodie of our state now assembled shall
come vnto vs, at wch tyme we are pleased he shall also–   25
come to our presence, for yt as it is on vs that his only hopes
depend, so we will reserue those workes of further favoures vntill
the tyme he beholdes our own eyes, whereof as we knowe the
comforte will be greate vnto hym, so it will be contentment to
vs to haue oportunitie to declare our estimation of him in any thing 30
herevnto belonging./ Wherein ye shall be doubtfull, we haue nowe
by our letters directed our servant the Lord of kynlos to gyve you
satisfaction, who bothe before his commynge in parte, and nowe by
these our letters sent after hym is best instructed therin./ We

have also wrytten to our forsaid Lieftenaunt for the present –   35
delyuery of Henry Nevill knight. whom we are pleased you
of our counsell shall bring wth you when you shall wayte –
vpon vs./ From our Pallace of Holyrude howse the
.5. of Aprile.   *I.R.*   .1603.

[14   7 May 1603 or 15 March 1604   see Commentary]

An Oration delyuered to the Kinge   1
as he came to the Citie of London
Long the hope, and nowe the assurance: there was no way
for vs but a death in mourninge, save in the howre wherin we had
iust cause to weepe, we founde in the verie moment as Iust a cause   5
of Trivmphe: our Black yt should haue lasted tyll the *Zodiacke*
had gone rounde, we founde it worne to barenes ere the howre –
had ron out./ O excellent occasion of gladnes, yt in so capitall
and profounde a Theam of sorrow, woldst not suffer the weedes
of lamentacion to holde the putting on. O memorable restorer, yt   10
even in the exigent & pange of our generall death, not onlie didst recur
vs, but in suche a manner recover vs, yt we were not everie one alone the
better for our sufferaunce, but so put vs into a ravishment that we
forgat what we gron'd for./ Welcome renowned Emperor, and marke
how heaven envites thee; not onlie thy Ioyfull Subiectes vse all arte   15
to shew their love, but the highest hand of all hathe a finger in thy
welcome; Not a bird but singes, Not a plant but buddes, Not a Mead
but springes: Lame men goe wthout their Crouches, Olde men daunce
wthout their Cappes, all complections haue one appetite, all conditions
one consent: *Saturn* smyles as well as *Iupiter:* but aske who makes   20
this vniuersall vnion? all crye *kinge Iames:* wiser men can tell you more,
onlie this is my comfortable envie, boyes lesse then I can tell as muche.
let my mother recken myne age from the tyme of my Nativitie, I will
accompt my tyme from the commynge in of our Soveraigne *Iames:* Ye are
wthin fower myles of your London, where fowerscore thowsand Soules   25
attend you, everie one wth a prayer in his mouth, and a thowsand
in everie harte, all for your health, wealth, long raigne, & prosperitie

e are also wrytten to our forsaid Lieutenant for the present
delyvery of James Nevill knight: whom we are pleased yon
of our counsell shall bring vnto you when you shall wayte
vpon vs. / from our Pallace of Holyrinds howse the
5. of Aprile.   J.R. 1603.

An Oration delyvered to the Kinge
as he came to the Citie of London

Long the hope, and now the all instance: there was no way
for vs but at death in mowrninge, / als in the howre wherein we had
iust cause to weepe, we founde in the verie moment as iust a cause
of Triumphe: our Black night shoulde have lasted tyll the Zodiacke
had gone rounde, we founde it worne to baldnes ere the howre
had won out. / O excellent occasion of gladnes, y in so capitall
and profounde a Theam of sorrow, woldst not suffer the weedes
of lamentacon to holde their putting on. O memorable restorer, y
even in the exigent & pangs of our generall death, not onlie didst winn
vs, but in suche a manner recover vs, y we were not therie one alone the
better for our sufferance, but so put vs into a ravishment that we
forgat what we grond for. / Welcome renowned Emperor, and marke
how heaven enbites thee; not onlie thy joyfull Embrace vse all arte
to shew their love, but the highest hand of all hathe a finger in thy
welcome; Not a bird but singe, Not a plant but budds, Not a Meade
but springe: Lame men goe without their Crowches, Olde men daunce
without their Canes, all complexions have one appetite, all conditions
one consent: Saturn smylst as well as Jupiter; but aske who makes
this universall union; all cry, Kinge James: wiser men can tell you more,
onlie this is my comfortable endis, boyes lesse then I can tell as much:
let my mother recken myne age from the tyme of my Nativitie, I will
accompt my tyme from the cominge in of our Soveraigne James: Yee are
within fower mylis of yor London, where fowerscore thowsand Soules
attend you, everie one wth a prayer in his mouth, and a thowsand
in everie harte, all for yor health, wealth, long raigne, & prosperitie

The god of grace, peace, and plentie,
give happie blessinge to yo.r Royall Ma.tie /

I humblie besech yo.r most excellent Ma.tie, that when youre
most gratious disposition shall be pleased to see the sportes
of Cock fightinge: yo.r Highnes wolde vouchsafe me youre
humblest servaunt to attend yo.r Royall greatnes in those
pleasing sportes. ffor well vnderstanding the conditions
of those pleasures, I humblie recommend the best of my
service to yo.r Highnes in them. / Thus w.th my dewest
dutie tendered at yo.r graces feete, I pray to god
to preserve yo.r Ma.tie, and gyve his gratious blessinge to all
youre Princely and right Royall posteritie. /

Right trustie and right welbeloved, we greete you well :
Where we have bene pleased to graunt to william Hyolby
a Reversion of the office of a waitershyp in the custome
house of London the next y.t shall happen. And
have passed it vnder our Signature. We wyll
and require you that you give allowance therof
vnder yo.r hand, w.ch we shall also accept in good
parte. Geaven at our Castell of Windsor this
20 of Iulij. 1603.

To our Right trustie and
right welbeloved Counsello.r
the Lord Buckhurst, our
Lord high Treasurer of
England. /

[15   *c.* mid-1603–1604 (?)   see Commentary]

The god of grace, peace, and plentie,   1
    give happie blessinges to your Royall Maiestie/
I humblie besech your most excellent Maiestie, that when youre
most gratious disposition shall be pleased to see the sportes
of Cock fighting: Your highnes wolde vouchsafe me youre   5
humblest servaunt to attend your Royall greatnes in those
pleasing sportes. For well vnderstanding the conditions
of those pleasures, I humblie Commend the best of my
service to your highnes in them./ Thus wth my dearest
dutie tendered at your ⟨highnes⟩ graces feete, I pray to god   10
to preserue your Maiestie, and gyve his gratious blessinges to all
youre Princely and Right Royall posteritie./.

[16   20 July 1603   see Commentary]

Right trustie and right welbeloved, we greete you well: 1
Where we haue bene pleased to graunt to William Huxley
a Reversion of the Office of a waitership in the custome
house of London the next yt shall happen. And
haue passed it vnder our Signature. We wyll   5
and require you that you give allowance therof
vnder your hand, wch we shall also accept in good
parte. Yeaven at our Castell of Windsor this
20 of Iulij .i603.

                        To our Right trustie and   10
                        right welbeloved Counsellor
                        the Lord Buckhurst, our
                        lord high Treasurer of
                        England ./.

[17   23/24 April 1602   see Commentary]

      The Copie of a lettere sent from Therle of   1
      Northumberland, to Sir Frauncis Vere, by
      Captain Whitlocke the .24. of Aprile./.
        To the Valerous and worthie Captein
        Sir Frauncis Vere, Lord Governor of   5
        the Brill, and Commaunder of the
        English vnder the States./.
I tolde you at Ostend, that then was no fytt tyme to expostulate
matters, nowe I holde it proper: I call you to accompt of those
wronges you haue done me, You love to take the ayre and ryde   10
abrode, apoint therfore a place & tyme to your lykinge that I
may meete you: bring + you + a frend wth you, and I will be accom =
panied wth another, that shall be wytnesse of the thinges I will
lay to your charge: Yf you satisfie me, we will return good
Frendes; Yf not, we shall doe as god shall put in our myndes.   15
I will eschew all bitter wordes, as vnfyt for men of our condition,
Seeke not by fryvolous shyftes to divert this course of satisfac =
tion, wch will cause me to proceede in rightinge my self as the
wronges require: Make no replies by lettere, but send me your wyll
by this bearer directly that you will or you will not, for from   20
me you shall heare no more. Gyve no cause of Noyses to the
worlde to hinder this course, least you baffle youre owne –
reputation./.

[18   25 April 1602   see Commentary]

The Sonday morninge, the .25. of Aprile: Captain Ogle   1
came to th'erle of Northumberlands lodginge, and tolde his Lordshippe,
that Sir Fraunces Vere vpon the receyte of his lettere, had
no disposition to lay him self so open + to + the bearer thereof,
as to let hym vnderstand his mynde: But yt he had advysed   5
since wth hym self, and sent him an answere of his letter in
another: wch Captain Ogle intreated his Lordship to receyve./.

The copie off a lre sent from Thearle off
Northumberland, to Sr ffrancis Vere, by
Capt Whitlocke the .24. off Aprill. /

To the valorous and worthie Captain
Sr ffrancis Vere, Lord Governor off
the Brill, and Commaunder off the
English under the Estates. /

J tolde you at Ostend, that then was no fytt tyme to expostulate
matters, nowe J holde it proper: J call you to accompt off those
wronges you have done me, you love to take the ayre and ryde
abrode, apoint therfore a place & tyme to yor lykinge that J
may meete you: bring a frend wth you, and J will be accom=
panied wth another, that shall be wytnesse off the thinge J will
lay to yor charge: Eff you satisfie me, wee will retturn good
frends; eff not, wee shall doe as god shall putt in our myndes.
J will eschew all bitter woordes, as unfytt for men off our condition
Seeke not by frivolous Jeste to divert this course off satisfaction, wch will cause me to proceede in wrytinge my selff as the
wronges requires: Make no replies by lre, but send me yor wytt
by this bearer directly that you will or you will not, for from
me you shall have no more. Give no cause off Noyse to the
worlde to hinder this course, least you baffle youre owne
reputation. /

The sonday morninge, the .25. off Aprill: Captain Ogle
came to thearle off Northes lodginge, and tolde his Lordshippe,
that Sr ffrancis Vere upon the receypt off his lre, had
no disposition to lay him selff so open to the bearer therof,
as to let him understand his mynde: But yt he had addrest
since wth him selff, and sent him an answere off his letter in
another: wch Capt: Ogle intreated his Lordship to receyve. /

Sr ffrauncis Vere was desyrous that they might meete in some
place in London, and either of them accompanied wth a man of quallitie
and of some ranke in the State: This hod my Lord refused ab~
surdely, alledginge y suche men were likely to acquaint y Queene
and Counsell wthall, yf they shoulde see any dyfference betwene
vs y might breede further contention: And so bringe vs bothe
under the power of her Ma:tie comaundm:t by theire information.
At the least, yf they should not doe this: they wolde hynder
vs from going togither to the fielde (iff either of vs should habe
iust cause so to doe) A proceeding flatt against his meaninge
bycause he desyred no noyse, but privately to be satisfied. /.

Afterwards when the Earle was commaunded by her Ma:tie whom
in all dutie he obeyed: He onlie made the company there present
to understand, that he referred himselfe to all men of iudgement,
that made profession of Honor: / And that he hoped they
wolde not blame hym iff in attending his better satisfaction, he
protested y Sr ffrauncis Vere was a knabe, and a Coward.
that in sleaving and praving like a common Buffone, wold wronge
men of all conditions: and had neither the honestie nor the
cariage to satisfie any. /.

            Sr ffrauncis Vere his letter to the
            Earle of Northumberland. /.
                  Directed.

To the right honorable, the Earle of
Northumberland, knight of the most noble
      Order of the Garter. /.

Yor Lordship required in the letter sent by Captaine Whitlockes,
that I should returne a direct answere by wordes of mouthe to
the contente: Wch at the instant I forbare, the matter being
of moment and not to be resolved of so suddainly, and none for

Sir Frauncis Vere was desyrous that they might meete in some
place in London, and either of them accompanied wth a man of gravitie,
and of some ranke in the state: The wch my Lord refused as –   10
vnmeete, alledginge yt suche men were likely to acquaynt ye Queene
and Counsell wthall, Yf they shoulde see any dyfference betwene
vs yt might breede further contention: And so bringe vs bothe
vnder the power of her Maiesties commaundement by their information./
At the least, yf they should not doe this: they wolde hynder   15
vs from going togither to the fielde (if either of vs should have
iust cause so to doe) A proceeding flatt against his meaninge
bycause he desyred no noyse, but pryvately to be satisfied./.

Afterwarde when the Earle was commaunded by her Maiestie whom
in all dutie he Obeyed: he onlie made the company their present   20
to vnderstand, that he referred him self to all men of Iudgement,
that made profession of honor:/ And that he hoped they
wolde not blame hym if in attending his better satisfaction, he
protested yt Sir Frauncis Vere was a knave, and a Coward:
that in flearing and gearing like a common Buffone, wold wronge   25
men of all conditions: and had neither the honestie nor the
cariage to satisfie any./.

[19   26 April 1602   see Commentary]

                    Sir Frauncis Vere his letter to the   1
                      Earle of Northumberland./.
                            .Directed.
                 To the Right honorable, the Earle of
                 Northumberland, knight of the most Noble   5
                      Order of the Garter./.
Your Lordship required in the letter sent by Captain Whitlocke,
that I should return a direct answere by worde of mouthe to
the contentes: Wch at the instant I forbare, the matter being
of moment and not to be resolved of so suddainly, and nowe for   10

good respectes I choose rather to let your Lordshippe to knowe my mynde
by wryting, then by any mans reporte; Yf your Lordshippes meaning bee by
the meetinge you apoint, to draw a Verball satisfaction from me
in the obiections you are to make: The manner of the meeting
in my opinion is not the best: In regarde that he delyvered –   15
where swordes may be drawne, is subiect to hard construction,
wch I desyer to avoyde./ Your Lordshippe shall therfore be pleased to
nominate some fytt place for communication, whether I will
repayre wth muche willingnes to cleere my self of having gyven
to your Lordshippe the fyrst cause of offence: For truthes sake, for the   20
respect of your greatnes, and for that I despise private combatting.
Especially at this tyme, that I am ingaged in so greate and
Ymportant an accion as your Lordshippe well knoweth: This course
reiected by your Lordshippe I shall not leave to follow the occasions yt
drewe me over, wth my poore trayne attending on me ordinarilie./   25
Confident yt your Lordshippe will attempt nothing vnfytting your self
vpon me, that haue alwayes lyved in good reputation, and am
discended from a Grandfather of your owne ranke: my lodging
in Aldersgate streete this .26. of Aprile./

                          F.V./.   30

[20   see Commentary]

After her Maiestie had Commaunded Th'erle as aforesaid./   1
Then the Earle published the manner of his proceedinges
in Englishe, French, and Italian: Whereof Sir Frauncis
Vere coulde not procure a copie, tyll some fewe dayes before
his departure, nor answere ye same so presently as he willingly   5
wolde for his affayres otherwyse. And for the same Earle went
beyond ye true groundes of Iudgment & honor: Sir Frauncis Vere. thought
it necessarie to send to ye Earle this letter, wch he offreth to the
worlde wth the rest of his proceedinges to be Iudged of./.

good reporte & choose rather to let yo.r Lo: to knowe my mynde
by wryting, then by any mans reporte; Iff yo.r Lo: meaning bee by
the meetinge you apoint, to draw a verball satisfaction from me
in the obiections you are to make: The manner off this meeting
in my opinion is not the best; In regards that the dolyvered
wordes sodded may be drawne, is subiect to hard construction,
wch I desyre to avoyde. / yo.r Lo: shall therfore be pleased to
nominate some fytt place for communication, whether I will
repayre wth muche willingnes to cleare my selff off having gyven
to yo.r Lo: the fyrst cause off offence: ffor truthes sake, for the
respect off yo.r greatnes, and for that I despise private combatting
Especially at this tyme, that I am ingaged in so greate and
ymportant an action as yo.r Lo: well knoweth : This comes
reiected by yo.r Lo: I shall not leave to follow the occasions yt
drewe me over, wth my poore trayne attending on me ordinarilie,
Confident yt yo.r Lo: will attempt nothing vnfytting yo.r selff
vpon me, that have alwayes lyved in good reputation, and am
discended from a Grandfather off yo.r owne ranke : My lodging
in Aldersgate streete this. 26. off Aprill. /   F. V. 1.

After her Ma.tie had Commaunded these as aforesaid. /
Then the Earle published the manner off his proceedinge
in Englisshe, ffrench, and Italian: whereof S.r ffrauncis
Vere coulde not procure a copie, tyll some fewe dayes before
his departure, nor answere ye same so presently as he willingly
woulde for his affayres otherwyse. And for the same Earle went
beyond ye true grounde off iudgment & hono.r. S.r ffra. Vere. thought
it necessarie to send to ye Earle this letter, wch he offreth to the
worlde wth the rest off his proceedinge to be iudged off. /

Bycause I refused to meete you vpon yo[u]r peremptorie and
foolishe Commons: you conclude me in a discourse sent
abroade vnder yo[u]r name, to be a knave, and a Coward, and
a Buffone: Wherein you have provoked me to set aside
all respecte to yo[u]r person, and say that you are a most
lying, and an vnworthie Lord: you are bounde to her M.[ties]
Commaundement not to assaile me, and I by the busynes
committed vnto mee, not to seeke you: when we shall be
freed, or god shall make vs meete, I will maintein it w[i]th
my sworde./

Fra: Vere:

My good friend, I take it in exceeding kindnes y[t] you are so
carefull ouer my poore distressed fronde in these sorrowfull dayes,
I pray proceede according as you have begon in yo[u]r friendly assistance w[i]th yo[u]r good counsell & comforte wherewith you rightlye abownd
I assure ye you shall infinitely deserve my love, yf you shall
freely & helpfully rayse & relieve their deiected & heavy spirritte./
I pray take vpon you y[e] deliuery of my lres to doct[r] lodge & m[r]
sheld, read them & seale them vp, & vrge them (as needs shall
require) to performe the same:/ My prayers I exhibite dailie
& howerly vnto god y[e] Creation of men, y[t] it might please him
to shed his comforte into yo[u]r hartes, & acquit ye from y[t] evill
spirritt y[t] furiously rageth in the bowells of the desolate
cittie. Amen./
My trust is in god y[t] we shall meete in better dayes then euer we
sawe yet, or hetherto inioyed; I desyer it may be so in the
earnest of my soule: w[ch] he graunt in whose power all per=
formance consyste. Amen./

Hitchin

I pray you beare w[i]th my imperfect wrything, when I thinke of
yo[u]r estate I am not w[i]thout disturbance of my spirritte./

Bycause I refused to meete you vpon your peremptorie and 10
foolishe Summons: You conclude me in a discourse sent
abrode vnder your name, to be a knave, and a Coward, and
a Buffone: Wherein you haue provoked me to set asyde
all respectes to your person, and say that you are a most
lying, and + an + vnworthie Lord: You are bounde to her Maiesties 15
Commaundement not to assaile me, and I by the busynes –
commytted vnto mee, not to seeke you: When we shall be
freed, or god shall make vs meete, I will maintein it wth
my sworde./.

Fra: Vere : 20

[21   mid- to late-1603 (?)   see Commentary]

My good Frend, I take it in exceeding kindnes yt you are so – 1
carefull over my poore distressed frendes in there sorrowfull dayes,
I pray proceede according as you have begon in your frendly assist =
ance wth your good counsell & comforte wherewth you ritchlye abound,
I assure ye you shall infinitely deserue my love, yf you shall – 5
freely & helpfully rayse & releeve their deiected & heavy spirrittes./
I pray take vpon ye ye delyuery of my letteres to doctor lodge & Mr
Field, read them & seale them vp, & vrge them (as neede shall
require) to performe the same:/ My prayers I exhibite dailie
& howerly vnto god ye Saviour of men, yt it might please him 10
to shed his comforte into your hartes, & acquit ye from yt evill
spirritt yt furiously rageth in the bowells of the desolate
cittie. *Amen./.*
My trust is in god yt we shall meete in better dayes then ever we
sawe yet, or hetherto enioyed; I desyer it may be so in the 15
earnest of my soule: wch he graunt in whose power all per =
formance consystes. *Amen./.*   *Hitchin*

I pray you beare wth my imperfect wryting, when I thinke of
your estates I am not wthout disturbance of my spirrittes./.

[22]

               A letter to her Maiestie./   1
Being bounde (most gratious Lady) by the streight Chaines of
Nature in all dutie vnto your Maiestie and lincked vndivisiblie –
vnto the service of the same by the free and fatall affection
of my harte: I holde it meere impietie not to present your highnes   5
wth the register of myne actions: yea were it possible, wth the
iust inventorie of my verie thoughtes./ In this discontinuance
being at Sea, I founde sea roome, wthout myndes rest; open ayr:
yet sweltring cogitacions; Sunshine to the eye, not the Sun yt
lightens my harte: and so many dayes, so many deathes: and no   10
more nightes then hells haue I passed thorough; O the simpli =
citie of men, yt Imagines any passage, pollicie, place, or circum =
stance, can Medicine the love wounded cogitacion./ As yet –
gratious Madam: my bodie hathe not cast of the desaster it
suffred for companies sake of my mynde: but no sooner shall my   15
health be obtayned, then I must offer my harte personally vnto
your divine presence, to suffer wth the Sundyinge Egle ye last
of my Martirdome; wherin I doe & shall everlastingly reioyc
endinge the worlde in so glorious a cause, & passinge vnto –
heaven wth so sufficient a warrant./   20
                    The Subiect, Servaunt,
                    and Martir: of your celestiall
                    perfections:

[23]

             Another letter to her Maiestie./   1
I leave it to be determyned by your self (Most gratious Madame)
whether I should stand vpon the merittes of my long endured passion
and therby plead the recompence of most faithefull love: or refer =
ring my case vnto the Chauncerie of your divine perfections, be   5
ordered by a Iewrie of conscience: It can not be vnknowne –
vnto your Maiestie for I haue often said it, and you haue often –
heard it: I haue suffred, and you haue seene: how my devotion
is no daliance, & yt my carefull service, can be no tryfeling atten =
dance./ I was borne to serue you, Raigninge the blessed Queene   10
of England: brought to honor you being the Miracle of Ages:

A letter to her Maiestie.

Being bownde (most gratious La:) by the stronngest chaines off
Natur in all dutie vnto yor Matie: and linked vndivisblie
vnto the servic off the same by the free and fatall affection
off my harte: I holde it meere impietie not to present yor highnes
wth the register off myne actions: yea were it possible, wth the
inst inventorie off my verrie thoughte. In this discontinuance
being at Sea, I fownde sea roome, wthout myndes rest; open ayre
yet smothring cogitations: Sunnshine to the eye, not the storm of
highstorms my harte: and so many dayes, so many deathes: and no
more nighttes then hell have I passed thorowe; O the simplicitie off men, y Imagind any passage, pollicie, place, or circumstance, can Medicine the love woonded cogitacion. I Ah not
gratious Madam: my bodie hathe not cast off the disaster it
suffred for companies sake off my mynde: but no sooner shall my
healthe be obtaynd, then I must offer my harte personally vnto
yor divine presence, to suffore wth the remedyinge either the last
off my martirdome, wherein I doe & shall everlastingly vioye:
ending the worlde in so glorious a cause, & passinge vnto
heaven wth so sufficient a warrant.

                    The Subiect, Servante,
                    and Martir: of yor celestiall
                    perfections:

Another letter to her Maiestie.

I leave it to be determyned by yor selfe (most gratious madame)
wether I should stand vpon the meritte off my long endured passion
and therby plead the recompence off most faithefull love: or referring my case vnto the Champione off yor divine perfections, be
ordered by a feavrie off conscience: it can not be vnknowne
vnto yor Matie: for I have often said it, and you have often
heard it: I have suffred, and you have seene: sure my devotion
is no duliance, & y my carefull service, can be no trifeling attendance. I was bound to serve you, sithe singinge the blessed Queene
off England: brought to honor you being the Miracle off Age:

induced to admyre yow the Angell of owr good thoughts,
but constraynod to love (that is all the rest, & more then all)
as yow are the onlie Quene, Miracle, Angell, and excellency
of all tymes: Seme not strange Madam to be ignorant of
yor might, yow rule not the authoritie of yor Scepter: nor
yow overrule not the influens of yor beauties: yow commande
by the prerogative of yor estate, yow compell mee by the
power of yor vertues: and more then yow can do as a Quene
yow doe in mee as yor sole and divine selff. To conclude
briefly the length of my infinite desyres: I am gratious Lady,
nothing but yor pleasure, either to have the hope & holde
my lyfe strengthned by yor free mercye, or by cruell denyall
to have the twyne sundered, and sincking downe to dye
in the fyer of yor beauties. ./

                    The most contented & resolute
                    Martir of yor Excellencies:

          To the Quenes most excellent Matis. ./

Most excellent Matis, vouchsafe I beseech yow out of yowr
sacred regardes, the reading of a poore Ladies humble petition,
preferred by her sonne in her husbande behalf and her
owne, for relief of them: whose infancie & miserie blusshes
not to begge. / Once is the hono'' of yor Matis: ever vouch-
safinge pittie to distresse, & rewardes to any service: as succour
in either of these cases are not violated at any tyme. / But
it is necessitie and not desert & is the mover of my sute:
wch is: That yor gracious and bountious Matis: will pleass
to bestowe the benefitt of the fyne worthship imposed upon
some of the late offendors: upon yor Matis: true & faithfull
(though unfortunate) Servant, Sr Edwarde Wingfield:

f. 20v

induced to admyre you the Angell of our good thoughtes,
but constrayned to love (that is all the rest, & more then all)
as you are the onlie Queene, Miracle, Angell, and excellency
of all tymes: Seeme not sweete Madam to be ignorant of   15
your might, You rule wth the authoritie of your Scepter: mee
you overrule wth the influence of your beauties: You commaunde
by the prerogative of your estate, you compell mee by the
power of your vertues: and more then you can do as a Queene,
you doe in mee as your sole and divine self./ To conclude   20
briefly the length of my infinite desyers: I am gratious Lady,
nothing but your pleasure; either to haue the hope yt holdes
my lyfe strengthned by your free mercye, or by cruell denyall
to haue the twyne sundered, and sincking downe to dye
in the fyer of your beauties./.   25

                    The most contented & resolute
                    Martir of your Excellencies:

[24   February 1601 – March 1602 (?)   see Commentary]

            To the Queenes Most excellent Maiestie./.   1
Most excellent Maiestie: Vouchsafe I besech you out of youre
sacred regarde, the reading of a poore Ladies humble peticion,
preferred by her Sonne in her husbandes behalf and her
owne, for reliefe of them: whose infancie & miserie blusshes   5
not to begge./ Such is the honor of your Maiestie ever vouch =
safinge pittie to distresse, & rewarde to any service: as sutors
in either of these cases are not reiected at any tyme./ But
it is necessitie and not desart yt is the mover of my Sute:
wch is: That your gracious and bounteous Maiestie will please   10
to bestowe the benifitt of the fyne worthelie imposed vpon
some of the late Offendors: vpon your Maiesties true & faithfull
(though vnfortunate) Servaunt, Sir Edwarde Winckfield:

Who is nowe in Your Maiesties service in Ireland Private wthout
imployment: having small maintenaunce their, his debtes being   15
many, and his charge of children great at home, and no
meanes lefte to satisfie and maintein them: wch the rather
makes this boldnes in your Maiesties poore suppliant to implore youre
princely ayde in this kynde./ So shall the Children
god hathé gyven hym be brought vp in his feare to pray   20
for your highnes tyll they be of strength to serue your most
Royall Maiestie as your true subiectes ought: And him self
thinke all services of labor and hazard too little wch is
done for your Maiestie./.

   Most gratious Maiestie let it please your highnes to   25
   referre this humble sute to the Right honorable
   the Lord Admyrall and Mr Secretarie./.

[25   February 1601 (1602?)   see Commentary]

   A letter to the Queenes Atturney Mr *Cooke*./   1
Good Sir: I holde my self so interessed in the distressed
estate of that poore man *Neweby*, the post of dartfoord, yt
I should be sorie her Maiesties mercyfull disposition towardes him
should offend any, though it seeme extended in some extra =   5
ordinarie manner./.
howe soever his case be by the sentence of the lawe, The
specyall affection, testimonye, & sute of the knightes and
Esquiers, Iustices of the Countie, on his behalf, together
wth the Iuryes owne remorce and relenting of their verdict   10
vnder their handes vpon better advice (wch her highnes was
pleased to apprehend and harken vnto) dyd so inclyne her
to mercye, that where she had twyce before commaunded –
their lordshippes to do for his repryve, she was willing by
her owne hand to ratifie and to make hym as it were her owne   15

who is now in yo[ur] Ma[jes]tie: service in Ireland w[i]thout
imployment: havinge small maintenanc[e] there, his debte beinge
many, and his charge of children great at home, and no
meanes lefte to satisfie and maintein them: w[hi]ch the rather
makes this beadns in yo[ur] Ma[jes]tie: poore supp[lian]t: to implore yo[ur]
p[ri]ncely ayde in this kynde. / So shall the children
(god saith) geven hym be brought vp in his feare to pray
for yo[ur] highnes tyll they be of strength to serve yo[ur] most
Royall Ma[jes]tie: as yo[ur] true subiectes ought: And hym self
thinke all s[er]vice of labo[ur] and hazard too little w[hi]ch is
done for yo[ur] Ma[jes]tie: /

Most gratious Ma[jes]tie: let it please yo[ur] highnes to
referre this humble sute to the Right honorable
the Lord Admyrall and M[aste]r Secretarie. /

A letter to the Generall Attourney M[aste]r Cooke. /

Good S[i]r. I holde my self so interessed in the distressed
state of that poore man Newby, the post of Dartfood, &
I should be sorie her Ma[jes]ties: m[er]cyfull disposition towarde hym
should offend any, though it seeme extended in some extra=
ordinarie manner. /

Howe soever his case be by the sentence of the lawes, The
Royall affection, testimonye, & sute of the knightes and
esquiers, Justices of the Countie, on his behalf, together
w[i]th the iuryes owne remorse and relenting of their verdict
vnder their hand vpon better advice (w[hi]ch her highnes was
pleased to apprehend and harken vnto) dyd so inclyne her
to mercye, that whe[n] she had twyse before comaunded
their Lordshippe to do for his reprieve, she was willing by
her owne hand to ratifie and to make hym as it were her owne

prisoners, in such form as the inclosed will shewe vpon,
Drawne from a president of the like, procured by the
late Lo: Thresurer. about the .24. of her raigne, ~
grounded vpon her Ma:^{tie} royall prerogatiue./

The fittues of the tyme wch only attended, makes me
acquaint yor therof, now against the Assises, rather then
sooner: And soe may yo^u gerawnsall to afforde the wretched
man yor commiseration & fauours, the rather for that
(as I am enformed) the Vicar of Dartford, (a speciall
instrument of his heavy doome) stricken sins wth an
extraordinarie sickues, lyeth disquieted in conscience, and
by the pursaches and troubles theire, wth the poore man
mercyes for the wrong his tongue dyd him at his ar=
waignement. Thus still recommendinge the poore man
to yor speciall fauor, wth my hartiest commendations I
leaue yo^u to the protection of god. ffrom the Courts
at Westher all this   of ffebruarij. 1601 /

G.N. his letter to the Lo: cheefe Justice./

Right honorable Lords:/

Pardon me I besseghe yor Lo: thoughs./ I still perseuer in my desire
of my wyues enlargement, who throughe the infamye of the
place, the griefe of her owne infirmitie, and feare of beinge by me
abandoned, wch am bounde to mainteine her. her wytte & healte
are so impayred, y^t she is in hazard bothe of bodye and soule;
for she being thus oversweayed wth troubles, & also rashly refused,

prisoner, in such form as the inclosed will shewe you,
drawne from a president of the like, procured by the
late Lord Treasurer: about the .24. of her raigne, –
grounded vpon her Maiesties royall prerogative./
The fyttnes of the tyme wch I only attended, makes me   20
acquaint you therwth, now against the Assises, rather then
sooner: And pray you herewthall to afforde the wretched
man your commiseration & favoure, the rather for that
(as I am enformed) the Vicar of Dartford, (a speciall
instrument of his heavy doome) stricken since wth an   25
extraordinarie sicknes, lyeth disquieted in conscience, and
by the preacher and Scholemaster their, cryes the poore man
mercye for the wrong his tongue dyd him at his ar =
raignement. Thus still recommendinge the poore man
to your specyall favour, wth my hartiest commendations I   30
leave you to the protection of god. From the Courte
at Whitehall this   of Februarij . i60i /

[26]

       G.N. his letter to the Lord chiefe Iustice./   1
       Right honorable Lorde:/
Pardon me I beseche your Lordshippe though I still persever in ye desier
of my wyves enlargement, Who through the infamye of the
place, the griefe of her owne infirmitie, and feare of beinge by me   5
abandoned, wch am bounde to maintein her. her wyttes & health
are so impayred, yt she is in hazard bothe of bodye and soule;
for she being thus overwayed wth trobles, hathe rashly refused

suche punyshmentes as were offered to be Imposed vpon her./ Yet
your good Lordshippe of your high discretion knowing how vnable weake   10
weomen ar to beare such greevous trobles and disgraces, especially
being borne and brought vp to better effectes, will I trust in mercy
and charitie heap no more miseries vpon her, then may brydle her
affections, but not destroy her sence or bring her to dispayre./
My good lord: her fall was my falt, Who being my self in troble,   15
sent her about such sutes as were vnmeete for her youth or sexe,
Wherby through her wandering abrode she grewe more infamous
by mens vnbrideled tongues (wherewth this Cittie overfloweth)
then I trust she was by her incontinent factes./ For no particular
offence can be proved against her whereby (in the mynde of the   20
common sorte) she should be subiect to punyshment in so high
degrees; Yet god having chosen your Lordshippe to distribute equall
Iustice, I knowe the same god hathe endued you wth those three
especyall graces wch are annexed to the same./ The first,
vprightnes of Counsell, by wayes & tymes most Congruent: 25
The second, to do the workes of Iustice stricktly accordinge
to the lawes: The third, (wch is the high gyfte of god),
a discretion lefte in your brest when all lawes do fayle for
the sodaine necessitie of the service of god and ye common
wealth, wch must direct your Lordshippe in my case, as from a   30
higher begynnyng: And therfore do humbly intreate youre
Lordshippe yt you will be pleased to exercise yt clemencye yt is appropri =
ate to your person and place. The offence is hirs, the occasion
was myne, and the harme is myne, & shall hereafter be no mans els:
God in repentaunce will forgyve her, wherevpon I trust he wyll   35
instill the like mercye into your mynde in furtheraunce of vnitie betwixte
man and wyfe, since we are determyned to lyve in the feare of god
and amendement of lyfe./.

               Ever bounde to do your Lordshippe
                 honor and service./.   40

suche punyshmente as were offered to be imposed upon her. yet
yo[r] good Lo: off yo[r] highe discretion knowinge how vnable weake
woomen are to beare suche greevous troubles and disgraces, especially
being borne and brought vp to better estate, will I trust in mercy
and charitie heap no more miseries vpon her, then may brydle her
affections, but not destroy her senses or bring her to dispayre.

My good Lord: her fall was my falt, who being my selfe in trouble,
sent her about suche sutes as were vnmeete for her youth or sexe,
whereby through her wandring abrode she growe more infamous
by mens vnbridled tongues (wherewth this dittie ouerflowethe)
then I trust she was by her incontinent factes. If no particular
offence can be proved against her whereby (in the myndes off the
common sorte) she should be subiect to punyshment in so highe
degrees; yet god hauing chosen yo[r] Lo: to distribute equall
iustice, I knowe the same god hathe endued you wth those three
especyall graces wth are annexed to the same. The first,
knowledge off counsell, by wayes & tymes most convenient:
The second, to do the workes off iustice strickly accordinge
to the lawes: The thurd, (wch is the highe gyfte off god,)
a discretion lefte in yo[r] brest when all lawes do fayle for
the sodaine necessitie off the seruice off god and y common
wealthe, wch must direct yo[r] Lo: in my case, as from a
highe beginnyng: And therefore do humbly intreate yo[u]r
Lo: y you will be pleased to exercise y clemencye y is appropriate to yo[r] person and place. The offence is hers, the occasion
was myne, and the harme is myne, & shall hereafter be no mans els:
God in repentannce will forgyve her, whereupon I trust she wyll
instill the like mercye into yo[r] mynde in furtherance off amitie betwixte
man and wyfe, since we are determyned to lyve in the feare off god
and amendment off lyfe.

Her bounde to do yor Lo:
honor and seruice.

Most Honorable, and my onlie singular good Lord:

About twelue yeeres past, throughe lyttle regarde to my selfe I
fell into some misgovernement, for the whiche (as other) I might
alledge youthe for my excuse (if is not for warrantise) But
trustinge especyally ý my humble willing and ready endevours
in the service of Her Ma: & my Contrie, had cancelled those
former errors, I gabe lyttle heede vnto them: The vngile (now
of late) mallice makinge large blotts of those heedes stayned
hathe vrged them (by false and fimmisions evidence) against me,
and caused them to be considered against my reputation and fame.

In my distresses heretofore (most Honorable) hauinge found
your Lo: the onlie hopefull Starr ý hathe avayled me,
may it nowe please the same to shyne vpon me fauorablie,
before I perishe vtterly. A most happie (vous appoie) man
conlde I bee (yor honor ablinge me theervnto) yf I might in
forraigne trabayle employed (I recke not ý daunger whatsoever)
either by industrious service and daringe adventure, wype out
this my homebred blemyshe, or wth my blond sheddinge testifie
the dutie I owe to yor honor, and get beyond fortunes and the
worldes spite. Vnto this my humble petition these Noble
Lordes lysten, by the excellencye of those vertues ý renownes
you for ever: And my perpetuall prayers to god shall bee,
ý yor honor pittie in this case may be accepted of Hym as
greate pietie, and to rewarde it wth present and ever
followinge vnfaylinge happinesse. The 20 of Ianuary
1594 : /.

f. 22v

[27   20 January 1594 (1595?)]

    Most honorable, and my onlie singular good lord: 1
About twelue yeeres past, through lyttle regarde to my self I
fell into some misgovernement, for the wch (as others) I might
alledge Youthe for my excuse, (if not for warrantise) But
trustinge especyally yt my sundrie willing and ready endevours   5
in the service of her Maiestie & my Countrie, had cancelled those
former errores, I gave lyttle heede vnto them: The while (now
of late) Mallice makinge large blottes of those heedles staynes,
hathe vrged them (by falce and Iniurious evidence) against me,
and caused + them + to be censured against my reputation and fame./ 10
In my distresses heretofore (Most honorable) havinge founde
your Lordshippe the onlie helpfull Starr yt hathe avayled me,
may it nowe please the same to shyne vpon me favorablie,
before I perish vtterly: A most happie (vnhappie) man
shoulde I bee (your honor ablinge me thervnto) yf I might in   15
forreigne travayle employed (I recke not ye daunger whatsoever)
either by industrious service and daringe adventure, wype out
this my homebred blemyshe, or wth my bloud shedding testifie
the dutie I owe to your honor, and get beyond fortunes and the
worldes spite./ Vnto this my humble peticion thryse Noble   20
Lorde lysten, by the excellencye of those vertues yt renownes
you for ever: And my perpetuall prayers to god shall be,
yt your honores pittie in this case may be accepted of hym as
greate pietie, and to rewarde it wth present and ever –
followinge vnfaylinge happinesse. The .20. of Ianuarij   25
1594./.

[28]

Right Worshipful let me once again intreate and humblie beseche   1
you, to consyder and pittie the hard extreemes of a poore
olde man: and let him not perishe in youre defalt, whose
better yeeres was then best spent, when he toke pleasure
in pleasuringe others./ My self, and what I esteemed most,   5
was alwayes ready at your commaundes./ Conceyt what a
Tyrant is auncyent povertie: O, it is a devill and furye
of hell: It breakes all lawes, respectes no persons, nor feares
no perilles./ It observes neither reason, sence, humanitie, –
scilence, nor secresie./ Were I a straunger vnknowne to   10
your Worship and therewthall voyde of the least desarte: my
aged yeares and wofull estate, might make me fytt matter
for your goodnes to worke on./ I am lothe to expostulate wth
your Worship: I still regarde you as becomes me./ Yf you –
thinke me to bolde to importune you thus, it is not my –   15
custome, but my want yt compelles me: for while I had –
meanes to relieve my self, I made no demaundes, nor pleaded
no wantes./ May it please you therefore to loke backe –
but a lyttle, to those former tymes I must put you in mynd
of, and former matters I haue reason to speake of: bothe –   20
what I was then (I beseche you remember) and what I am
nowe, and what is the poore demaunde I haue made, & howe
my extreemes constrayne & enforce me./ I hope you will
showe me your speedy favoure, and free your self from my
importunitie: So shall you bothe stead me, relieve me, and   25
ryd me; and gyve me iust cause to love and honor you ./.
What more I should wryte or say in this matter, I leave
to your Worships far better discretion, to be consydered by your
self: and so most humblie take my leave ./.

Right wo[rshipfull]: let me once again intreate and humblie besoughe
you, to consyder and pittie the hard estreeme of a poore
olde man: and let him not perishe in youre defalt, whose
better yeares was then best spent, when he toke pleasure
in pleasinges of you. My selfe, and what I esteemd most,
was alwayes ready at yo[ur] commande. Conceyt what a
Tyrant is annoyent povertie: O, it is a devill and furye
of hell: It breakes all lawes, respectes no persons, nor feares
no perilles. It observes neither reason, sence, humanitie,
silence, nor secresie. Were I a straynger unknowne to
yo[ur] wo[rshipp]: and therewithall voyde of the least desartes: my
aged yeares and wofull estate, might make me fytt matter
for yo[ur] goodnes to worke on. I am lothe to expostulate w[i]th
yo[ur] wo[rshipp]: I still regarde you as becomes me. Lest you
thinke me to bolde to importune you thus, it is not my
custome, but my want y[t] compelles me: for while I had
meanes to relieve my selfe, I made no demaundes, nor pleaded
no wante. May it please you therefore to loke back
but a lyttle, to those former tymes I must put you in mynde
of, and former matters I have reason to speake of: bothe
what I was then (I beseche you remember) and what I am
nowe, and what is the poore demaunde I have made, & howe
my estreemes constrayne & enforce me. I hope you will
shewe me yo[ur] speedy favours, and free yo[ur] selfe from my
importunitie. So shall you bothe stead me, relieve me, and
ryd me; and gyve me iust cause to love and hono[ur] you.
What more I should wryte or say in this matter, I leave
to yo[ur] wo[rshipps] farr better discretion, to be consydered by yo[ur]
selfe: and so most humblie take my leave.

Sonne Micah: youre meanes of prosperitie & wastes are
nowe in yor hand: iff you lose them (as you may) you are
made, iff abuse them (as I feare) you aar marrd for ever.
Iff the same pleasures of thee place you lyve in possesse
you, the tormentinge griefe therof possesseth me. Iff sloath
(wch sometymes assalted you heare) have there gotten the
upper hand off you, I se no remedie but you must be a
slave as well to miserie the daughter, as follows the mother.
Studye earnestlye therfore to acquite yor self from so
hard a yoake, & labour to make some amendes wth diligence
for the greate charges wch the love off yor parentes is willing
to bestowe upon the hope off yor preferment. Be not you
a barre to yor owne advancement, but take holde off the
occasion wch presentes it self unto you: wch iff you nowe
let passe, you let passe wthall yor parentes further care
off you. Yor father you knows hath strayned hym self to
do you good: iff he see no frute off his long expectation,
what can you expect, but a slacking off his liberall hand,
iff not a wthdrawinge off it smallie? And as for me, presume
not overmuche off my too tender affection, since you can not
be ignorant my hoysome love (being answered wth an ingrate=
full unkindenes) will turn it self into an extremitie off
loathinge, iff not hatinge. Flatter not yor self wth my
favouringe you, since as iff you studie to deserve ill you shall
have it, so iff you herein neglect it, I have others as neere
and as deere unto me as yor self on whome to bestowe it:
Iff you desyre to go before yor brother & sister in my love,
endevoure yor self to go even wth them in theire deserte. Iff you
be carelesse in this pointe, as nowe yor self you discharge me
off my carefullnes, whereof I accompte yor negligence a full
acquittance. This is the last offer wch you shall have off
lykinge as a gentleman or an unthriste: Nowe you may

[29   13 February 1601 (1602?)   see Commentary]

Sonne *Micah:* youre meanes of prosperitie hereafter are   1
nowe in your hand: if you vse them (as you may) you are
made, if abuse them (as I feare) you are mard for ever./
Yf the vaine pleasures of the place you lyve in possesse
you, the tormentinge griefe therof possesseth me. Yf sloath   5
(wch sometymes assalted you here) haue their gotten the
vpper hand of you, I se no remedie but you must be a
slave as well to miserie the daughter, as Idlenes the mother./
Stryve earnestlye therfore to acquite your self from so
hard a yoake, & laboure to make some amendes wth diligence   10
for the greate charges wch the love of your parentes is willing
to bestowe vpon the hope of your preferment. Be not you
a barre to your owne advauncement, but take holde of the
occasion wch presentes it self vnto you: Wch yf you nowe
let passe, you let passe wthall your parentes further care   15
of you. Your father you knowe hathe strayned hym self to
do you good: if he see no fruyte of his long expectation,
What can you expect, but a slacking of his liberall hand,
if not a wthdrawinge of it finallie? And as for me, presume
not overmuche of my too tender affection, since you can not   20
be ignorant yt extreeme love (being answered wth an vngrate =
full vnkindenesse) will turn it self into an extremitie of
loathinge, if not hatinge./ Flatter not your self wth my –
favouringe you, since as if you studie to deserue it, you shall
haue it, so if you herein neglect it, I haue others as neere   25
and as deare vnto me as your self on whom to bestowe it:
Yf you desyer to go before your brother & syster in my love,
endevour your self to go even wth them in their desertes. Yf you
be carelesse in this pointe, assure your self you discharge me
of my carefullnes, whereof I accompte youre negligence a full   30
acquittaunce. This is the last offer wch you shall haue of
lyvinge as a gentleman or an vnthrifte: Nowe you may

chuse: and in your choyse remember this, that you do either
binde vs to care for you, or ⟨cast you of⟩ drive vs to cast
you of. Thus leaving you to deliberate of yt wch I hope   35
needes no deliberation. I beseche god to guyde you into the
better path wch yet lyeth before you, in wch no doubt he
will blesse you. Farewell *Danburie:* februarij .13. i60i.
                                    Your carefull mother
                                    Marie Wither   40

Your money was demaunded of Robert Barnard who seemes
to wonder that you should aske that by another wch he repaide
to your owne handes before your departure. Yf he dyd so, you
are worthely blamed for discreditinge your self so: yf he dyd
not pay you and yet say he dyd (wch in your conscience you   45
can decyde) you may see the good wch comes of suche companye
and seeing it learn to avoyde that or the like hereafter./.

[30   13 February 1601 (1602?)   see Commentary]

Sonne *Abell*, as I haue alwayes desyred your good, so you know not   1
what good it dyd me of late to heare of youre well doinge. Continue
(in godes name) yt good course, wch will in the meane bringe Ioye to your
frendes, and in the ende pleasure to your self: Let not the ill example
of any (though never so neere vnto you) wthdraw you from an –   5
earnestnes of your studyes, your diligence wherein I delight to heare of,
& commend you for gyving occasion of a good reporte; but muche more
wolde my Ioye be, yf myne eyes might accompanie myne eares in their
delight: I meane, yf I might by often letters from you assure my
self of your proceedinges, as well in wryting, as in other literature: and   10
by that meanes be in some sorte an eye wytnesse of yt wch I heare./
Yf you do not wryte often vnto me, though I heare never so often, &
heare well of you, yet shall I haue a kinde of doubt still yt reporte
multiplies: whereas if I might see your lettere produced as a wytnesse
of your good behaviour, I should the sooner graunt peace to myne vnquiet   15
thoughtes. Let these fewe lynes (in the meane tyme) be a provocation, &
a commendation, of yt wch is to come, & of what is past. Serue god, & god
will blesse you, to whom I commend you wth the rest of your brethren
& frendes: *Danb: Febr:* 13. 160i./ Your loving mother: *Marie Wither*

...: and in yo.r cheyst remember this, that you do either
binde vs to care for you, or ~~strike~~ drive vs to cast
you off. Thus leaving you to deliberate of y.t w.ch I hope
needes no deliberation. I beseech god to guyde you into the
better path w.ch yet lyeth before you, in w.ch no dowbt he
will blesse you. Farewell Danburie: February .13. 1601.

yo.r carefull mother
Marie Wither.

yo.r money was demaunded of Robert Barnard who seemes
to wonder that you should aske that by another w.ch he payde
to yo.r owne hande before yo.r departure. If he dyd so, you
not pay you and yet say he dyd (w.ch in his conscience you
can deny:) you may se the good w.ch comes of such company,
and seeing it learne to avoyde that or the like hereafter. / !

Sonne Abell, as I have alwayes desyred yo.r good, so you know not
what good it dyd me of late to heare of yo.r well doings. Continue
(in gode name) y.t good comse, w.ch will in the meane bringe ioye to yo.r
frende, and in the ende pleasure to yo.r selfe: Let not the ill example
of any (though never so neere vnto you) w.th draw you from an
barenes of yo.r studyes, yo.r diligence wherein I delight to heare of.
I commend you for gyving occasion of a good reporte; but muche more
wolde my ioye be, yf myne eyes might accompanie myne eares in their
delight: I meane, y.t I might by often letters from you assure my
selfe of yo.r proceedings, as well in wryting, as in other literature: and
by that meanes be in some sorte an eye wytnes of y.t w.ch I heare. /
If you do not wryte often vnto me, though I have never so often
heare well of you, yet shall I have a kinde of dowbt still w.ch reportes
multiplies: whereas if I might see yo.r lyfe proudnes as a wytnesse
of yo.r good behaviour, I should the sooner permit peace to myne vnquiet
thoughts. Let these fewe lynes (in the meane tyme) be a provocation,
a commendation, of y.t w.ch is to come, & of what is past. As one god is good
will blesse you, to w.hom I commend you w.th the rest of yo.r bretheren
& frende: Danb: Febr: 13. 1601. / yo.r loving mother: Marie Wither.

Right honourable good Lord, these lynes present unto you
the true servize of hym that acknowledgeth him self
most unto you: Insufficient in any sorte to deserve well
saving in desyer. The testimonie whereof hathe alwayes
awayted yo' good Lordshyps commaundement, wch I have
ever embraced as a favour. I know not whether ever
it shall please god to make me a man half so fortunal
personally to vysit you: Notwthstanding my care shall
be to preserve the remembrannce of my name wth you,
least it dye by defalts of myne owne understandinges and
idle hand. My studyes hitherto have bene more accompanied wth melancholye then musike: whose fruytes yeld
neither content to mee, nor pleasure to another. How be it,
my desyre shall never be restraynd to lay before yo' Lo:
as suche poore skilless notes as Pan (a musition for
so obscure a place) hathe lent me. Thoughe they tell
a tale playne & countrielike, yet am I bolde to preferre
them to wayte on you at home. Humbly beseechinge
you to receyve them as true witnesses of the honour I
beare you, and simple messengers for the continuaunce of
yo' lordshipe good favour. Whose entertaynment (yf the
rather for my sake) shall the better enable their yonger
brothers (yet in the cradle) to do yo' Lo: y' pleasing
servize wch I my selfe have ever desyred to doo.
Who lyveth to honour you wth all his powers in true
faithe: ——— And ever shall be,

yo' Lo: unremoveably
the unfortunate:

Anto: Hoborne

[31   late 1597 (?)   see Commentary]

Right honorable good Lord, these lynes present vnto you   1
the true service of hym that acknowledgeth him self
most vnto you: Insufficient in any sorte to deserue well
saving in desyer. The testimonie wherof hathe alwayes
awayted your good Lordshippes commaundement, wch I haue   5
ever embraced as a favour. I know not whether ever
it shall please god to make me a man half so fortunate
personally to vysit you: Notwthstanding my care shall
be to preserue the remembraunce of my name wth you,
least it dye by defalte of myne owne vndeservinges and   10
Idle hand./ My studyes hitherto haue bene more accom =
panied wth melancholye then musicke: whose fruytes yelde
neither content to mee, nor pleasure to another. How be it,
my desyer shall never be restraynd to lay before your Lordshippes
eyes suche poore skillesse notes as *Pan* (a Musition for   15
so obscure a place) hathe lent me. Though they tell
a tale playne & countrielike, yet am I bolde to preferr
them to wayte on you at Courte. Humbly beseechinge
you to receyve them as true witnesses of the honor I
beare you, and simple messengers for the continuance of   20
your lordshipes good favour. Whose entertaynment (yf the
rather for my sake) shall the better enable their yonger
brothers (yet in the cradle) to do your Lordshippe yt pleasinge
service wch I my self haue ever desyred to doe.
Who lyveth to honor you wth all his powers in true   25
faithe: _____ And ever shall be,

                      Your Lordshippes vnremoveably
                      the vnfortunate:
                      Anto: Hoborne

[32   7 April 1599   see Commentary]

Good Madam: I haue bene most sorie to heare of your   1
late hard happe, wch if you remember I tolde you I feared
but good Lady suche is the worlde, and godes ordinaunce
for vs that lyves in it, to passe many cares and afflictions,
wherof I haue had deepely my parte: it is his mer =   5
cifull schoole for his children, to make them seeke after
the ioyes of heaven, wch he hathe ordeyned for them./
And for Mr Morrison, he is happier then those
he hathe lefte behinde him, whom god blest to passe
great matters in his lyfe tyme, and lefte behinde him   10
muche to performe: As yet I haue hardly pulled vp
my spirites to see my present estate: Yet not knowing
your want, haue by this bearer your frend, sent you 4 li.
to passe these hollydayes wthall: Wherein I pray you
accept my good will, who hathe ever shewed my love   15
to your brother and his: And so good lady wishinge
you patience, & my self the like, wth all good wishes
I leave you to god. Caisho the .7. of Aprile. 1599.
                    Your loving Sister
                    Dorothie Moryson   20

[33]

Althoughe sorie yt you followed not my counsell: yet glad   1
yt your will hathe removed your woe: and perhapes altred
your disease from the .P. to the .G. wch will somwhat save
your honestie: I thanke you muche fror the Caveat you gave
me, but more for the redynes you promysse me: but yf I   5
be distressed a horssebacke, I doubt me your paine in youre
Ancle will not suffer you to come to me on foote./ I haue
provyded for your men & yt for a grote a meale or their aboutes.
wherefore send them hether as soone as you will: And when
your self comes (although I can hardly afforde you any more   10
phisick money ⟨ ⟩ yet) I will helpe to purge you the best I can
And so good harry farewell./ To Captaine henry Catlain
                    at Margate ./.

Good Madam: I haue bene most sorie to heare of yo:r
late hard happe, w:ch if you remember I tolde you I feared
but good La: suche is the worlde, and gods ordinance
for us that lyves in it, to passe many cares and afflictions,
wherof I haue had deeply my parte: it is his mer=
cifull schoole for his children, to make them seke after
the joyes of heaven, w:ch He hath ordeyned for them.
And for M:r Morrison, he is happier then those
he hathe leste behinde him, whom god blest to passe
great matters in his lyfe tyme, and leste behinde him
muche to performe: As yet I haue hardly pulled vp
my spirites to see my present estate: Yet not knowing
yo:r want, haue by this bearer yo:r frend, sent you 4.:th
to passe these holydayes w:th all: wherein I pray you
accept my good will, who hathe ever shewed my love
to yo:r brother and his: And so good La: wishinge
you patience, & my selfe the like, w:th all good wishes
I leave you to god. Dated the .7. of Aprile. 1599.
                                    yo:r loving Sister
                                    Dorothie Moryson

Although I sorie y:t you followed not my counsell: yet glad
y:t yo:r will hathe removed yo:r woe: and perhappe altered
yo:r disease from the .P. to the .G. w:ch will somewhat save
yo:r honestie: I thanke you muche for the advise you gave
me, but more for the redynes you promyse me: but if I
be distressed a horssbacke, I doubt me yo:r paine in some
Uncle will not suffer you to come to me on foote. I haue
provyded for yo:r men & y for a grots a meale or there abouts
wherefore send them either as soone as you will: And when
yo:r selfe comes (although I can hardly afforde you any more
profitt money) yet if I will helpe to pinche you the best I can.
And so good Harry farewell. / To Captaine Henry Catlin
                                    at Margate. /

Right Noble, discreet, most vertuous and curteous Ladie: I
comend my humble service, & hartie love to yor honor: humblie
craving pardon off yor La: for my long absence before
yor departure, and for amende, I woold have seene yor
honor in the cuntrie, had not some occasions faln out to
the contrarie, wch hereafter you may knowe: But off
this good Madam be ever assured, you have power to
commaunde me in all yt shall please you so long as I
lyve. I wolde not off comfort, nor fashion my lyve to the
fashion off the world: you may beleve me I wolde as I
thinke, my lyves and my woordes shall ever be true: and
my selfe and my service shall ever be yor. Theise
woordes as be greater yor than can reporte, I neede not informe
at this tyme to wryte them: I am most glad to heare
off yor healthe, and wisshing all happines still to attend
you, wth all the best good yt yor harte can desyre, shall
so most humblie take my leave. London. 23. Julij.

                        yor honor most humblie & ever
                    most ready to be comaunded.

Standing thus doblye perplexed, one way in healthe, and
otherwyse in the conscience off my defalt: you sent me
opportunely (thanke to yor sweetnes) yor inestimable favor
yt wrought like a divine balme so presently & pleasantlie
uppon my straynings perplexities: yt at the instant my bodie
fought to be sick, my mynde to be molested, and I so stande
off bothe, stand wth bodie & mynde alwayes to honor you, as
redeemed onlie to yor service by yor invaluable curtesie
                        Not without longing:

Good ladie return me backe those unhappie letters, seing I
can not dispose off my selfe according to my desyre, I will
return into ye cuntrie & theire play the hermytt: not for religious
sake, but for hir cause yt hath cast me into these disgraced
fortunes: wisshing you possessed off all yt doe yor good honor so:
                        bound to your Curtesie:

[34   23 July]

Right Noble, discrete, most vertuous and curteous Ladie: I   1
commend my humble service, & hartie love to your honor: humblie
craving pardon of your Ladyship for my long absence before
your departure; and for amendes, I wolde haue seene your
honor in the countrie, had not some occasions faln out to   5
the contrarie, wch hereafter you may knowe: But of
this good Madam be ever assured, you haue power to
commaunde me in all yt shall please you so long as I
lyve./ I wryte not of course, nor fashion my lynes to the
fashion of the worlde: you may beleue me I wryte as I   10
thinke, my lynes and my wordes shall ever be true: and
my self and my service shall ever be youres./ Suche
newes as be heare your man can reporte, I neede not yerfore
at this tyme to wryte them: I am most glad to heare
of your health, and wishing all happines still to attend   15
you, wth all the best good yt your harte can desyer, shall
so most humblie take my leave. London .23. Iulij./
                          Your honores most humblie & ever
                          most ready to be commaunded:/

[35]

Standing thus doblye perplexed, one way in health, and   1
otherwyse in the conscience of my defalt: you sent me
oportunely (thankes to your sweetenes) your inestimable favour
yt wrought like a divine balme so presently & pleasantlie
vpon my strayninge perplexities: yt at the instant my bodie   5
forgat to be sicke, my mynde to be molested, and I ⟨to⟩ sounde
of bothe, stand wth bodie & mynde alwayes to honor you, as
redeemed onlie to your service by your vnvaluable Curtesies
                          Not without longing:

[36]

Good ladie return me backe those vnhappie letters, seing I   1
can not dispose of my self according to my desyers, I will
return into ye countrie & their play the hermytt: not for religions
sake, but for hir cause yt hathe cast me into these disgraced
fortunes: wishing you possessed of all your desyres, god holde you so: 5
                          bound to your Curtesie:

[37]

Most honorable, Most noble, and ever most kinde & curteous   1
Ladie./ Emongst so many my discontentes and adverse for =
tunes yt haue followed me of late: I protest, their is not
any of them all haue more hartely greeved me, then the late
reporte of your Ladyships sicknes./ And so muche the more, as I   5
have good cause to feare the losse of my dere, best worthie,
& well esteemed Frendes./ This worlde enioyes the good but a
while, to shorte are the dayes of the noble and vertuous, and
the nomber to fewe yt are truely enobled./ Lyve long Sweete
Lady to the comforte of your frendes and your hartes desyer./   10
plucke vp your sprytes and cherishe your self, to confirme yt
good that your noble birthe, and farr nobler mynde have still
produced: lyve ⟨longe⟩ still and florishe fayre flower of
vertue and honorable curtesie: yt all your frendes that knowe
you and love you, may still remember to speake of your goodnes./   15
Beleue me faire lady my griefe was the more, that I could
not be present to performe suche dutyes & frendly offices,
as my love & dutye at all tymes dothe owe you./ Pardon
good lady I humblie beseche you my long discontinuaunce./
plead you my excuse & say to your self, I knowe he will   20
not, nor can not forget me; for he hathe sworne to love and
honor me in the greatest degree yt his hart can Imagine./
This bearer of late hathe brought the good newes of your
happie amendes: and although not so thorowly as I coulde
wishe, the good begynnyng gyves hope of the rest, wch I ever   25
desyer & most hartely pray for./ I hope ere longe to see
you my self, tyll when and ever as best becomes me, I rest
in all humble dutie & service at your good pleasure to be
commaunded./.

Most honorable, Most noble, and her most kinde & curteous
Ladie. / Emongst so many my discontents and adverse fortunes ŷ have followed me of late: I protest, there is not
any of them all have more hartely greeved me, then the late
reportes of yo[ur] La: sicknes. / And so much the more, as I
have good cause to feare the losse of my deare, best woorthie,
& well esteemed frende. / This worlde enioyes the good but a
while, to shorte are the dayes of the noble and vertuous, and
the number to fewe ŷ are trewly enobled. / Lyve long sweete
Ladie to the comfortes of yo[ur] frende and yo[ur] hartes desyer. /
plucke vp yo[ur] spyrytes and cherisse yo[ur] selfe, to confirme ŷ
good that yo[ur] noble birthe, and faire nobler mynde have still
produced: Lyve still and flowrisshe fayrer flower of
vertue and honorable curtesie: ŷ all yo[ur] frendes that knowe
you and love you, may still remember to speake of yo[ur] goodnes.
Beleve me faire lady my greife was the more, that I could
not be present to performe suche dutyes & frendly offices,
as my love & dutye at all tymes dothe owe you. / Pardon
good lady, I humblie beseche you my long discontinuance. /
plead you my excuse & say to yo[ur] selfe, I knowe he will
not, nor can not forget me; for he hathe sworne to love and
honor me in the greatest degree ŷ his hart can imagine. /
This bearer of late hathe brought the good newes of yo[ur]
happie amendes: and although not so throwly as I could
wisshe, the good beginnyng gyves hope of the rest, wch I ever
desyer & most hartely pray for. / I hope ere longe to see
you my selfe, tyll when and ever as best becomes me, I rest
in all humble dutie & service at yo[ur] good pleasure to be
commaunded. /

Right noble, discreete, and most honorable Lady: whose birth,
behaviour, & honorable curtesie, deservedly meritte greate titles
of honor: I do not commend you so muche as I coulde, nor
can I commend you so muche as I shoulde: let this suffise,
my pen & my mynde: my hand & my harte: shall alwayes
doe honor & sett forthe yor goodnes. I wryte not now but as I
wryte alwayes, and alwayes must wryte bycause it is true.
I soe it, I know it: and still must I praysse, and ever commend it.
If therfore sweete Lady you seeme to mislike, or take the
advantage of my longe absence, I pray yor pardon with all my
harte for my discontinuance. And know fayre lady my
troubled estate and unquiet thoughte hathe made me a straunger
not onlie to yor honor and other my frendes: but even to my selfe
and my best endevor. My discontents I kept to my selfe
not willing to shew or imparte them to any, for that I well
hoped to bring them to ende: and I had made ende of the
most & greatest, and shoulde have done the rest not a lyttle
more respite: but in the meane season (at the worst of all
tymes) I was arrested, when least I expected, & brought
to pryson, where now I remayne in woodstreete counter, and
so have I done these twentie dayes in execution. And for
all this I may thanke my good frendes. I have done my selfe
wronge in pleasuring others to displeasure my selfe: especiallie
suche as but badly deserve it: and if onlie good I shall get
hereby, I shall be well taught to be wyser hereafter.
If therfore good Madam it may please you at this tyme to stede
me so muche as to lend me to till Michallmas nexte, you shall
do me a greate and honorable curtesie bycause it will worke
my present delyverie. And for yor assurance to repay yor money
at the tyme apointed: I will give you my worde my hand & my
deede, my credytt & my lyfe for the due performance. I will
not trouble yor honor in this, I valewe you more a thowsand
degrees, & my credett to me is far more dere then the common
opinion perhaps will imagine. It is not my losse (most honorable

[38   29 February 1599/1600 (?)   see Commentary]

Right noble, discreete, and most honorable Lady: whose birth,   1
behaviour, & honorable curtesie, deservedly merittes high titles
of honor: I do not commend you so muche as I coulde, nor
can I commend you so muche as I shoulde:/ let this suffice,
my pen & my mynde: my hand & my harte: shall alwayes –   5
declare & set forthe your goodnes./ I wryte not nowe but as I
wryte alwayes, and alwayes must wryte bycause it is true./
I see it, I knowe it: and still must I prayse and ever commend it:
Yf therfore sweete lady you seeme to mislike, or take the – –
advantage of my longe absence, I pray your pardon wth all my   10
harte for my discontinuaunce./ And knowe fayre lady my
trobled estate and vnquiet thoughtes hathe made me a straunger
not onlie to your honor and other my frendes: but even to my self
and my best endevoures./ My discontentes I kept to my self,
not willing to shew or imparte them to any, for that I well   15
hoped to bring them to ende: and I had made ende of the
most & greatest, and shoulde haue done these wth a lyttle
more respite: but in the meane season (at ye worst of all
tymes) I was arrested, when least I expected, & brought
to pryson, where nowe I remayne in woodstreete counter, and   20
so haue I done these twentie dayes in execution./ And for
all this I may thanke my good frendes, I haue done my self –
wronge in pleasuring others to displeasure my self: especially
suche as but badly deserue it: and ye onlie good I shall get
hereby, I shall be well taught to be wyser hereafter./.   25
Yf therfore good Madam it may please you at this tyme to favour
me so muche as to lend me. v li. tyll Michallmas nexte, you shall
do me a greate and honorable curtesie, bycause it will worke
my present delyuerie. And for your assuraunce to repay your money
at the tyme apointed: I will give you my worde my hand & my   30
deede, my credytt & my lyfe for the due performance./ I will
not breake wth your honor in this, I value you more a thowsand
degrees, & my creditt to me is far more dere then the common
opinion perhapes will Imagine./ It is not my vse (most honorable

ladie) I make it no custome to be beholdinge. I protest, it is　　　　　35
muche contrarie to my mynde: let me then intreate your pardon
in this, and censure me still wth your discrete Iudgement./
So shall I be nowe, as I haue bene alwayes, your honores most
true and ever devoted, to do you all humble dutie & service.
And so good Madam I wishe you all health & continuall　　　　　40
hapines, wth many good dayes to your hartes desyer, and all
the good fortunes that the worlde affordes./.

[39]

Pardon (sweete mystresse) my Importunitie, and prowdlie　　　　　1
tryvmphe in this your victorie./ The sight of your sweete perfections
haue caught me, though no extreemes coulde ever enforce me. I sewe
and serue yt worthinesse of youres, wch the eyes of my Iudgment have
founde to be singuler./ I rest in all dewtie at your devotion, and　　　　5
still I crave to be commaunded. When ought in me shall seeme to
content you, even then begyns my greatest happines./ I make you
Iudge, & fall at your feete to sewe for Iustice. I appeale to youre
vertues, wch can not wronge me: nor stand vpon tearmes of ever =
lasting Iniurie./ You sewe to others to haue your right: I sewe　　　　10
to you and crave but equitie. You sewe to a Lord, and I to a
Sainct: and sweete commaunder of my sences, my service, my self
and whatsoever./ All yt I am, I freelye gyve you: no more his
owne, but onlie youres whose greatest comforte is your commaundement.
Sweete Mistresse vse your newe Authoritie on him yt vowes all　　　　15
humble service to you: and still will live to be obedient./ for ende
(faire sweete) I lyve in contemplation of your divine beauties and
alwayes rest
　　　　　　　　　　　　　　　At your good pleasure:
Paper make haste & tell my Mistresse this:　　　　　　　　　　　20
Faithe sealed vp this letter wth a kysse:
and yt I vowe howe ere my fortunes bee:
to love but one, and yt same one is shee:
　　　　　　　　　　　　　To the fayre handes
　　　　　　　　　　　　　of his sweete Mistresse　　　　25

Ladie) I make it no custome to be beholdinge. I protest, it is
moche contrarie to my mynde: let me then intreate yo[u] pardon
in this, and censure me still w[i]th yo[ur] discrete Iudgement.
So shall I be now, as I have bene alwayes, yo[ur] honor most
bounde and ever devoted, to do you all humble dutie & service.
And so good Madam I wishe you all healthe & continuall
happines, w[i]th many good dayes to yo[ur] hartes desyre, and all
those good fortunes that the worlde affordes.

Pardon (sweete Mistresse) my importunities, and proude this
tryumphes in this yo[ur] victorie. The sight of yo[ur] sweete perfections
have taught me, thoughe no experience coulde ever enforce me. I love
and serve w[i]t[h] worthinesse of yo[u], w[i]th the eyes of my Iudgement have
founde to be singuler. I rest in all dewtie at yo[ur] devotion, and
still I crave to be commaunded. When ought in me shall seeme to
content you, even then beginns my greatest happines. I make you
Iudge, & fall at yo[ur] feete to sue for Iustice. I appeale to yo[ur]
vertues, w[hi]ch can not wronge me: nor stand vpon teармes of ever=
lasting frindshie. You sue to others to have yo[ur] right. I sue
to you and crave but equitie. You sue to a Lord, and I to a
saint: and sweete commaunder of my deedes, my service, my selfe
and whatsoever. All y[a]t I am, I freelye give then: no more this
owne, but onlie yo[urs]. whose greatest comforte is yo[ur] comaundement.
Sweete Mistresse w[i]th yo[ur] newe Authoritie on him y[a]t avowes all
humble service to you: and still will live to be obedient. for such
(faire sweete) I lyve in contemplation of yo[ur] divine beauties. and
alwayes rest

                              At yo[ur] good pleasure:

Paper made haste & tell my M[istres]s this:
faithe sealed vp this letter w[i]th a kisse:
and y[a]t I vowe howe ever my fortunes bee:
to love but one, and y[a]t same one is shee:

                              To the fayre hande
                              of this sweete Mistresse

Where helpe doth want, what hope of remedie: where comforte
killed, straunge is the maladie: where good condition is evell
disposition, what availes the frutes of frendshippe. / Marvell not
(good frend) ye I wryte in this manner: my truthe is mistrusted,
my travell suspected, and my selfe most earnestly intreated to
doe you no more. I esteeme yor merites & good desarte, wth
muche more regardes then you imagine: even so will I seeke
to satisfie my frende, yf they passe not the lymitte of reason
too muche. The small government I have alwayes allowed my
selfe, is sore abused. And slender practise, bewrayes ye worker,
for lacke of colours to shadow the matter. / I have muche
more to say, but thinke it not meete in this manner to tell you. /
My penn shall geve place to a better conference, wch ißf I may
intreate you to graunte, you binde me in the best sorte I may
to requite yor curtesie. / Onely this favor let me crave, &
render a clowde to Mrs Awndam you will convey yor selfe
to a convenient place, where I will rest to attend yor comminge. /
Not for any ende, desyre, or request, yt may breede you offence:
but to disclose suche matter as concerns you neere. / And so
shall diverse doubtes be determined, many objections fully answered, reportes & tales well reconciled, my selfe contented, & you
best satisfied. / At our last meeting, you tolde me how muche
I might presume, my answere was, you shoulde commaunde a great
deale more: and yet I ment to lay holde of yor offer, and in this
sorte have made the tryall. As for any other partie or person
but wholie & meerely from my selfe, I protest as I am a gentleman
I meane simplie & truelie, wthout any practise of undecency. therefor
Condemne me not good frend, nor enter not into the least suspition
of frunorie, for before god I meane it not. The case is altered
since I sawe you last, and ißf it please you to take the paines,
I pray you bring this lre wth you: so shall I resolve you of
all the contentes. / Ißf you can not come, read and returne it by
this bearer: and committ the matter to silence. / Thus trusteth
hopeth, & desyre: I rest bothe now and alwayes

&c.

f. 27v

[40]

Where helpe dothe hurt, what hope of remedie: where comforte   1
killes, straunge is the Maladie: where good Condition is helde
suspition, what availes the fruytes of frendship./ Marvell not
(good frend) yt I wryte in this manner: my trothe is mistrusted,
my travell suspected, and my self most earnestly intreated to   5
see you no more./ I esteeme your merites & good desertes, wth
muche more regarde then you Imagine: even so will I seeke
to satisfie my frendes, yf they passe not the lymittes of reason
too muche./ The small goverment I haue always allowed my
self, is far abused. And slender practise, bewrayes ye worker,   10
for lacke of coloure to shadow the matter./ I haue mche
more to say, but thinke it not meete in this manner to tell you./
My pen shall geue place to a better conference, wch if I may
intreate you to graunte, you binde me in the best sorte I may
to requite your Curtesie./Onely this favour let me crave, yt   15
vnder a Clowde to Mistresse Trentam you will convey your self
to a convenient place, where I will rest to attend your commynge./
Not for any ende, desyer, or request, yt may breede you offence:
but to disclose suche matter as concerns you neere./ And so
shall divers doubtes be determined, many obiections fully answe =   20
red, Reportes & tales well reconciled, my self contented, & you
best satisfied./ At our last meeting, your tolde me how muche
I might presume, my answere was, you shoulde commaunde a great
deale more: and yet I ment to lay holde of your offer, and in this
sorte haue made the tryall. As for any other partie or person,   25
but wholie & meerely from my self, I protest as I am a gentleman
I meane simplie & trulie, wthout any practise of vnseemely trechery.
Condempne me not good frend, nor enter not into the least suspition
of Iniurie, for before god I meane it not./ The case is altred
since I saw you last, and if it please you to take the paines,   30
I pray you bring this lettere wth you: so shall I resolue you of
all the contentes./ Yf you can not come, read and return it by
this bearer: and commytt the matter to scilence./ Thus twixte
hope, & desyer: I rest bothe now and alwayes
                                        Youres: 35

[41]

Madam: I haue bene alwayes so throughlie possest wth so   1
great an opinion of your honorable & courteous behauiour to all
sortes, that I thinke it now straunge + for me + to finde the least point
of disdain in you, yt might crosse my conceite, or diminishe your
deseruinge. ⟨Yf this your vnkindenes were through myne owne   5
fault, I should be content to commytt it to scilence⟩: But thus
it falles out (in this worlde) many tymes, that we finde our
misfortunes when we least expect them: and faile our best
hopes when we most desyer them./ I came, (not long since)
to haue seene your Ladyship and had (wth my dutie) a message to   10
tell you: but it was not (at that tyme) your pleasure to see
me, you founde your self then so earnestlye busyed. The sleight
esteeme you helde of the bearer, did verie well shew how
lyttle regarde you tooke of the message, or him yt brought it./
Your busines serv'd for a good excuse, to be ryd of him you   15
so muche misliked./ My commynge to see you (were it no more)
might verie well shewe the continuall love and dutie I owe you.
But your refusall ⟨(take it as it was) was⟩ (needes must I tell you)
was against all kinde of curtesie, wch other Ladies of as high
degree, and no lesse Iudgment, wolde not willingly haue offred.   20
Pardon these rewd lynes good Madam, my meaninge is not
herein to controll above my reatch: neither yet will I take
vpon me to correct a better wytt then myne owne./ My onlie
intent is to let you vnderstand, wth what iniustice you haue
reiected him, whose especiall care & studie hathe alwayes   25
bene, how he might most honor you./ Beleue me right honorable
Ladie, it displeased me not so muche at that tyme to loose
my labor, as it greeved me to see my self deceyved in her,
in regarde of whose excellencie, I accompted all others els in
this worlde inferior./ Beare wth my presumption good   30
Madam in wryting to you, for suche is my fault in regarde

Madam: I haue bene alwayes so throughlie possest w{th} so
great an opinion o{f} yo{r} honorable & curteous behauiour to all
sortes, that I thinke it now straunge (for me) to finde the least point
o{f} disdain in you, {that} might crosse my conceite, or diminish yo{r}
deseruinges. ~~~~~~ But thus
it falles out (in this worlde) many tymes, that we finde our
misfortunes when we least expect them: and faile our best
hopes when we most desyer them. I came, (not long since)
to haue seene yo{r} La: and had (w{th} my dutie) a message to
tell you: but it was not (at that tyme) yo{r} pleasure to see
me, you founde yo{r} selfe then so earnestlye busyed. The slight
esteeme you helde o{f} the bearer, did verie well shew how
lyttle regarde you tooke o{f} the message, or him {that} brought it.
Yo{r} busines serued, for a good excuse, to be ryd o{f} him you
so muche misliked. My comynge to see you (were it no more)
might serue well shew the continuall loue and dutie I owe you
But yo{r} refusall ~~~~~~~~~~~~~~~~~ (needes must I tell you)
was against all kinde o{f} curtesie, w{ch} other Ladies o{f} as high
degree, and no lesse iudgment, wolde not willingly haue offred.
Pardon these warme lynes good Madam, my meaninge is not
geuin to controll aboue my water: neither yet will I take
vpon me to correct a better wytt then myne owne. My onelie
intent is to let you vnderstand, w{th} what iniustice you haue
reiected him, whose especiall care & studie hathe alwayes
bene, how he might most honor you. Beleue me right ho:
Ladie, it disholwased me not so muche at that tyme to loose
my labo{r}, as it greeued me. to see my selfe deceyued in her,
in regarde o{f} whose excellencie, I accompted all others els in
this worlde inferiour. Beare w{th} my presumption good
Madam in wryting to you, for suche is my fault in regarde

off yor degree. These lynes be the first and the last wherwith
wer you have bene or shall be troubled without some better
warrant. | And though you have bene pleased to
wreck me in such wise as you know, yet for many respecte
will I honor you still, in that sort as best becommeth me. |
Thus I comytt my self & my cause to yor Judgment; and
leave yor fault to be amended by yor owne discretion. |
And so I most humblie take my leave off yor La: wishing
health to yor person, prosperous successe to yor sutes
in lawe, and good fortune to all yor lyfe. |

The humble peticion off Josias Kirton prisoner
in the fleete :| to the Lo: off the counsell :|

The great moderation off yor honor displeasure, together with
yor Clemencies: with never inflictete all due punishmente upon
offenders. hathe verie well taught me to acknowledge my fault,
and holie to learne from so noble a spiritte, that yor honorable Justice is to have peace wi^th men, and warres wi^th there
vices. | My good lorde, I presume not to aske favours off
any meritt off myne owne, but humble my self before you :
y^t yor Lo: will be pleased to move her ma^tie to mercy on my
behalfe. having before made relation vnto yor honor, how vn-
hable I am to satisfie her fyne, or maintaine my self in
pryson. And how able I am in bodie and mynde, to doe her
ma^tie: and yor honor service. being bounde thervnto by parti=
culer dutye. Off therfore it shall please yor honor to further
y^t libertie wi^th you have so graciously begon: and deliver
by yor wysedomes & opinions what my poore estate is. I
doubte not but god will blesse me wi^th the benefitt off
libertie, and yor honor wi^th all happinesse: for giving newe
lyfe to a mortified offender: that will be readye in your
service to wonder y^t lyfe wi^th yor honor have vppon me
in satisfaction & acknowledgment off my dutye. |

of your degree. These lynes be the first and the last where =
wth you haue bene or shall be troubled wthout some better
warrant./ And thoughe you haue bene pleased to
reiect me in suche wise as you knowe, yet for many respectes   35
will I honor you still, in that sort as best becommeth me./
Thus I commytt my self & my cause to your Iudgment, and
leave your fault to be amended by your owne discretion./
And so I most humblie take my leave of your Ladyship wishing
health to your person, prosperous successe to your sewtes   40
in lawe, and good fortune to all your lyfe./.

[42   before 24 March 1603   see Commentary]

         The humble peticion of Iosias Kirton prisoner   1
         in the Fleete:/ to the Lords of the counsell./.
The high moderation of your honores displeasures, together wth
your Clemencies: wch never inflicteth all due punishmentes vpon
offenders. hathe very well taught me to acknowledge my fault,   5
and ⟨. . st⟩ trulie to learne from so noble spirittes, that your honora =
ble Iustice is to haue peace wth men, and warres wth there
vices./ My good lordes, I presume not to aske favoure of
any meritt of myne owne, but humble my self before you:
yt your honors will be pleased to move her Maiestie to mercy on my   10
behalfe. having before made relation vnto your honores, howe
vnable I am to satisfie her fyne, or maintaine my self in
pryson. And how able I am in bodie and mynde, to doe her
Maiestie and your honores service. being bounde thervnto by perti =
culer dutye. Yf therfore it shall please your honores to further   15
yt libertie wch you haue so graciously begon: and delyver
by your wysdomes & opinions what my poore estate is./ I
doubte not but god will blesse me wth the benefytt of
libertie, and your honores wth all happinesse: for gyving newe
lyfe to a mortified offender: that will be redye in your   20
service to render yt lyfe wch your honores have gyven me
In satisfaction & acknowledgment of my dutye./.

f. 29r

[43   see Commentary]

Right honorable and most noble lorde: 1

I humblie beseche you to thinke of my true and vnfayned affec =
tion to love and honor you. And as my first fruytes were
graste by your Lordshippes most honorable favoures, so wolde I be glad
to serue and attend you wth all whatsoever my painfull tra =   5
vells or best endevores haue made more able for your lordshippes service.
I coulde be commaunded by some yt be great, in honors high
rancke bothe powerfull & mightie: and yet for some reasons
I make to my self, I haue not bene forward to follow that
course./ Since I can be myne owne, I will be no others,   10
onlesse I be his, whose truborne vertues and honorable mynde
in all that I am shall ever commaunde me./ It is not of
course most honorable Lorde, that thus I presume to importune youre
Lordshippe but out of a setled & long resolution, as wholie devoted
to lyve at your service./ Then pardon my Lord this boldnes   15
of myne, and wth your good favour let me put you in mynde of
your honorable promysse: that you wolde vouchsafe when you
come into wales to remember me their, and send me / youre
⟨mynde⟩ pleasure by your Lordshippes letters, whereby you shall binde
me (as you haue done ever) wth all my best powers to   20
acknowledge your goodnes./ Thus Noble Lorde I attend
your good pleasure. And wishing you all true honores increase,
good health, longe lyfe, and perpetuall happiness. shall so
most humblie take my leave./.

Your Lordshippes in all humble dutie   25
& service to be commaunded

[44]

Mr Feryman: 1
Yf my love to you were not more then my fortunes: I should
hardlye answere your request./ But I will expose my poore
creditt for you. And wishe your preferment answerable to
your hopes as your true frend./   5

A.G. /

29

Right honorable and most noble lords:

I humblie beseech you to thinke of my trew and unfayned affection to love and honor you. And as my first frutes were
graste by yor Lo: most honorable favor, so would I be glad
to serve and attend you wth all ... should my painfull tra-
velles or best endebo... have made more able for yor Lo: service.
I could be commaunded by some yt be great, in honors highe
rancke bothe powerfull & mightie: and yet for some reasons
I make to my self, I have not bene forward to follow that
course. / Since I can be myne owne, I will be no others,
onlesse I be his, whose honorable vertues and honorable mynde
in all that I am shall ever commaunde me. / It is not of
course most Ho: Lords, that thus I presume to importune yor
Lo: but out of a setled & long resolution, as wholie devoted
to lyve at yor service. / Then pardon my Lord this boldnes
of myne, and wth yor good favor let me put you in mynde of
yor honorable promyse: that you woulde vouchsafe when you
come into wales to remember me their, and send me / yor
... pleasure by yor Lo: letters, wherby you shall binde
me (as you have done ever) wth all my best powers to
acknowledge yor goodnes. / Thus Noble Lords I attend
yor good pleasure. And wishing you all trew honor increase,
good healthe, longe lyfe, and perpetuall & happines. shall so
most humblie take my leave. /.

Yor Lo: in all humble dutie
& service to be commaunded

Mr fferryman:

Yf my love to you were not more then my fortune: I should
hardlye answere yor request. / But I will expose my poore
creditt for you. And wishe yor preferment answerable to
yor hopes as yor trew frind. /

A. G. /

My good   Iff you will but looke into your owne
merritt, and consider the affection I have ever borne to yo[ur]
vertues: you shall easely perceyve bothe what sorrowe I
sustaine for yo[ur] imprysonment, and what myndes I carrie
to procure yo[ur] libertie./ To make therfore a long discourse
of either, I accompt it needles./ My estate you know,
Iff either my friendes, myne owne, or my servante Trabell, may
any way stedd you, Command it or any thing els that
lyes w[i]thin the compasse of my fortune to performe./
To counsell you how to beare this present Crosse, wolde
argue bothe presumption and want of Iudgement in mee./
Presumption, to take that on me, I can so slenderlye
performe: Defect of Iudgement, in that having knowne
you so longe, I shoulde be ignorant of yo[ur] trewe fortitude
and constant mynde; Sufficient not onlie to supporte yo[ur]
owne misfortunes, but partes of yo[ur] friendes w[i]thall./ And
to counsell and comforte w[i]th yo[ur] sounde advice, even those
that taste of the greatest extremities./ Wherfore, no
office of friendship restinge nowe at this instant in my
power to performe./ W[i]th many earnest prayers to God,
to deliver you bothe from this, and all other miseries:
that holde you downe from mountings to that height
of honor and content, I accompt you worthie of: I
take my leave./
                                   Euer as I am Domus

To my trewe friend
libertie, honor, and all content:

[45]

My good   Yf you will but looke into youre owne   1
meritt, and consider the affection I haue ever borne to your
vertues: you shall easely perceyve bothe what sorrow I
sustaine for your imprysonment, and what mynde I carie
to procure your libertie./ To make therfore a long discourse   5
of either, I accompt it needles./ My estate you know,
Yf either my frendes, myne owne, or my servantes travell, may
any way steede you, Commaunde it or any thing els that
lyes wthin the compasse of my fortune to performe./
To counsell you how to beare this present Crosse, wolde   10
argue bothe presumption and want of Iudgment in mee./
Presumption, to take that on me, I can so slenderlye
performe: defect of Iudgment, in that having knowne
you so longe, I shoulde be ignorant of your trew fortitude
and constant mynde; Sufficient not onlie to supporte your   15
owne misfortunes, but parte of your frendes wthall./ And
to counsell and comforte wth your sounde advice, even those
that taste of the greatest extremities./ Wherefore, no
office of frendship restinge more at this instant in my
power to performe. Wth many earnest prayers to God,   20
to delyver you bothe from this, and all other miseries:
that holde you downe from Mountinge to that height
of honor and content, I accompt you worthie of: I
take my leave./   Suche as I am Youres

    To my trewe frend   25
      libertie, honor, and all content:

f. 30r

[46   see Commentary]

Yf you be mynded to chaunge, I see no way to stay you: since my   1
faithfull affection can not holde you: neither your owne assured
promysses so often sworne keepe you./ Yf I haue gyven you
cause of vnkindenes in one thinge, you haue gyven me occasion
of griefe in an hundred./ But you having glutted your self wth   5
mee: goe to deceyve an other as vnhappie as my self./ and
sithe my fault hathe bene suche as to be deceyved by youre –
flatterye, I will hensforthe take heede of suche as you are
for ever. And bewayle the rest of my lyfe in contynuall
teares: wch the sooner it endes the better./ I had not thought   10
to have wrytten thus, but yt you compell me./.

[47   see Commentary]

Who hathe bene first glutted, my frendly requestes so often most   1
vncurteously denyed, and your owne desyer of chaunge can very well
witnesse./ The Oddes of an hundred for one is too greate, yet is
your one fault of vntruthe most worthie to be blamed, when an
hundred other might deserue to be pardoned./ What I haue promised   5
& sworne, I haue most faithfully kept: when I never heard you
promysse any ⟨d . .⟩ thinge on the one day, but you brake it on
the nexte./ The light stay you make of my goinge, thoughe
it contenteth me best, showeth a proofe of my former thoughtes./
But as you haue wished & wrought secretly for my departure,   10
so shall you fynde me most vnwillinge to be stayed./ The
vnhappines of yt other what soever she be, shall consist in no
one thinge more, then in yt you haue bene before her./ Youre
teares will proceede from eyes watred wth an Onnyon. For
your Ioye begynneth even now at the speaking of my departure.   15
I wishe not the ende of your lyfe, but I muche repent me of
the begynnynge of our acquaintance./ And thus is youre
vnfrendly letter answered./

[48   see Commentary]

My sweete frend, yf I haue ever done any thinge yt liked   1
you, requite me at this tyme wth stay of all thinges: tyll I
may speake or wryte more./.

30

If you be mynded to chaungs, I see no way to stay you: since my faithfull affection can not holde you: neither your owne assured promysses so often sworne kepe you. / If I have gyven you cause of vnkindenes in one things, you have gyven me occasion of greife in an hundred. / But you having glutted your sslfe with mee: goe to discrybe an other as vnhappie as my sslfe / and sithe my fault hath bene suche as to be discryved by yours flatterye, I will henceforth take hede of suche as you are for ever. And bewayle the rest of my lyfe in contynuall teares: yet the sooner it endes the better. / I had not thought to have wrytten thus, but that you compell me. /

Who hath bene first glutted, my frendly request so often most vnreasonsly denyed, and your owne desyre of chaungs can bere wytnesse. / The odds of an hundred for one is too greate, yet is your one fault of vnkindnes most worthie to be blamed, when an hundred other myght desyne to be pdoned. / What I have promised & sworne, I have most faithfully kept: when I never heard you promysse any things on the one day, but you breake it on the nexte. / The light stay you make of my goinge, thoughe it contentes me best, shewes a proofe of my former thoughts. / But as you have wisshed & wrought secretly for my departure, so shall you fynde me most vnwillinge to be stayd. The vnhappines of the other what soever she be, shall consist in no one things more, then in that you have bene before her. / Your teares will proceede from eyes watred with an Onyon. for your joye begynnes even now at the speaking of my departure. I wisshe not the endes of your lyfe, but I muche repent me of the begynnyngs of our acquaintance. / And thus is youre vnfrendly letter answered. /

My swete frend, yf I have ever done any things that liked you, requite me at this tyme with stay of all things: tyll I may speake or wryght more. /

S.r I haue enquir'de for the widdow, and am advertised by
some in her howse, y.t she lyes at a place cald Grayes, nere
Gravesende, by the water syde in Essex at one M.r Dwninges
howse: And bycause it is necessarie she sould be saluted
w.th some preparation to my comminge (that I may knowe
by her answere, yf she remaine as I left her, before I
venture the forfaite off fyndinge her bow'de to another)
I haue drawne this enclosed letter, to w.ch I wold intreate
yo.r hand: wherein, though I wright it, there is no prayse
off myne owne. / I hope you will not looke I should lose
any cou.rtesybe tearmed for my former soddaine departure. but
rather pout the fault in your footman or other servaunt,
not expressing yo.r pleasure, then in my ouer tender appre=
hension off youre unintended unkindnes, w.ch being to my
guiltles conceyt so exceedingly questions, none will imagine,
I tooke it w.thout evident & speaking occasions; for I can
not be so dull, but I must easyly apprehend how worthie
yo.r loue is off a much worthier mans respect. / And
therfore for me to stomacke or sleight any comon or free
kyndnes in yo.r actions y concerne me, were no lesse then
iniuryous: But (how poore soever I am & professe my
self) to expresse as much freedome & scorne in the tonge,
off an open y contemptuous neglect, as the richest man =
lyvinge: I know you will not blame me. w.ch for me to
imagine was offered on yo.r parte (hauing heard what my
Brother related out off yo.r solemne and honorable letter)
were on my parte too proude and foule an ingratitude;
And therfore I hope all misconstructions are here ended;
you know my bashfull and uncomely simplicitie: alwayes
fearefull to be thought irksome, where I haue bene welcome;
how as it is a rudenes to generouse and childish, for a

f. 30v

[49 see Commentary]

Sir. I haue enquir'de for the widdow, and am advertisd⟨.⟩ by 1
some in her howse, yt she lyes at a place cald Grayes, nere
Gravesende: by the water syde in Essex at one Mr durainges
howse: And bycause it is necessarie she should be saluted
wth some preparation to my commynge (that I may knowe 5
by her answere, yf she remayne as I lefte her, before I
⟨ver⟩ venture the forfaite of fyndinge her vow'de to another)
I haue drawne this enclosed letter, to wch I wolde intreate
your hand: wherein, though I wrytt it, there is no prayse
of myne owne./ I hope you will not looke I should vse 10
any excusyve termes for my former soodaine departure. but
rather put the fault in your footeman or other servaunt,
not expressing your pleasure, then in my over tender appre =
hension of youre vnintended vnkindenes; wch being to my
guyltles conceyt so exceedingly greevous, none will Imagine, 15
I tooke it wthout evident & speaking occasions; For I can
not be so dull, but I must easely apprehend how worthie
your love is of a muche worthier mans respect./ And
therfore for me to stomacke or sleight any common or free
lycence in your actions yt concerne me, were no lesse then 20
sawcynesse; But (how poore soever I am & professe my
self) to expresse as muche freedome & skorne in the touch
of an open & contemptuous neglect, as the richest man –
lyvinge: I know you will not blame me. wch for me to
Imagine was offred on your parte (having heard what my 25
Brother related out of your spleneles and honorable letter)
were on my parte too prowde and fowle an Ingratitude;
And therefore I hope all misconstructions are here ended;
You know my bashfull and vncourtly simplicitie: always
fearefull to be thought ircksome, where I haue bene welcome; 30
For as it is a rudenes to humorouse and childishe, for a

man to mistake wthout cause, the vsage of his frend. So
is it an Impudence too base and servile, to be so bould an
intruder, as to looke for a verball and direct casting of,
before he forbeare to charge hym./   35

[50   see Commentary]

Good Wyddow, I am to put you in mynde (wth all kyndenes)   1
of the Motion lately made betwixt you and my Frend Mr
Chapman: who (it seemeth) did me the wronge of his
sodaine departure, to do you all the right of a more true
then professed lover: For he hathe in this tyme so   5
wrought wth his brother (whom I well knowe) that
by his meanes he is able to make you that Iointure you
demaunded: wherein the coldnes of his affection towardes
you (wch wth good cause you might Imagine) is sufficient =
ly excused: And his disposition muche the better to be   10
lik't, that he will haue his deedes prove his love to you
rather then his wordes: consider his desertes accordingly.
and remember what hathe bene tolde you of him, by all
yt vnderstoode his affection towardes you: Not forgetting –
your free kindenes in embracinge his motion: wch hathe made   15
him, out of the assurance of your constant inclination, take
this care & paines to provyde himself of as muche as you
desyred; that the Marriadge (wch it seemes god hathe
apointed) may to his honor and bothe your comfortes be effec =
ted; You neede stand on no further deliberation, you haue   20
had sufficient warrantes & proofes of his worthinesse,
wch will make him at all tymes appeare a creditt to your
choyce in the eyes and Iudgmentes of any worthie to –
Iudge him./ Let me therfore intreate you to thinke no =
thing you have or can bring wth you to muche to Ioine wth   25

man to mistake w{th}out cause, the vsage of his frend. So
is it an impudence too base and servile, to be so bould an
intruder, as to looke for a verball and direct casting of,
before he forbeare to harpe h{i}m./

Good Wyddow, I am to put you in mynde (w{i}thall kyndnes)
of the Motion lately made betwixt you and my frend M{r}
Chapman: who (it seemeth) did me the wronge of his
sodaine departure, to do you all the right of a more true
& profess{ed} lover: ffor he hathe in this tyme so
wronged w{i}th his brother (whom I well know) that
by his meanes he is able to make you that ioincture you
demanded: wherein the coldnes of his affection towards
you (w{i}th no good cause you might imagine) is sufficiently excused. And his disposition muche the better to be
likt, that he will haue his deedes proue his loue to you
rather then his wordes: consider his deserte accordingly.
and remember w{hat} hathe bene tolde you of him, by all
{tha}t vnderstoode his affection towards you: not forgetting
yo{r} first kindenes in embracinge his motion: w{hi}ch hathe made
him, out of the assurance of yo{r} constant inclination, take
this care & paines to prouyde himself of as muche as you
desyred; that the Marriadge (w{hi}ch it seemes god hathe
apointed) may to his hono{r} and bothe yo{r} comfortes be effec-
ted; you neede stand on no further deliberation, you haue
had sufficient warrante & proofes of his worthines,
w{hi}ch w{i}th make him at all tymes appeare a creditt to yo{r}
choyce in the eyes and iudgmente of any worthie to
iudge him./ Let me therfore intreate you to thinke no=
thing you haue or can bring w{i}th you to muche to ioine w{i}th

that he shall adde to your estate: for in his least tryall
I am well assured you will wishe you had muche more for
him./ His brother hathe vowytten to mee, to intreate me
to put you in mynde off him, and to tell you what he
will gladly do for him; being exceedingly pleasde w[th]
his disposition now framde to so sociable a course off
life: that hathe made him spend his youthe and all his
ofters off preferment hitherto (in regardes off the worlde)
so unprofitably and vainlie./

Good M[r] Henryman, I am hartely sorie, y[t] out off my
present estate, I can not tender y[t] true act off my love, w[ch]
bothe yo[r] fortune requireth, & my deare account off you should
lead me to. But be Iudge yo[r] olde frend M[r] Royden wooteth
I stand not in muche danger to come to y[t] place off
dead men, to y[e] Colgatha for want off present money my
selfe./ Howbeit, yff either my credit, or any frend off myne y[t]
you knowe y[t] can add to make myne better, or any travayle
or whatsoever y[t] you can imagine to be in my power or at my
commaund or intreatie, I will & stand most willing to spare
rise & imploy for you, set me but downe the meanes, & then
iff I doe it not, thinke me untrustworthy to be lovde off you./
Onlie belone I have not ready one quarter off so muche money
yff it wolde purchase yo[r] doliverie for w[ch] I am sorie: fort
I wolde have you perswaded I love you and make muche off
yo[r] knowledge./ And so wishing yo[r] advise & direction for
any thinge y[t] shall lye in my abilitie to worke for you./
I Letany my english thus: from where you are, good lorde
deliver us./

yo[r] true unfayned frend

William Strachey

that he shall adde to your estate: for in his least tryall
I am well assur'de you will wishe you had muche more for
him./ His brother hathe wrytten to mee, to intreate me
to put you in mynde of him, and to tell you what he
will gladly do for him; being exceedingly pleasde wth   30
his disposition now fram'de to so sociable a course of
lyfe: that hathe made him spend his youthe and all his
offers of preferment hitherto (in regarde of the worlde)
so vnprofitably and vainlie./

[51   early 1609 (?)   see Commentary]

Good Mr Ferryman, I – am hartely sorie, yt out of my –   1
present estate, I can not tender yt true act of my love, wch
bothe your fortune requires, & my deere accompt of you should
lead me to. But be Iudge your olde frend Mr Royden, whether
I stand not in muche daunger to come to yt ⟨play⟩ place of   5
dead men, to yt Golgatha for want of present money my
self./ howbeit, yf either my creditt, or any frend of myne yt
you knowe yt can add to make myne better, or any travayle
or whatsoever yt you can Imagine to be in my power or at my
commaunde or intreatie, I will & stand most willing to exer   10
cise & imploy for you, set me but downe the meanes, & then
if I doe it not, thinke me vnworthy to be loved of you./
Onlie beleue I haue not ready one quarter of so muche money
yf it wolde purchase your delyverie. for wch I am sorie: for
I wolde have you perswaded I love you and make muche of   15
your knowledge./ And so wishing your advice & direction for
any thinge yt shall lye in my abilitie to worke for you./
*I Letany my english thus: from where you are, good lorde
deliuer us./*

                  Your true vnfayned frend   20
                  William Strachey

[52   28 May 1594 – 30 April 1596   see Commentary]

A Specyall Protection   1
For three yeeres:/.
Elizabeth by the grace of God + *queene* + of England Fraunce and
Ireland, defendor of the Faithe &c./. To our Trustie and
welbeloved Chauncellor Sir Iohn Puckeringe knight, Lord   5
Keeper of the great Seale of England now beinge, and to
any other Lord keeper of keepers, of our said greate Seale,
or Chauncelor of England for the tyme beinge. To our
High Treasurer of England, To our Chauncelor, vnder =
treasurer, Chamberlaines, and Barrons of our Exchequer.   10
To our chiefe Iustice of England, and to all other our Iudges,
Iustices, Mynisters, & Subiectes whatsoever wthin all our dominions
and to every of them wch now be, or at any tyme hereafter shall
be, and to all Mayors, Sheryffes, Baylyffes, Constables, Ser =
geantes, yeomen, and to all and every other Officer, or Officers,   15
person, and persons whatsoever, greetinge./. Knowe ye, that
wee of our Prerogative Royall, wch we will not have to
be argued or brought in question: and at the humble Suyte
and peticion, as well of sondrie the Creditores of our trustie
and welbeloved Sir Walter Leveson of Lilleshall in the   20
countie of Salop Knight, as of the said Walter Leveson
and his Suerties, and for certaine other good causes and
considerations vs hervnto especyally movinge, doe take into our
Royall protection and defence, the said Sir Walter Leveson
of Lilleshall aforesaid Knight, or by what other name or   25
names, additions of name or names or place he is called or
knowne: and all and every his suretie or sureties, wch stand
bounde wth or for the said Sir Walter Leveson for his debte
or cause, and all his and their, and everie of their Mannors
landes, tenementes, goodes, chattells, rentes, Annuities & possessions.   30

32

A Speciall Protection
ffor three yeres :.

queene

Elizabeth by the grace off God, off England ffraunce and
Ireland, defendo off the ffaithe &c. :. To our Trustie and
welbeloved Chauncellor Sr John Puckerings knight, Lord
keeper off the great Seale off England now beinge, and to
any other Lord keeper or keepers, off our said greate Seale,
or Chauncelor off England for the tyme beinge. To our
high Treasurer off England, To our Chauncelor, vndertreasurer, Chamberlaines, and Barrons off our Exchequer.
To our chiefe Justice off England, and to all other our Judges,
Justices, Mynisters, & Subiectes whatsoever within all our dominions
and to every off them wch now be, or at any tyme hereafter shall
be, and to all Mayors, Sheriffes, Bayliffes, Constables, Ser=
vantes, yeomen, and to all and every other Officer, or Officers,
person, and persons whatsoever, greetinges. / Knowe ye, that
wee off our Prerogative Royall, wch we will not have to
be argued or broughtt in question: and at the humble Suyte
and petition, aswell off Sondrie the Creditors off our trustie
and welbeloved Sr Walter Leveson off Lilleshall in the
countie off Salop knight; as off the said walter Leveson
and his Sureties, and for certaine other good causes and
considerations vs herevnto especially movinge, doe take into our
Royall protection and defence, the said Sr Walter Leveson
off Lilleshall aforesaid knight, or by what other name or
names, additions off name or names or place he is called or
knowne: and all and every his Suretie or Sureties, wch stand
bounde wth or for the said Sr walter Leveson for his debtes
or causes, and all his and their, and everie off their Mannours,
Landes, tenementes, goodes, chattelles, rentes, Annuities & possessions

And therfore we will and by theis presente of our Princely
power and authoritie ne of grace and Commande for us our
heyres & successors, you and every of you, that the said Sr
Walter Leveson, and all and every his said suretie, and
theyr Mannors, Lande, tenemente, good, chattells, rente, imm=
nities and possessions of the said Sr Walter Leveson, and of
all and every his said suretie ye doe protect and defend,
not suffering him or them to be hindred, molested, troubled,
arrested, attached, dystrayned, imprysoned, or in any wyse
hindred, for any debt, dutye or cause of the said Sr Walter
Leveson; And if any impeachment, molestation, trouble, arrest,
attachment, distresse, imprysonment or hindrance be to him
or them or any of them done or offred, the same to him
or them w[i]thout delay ye cause to be released, amended,
discharged, and to their former estates to be restored,
We will also and by theis presente do graunt y[t] the said
Sr Walter Leveson and all and every his said suretie,
and all theyr, and every of their Mannors, Lande & tenemente,
thinge, rente, good, chattells, Annuities and possessions shall
be acquited, discharged, and exonerated of and from all
and singuler Pleas, suite, plainte, sentences, outlawries,
Judgmente, execucions, districcions, attachmente, disquietinge,
and imprysonmente whatsoever; And moreover we will
and our pleasure is, and by theis presente we doe gyve
further power and authoritie to the Lo: Chauncellor, or keeper,
or keepers of our great Seale of England for the tyme
being. To our high Treasurer of England Chauncellor
vndertreasurer Chamberlaines & Barrons of our said
Exches for the tyme beings, & to all & singuler our
Judges & Justices of our Courte of Recorde for the tyme

f. 32v

And therfore we will and by these presentes of our Princely
power and authoritie we charge and Commaunde for vs our
heyres & successors, you and every of you, that the said Sir
Walter Leveson, and all and every his said suerties, and
the Mannors, Landes, tenementes, goodes, chattells, Rentes, Annu =　　35
ities and possessions of the said Sir Walter Leveson, and of
all and every his said suerties Ye doe protect and defend,
not suffringe him or them to be Iniured, molested, troubled,
arrested, attached, dystrayned, imprysoned, or in any wyse
hindred, for any debt, dutye or cause of the said Sir Walter　　40
Leveson; And if any impeachment, molestation, trouble, arrest,
attachment, distresse, imprysonment or hindraunce be to him
or them or any of them done or offered, the same to him
or them wthout delay ye cause to be released, amended, –
discharged, and to their former estates to be restored, /　　45
We will also and by these presentes do graunt yt the said
Sir Walter Leveson and all and everye his said sureties,
and all their, and every of their Mannors, Landes, Tenementes,
thinges, rentes, goodes, chattells, Annuities and possessions shall
be acquited, discharged, and exonerated of and from all　　50
and singuler Pleas, suetes, plaintes, sentences, Outlawries,
Iudgmentes, executions, districtions, attachmentes, disquietinges,
and Imprysonmentes whatsoever; And moreover we will
and our pleasure is, and by these presentes we doe gyve
further power and authoritie to the Lord Chauncelor, or keeper,　　55
or keepers of our great Seale of England for the tyme
being. To our high Treasurer of England Chauncelor
vndertreasurer Chamberlaines & Barrons of our said
Exchequer for the tyme beeinge, & to all & singuler our
Iudges & Iustices of our Courtes of Recorde for the tyme　　60

beinge and every of them, vpon request or peticion to them or
any of them to be made by the said Sir Walter Leveson &
his ⟨Suerties⟩ said Suerties or any of them, to take or gyve
suche order & commaundement to the Clerke or Clerkes, Officer,
or Officers, Minister or Ministers, of all our said Courtes,   65
to stay and surcease all suche processe, suytes, & Actions, as
shall or may be procured or attempted to be sued prosecuted
or awarded against the said Sir Walter Leveson & his
said suerties, & every ⟨of⟩ or any of them or his or their
Mannors, landes, goodes, chattells, Annuities and possessions   70
for any debt dutye or other cause of the said Sir Walter
Leveson or his said suerties: duringe the space of three
yeeres next ensewinge the date hereof, wthout any other
or further ⟨wth⟩ warrant or warrantes to be had or sued
for, other then the sight of these our letters Patentes, or   75
the Inrollmentes thereof. In Wittnesse whereof &c:/.

thinges and every off them, vpon request or peticion to them or
any off them to be made by the said Sr walter Leveson or
his said Sueties said Sueties or any off them, to take or give
suche order & commaundement to the Clerk or Clerke, officer,
or officers, Minister or Ministers, off all our said Courts,
to stay and surcease all suche proces, suytes, & Accions, as
shall or may be prosewed or attempted to be sued prosented
or awarded against the said Sr walter Leveson & his
said Sueties, & every off or any off them or his or their
Mannors, Landes, goods, Cattells, Amunicion and possessions
for any Debt Dutye or other cause off the said Sr walter
Leveson or his said Sueties! Duringe the space off three
yeres next ensewinge the date hereof, without any other
or further writt warrant or warrants to be had or sued
for, other then the first off these our Letters Patents, or
the Inrollmentes thereof. In wittnesse wherof &c ij.

To the most highe and most mightie Prince,
Sultan Mahumet Chan, of the Ottomanicall
Empire and dominion of the East partes, most
puissant, Sole, & Supreme Lord & Monarch:

Elizabeth (by the grace of God, almightie creator of
the worlde) of England, ffraunce, and Ireland Queene,
and of the true Christian ffaith against Idolatous falsely
professing the name of Christ, the Constant, perpetuall,
and victorious Defender. | To the most highe, & most
mightie Prince, Sultan Mahumet Chan, of y.e Ottomanicall
Empire and dominion of the East partes, Most puissan.
Sole, & Supreme Lord & Monarch. | Greeting. . |.

Most highe and most puissant Prince, It is no small con=
tentment to vs, that the Amitie we have w.th so highe and
renowned a Prince, as yo.u: is by our neighbour Princes &
their subiects so well knowne, that when they have neede
to seke any favour or kindnes from yo.u, they implore our
mediacion, as the readiest way to obtaine their desyres, w.ch
as at other tymes we have bene importuned to doe towardes yo.u,
and receyved therein great satisfaction, So are we
pressed at this tyme by the earnest suyte of the frendes of
certaine distressed gentlemen, to intreate yo.ur ffavorie ffavor
& reliefe of their extreamities; whose Names are Lawrence
Oliphant Master of Oliphant, and Robert Douglas Master
of Morton, two sonnes & Heyres of two Noble men, subiectes
of our Neighbour and good brother, the Kinge of Scotland,
who havinge bene many yeares since taken prisoners or takē in battle taken
at Sea by Pirates, and by them solde in Barbarie for
Bondmen, have ever since remayned in y.e state of Captivitie

[53   20 January 1600/1601]

ye direction ⎱ To the most high and most mightie Prince,   1
of ye letter ⎰ Sultan Mahumet Cham, of the Ottomanicall
                 Empire and dominion of the East partes, most
                 puissant, Sole, & Supream Lord & Monarch.
Elizabeth (by the grace of God, almightie creator of   5
the worlde) of England, Fraunce, and Ireland Queene,
and of the true Christian Faith against Idolators falcely
professing the name of Christ, the Constant, perpetuall,
and victorious defender./ To the Most high & most
mightie Prince, Sultan Mahumet Cham, of ye Ottomanicall   10
Empire and dominion of the East partes, Most puissant,
Sole, & Supreame Lord & Monarch. Greeting ./.

Most high and most puissant Prince, It is no small con =
tentment to vs, that the Amitie we have wth so high and
renowned a Prince, as you: is by our neighboure Princes &   15
their subiectes so well knowne, that when they have neede
to seeke any favoure or kindenes from you, they implore our
mediacion, as the rediest way to obtaine their desyers, wch
as at other tymes we have bene importuned to vse towardes you,
and receyved therin great satisfaction, So are we –   20
pressed at this tyme by the earnest suyte of the frendes of
certaine distressed gentlemen, to intreate youre Princely favour
& reliefe of their extremities; Whose Names are Lawrence –
Oliphant Master of Oliphant, and Robert Douglas Master
of Morton, two sonnes & heyres of two Noble men, Subiectes   25
of our Neighbour and good brother, the kinge of Scotland.
Who havinge bene many yeeres since taken prysoners casuallie
at Sea by Pirates, and by them solde in Barbarie for
Bondmen, have ever since remayned in yt state of Captivitie,

and so muche the more miserable, bycause none of their Frendes   30
knewe of their beinge, vntill yt of late it hath bene vnderstood
(though not of certeintie) yt they are prysoners in Argier –
vnder the Viceroy their your Tributarie: vpon knowledge
whereof, their Friendes & kinsfolke have sent & authorised
this bearer Robert Oliphant, one of their kinred, to seeke   35
& enquier of their estate, & to procure their redemption from yt
Servitude; who knowinge ⟨.⟩ no other way of addresse to you,
(bycause they are of a Nation yt have lyttle trade in those
quarters of the worlde) have humblie besought our letters and
furtherance to you, wch wee as willinglye have yeelded, for yt   40
the said persons were not taken in action of Warre by Sea
or Land against you, or your people; whereby you might have
cause of iust indignation against them, but onlie by meere casu =
altie of fortune, deservinge the compassion of all Princes:
whereof our earnest desyer is, yt you interpose your authoritie   45
towardes the said Viceroy of Argier: that he will sett
the said Laurence Oliphant and Robert Douglas at libertie,
if they be founde vnder him, or any other of your dominions:
to return home into their Native Countrey, whereby you shall
increase in vs the kinde remembraunce we have of your former   50
frendshippes, and obligue vs to requite it in any like matter you
may require at our handes: as more at Large shall declare to
you our ⟨Emb⟩ Ambassador there, to whom we pray you
to gyve credytt & favour in this matter;   Gyven vnder
our privie Seale at our Pallace of Westmynster, the   55
20. day of Ianuarij, in the yeere of our Lord God. 1600./
and of our Raigne the .43. /.

                        Elizabeth .I.

and so muche the more miserable, bycause none off their frinde
knewe off their beinge, untill the off late it hathe bene understood
(thoughe not off certaintie) the they are prysoners in Argier
under the Viceroy their yet Tributarie: upon knowledge
whereoff, their friende & kinsfolke have sent this aunt prysed
this bearer Robert Oliphant, one off their kinred, to seeke
& enquire off their estate, & to procure their redemption from the
servitude; who knowinge the no other way off addresse to you,
(bycause they are off a Nation that have lytle trade in those
quarters off the worlde) have humblie besought our lettres and
furtherance to you, which wee as willinglye have yeelded, for the
the said persons were not taken in action off warres by Sea
or land against you, or yor peoople; whereby you might have
cause off just indignation against them, but onlie by meere casu=
altie off fortune, deservinge the compassion off all Princes:
wherof our earnest desyer is, that you interpose yor authoritie
towarde the said Viceroy off Argier: that he will sett
the said Lawrence Oliphant and Robert Douglas at libertie,
iff they be founde under him, or any other off yor Dominions:
to retourne home into their Native Countrey, wherby you shall
increase in vs the kinde remembrance we have off yor former
freundshippe, and oblige vs to requite it in any like matter you
may require at our hande: as more at large shall declare to
you our Ambassador there, to whom we pray you
to gyve credytt & favor in this matter;   Gyven under
our privie Seale at our Pallace off Westmynster, the
20. day off January, in the yeare off our Lord God. 1600.
and off our Raigne the. 43.

Elizabeth.

The Emperor of China his letter
to the Queene of England. 1.

Il Potentissimo et vittoriosissimo Principe Tacosama, Incomparabil
gran Signor del Mondo, Figlio del Sole, al cui potente Nome tutte le
Nationi Orientali prostrandosi l'adorano: Imperatore et gran Signor
di tutti i Regni di China, et delle Territorij et Isole agiacenti;
Dayry ouer gran Re di Coray, Tambano, Bungo, Giamaco,
Xumoto, Ciazzura, Mino, Voari &c: Alla sublime Stella
del Settentrione, Tramontana; alla quale tutti quanti i valorosi
Cuori tirano, Elizabeta Regina d'Inghilterra, di Francia,
d'Irlanda, delle Isole di Normandia, di Vuight, et di Man &c
Principessa di Wales, Duchessa di Yorke, di Lancastre, di
Cornuallia, et d'Essestre, Contessa di Chestre &c: l'unica
vittoriosa Imperatrice del Tempo, della Fortuna, et d'Amore;
l'Anima et vita della Isola Fortunata: La Phenice sotto le cui
Ale fioriscono le Muse, la Pace, et l'Abondanza: Raggio mira-
coloso di Natura Lampeggiante per tutto l'universo, Augura
con perpetua salute, il Colmo di felicita in ogni successo prospero
& glorioso. 1.

Benche i piu de i Potenti Prencipi Occidentali ci habbiamo per gli
loro Ambascitori con infinite importunita sollecitati riceuer i lor
Sudditi nelli nostri Territorij, a cio che, vi si stabilisse un
Comercio, et mutuo traffico tra noi et essi: Et che alle loro
requisitioni non ci siamo piu oltre allargati, che di acconsentire
alla venuta de i lor sudditi, solamente alle parti piu discoste
da i nostri Famosi Imperij, et alcune altre Isole possedute
da Prencipi che ci sono Vassalli; Nondimeno subito che
habbiamo sentito il Nome solo della Splendidissima Regina
d'Inghilterra, Francia, e d'Irlanda, &c: la cui gloria

f. 34v

[54   1600]

.1600.   1
The Emperor of China his letter
to the Queene of England./.
Il Potentissimo et Vittoriosissimo Principe Ta+i+cosama, Incomparabile
gran Signor del Mondo, Figlio del Sole, al cui potente Nome tutte le   5
Nationi Orientali prostrandosi l'adorano: Imperatore et gran Signor
di tutti i Regni di China, et delle Territorij et Isole agiacenti; –
Dayry ouer gran Re di Coray, Tambano, Bungo, Giamaco, –
Xumoto, Ciazzura, Mino, Voari &c: Alla sublime Stella –
del Settentrione, Tramontana; alla quale tutti quanti i valorosi   10
Cuori tirano, Elizabeta Regina d'Inghilterra, di Francia, –
d'Irlanda, delle Isole di Normandia, di Vuight, et di Man &c:
Principessa di Wales, Duchessa di Yorke, di Lancastre, di –
Cornaullia, et d'Essestre, Contessa di Chestre &c: L'vnica
Vittoriosa Imperatrice del Tempo, della Fortuna, et d'Amore;   15
L'Anima et vita della Isola Fortunata: La Phenice sotto le cui
Ale fioriscono le Muse, la Pace, et l'Abondanza: Raggio mire =
colosa di Natura Lampeggiante per tutto l'vniuerso, Augura
con perpetua salute, il Colmo di felicita in ogni successo prospero
& glorioso ./.   20
Benche i piu de i Potenti Prencipi Occidentali ci habbiamo per gli
loro Ambasciatori con infinite importunita sollecitati riceu⟨e⟩r i lor
Sudditi nelli nostri Territorij, a cio che, vi si stabilisse vn
Comercio, et mutuo traffico tra noi et essi: Et che alle loro
requisitioni non ci siamo piu oltre allargati, che di acconsentire   25
alla venuta de i lor sudditi, solamente alle parti piu discoste
da i nostri Famosi Imperij, et alcune altre Isole possedute
da Prencipi che ci sono Vassalli; Nondimeno subito che
habbiamo sentito il Nome solo della Splendidissima Regina
d'Inghilterra, Francia, e d'Irlanda, &c: la cui gloria –   30

f. 35r

(per esser la piu casta tra tutti i Signori che seguono Giesu,
come singolarmente Eletta fra i Potentissimi della legge Chri =
stiani) si distende et sparge per tutte le parti del Mondo : –
Siamo stati talmente rapiti d'ammiratione di quelle cose miracolose,
che (ci ha riferite quel famoso Nauarca Beniamino Vuod) della   35
perfettione et splendore Fulgentissimo della Persona (presentandosi
le vostre lettere segnate dalle vostre Bellissime Mani proprie) che
non solamente l'habbiamo con ogni fauore distessamente ascoltato:
Ma ci siamo etiandio prestamente risoluti di donarui il primo et
supremo grado con ogni honore et Priuilegij in questi Nostri –   40
Reami, con offerta a tutti i vostri (Mentre saranno vostri)
di ogni sicurtà di Passagio et libero traffico, come nè Regni vostri
proprij. Di che per intera fede, habbiamo voluto accompagnare
queste nostre, d'vn' altro pegno et indicio del Nostro Amore: Il
quale vi piaccia accettare non altrimente che come vn segno este =   45
riore della nostra interiore amicitia Reale che vi portiamo; Et
piu ampiamente lo dimostraremo, se ce ne fia concesso il modo
di poterlo fare. In contracambio di questo, noi vi pregheremo
solamente di rimandarei con Ispeditione il presente Portatore,
con le gratissime nuoue della vostra buona et prospera costan =   50
te sanità. Dalla Nostra Real Porta Aurea di Cantonfu,
alli dieci della Luna Prima, l'Anno dalla Creatione del –
Mondo ./.

25000

C per esser la piu casta tra tutti i Signori che seguono Giesu,
come singolarmente Eletta fra i Potentissimi della legge Chri=
stiani) si distende et sparge per tutte le parti del Mondo: ~
Siamo stati talmente rapiti d'ammiratione di quelle cose miracolose,
che (ci ha riferite quel famoso Nauarca Beniamino vuod) della
perfettione et splendore Fulgentissimo della Persona (presentandosi
le vostre lettere segnate dalle vostre Bellissime Mani proprie) che
non solamente l'habbiamo con ogni fauore distessamente ascoltato:
Ma ci siamo etiandio prestamente risoluti di donarui il primo et
supremo grado con ogni honore et Priuilegij in   questi Nostri ~
Reami, con offerta a tutti i vostri (Mentre saranno vostri)
di ogni sicurtà di Passagio et libero traffico, come nè Regni vostri
proprij. Di che per intera fede, habbiamo voluto accompagnare
queste nostre, d'un altro pegno et indicio del Nostro Amore: Il
quale vi piaccia accettare non altrimente che come un segno este=
riore della nostra interiore amicitia Reale che vi portiamo; Et
piu ampiamente lo dimostraremo, se ce ne sia concesso il modo
di poterlo fare. In contracambio di questo, noi vi pregheremo
solamente di rimandarci con Espeditione il presente Portatore,
con le gratissime nuoue della vostra buona et prospera costan=
te sanità. Dalla Nostra Real Porta Aurea di Cantonsu,
alli dieci della Luna Prima, l'Anno dalla Creatione del ~
Mondo. /.

                        /25000/

Oh quam decepta fui: Expectaui Legationem tu vero querelam,
mihi adduxisti, Per literas accepi te esse Legatum, inueni vero
Heraldum, Nunquam in vita mea audiui talem orationem; Miror
sane, Miror tantam: et tam insolitam in publico audatiam, Neque
possum credere, si Rex tuus adesset; quod ipse talia verba pro=
tulisset, sin vero tale aliquid tibi fortasse; in mandatis comisit,
(quod quidem valde dubito) eo tribuendum, quod cum Rex tuus
sit Iuuenis, et non tam Iure sanguinis, quam Iure electionis; ac
nouiter electus, non tam perfecte; Inteligat rationem
tractandi istiusmodi negotia Cum alijs Principibus; quam vel
Maiores illius nobiscum obseruarunt, vel fortasse obseruabunt
alij qui locum eius post hac tenebunt. /.

Quod ad te attinet, tu mihi videris libros multos per legisse; libros
tamen Principum ne attigisse, sed prorsus ignorare, quid inter
reges conueniat, Nam quod Iuris natura gentiumqs tantopere
mentionem facis, hoc scito iuris natura Gentiumqs esse vt cum
bellum InterReges intercedit, liceat alteri alterius bellica subsidi
vndecumqs allata intercipere et ne in damnum suum conuertan
tur precauere; (Hoc inquam) est ius nature et Gentium. /.

Quod nouam affinitatem Cum domo Austriaca Commemores; quam
tanti Iam fieri velis: non te fugiat ex eadem domo non de fuisse
qui Regi tuo Pollonia Regnum preripere voluisset. /.

De ceteris vero qua non sint huius Loci et temporis cum plura
sint, et singilatim Consideranda illud expectabis quod ex
quibusdam meis Consiliarijs huic rei designandis, intelliges,
Interia vero valeas et quiescas. /.

f. 35v

[55   25 July 1597   see Commentary]

Her Maiesties Answer to the   1
Polands Ambassador ./.

Oh quam decepta fui: Expectaui Legationem tu vero querelam,
mihi adduxisti, Per literas accepi te esse Legatum, inueni vero –
Heraldum, Nunquam in vita mea audiui talem orationem; Miror
sane, Miror tantam: et tam insolitam in publico audatiam, Neque   5
possum credere, si Rex tuus adesset; quod ipse talia verba pro =
tullisset, sin vero tale aliquid tibi fortasse; in mandatis comisit,
(quod quidem valde dubito) eo tribuendum, quod cum Rex tuus
sit Iuuenis, et non tam Iure sanquinis, quam Iure electionis; ac
nouiter electus, non tam perfecte; Inteligat rationem –   10
tractandi istiusmodi negotia Cum alijs Principibus; quam vel
Maiores illius nobiscum obseruarunt, Vel fortasse obseruabunt
alij qui locum eius post hac tenebunt. /.

Quod ad te attinet, tu mihi videris libros multos per legisse; libros
tamen Principum ne attigisse, sed prorsus ignorare, quid inter   15
reges conueniat, Nam quod Iuris naturæ gentiumque tantopere
mentionem facis, hoc scito iuris naturæ Gentiumque esse vt cum
bellum Inter Reges intercedit, liceat alteri alterius bellica subsidia;
vndecumque allata intercipere et ne in damnum suum conuertan =
tur precauere; (Hoc inquam) est ius nature et Gentium./.   20

Quod nouam affinitatem Cum domo Austriaca Commemores; quam
tanti Iam fieri velis: non te fugiat ex eadem domo non de fuisse,
qui Regi tuo Polloniæ Regnum preripere voluisset./.

De ceteris vero quæ non sint huius Loci et temporis cum plura
sint, et singilatim Consideranda illud expectabis quod ex   25
quibusdam meis Consiliarijs huic rei de signandis, intelliges,
Interia vero valeas et quiescas./.

[56   25 July 1597   see Commentary]

The same in english:/   1

O how haue I bene deceaued, I expected an Imbassadge, but you haue
brought to me a complaint, I was certified by letters that you were an
Imbassador, But I haue found you an Herald; Neuer in my life tyme
haue I heard such an Oration; I maruell much at so great and insolent a   5
boldnes in open presence: Neither doe I beleue yf your Kinge were pre =
sent, that hee himselfe wolde deliuer such speeches; But yf you haue bene
commaunded to vse such like speeches (whereof I greatly doubt) it is here =
vnto to be attributed, yt seeinge your kinge is a yonge man, and newlie Cho =
sen, not so fullie by right of blood, as by right of Election; yt he doth not   10
soe perfectlie knowe the course of managinge affayres of this Nature wth
other Princes, as his elders haue obserued with vs, or perhaps others will
obserue, which shall succeed him in his place hereafter./.

And as concerninge your selfe, you seeme to haue redd manye bookes, but
the bookes of Princes you haue not so much as touched, but shewe your   15
selfe vtterlie Ignorant what is conuenient betweene kinges; and –
where you make mention so often of the Lawe of Nature and of
Lawes of Nations: know you, yt this is the Lawe of Nature and of
Nations; That when Hostilitie Interposeth her selfe betwene Princes;
It is lawefull for either partie to Cease on eithers prouisions for war,   20
from whence soeuer deryued, and to foresee yt they be not conuerted
to their own hurts; This I saye is ye Lawe of Nature, & of Nations./.

And where you recite the newe affinitie wth the House of Austria:
what accompt soeuer you make thereof, You are not Ignorant yt
some one of that House wolde haue had the kingdome of Pollonia –   25
from youre kinge./.

For other matters, for which tyme and place serue not: Seeinge –
they are many, & must be considered by them selues; This you shall
expect, to be certified of them by some of our Councellors, yt shall
be appointed to those matters; In the meane tyme, fare you well   30
and repose youre selfe. /.

The same in english : /

O how haue I bene deceaued, I expected an Imbassadge, but you haue
brought to me a complaint, I was certified by letters that you were an
Imbassador, But I haue found you an Herald; Neuer in my life tyme
haue I heard such an Oration; I maruell much at so great and insolent a
boldnes in open presence: Neither doe I beleue yf your kinge were pre=
sent, that hee himselfe wolde deliuer such speeches; But yf you haue bene
commaunded to vse such like speeches (whereof I greatly doubt) it is here=
vnto to be attributed, y seeinge your kinge is a yonge man, and newelie Cho=
sen, not so fullie by right of blood, as by right of Election; y he doth not
see perfectlie knowe the course of managinge affayres of this Nature w
other Princes, as his elders haue obserued with vs, or perhaps others will
obserue, which shall succeed him in his place hereafter. /.

And as concerninge your selfe, you seeme to haue redd manye bookes, but
the bookes of Princes you haue not so much as touched, but shewe your
selfe vtterlie Ignorant what is conuenient betweene kinges; and
where you make mention so often of the Lawe of Nature, and the
Lawes of Nations: know you, y this is the Lawe of Nature and of
Nations; That when Hostilitie Interposeth her selfe betwene Princes;
It is lawefull for either partie to Cease on eithers prouisions for war,
from whence soeuer deryued, and to foresee y they be not conuerted
to their own hurts; This I saye is y Lawe of Nature, & of Nations. /.

And where you recite the newe affinitie w the House of Austria:
what accompt soeuer you make thereof, You are not Ignorant y
some one of that House wolde haue had the kingdome of Pollonia
from youre kinge. /.

For other matters, for which tyme and place serue not: Seeinge
they are many, & must be considered by them selues; This you shall
expect, to be certified of them by some of our Councellors, y shall
be appointed to those matters; In the meane tyme, fare you well
and repose youre selfe. /.

fforasmuche as Almightie God hathe ordeyned Kinges,
Quenes, and Princes: to have dominion and rule over all
their Subiectes, and to preserve them in the profession and
observation off the true Christian Religion, according to his
holye worde & Commaundementes. And in like sorte y all
Subiectes shoulde love, feare, and obey their Soveraigne Princes, beinge Kinges or Quenes; and to the vttermost off their
powers at all tymes to withstand, pursue, and suppresse
All manner off persons that shall by any meanes intend
& attempt any thinge dampgerous or hurtfull, to the Honor
Estates, or persons, off their Soveraignes. Therefore,
Wee whose names are or shall be subscribed to this
wrytinge, beings naturall borne subiectes off this Realme
off England, and havinge so gratious a Lady our Soveraigne Elizabeth, by the ordinance off God, our most
rightfull Quene raigninge over vs these many yeares
with great felicitie to our inestimable Comfortes. And
fyndinge off late by dyvers disposicions, confessions, and
sundrye advertisementes out off forreine partes from credible
persons well knowne to her Ma:tie Counsell, and to diverse
others; That for the furtherance & advauncement off
some pretended Titles to the Crowne off this Realme,
It hathe bene manifest that the lyfe off our gratious ~
Soveraigne Lady Quene Elizabeth, hathe bene most
trayterously and devillishly sought; and the same ~
followed most dampgerously to the perill off her person
Iff Almightie God her perpetuall defendor, off his great
mercye had not revealed and withstoode the same.
By whose lyfe, we and all others her Ma:tie loyall

[57   19 October 1584   see Commentary]

The Oath of assotiation   1
Forasmuche as Almightie God hathe ordeyned Kinges,
Queenes, and Princes: to have dominion and rule over all
their Subiectes, and to preserve them in the profession and
observation of the true christian Religion, accordinge to his   5
holye worde & Commaundementes. And in like sort yt all
Subiectes should love, feare, and Obey their Soueraigne Prin =
ces, beinge Kinges or Queenes; and to the vttermost of their
power at all tymes to wthstand, pursue, and suppresse:
All manner of persons that shall by any meanes intend,   10
& attempt any thinge daungerous or hurtfull, to the honores
estates, or persons, of their Soueraignes./ Therefore,
Wee whose names are or shall be subscribed to this
wrytinge, (beinge naturall borne subiectes of this Realme
of England, and havinge so gratious a Lady our Sove =   15
raigne Elizabeth, by the ordinaunce of God, our most
rightfull Queene Raigninge over vs these many yeeres
wth great Felicitie to our inestimable Comforte: And
fyndinge of late by dyvers deposicions, confessions, and
sondrye advertisementes out of forreine partes from credible   20
persons well knowne to her Maiesties Counsell, and to divers
others; That for the furtheraunce & advauncement of
some pretended Titles to the Crowne of this Realme,
It hathe bene manifest that the lyfe of our gratious –
Soueraigne Lady Queene Elizabeth, hathe bene most   25
trayterously and devillishly sought; and the same –
followed most daungerously to the perill of her person,
Yf Almightie God her perpetuall defender, of his great
mercye had not revealed and wthstoode the same./.
By whose lyfe, we and all others her Maiesties loyall   30

and true subiectes doe enioye an Inestimable benefitt of peace
in this land) doe, for the reasons & causes before alleaged,
not onlie acknowledge our selues most iustlye bounde, wth our
bodies, lyves, landes and goodes, in her defence and her safetie
to wthstand, pursue, & suppresse, all such mischievous   35
persons, and all her enemyes: of what Nation, condition, or
degree soever they shall bee, or by what coulor or title
they shall pretend to be her enemyes, or attempt any harm
vnto her person: But we doe also thinke it our most
bounden dutyes, for the great benefites of peace, wealth,   40
and godly government, wch we have more plentifully recey =
ved these many yeeres vnder her Maiesties most happie govern =
ment, then our forefathers have done in +any+ ⟨muche⟩ longer tyme
of any other her progenitors kinges of this Realme, to de =
clare, & by this wrytinge make manifest, our loyall & bounden   45
dutyes to our said soueraigne Ladie for her saffetye: –
And to that ende, we: and everie of vs, First callinge
to witnesse the holie name of Almightie God: Doe
voluntarilie & most willinglye, binde our selues ⟨our
soules, & bodyes⟩ : everie one of vs to the other, Iointlye &   50
seuerallye in the bond of one fyrme & loyall societie, and
doe hereby vowe & promysse before the Maiestie of Al =
mightie God, That wth our whole powers, bodyes, lyves,
landes & goodes: and wth our Children & servantes and
vttermost habilities: wee, and every of vs, will faithfully   55
serve & humblye Obey our said soueraigne Ladie Queene
Elizabeth, against all estates, dignities, and earthlye
powers whatsoever; And will aswell wth our Ioynte
& perticuler forces, duringe our lyves, wthstand, offend, and

and true subiecte dos enioye an Inestimable benefitt off peace
in this lande) dos, for the reasons & causes before alleaged,
not onlie acknowledge our selues most instlye bounde, wth our
bodies, lybes, lande and goode, in her defence and her safetie
to withstande, pursue, & suppresse, all such mischievous
persons, and all her enemyes: off what Nation, condition, or
degree soever they shall bee, or by what colour or title
they shall pretende to be her enemyes, or attempt any harme
vnto her person: But we do also thinke it our most
bownden dutyes, for the great benefites off peace, wealth,
and godly governmente, wth we have more plentifully enioy=
ed theise many yeares vnder her Ma:tie most happie govern=
ment, then our forefathers have done in any longer tyme
off any other her progenitours kinge off this Realme, to de=
clare, & by this writinge make manifest, our loyall & bownden
dutyes to our said soueraigne Ladie for her safftye: ~
And to that ende, we: and everie off vs, first callinge
to witnesse the holie name off Almightie God: doe
volumtarilie & most willinglye, binde our selues ~~and~~
~~faith, & bodie~~: everie one off vs to the other, iointlye &
severallye, in the bond off one fyrme & loyall societie, and
doe herby vowe & promyse before the Ma:tie off Al=
mightie God, that wth our whole powers, bodyes, lybes,
lande & goode: and wth our children & servauntes and
vttermost habilities: we, and everie off vs, will faithfully
serve & humblye obey our said soueraigne Ladie Queene
Elisabeth, against all estates, dignities, and earthlye
powers whatsoever: And will aswell wth our ioynte
& particuler forces, duringe our lybes, withstande, offend, and

pursue, as well by force of Armes, as by all other meanes
of revenge, all manner of persons of what estate soever
they shall be, and their abettors, that shall attempt by any
acte, counsell, or consent, any thinge that shall tend to
the harme of her Ma:ties Royall person; and wee shall
never desyst from all manner of pursute against such
persons to the vttermost extermination of them, theire Counsellors, aydors, & abettors; And iff any suche wicked
attempt against her most Royall person shall be taken
in hand or procured, whereby any that have, may, or
shall pretend title to come to this Crowne by the vn-
tymely death of her Ma:tie so wickedly procured (which
God for his Mercyes sake forbid) may be advanced;
wee doe not onlie vowe and binde our selues bothe jointlye
& severallye, never to allowe, accept, or favour any such
pretended successor, by whome any suche detestable acte
shall be attempted or commytted, or any y[at] may any way
clayme by, or from suche person or persons as is aforesaid, by whome or for whom suche an acte shall be attempted or commytted, as vnworthie of all government in any
Christian Realme or Civill Societie; But doe also
further vowe & protest as wee are most bounde, and y[at] in
the presence of the Eternall and everlasting God, to
prosecute suche person or persons to the death, w[i]th our
joynts & particuler forces, and to take the vttermost
revenge on them y[at] by any possible meanes wee or any of
vs can devyse or doe, or cause to be devysed and done
for theire vtter overthrow and extirpacion; And to the
better Corroboration of this our loyall bond and

pursue, aswell by force of Armes, as by all other meanes   60
of revenge, all manner of persons of what estate soever
they shall be, and their abbetters yt shall attempt by any
acte, counsell, or consent, any thinge that shall tend to
the harme of her Maiesties Royall person; and we shall
never desyst from all manner of pursute against suche   65
persons to the vttermost extermination of them, their Coun =
sellors, ayders, & abetters; And if any ⟨s.⟩ suche wicked
attempt against her most Royall person shall be taken
in hand or procured, Whereby any that have, may, or
shall pretend title to come to this Crowne by the vn =   70
tymely death of her Maiestie so wickedly procured (wch
God for his Mercyes sake forbid) may be advaunced;
we doe not onlie vowe and binde our selues bothe Iointlye
& seuerallye, never to allowe, accept, or favour any such
pretended successor, by whome any suche detestable acte   75
shall be attempted or commytted, or any yt may any way
clayme by, or from suche person or pretence as is afore =
said, by whome or for whom suche an acte shall be attemp =
ted or commytted, as vnworthie of all government in any
Christian Realme or Civill Societie; But doe also   80
further vow & protest as we are most bounde, and yt in
the presence of the Eternall and everlasting God, to
prosecute suche person or persons to the death, wth our
Ioynte & perticuler forces, and to take the vttermost –
revenge on them yt by any possible meanes wee or any of   85
vs can devyse or doe, or cause to be devysed and done
for their vtter overthrow and extirpacion; And to the
better Corroboration of this our loyall bond and —

Association: we doe also testifie by this wrytinge, yt
we doe confirme the contentes hereof, by +our+ oathes Corporally   90
taken vpon the holie Evangelistes, wth this expresse
condition: that no one of vs shall for any respect of
persons or cawses, or for feare or rewarde, seperate
our selues from this Assotiacion, or fayle in the pro =
secution hereof duringe our lyves: vpon payne, to be   95
by the rest of vs prosecuted and suppressed as periur'de
persons, and publike enemyes, to God, our Queene, and
our Natyve Countrey./ To wch punyshement and
paynes, we doe voluntarilye Submytt our selues, and
every of vs: wthout benefyt of any exception to be hereafter   100
challenged by any of vs, by any coloure or pretexte./
In Wittnes of all wch premysses to be inviolablye
kept: we doe to this wrytinge put our handes & seales
and shall be most ready to accept and admytt any others
hereafter to this our Societie and Association ./.   105
Dated at Hampton Courte this .19. day of October.
1584. In the Sixe & twentith yeere of her Maiesties
Reigne./.

Association: we doe also testifie by this wrytinge, &
we doe confirme the contents hereof, by oathe Corporallie
taken upon the holie Evangeliste, with this expresse
condition: that no one of us shall for any respecte of
persons or cause, or for feare or rewarde, separate
our selues from this Association, or fayle in the pro=
secution hereof duringe our lyues: upon payne, to be
by the rest of us presented and suppressed as periured
persons, and publike enemyes, to God, our Queene, and
our Natyve Countrey. To w[hi]ch punyshment and
payne, we doe voluntarilye submytt our selues, and
every of us: w[i]thout benefyt of any exception to be hereafter
challenged by any of us, by any coloure or pretexte.
In Wittnes of all w[hi]ch premysses to be inviolablye
kept: we doe to this wrytinge putt our handes sealed
and shall be most readie to accepte and admytt any others
hereafter to this our Societie and Association.
Dated at Hampton Courte this 19. day of October
1584. In the xxvjth e twentithe yeare of the raigne of her Ma[ies]tie
Raigne.

Salutem in Christo: I have receyved late from yo~ Lo: and
others of his Matie honorable privie Counsell, contayninge
twoo pointes; one, that the Puritanes be proceeded against
accordinge to lawe, except they reforme themselves: The other,
y^t good care be had unto greddie Patrones, y^t none be admitted in their Places, but such as be conformable, & otherwise
worthie for their vertue & learninge. | If have written to
the Bisshopps of this Province, and in their absence to their
Chauncellors: to have speciall care of these thinges, & therein
have sent Coppies of yo~^r honor^s Lett^r, and will take present
order w^thin myne owne Diocess. I wisshe wth all my harte y^t
the like order Were given not onlie to all Bisshopps, but
to all Magistrates & Justices of Peace, to proceede against
Papistes and Recusantes, who of late: partlie by this common
Dealinges against the Puritanes, & partlie by extraordinary
favor; they are growen mightie in Number, corradge & Insolencie.
The Puritanes (whose fantasticall Zeale I mislike) though
they differ in Ceremonies and Accidentes, yet they agree
not wth us in substance of Religion, and I thinke all, or ye most
parte of them, love his Matie & the present State, and
I hope will yeelde to conformitye; but the Papistes are
opposite & contrarie in many verie Mayne pointes of Religion
& can not but wisshe the Popes authoritie & Popishe Religion
to be established; I assure yor honor, it is highe tyme to
looke unto them, besides many are gone from all partes to
London, & some are come downe into the Countrey in greate
Jollitie, almost triumphantly: but his Matie as he hath
bene brought upp in the Gospell, & understands Religion
excellently well, so he will (wee doubt not) perfect, ~
maintayne, and advaunce it even to the ende; so y^t if the Gospe[ll]

[58   18 December 1604   see Commentary]

The Archbushop of Yorke his   1
Answere to my Lord of Salisburie
Salutem in Christo: I have receyved letteres from your Lordshippe and
others of his Maiesties honorable privie Counsell, conteyninge
two pointes; one, that the Puritanes be proceeded against   5
accordinge to lawe, except they reforme themselues: Th'other,
yt good care be had vnto greedie Patrons, yt none be admit =
ted in their Places, but such as be conformable, & otherwise
worthie for their vertue & learninge./ I have wrytten to
the Busshops of this Province, and in their absence to their   10
Chauncellors: to have speciall care of the service, & therein
have sent Coppies of your honores Letteres, and will take present
order wthin myne owne Dioces. I wishe wth all my harte yt
the like order Were gyven not onlie to all Busshops, but
to all Magistrates & Iustices of Peace, to proceede against   15
Papistes and Recusantes, who of late: partly by this rounde
dealinge against the Puritans, & partly by extraordinary
favour, they are growne mightie in Nomber, courage & Insolence./
The Puritans (whose fantasticall zeale I mislike) though
they dyffer in Ceremonies and Accidentes, Yet they agree   20
wth vs in substance of Religion, and I thinke all, or ye most
part of them, love his Maiestie & the present State, and
I hope will yeelde to conformitye; but the Papistes are
opposite & contrarie in many verie Mayne pointes of Religion,
& can not but wishe the Popes authoritie & Popishe Religion   25
to be established; I assure your honor, it is high tyme to
looke vnto them, verie many are gone from all partes to
London, & some are come downe into the Countrey in greate
Iollitie, almost tryvmphantly: but his Maiestie as he hathe
bene brought vp in the Gospell, & vnderstandes Religion –   30
excellently well, so he will (wee doubt not) perfect, –
mainteyne, and advaunce it even to the ende; so yt if ye Ghospell

shall quaile & Poperie prevaile, it will be imputed princi =
pally to you (great Counsellores) who either procure, or
yeelde to graunt tolleracion to some &c./. Good my Lord   35
Cranborne, let me put you in mynde that you were borne, &
brought vp in true Religion, Your honorable Father was an
Instrument to banish supersticion & to advaunce ye Gospell:
Imitate him in this service especially: 〈A.〉 As for other
thinges, I confesse I am not to deale in State Matters,   40
Yet (as one that honoreth & loveth his Maiestie wth all my
harte) I wishe les wastinge of the Treasure of the
Realme, & more moderation in the lawfull exercise of hun =
tinge, bothe yt poore mens Corne may be lesse spoyled, and
other his Maiesties Subiectes more spared./ The Papistes   45
gyve out yt they hope the Ecclesiasticall Commyssion shall
not be renewed any more, indeede it stayeth verie longe, albeit
there is heere great want of it, I pray your honor to further
it, Sir Iohn *Bennett* will attend you./ Thus beseeching
God to blesse your Lordship wth his manifolde graces, that   50
you may as longe serve his Maiestie as your Most wyse
Father dyd serve our Late worthie Queene Elizabeth:
I byd you most hartely Farewell: From Thorpe the
&c./.

If all quaile & Poperie prevaile, it will be imputed principi=
pally to you (great Counsellors) who either permitt, or
yourselfe by greate followance to some &c. / God my Lord
Cranborne, let me put you in mynde that you were borne, &
broughte up in true Religion, yo[ur] honorable ffather was an
Instrument to banish Superstition & to advannce y[e] Gospell:
imitate him in this service especially: As for other
thinge, I confesse I am not to deale in State Matters,
yet (as one that honoreth & loveth his Ma[jes]tie w[i]th all my
harte) I wishe les wastinge of the Treasure of the
Realme, & more moderation in the lawfull exercise of Hun=
tinge, bothe y[at] poore mens Corne may be lesse spoyled, and
other his Ma[jes]ties Enworke more spared. / the Papistes
gyve out y[at] they hope the Ecclesiasticall Commission shall
not be renewed any more, indeede it stayeth verie longe, albeit
there is great want of it, I pray yo[ur] hono[r] to further
it, S[ir] John Bennett will attend you. / Thus beseeching
God to blesse yo[ur] Lordshipp w[i]th his manifolde graces, that
you may as longe serve his Ma[jes]tie, as yo[ur] most worthie
ffather did serve our Late worthie Queene Elizabeth:
I bid you most hartely farewell: from Thorpe the
&c. /

Sir ffrauncis Drake his letter to
Mr John ffoxe .1.

Mr ffoxe, whereas we had of late thappie onsett
against the Spaniardes, I doe assure my selfe that you
have thapposstly remembred vs in your good prayers, And
therefore I have not forgotten briefflye to make you pertaker
thereof. The .19. daye of Aprill. 1587. we arryved within
the Roade of Cales: where we founde many shippinges. |
But amongst the rest. 32. of verie great burthen, Laden
& to be laden wth provision: and prepared to furnish the
kinge Navie, intendinge wth all speede against England;
The wch (when we had boorded & also furnished our
severall shippes wth provision as we thought sufficient)
we burnt. And althoughe by the space of two dayes &
two nightes yt we contynued theere, we were still in daunger
bothe wth the thunderinge shott from the towne, & assaulted
wth the rowinge Cannons of .12. Gallies: yet we suncke
two of them, and one great Argosie, & still annoyed them
wth theire small hurt to our selves. And so at our departure
we broughte away. 4. shippes of provision to the greate
terror of our enemye, & good to our selves: as it might
appeare by a most curteous letter wrytten vnto me wth a
flagge of Truce by Don Pedro Generall of the Gallies.
But whereas it is most certaine, that the kinge dothe not
onlie make speedie preparation in Spayne, but likewyse ex-
pectethe a verie great fleete from the Straightes & diverse
other places, yt shoulde Joyne wth his forces to invade England
We suppose yt sett aparte all feare of daunger, and by
Gods sufferaunce to proceede by all good meanes
we can devyse to prevent theire comynge. | Wherefore I
shall desyre you to continue yor faithfull remembraunce

[59   April 1587   see Commentary]

        Sir Fraunces drake his Letter to   1
        Mr Iohn Foxe./.
Mr Foxe, whereas we had of late happie Successe –
against the Spaniardes, I doe assure my self that you
have happely remembred vs in youre good prayers, And   5
therfore I have not forgotten brieflye to make you pertaker
therof. The .19. daye of Aprile.1587.we arryved wthin
the Roade of *Cales*: where we founde much shippinge./
But emongst the rest .32. of verie great burthen, Laden
& to be Laden wth provision: and prepared to furnish the   10
Kinges Navie, intendinge wth all speede against England;
The wch (when we had boorded & also furnished our
severall shippes wth provision as we thought sufficient)
we burnt. And althoughe by the space of two dayes &
two nightes yt we contynued there, we were still in daunger   15
bothe wth the thundringe shott from the towne, & assaulted
wth the roaringe Cannons of .i2. Gallies: yet we sunck –
two of them, and one great Argosie & still anoyed them
wth verie small hurt to our selves. And so at our departure,
we brought away .4. shippes of provision to the greate   20
terror of our enemyes, & honor to our selues: as it might
appeare by a most curteous letter wrytten vnto me wth a
Flagge of Truce by *Don Pedro* Generall of the Gallies./
But whereas it is most certaine, that the Kinge dothe not
onlie make speedie preparation in Spayne, but likewyse ex =   25
pecteth a verie great Fleete from the Straightes & divers
other places, yt should Ioyne wth his forces to invade England:
We purpose to set aparte all feare of daunger, and by
God his Furtherance to proceede by all good meanes
we can devyse to prevent their commynge./ Wherefore I   30
shall desyer you to continue your Faithfull remembraunce

of vs in your prayers, that our present service may take
good effect, as God may be glorified, his Churche, our
Queene & Countrey preserved, and the enemyes of his –
truthe vtterly vanquished, that we may have contynuall   35
peace./ From a Boorde her Maiesties good Shippe
the *Elizabeth Bonauenture*./

                Your loving Frend and
                Faithfull Sonne in
                Christ Iesus :/   40
                   Fraunces Drake
Our enemyes are many, but our Protector
commaundeth the whole Worlde./ Let vs all
pray contynuallye, and our lord Iesus will
helpe in good tyme mercyfullye./   45

        Haste Fra: Drake

off vs in yo[r] prayers, that our p[re]sent s[er]vice may take
good effect, as God may be glorified, his Churche, our
Quene & Country p[re]served, and the enemyes of his &
hers vtterly vanquished, that we may have contynuall
peace. | From a Boorde her Ma[ty] good ship the
the Elizabeth Bonaventure . |

yo[r] loving frend and
faithfull sonne in
Christ Jesus ./

Fraunces Drake

Our enemyes are many, but our p[ro]tecto[r]
comaundeth the whole woorlde. | Let vs all
pray contynuallye, and our lord Jesus will
helpe in good tyme mercyfullye. |

Haste Fra: Drake

To the Right ho: the Lordes and others
of the Queenes Ma:tie most ho: pryvie counsell

In all humble manner do beseech yo:r Honor, yo:ur poore
suppl:t, the prisoners of her Ma:tie Bench: whereas it
pleased her Ma:tie of her aboundant mercie, considering
the greate Calamities of sondrie her Highnes subiectes
imposed on them parthly by meere iniurie through
extremitie of lawe against all conscience, and parthly
by the rigorous dealinges of Mercilesse Creditors, [to]
grannt her Highnes most gratious Commyssion, through
w:ch (to the content of the divers creditors by the industrie
& travaile of the said commyssioners) many hundreds
of poore people have bene enlarged, extremities qualified,
& good and vprighte dealinges cherisshed; But so it is
right ho: Lordes, y:t sithence the suppression of the said
Commyssion, the said prison is pestred w:th a greate
nomber of poore people wended thither from all places
in England in hope of w:ch, according to equitie by
vertue of the said Commyssion suppressed. Notwithstandinge
the Justices have vndertaken to take some order for the
enlarginges of yo:r poore suppl:t in some consionable manner;
yet the said Justices vpon humble complainte to them
made albeit they confesse dyvers yo:r poore oratours endure
herein most extreme wronge by the practisse and oppression
of their adversaries as hathe bene manifested and proved
to the said Justices, yet they say they are sworne to the
lawe, so as howe lamentable the case of the poore prisoner

f. 40v

[60   *c*. 1585 – 1589 (?)   see Commentary]

To the Right honorable the Lordes and others   1
of the Queenes Maiesties most honorable pryvie counsell

In all humble Manner do beseech your honores, youre poore
suppliantes, the prisoners of her Maiesties Bench: where it
pleased her Maiestie of her aboundant Mercie, considering   5
the greate Calamities of sondrie her highnes subiectes
imposed on them partlye by meere Iniurie through
extremitie of lawe against all conscience, and partlie
by the rigorous dealinge of Mercilesse Creditores./To
graunt her highnes most gratious Commyssion, through   10
wch (to the content of the verie creditores by the Industrie
& travaile of the said commyssioners) many hundredes
of poore people have bene enlarged, extremities qualified,
& good and vpright dealinge cherished; But so it is
right honorable lordes, yt sithence the suppression of the said   15
Commyssion, the said pryson is pestred wth a greate
nomber of poore people removed thither from all places
in England in hope of releife, accordinge to equitie by
vertue of the said Commyssion suppressed. Notwthstandinge
the Iustices have vndertaken to take some order for the   20
enlarginge of your poore suppliantes in some conscionable Manner;
Yet the said Iustices vpon humble Complaintes to them –
made albeit they confesse dyvers your poore Oratores endure
herein most extreme wronge by the practise and oppression
of their adversaries as hathe bene manifested and proved   25
to the said Iustices, Yet they say they are sworne to the
lawe, so as howe lamentable the case of the poore prisoner

is, & how ever it standeth wth equitie, the said Iustices
do nothinge at all in performance of your honorable direc =
tions herein. / In tender consideration whereof, pleaseth   30
it your honores for godes cause to prefer into the high Court
of parliament a Statute by learned advise penned, in
parte agreable to the former Commyssion, qualified accordinge
to all good conscience, and not dyfferinge from the sincere
meaninge of the Common lawe, or otherwyse to order that   35
a newe Commyssion may be by her Maiesties Royall prerogative
apointed for the determyninge of the cawses of ye oppressed
in the said Gaole, in such sorte as the Court of Chauncerie
it self wolde order, had your poore Oratores abilitie to pursue
their Iust plaint in yt Courte. And your poore Oratores   40
who are otherwyse Remediles to reforme most extreeme wronges,
on them by slight & subtile devyses Imposed, but like to
perishe in this myserable pryson, and their wyves and
children goe a begginge; shall accordinge to their bounden
dutyes dailye pray to God for your honors estates in all   45
health and happines longe to ⟨continue⟩ endure. / .

is, & howe ever it standeth wth equitie, the said Justices
do nothinge at all in performance of yo[u]r honorable direc=
tions herein. In tender consideration whereof, please[th]
it yo[u]r hono[u]r for gode cause to preferre into the highe Court
of parliament a statute by learned advise penned, in
partes agreeable to the former Commyssion, qualified accordinge
to all good conscience, and not disferringe from the sincere
meaninge of the Common lawes, or otherwyse to order that
a newe Commyssion may be by her ma[ties] Royall prerogative
apointed for the determyninge of the causes of y[e] oppressed
in the said Gaole, in such sorte as the Court of Chancerie
it selfe wolde order, had yo[u]r poore Orato[u]rs abilitie to pursue
their Just plaint in y[e] Courte. And yo[u]r poore Orato[u]rs
who are otherwyse Remediless to reforme most grievous wronges,
on them by sleight & subtile devyses imposed, but like to
perishe in their myserable pryson, and their wyves and
children goe a begginge; shall accordinge to their bounden
Dutyes dailye pray to God for your ho[nor]: estate in all
healthe and happines longe to continue endure.

To the Right ho: Sr walter Mildmay,
knight, Chauncelor off the Queenes Ma[ties]
Courte off Eschequer: and off her Ma[ties] most
ho: privie Counsell.

In all humble manner besecheth yor hono. yor poore
suppl. the prysoners in her Ma[ties] Benche there
detayned. That where sins the supervision off her
Ma[ties] Commyssion, yor poore suppl. have caused by
learned advyse to be penned & drawen a most godlye
act and estatute for the wronginges off extreme wronge
imposed vpon yor poore suppl against all equitie, and
against the sincere meaninge off the common lawe, And
for the furtheringe off whiche to these poore persons
as mitely faver: wch hathe bene perused & thought
meete by dyvers worshipfull personages to passe,
tendinge also to the common weale off this lond.
Pleasethe it your hono. for God cause, and for as
muche as yor poore suppl have no other good meanes
to procure the said motion. To preffer the same
vnder yor honorable patronage to be well in the righte
highe Courte off parliament. And yor poore suppl
& dyvers othere in all posteritie shall be bounde to
pray for yor honorable estate.

[61   *c.* 1585 – 1589 (?)   see Commentary]

To the Right honorable Sir walter Mildemay,   1
knight, Chauncelor of the Queenes Maiesties
Courte of Eschequer and of her Maiesties most
honorable privie Counsell./.

In all humble manner besecheth your honor, your poore   5
suppliants the prysoners in her Maiesties Benche & fleete
deteyned./ That where since the suppression of her
Maiesties Commyssion, your poore suppliants have cawsed by
learned advyse to be penned & drawne a most godlye
act and estatute for the repressinge of extreme wronges   10
imposed vpon your poore suppliants against all equitie, and
against the sincere meaninge of the common lawe, And
for the sheweinge of reliefe to suche poore persons
as meriteth favor: wch hathe bene pervsed & thought
meete by dyvers worshipfull personages to passe;   15
tendinge also to the common ⟨wealth⟩ weale of this land./
Pleaseth it youre honor for Godes cawse, and for as
muche as your poore suppliants have no other good meanes
to procure the same moved. To prefer the same
vnder your honorable patronage to be redd in the presente   20
high Courte of parliament. And your poore suppliants
& divers others in all posterities shall be bounde to
pray for your honorable estate./

[62   9 July 1582   see Commentary]

Elizabeth Regina./.   By the Queene: 1
Trustie and welbeloved we greete you well, where as
william Poole gentleman, lately indicted, arrayned & condempned
for a robberye commytted by hym and others in our Countie
of Surrey, remayneth yet by repryve in our Gaole at the   5
Whyte Lyon in Southwarke in the said Countie vnder your
charges; We let you wytt that for certeyne consi =
derations movinge vs, we are pleased: that in case he can
and doe put in good surties wth sufficient bonde vpon your
consyderations to our vse, that he shall departe out of   10
this our realme and dominions wthin fyftene dayes then
next followinge, and shall not retorne into the same here =
after wthout our speciall pardon; you shall then after suche
bonde put in, discharge him (for any thinge towardes vs, or
our lawes for the said Fellonye) & set him to his full libertie,   15
yt he may then departe as banished./ The said condempnation
& Iudgment therevpon given or not gyven, or any other thinge tou =
chinge the same, in any wyse notwthstandinge; wth the wch we doe
dispence by these our speciall letteres, wch shall be to you the
Sheryffe, & to the keeper of our said Gaole sufficient warrant   20
& discharge in this behalffe. And for yt these our letters are
to remayne wth you ye Sheryff, they may be recorded, and the
constat yereof shall be to the said keeper of yt Gaile, as suffici –
ent warrant as this Originall./ Geven vnder our Signett
at our Mannor of Grenewich ye .9. day of Iulij .1582. In   25
the .24. yere of our Reigne./   *Concordat cum orig*:
    To our trustie & welbeloved the Sheryffe of our countie
    of Surrey, & to the keeper of our Gaile at the whyte
    Lyon in the Borough of Southwarke in the said countie
    & to either of them./.   30

Elizabeth Regina ./.   By the Queene:

Trustie and welbeloved we greete you well, wheras at
wikin Poole gent, lately indicted, arrayned & condempned
for a robbery commytted by hym and others in our Countie
of Surrey, remayneth yet by reprieve in our Gaole at the
white Lyon in Southwarke in the said Countie vnder yo'r
charge; We lett you witt that for certeyne considerations mooving vs, we are pleased: that in case he can
and doe pvtt in good suretie/w'th sufficient bonds vpon yo'r
consyderations to our vse, that he shall departe out of
this our realme and dominions w'thin fystene dayes then
next followinge, and shall not returne into the same hereafter w'thout our speciall pdon; you shall then after suche
bonds putt in, discharge hym (for any thinge towardes vs, or
our lawes for the said ffellonye) & sett hym to his full libertie,
yt he may then depte as banished. The said condempnation
& Iudgm't thereupon given or not gyven, or any other thinges ton-
chinge the same, in any wyse notw'thstandinge; w'th thy w'th we doe
dispence by these our speciall lres, w'ch shall be to you the
Sheryffe, & to the keeper of our said Gaole sufficient warrant
& discharge in this behalffe. And for y't these our lettres are
to remayne w'th you i'th' Sheryff, they may be recorded, and the
constat thoff shall be to the said keeper of y't Gaile, as sufficient warrant as this originall. / Geven vnder our Signett
at our Manno'r of Greenwich the 9. day of Iuly. 1582. In
the 24. yere of our Raigne. /
                                        Concordat cu orig:

To our trustie & welbeloved the Sheryffe of o'r countie
of Surrey, & to the keep of our Gaile at the white
Lyon in the Borough of Southwarke in the said countie
& to either of them. /

Pinchback: youre vnciuill seekings to waye twealt in the streete
vppon aduantage, muche confirmed the opinion J had off thee.
Nevertheles, bycause J haue promysed to answere thee in the
fielde, wether J thinke thou wilt neuer challenge mee, J
thought good to let thee knowe, that J meane this present
thursday morninge betwene 8. & 9. off the clocke, to ryde
my horsse in the fielde neer adioyninge to clarkenwell,
wether iff thou comest like a gentlema, J will be contented
to make thee for one, & answere to what soeuer thou haste to
say to mee; J had many waes bad to defenr the matter wh
yesterday thou wouldst haue vrged me to, without the wch J
coulde not haue endured thy vnsemly brablinges, the one wab
the consideration off the wronge J shoulde haue done my self
by drawinge my self and my brother wch wer onely then
knowest J was acompanied Jnto thy danger, and suche ab
followed thee, thou knowest thy self the number, and thou
wert bolde vppon the odde, wch wab so great, considringe
the cabe J wab in my self, ab the worlde wolde haue con=
demned mee off great follye, iff J had serued ye oportunitie
And yet thou knowst J vsed no base meanes; J sawe the
base manner off vetysinge wch thou vsest in the fielde.
(whereby thou sometymes cuttest mens fingers) will be a cause
that our fightinge will be ridiculous, & in vaine. Wherefore
J exceedinglye desyre that we were shutt together in some
chamber or tennyscourte, where J might easely ouertake the
This may be done, yff thou wilt; and we may ab well be
turned by a frend off either syde, into suche a place, ab into
the fielde; My rapier is scarce a yearde and a quarter long
from the pointe to ye pommell; yff thou be a gentlema seke no
aduantage. |

[63]

Chuetes Challenge to Pinchback 1

Pinchback: youre vncivill seekinge to rayse tumultes in the streetes
vppon advantage, muche confirmes the opinion I had of thee.
Nevertheles, bycause I have promysed to answere the in the
fielde, whether I thinke thou wilt never challenge mee, I 5
thought good to let the knowe, that I meane this present
thursday morninge betwene .8. & .9. of the clocke, to ryde
my horsse in the fieldes nere adioyninge to clarkenwell,
whether if thou commest like a gentleman, I will be contented
to take the for one, & answere to whatsoever thou haste to 10
say to mee, I had many reasons to deferr the matter wch
yesterday thou woldest have vrged me to, wthout the wch I
coulde not have endured thy ruffenly bravinge, the one was
the consideration of the wronge I shoulde have done my self
by drawinge my self and my brother, (wth whom only thou 15
knowest I was accompanied) into thy daunger, and suche as
followed thee, thou knowest thy self the nomber, and thou
wert bolde vppon the Oddes, wch was so great, consideringe
the case I was in my self, as the worlde wolde have con =
dempned mee of great follye, if I had served your oportunitie, 20
And yet thou knowst I vsed no base meanes; I feare thy
base manner of retyringe wch thou vsest in the fielde./
(wherby thou sometymes cuttest mens fingers) will be a cause
that our fightinge will be ridiculous, & in vaine. Wherefore
I exceedinglye desyer that we were shutt together in some 25
chamber or Tennyscourte, where I might easely overtake thee,
This may be done, yf thou wilt; and we may as well be
turned by a frend of either syde, into suche a place, as into
the fielde; My Rapier is scarce a yeard and a quarter long
from the pointe to ye pommell; yf thou be a gentleman seeke no 30
advantage./.

f. 43r

[64]

To Chute the Cabbidgeface: alias   1
great lippes: at Clarkenwell:/

Base Chute; more base then any birthe can well afforde, I
have receyved a laborinth of wrytinge, wch shewes a Con =
sumption of thy wyttes, thy excuse yesterday, was thy weake =   5
nes by reason of thy longe sicknes; Now thou hast written
a letter wthout either head or foote, wth some raylinge termes,
wch thou shalt ⟨fi.de⟩ finde contrarie, I am sorie it is my
hard fortune to happen on suche a fellow as is accounted
a foole, and called by the name of Cabbidge face; Chute,   10
at the tyme when thou didst me wronge, I reputed thee
a great gentleman, and now findinge the otherwise, & hearing
the worldes esteeme; I value thee as a drunkard, or a fellow
that had surfetted wth extreeme runnes; Therfore beinge
aforehand wth suche a Coward: I quitt my self of all   15
quarrells wth thee./ Thus fearinge thou wilt consume
thy self wth prayers that thou hast receyved so gentle
an answere, I leave: vowinge never to thinke of thee, before
thou gyvest me some other childishe occasion./.

To Chute the Cabbidgeface: alias
    great lippes: at Clarkenwell:

Base Chute; now base there any bridge can well afforde, I
have receyved a labarinte off writinges, which shewed a Con=
sumption off thy wytte, the which spronge yesterday, was thy weake=
nes by reason off thy longe sicknes; Now thou hast written
a letter without either head or foote, with some raylinge termes,
which thou shalt finde contraried; I am sorie it is my
hard fortune to happen on suche a fellow as is accompted
a foole, and called by the name off Cabbidge face; Chute,
at the tyme when thou didst me wronge, I reputed thee
a great gentleman, and now findinge thee otherwise, & hearinge
thy wordes esteeme; I value thee as a drunkard, or a fellow
that had surfotted with extreame wines; Therefore beinge
afowreand with suche a Coward: I quitt my selfe off all
quarrells with thee./ These hearinge thou wilt consume
thy selfe with prayeinge that thou hast receyved so gentle
an answere; I leave: havinge never to thinke off thee, before
thou gyvest me some other childishe occasion./

Sr. The noble discharge you have made of that trust reposed
in you by the last Lo: Cobham, assures me that those poore
fatherlesse infants lefte to the goodnes of yor Courteous,
shall fynde that good, that their Noble Grandfather intended
towardes them. / I am altogether ignorant how their state
standes: but am sure they are lefte upon my handes, whose
good dependes onlie on his Ma:ties favor. / And therfore would
be glad if their were any thinge for their good to understand
it before my goinge to ye Courte. / If your leysure would
afforde a poore distressed widow so muche favor, as to
make a Jorney hether, that I might have some conference
with you aboute their busynesse before my goinge, I would
holde my selfe especyally bounde unto you; But if yor
busynes will not geve you leave to afforde me that favour
I would make a Jorney of purpose to come to you to yor howse,
And will holde no travailes to hard, that may yeild those
poore distressed orphanes any good or comforte. Therfore
my request is that I may have some answere from you,
how I shall direct my selfe in these busynesses, by whom
I am resolved resolie to be guyded, and will rest ever in
any thinge I may at yor discretion to be directed. /.

f. 43v

[65   after 5 December 1603 – before 14 June 1610 (?)   see Commentary]

Sir The noble discharge you have made of the trust reposed   1
in you by the last Lord Cobham, assures me that those poore
fatherlesse infantes lefte to the goodnes of your Conscience,
shall fynde that good, that their Noble Graundfather intended
towardes them./ I am altogether ignorant how their state   5
standes; but am sure they are lefte vpon my handes, whose
good dependes onlie on his Maiesties favor./ And therfore would
be glad if their were any thinge for their good to vnderstand
it before my goinge to ye Courte./ Yf youre leysure would
affoorde a poore distressed wydow so muche favour, as to   10
make a Iourney hether, that I might have some conference
wth you aboute their busynesse before my goinge, I would
holde myself especyally bounde vnto you; But yf your
busynes will not gyve you leave to affoorde me that favour,
I would make a Iourney of purpose to come to you to your howse,   15
And will holde no travailes to hard, that may yeild these
poore distressed orphanes any good or comforte./ Therfore
my request is that I may have some answere from you,
how I shall direct my self in these busynesses, by whom
I am resolved wholie to be guyded, and will rest ever in   20
any thinge I may at your discretion to be directed./.

f. 44r

[66   after 14 June 1610 (?)   see Commentary]

To the Kinge./   1

Most humbly besecheth your highnes: That whereas it
hathe ⟨pleasethd⟩ pleased youre Maiestie of youre meere grace
longe since: to pronounce pardon and forgyvenesse of my
husbandes offence; it may now stand wth youre highe –   5
pleasure and Clemencie to Commaunde, that those gratious
woordes may not now loose their vertue by any new interpre =
tacion; nor my husband the fruyte of your Mercie, where =
vpon he onlye dependes./ Wch I most humbly even in the
bitternesse of my harte beseech of your Maiestie in considera =   10
tion of my poore Children, In whom the clearenesse of
my Fathers howse (that never offended) is like to be
stayned if your Maiestie relieve not, and their Innocencie –
punyshed who are not yet able to vnderstand the mis =
fortune of their parentes./ And I wth my poore children   15
shall daily pray as we are bounde for the longe lyfe of
your excellent Maiestie./

To the Kinge

Most humbly besecheth yo[ur] Highnes: That whereas it
hath pleased your Ma[jes]tie: of your meere grace
longe since: to pronounce pardon and forgyvenesse of my
husbande offence; it may now stand w[i]th your Highe[nes]
pleasure and Clemencie to Commaunde, that those gratious
woordes may not now loose their vertue by any new interpre=
tacion; nor my husband the forfeiture of yo[ur] Mercie, where=
upon he onlye depende./ W[hi]ch I most humbly even in the
bitternesse of my harte besech of yo[ur] Ma[jes]tie: in considera=
tion of my poore Children, (in whome the cleavenesse of
my [ ] howse (that never offended) is like to be
stayned if yo[ur] Ma[jes]tie wolieth not, and their Innocencie
punnyshed who are not yet able to understand the mis=
fortune of their parents./ And I w[i]th my poore children
shall daily pray as we are bounde for the longe life of
yo[ur] excellent Ma[jes]tie./

Most Royall, and most Sacred Queene,

Vouchesafe to read, or lend but yor Eare to these sorowfull
lynes, and heare the most wretched and wofull estate; off her
that lyvinge, perpetuallye dyes; by ffamyne, by want, and all
other extreames, wch a mercyless husband can inflict vpon me,
and never ceases nott to his endlesse crueltie; who by his
money, his ffrende, his meanes, and his never ceasinge ma=
lice: consumes me, tormente me, and starves me to death;
Suborninge false wytnesses, ffearinge my Neighbors, and
thwateninge my ffrende; And then wth his Countenance,
and wth his crueltie, oppresseth all those y^t wolde ayde
or relieve me; feared me Debyne most Gratious
Ladie, even out off yor ever accustomed pitie: but onely y^e
Justice wch all your good subiecte enioys by yours goodnyss.
My greate Calamities exceede all others; My wronges are
gryshous, my grieffe intollerable; I wryte that is true,
iff I prove not all this that is heare vnder wrytten,
let me dye in disgrace an example to all that lyve at
this day, or shall lyve hereafter, and never beholde your
most gracious Empresse or gladsome Countenance;
Read then, O Read most gracious Ladie; Or ells I perissh,
I starve, and dye; for want off Justice;

[67]

       Most Royall, and Most Sacred Queene   1
Vouchesafe to read, or lend but your Eare to these sorowfull
lynes, and heare the most wretched and wofull estate; of her
that lyvinge, perpetuallye dyes; by Famyne, by want, and all
other extreemes, wch a mercilesse husband can inflict vpon me,   5
and never gyves ende to his endlesse crueltie./ who by his –
money, his Frendes, his meanes, and his never ceasinge ma =
lice: confoundes me, tormentes me, and starves me to death;
Suborninge falce wytnesses, Fearinge my Neighboures, and
threateninge my Frendes; And thus wth his Countenaunce,   10
and wth his Crueltie, oppresseth all those yt woulde ayde
or relieve me; Afforde me devyne & most Gratious –
Ladie, even out of your ever accustomed pittie: but onlye yt
Iustice wch all youre good subiectes enioye by youre goodnesse.
My greate Calamities exceede all others; My wronges are   15
grievous, my griefes intollerable./ I wryte that is true,
if I prove not all this that is heere vnder wrytten,
let me dye in disgrace an example to all that lyve at
this day, or shall lyve hereafter, and never beholde youre
most gratious Sunshyne or gladsome Countenaunce./.   20
Read then, O Read most gratious Ladie: Or els I perishe,
I starve, and dye: for want of Iustice./.

[68]

Mr T: It is alwayes my Fortune to loose my frendes   1
wth my best deservinges, and your straunge construction of my kinde
endevores, hathe lefte me to thinke of your muche vnkindenes./ I
have byd the brunt and borne the burthen, onlie for the safetie
of youre reputation./ and I finde so small regarde of my love,   5
that you are content to increase the Loade, & make it heavier
then it was before; The fault was not myne, but the penaunce
is myne, if I must endure so many disgraces, suche travell and
paines, wth suche a charge; as I wolde not againe vndertake
the like for any man lyvinge, or any mans recompence./ The charge,   10
howsoever you may slight or put over wth a shew of carelessenes,
or a distrust yt it can be no suche as I have delyuered, yet (besides
the due proofes that shall make it apeare) youre owne reason
me thinkes should tell you plainly: that so many Sessions, and
so many weekes, & so many daies: And so many parsons of   15
the best, and the worst, as have bene pertakers, parties, or dea =
lers, since this begonne; could not be Maintainde wth a matter of
nothinge; You tolde me last day you were alwayes my frend,
and so I esteemde you in the best degree: otherwyse you should
have pardonde me for entringe into so vnhandsome a busynes./   20
Yf you had no more tryall of my frendship but this, it might
suffice to shew yt I lov'd you, consyderinge your absence, youre
vncertain returne (whether ever or never) and my extreemes so
sure and certaine in severall sortes./
     As we have bene frendes, so I wishe the continuance of our   25
frendship; if it must not be soe, you gyve me occasion to thinke
what is meete, and vse my discretion.
     You bobde me thryse when I saw you last; First, yt you
founde not your money in the streetes; Second, that I brought

Mr Ste: It is alwayes my fortune to loose my paine
wth my best deservinge, and yor strange construction off my kinde
endevor, rather leste me to thinke off yor muche unkindenes. I
have byd the brunt and borne the burthen, onlie for the safetie
off youre reputation. and I finde so small regarde off my labor,
that you are content to increase the loade, & make it heavier
then it was before; The fault was not myne, but the penaunce
is myne, iff I must endure so many disgraces, suche travell and
paines, wth suche a charge; as I wolde not againe undertake
the like for any man lyvinge, or any mans recompense. This charge,
how sever you may sleight or put over wth a shew off carelesnes,
or a distrust yt it can be no suche as I have deserved, yet (besides
the due proofes that shall make it apparent) youre owne reason
me thinkes sould tell you plainly: that so many Officiers, and
so many workes, & so many dawes: And so many parsons off
the best, and the worst, as have bene pertakers, paide, or dea=
led, since their begonne; could not be Maintainde wth a matter off
nothinge; you tolde me last day you were alwayes my frend,
and so I esteemde you in the best degree: otherwyse you sould
have pledde me for entringe into so roughandsome a busynes.
Iff you had no more tryall off my frendshipp but this, it might
suffice to shew yt I lovd you, consideringe yor absence, youre
uncertaine whence (wyether over or never) and my returne so
sure and certaine in severall sortes.

As we have bene frendes, so I wishe the continuance off our
frendshipp; iff it must not be so, you gyve me occasion to thinke
what is mete, and use my discretion.

You bode me thryse when I saw you last; ffirst, yt you
founde not yor money in the stocke; Second, that I brought

you first wearyed was wth my Importunities, and then the,
that you knew not how to gyve any money, least they might call
you to yor oathes hereafter. These are but slender and Idle
pollicies, to stop my demandes & leave me in the lappes for yor
owne proper causes. The kyndest brother wolde hardly endure
& suffer so muche as my selfe hathe done, and onlie for you
& the love I bore you. The trust frend could have done
no better, nor more then my selfe, the worlde can wyttnesse.
ffor all the extremities, labours, & paines, disgraces, & charges;
I have thus sustained; I finde no requitall nor thanke at all;
you stryve to acquite yor selfe off the charge, & care not how
heavy it lyes upon me. Iff this be all I must hope or looke
for, then it behoves me to looke to my selfe, and so I wyll.

My Lo: out off the love I beare to some off yor frends,
I have a care off yor preservation. I wolde wisshe you, as you
tender yor lyfe to devyse some excuse to shyfte off yor attendance
at the parliament; ffor God and man hathe concurred to
punysshe the wickednes off this tyme; And thinke not
slightlie off this advertisement, but retyre yor selfe into the
countrey where you may expect the event in saftie. ffor
thowgh there be no apparance off any styrre, yet I say they
shall receyve a terrible blowe this parliament, and they
shall not see who hurt them. This councell is not to
be contempned, because it may doe you good, and it can
doe you no harme. ffor the danger is past so soone
as you burne the letter; And I hope God will give
you the grace to make good use off it, to whose holie
protection I commytt you.

you first where she was wth my Importunities, and Thirdlye, 30
that you knewe not how to gyve any money, least they might call
you to your Oathe hereafter; These are but slender and Idle
pollicies, to stop my demaundes & leave me in the lappes for your
owne proper cawses./ The kyndest brother wolde hardly endure
& suffer so muche as my self hathe done, and onlie for you 35
& the love I bore you./ The truest frend could have done
no better, nor more then my self, the worlde can wyttnesse./
For all the extremities, laboure, & paines, disgraces, & charges;
I have thus sustainde; I finde no requitall nor thankes at all;
You stryve to acquite your self of the charge, & care not how 40
heavy it lye vpon me./ Yf this be all I must hope or looke
for, then it behoves me to looke to my self, and so I rest./.

[69   26 October 1605   see Commentary]

My Lord: out of the love I beare ⟨you⟩ to some of your Frendes, 1
I have a care of your preservation. I wolde wishe you, as you
tender your lyfe to devise some excuse to shyfte of your attendance
at the parliament; For god and man hathe concurred to
punyshe the wickednes of this tyme; And thinke not – 5
slightlie of this advertisement, but retyre your self into the
Countrey where you may expect the event in safetie. For
though there be no apparance of any styrre, yet I say they
shall receyve a terrible blowe this parliament, and they
shall not see who hurt them. This councell is not to 10
be contempned, bycause it may doe you good, and it can
do you no harme. For the daunger is past so soone
as you burne the letter, And I hope God will give
you the grace to make good vse of it, to whose holie
protection I commytt you./. 15

[70   1604   see Commentary]

The Great Turkes lettre to the   1
Emperor of Germanye:/.1604./
Wee by the grace of God, Welbeloved in heaven, and Lord of ye
Earthe: The most mightie Cæsar of all Cæsars; Invincible God
of the Earthe, Great Souldan of Babilon, kinge of Egipt, –   5
Europe and Asia: Great Souldan of Armenia, Lord of the
pretious pearles of India; Greatest helper of the Goddes./ Prince
from Turkie to the greatest Mountaines in Asia; Great kinge of
all kinges: from the East to the west: from the North to ye South.
keeper of the Paradice of the great god Mahomett; destroyer   10
& persecutor of the Christians and all yt enoiye that name./.
Emperor & wthholder of the Sepulchre of yt hanged God
at Ierusalem, and Trivmphant over the worlde./
We shewe to thee Rodulphus all my Fortunes & the overthrowe
of all thy kingdomes & dominions./ And bycause thou dost ascribe 15
to the title of the kingdome of hungarie; We sweare by our
Crowne, that we shall visitt the in most terrible manner; and
this know for certaine, that wth the Invincible power of our –
kingdomes; & wth many hundred thowsandes of foote & horssemen,
wth ⟨t.r⟩ Turkes, Armenians, & all sortes of peoples, And wth   20
so great power & strength, as neither thou nor any of thy Fathers
have ever heard of or seene the like at any tyme./ In Vienna &
Austria thy principall Iles, we shall chase the, And by our
Tyranny so oppresse the and the Inhabitantes therof: And then
see if yt God that thou beleevest in can either helpe or save thee./ 25
We shall destroye thee and all thy assistantes on earthe, and by
the force of our all conqueringe Arme overthrow & roote the
out from the face of the earthe; And that wth most cruellest
& vylest death: and wth all tortures & tormentes that can
be devysed, thee we shall slea & put in Oyle, and also   30

The Great Turke's lre to the
Emperor of Germanye :/. 1604 ./

Wee by the grace off God, Welbeloved in heaven, and lord off ye
Earthe: The most mightie Cæsar off all Cæsars; Invincible God
off the Earthe, Great Souldan off Babilon, kinge off Egipt, ~
Europe and Asia: Great Souldan off Armenia, lord off the
pretiouse pearles off India; Greatest Honor off the Goddes; / Prince
from Turkie to the greatest Mountaines in Asia; Great kinge off
all kinges: from the East to the West: from the North to ye Southe
keeper off the Paradise off the great god Mahomett; destroyer
& persecutor off the Christians and all ye enioye that name . /.
Emperor & recover off the Sepulchre off ye hanged God
att Jerusalem, and Triumphant over the worlde. /

We sweare to thee Rodulphus all my fortunes & the overthrowe
off all thy kingdomes & Dominions. / And bycause thou doste ascribe
to the title off the kingdome off Hungarie; We sweare by our
Crowne, that we shall visitt thee in most terrible manner; and
this know for certaine, that nott thy Invincible power off our ~
kingdomes; & nott many hundred thousandes off foote & horsmen,
nott but Turkes, Armenians, & all sortes off peoples, And nott
so great power & strength, as neither thou nor any off thy fathers
have ever heard off or seene the like at any tyme. In Vienna &
Austria thy principall flee, we shall feast thee, And by our
Tyranny so oppresse thee and the Inhabitants thereof: And then
see iff thy God that thou beleevest in can either helpe or save thee. /
We shall destroye thee and all thy assistante on earthe, and by
the force off our all conqueringe Name overthrow & roote thee
out from the face off the earthe; And that nott most cruelly
& by lost death: and nott all fortunes & tormente that can
be devysed, thee we shall swear put in Oyle, and also

thy Infante we shall slay like wretches. / This we advertise
thee, that thou and all thy Miserable captaines may beware
and foresee your miserie endure. By cause we have fynallye
determyned & concluded to w[i]th our Power and Empyre.
Even at Constantinople, out of the w[i]ch we spoiled
thy forefathers, and cruelly slayed their wyves and
Children, and ravisht their Maides and widowes, to
the fullfillinge of our lustes; / Of our Nativitie
the .28. yeer: And of our Raigne. 2. /.

The copie of a letter wrytten
from the State of Genoa, to y[e]
State of Venice; in answere to
one of theirs. /.

We have receyved your hignes letter, w[i]ch hath sownded
in to a divers effect from that you opposed at our
hande

thy Infantes we shall slay like whelpes./ This we advertise
thee, that thou and all thy Miserable captaines may beware
and foresee your wretchednes. Bycause we have fynallye
determynde & concluded so wth our Power and Empyre./
Gyven at Constantinople, out of the wch We exiled   35
thy Forefathers, and cruelly slayed their wyves and
Children, and ravished their Maides and Wydowes, to
the fullfillinge of our lustes;/   Off our Nativitie
the .28. yere: And of our Raigne. 2./.

[71]

         The copie of ⟨al.t⟩ a letter wrytten   1
         From the State of Genoa, to ye
         State of *Venice*: in answere to
         one of theirs./.

We have receyved your highnes letter, wch hath occasioned   5
in vs a divers effect from that you expected at our
handes

f. 47r

[72   June 1606   see Commentary]

The Copie of a letter wrytten from the   1
State of Genoa, to the State of Venice:
In answere to one of theirs:/
We have receyved your highnes letter, wch hathe occasioned
in vs a divers effect from that you expected at our handes;   5
For our yeildinge to the Popes desyer in revokinge the decrees
made against our Ambassadores, dothe not onlie not turne
to our preiudice, but is muche rather an argument of ye dignitie
of our Commonwealth, and a disgrace to all those who in
like case have bene repugnant to the pious intention of his holines./   10
We learn out of Stories, that your predicessores have at
some tymes defended the Authoritie of the Pope, but that
at other tymes they have resisted it, and have bene proclaymed
rebells against that holie Chaire; But we inherite this
glorie, not onlie to have bene defendours of the Catholike   15
fa+i+the, in the East and in the west, against Turkes, Moores,
& Sarazens; but alwayes to have defended Popes against
the Iuiuries of other Potentates, even Emperores: wthout
ever incurringe the offence of contumacye against their Sacred
dignitie./ Your State hathe alwayes kept her self   20
a *Virgine*, as touchinge the dominion of Straungers, albeit
many tymes she hathe bene in great hazard of fallinge –
into their handes; but ours hathe ever kept her Virginitie in
the *Catholike*, even till this day, pursuynge at all tymes wth
constant zeale the heretiques and enemyes of the holy Churche.   25
Wch at this present is not to be founde in your Cittie, –
beinge the receptacle of divers secktes and Religions./

The Copie off a letter wrytten from the
State off Genoa, to the State off Venice:
In answere to one off theirs:

We have receyved yo' Highnes letter, w'h hathe occasioned
in vs a divers effect from that you expected at our handes;
ffor our yeildinge to the Popes desyer, in wrekinge the wronge
made against our Ambassador, dothe not onlie not turne
to our preiudice, but is mutche rather an augmment off y' dignitie
off our Common wealthe, and a disgrace to all those who in
like case have bene repugnant to the pious intention off His Holines.
We learne out off Stories, that yo' predicessors have at
some tymes defended the Authoritie off the Pope, but that
at other tymes they have resisted it, and have bene proclaymed
rebells against that holie Chaire; But we inspairt this
glorie, not onlie to have bene defendours off the Catholike
faithe, in the East and in the west, against Turkes, Moores,
& Sarazens; but alwayes to have defended Popes against
the enimies off other Potentates, vea Emperours: w'h out
ever incurringe the offence off contumacy against their Sacred
Dignitie.   yo' State hathe alwayes kept her selfe
a Virgine, as touchinge the dominion off Strangers; albeit
many tymes she hathe bene in great hazard off fallinge
into their handes; but ours hathe ever kept her virginitie in
the Catholike, even till this day, pursuinge at all tymes w'h
constant scale the Heretiques and enimies off the holy Churche.
w'h at this present is not to be founde in yo' Cittie,
beinge the receptacle off divers Sectes and Religions.

Our weonblick lyves under the protection of the kings Ca=
tholique, without payinge him any tributs or donatives benett
or manifest; But you dependest upon a barbarous king,
unto whom, and to whose Ministers we know, that under
the name of a Donative you disbursse a Tribute of great
quantitie of Gold; and yet for all that when they ~
summone takes him, he makes warrs upon you and ill
intreatest your Ambassadors, which his Catholique Ma{tie}
dothe not to omd. / Your Commonwealth thinkes it an
honor not to yield one jott unto the Pope, yea even in ~
matters due unto him; And we judges it a greater repu=
tation for us to yield to the Successour of St Peter not
onlie his owne, but ours also; not havings regarde to this
present Pope (although of himself he meritesse much,
aswell for his holie intention & the integritie of his life,
as for the admirable meanes whereby he was advanced
to this degree) but onlie to the dignitie & person of him,
to whom he is Lieutenant. / The kings Catholique ~
hath always had a good inclination to the peace of Italie, and
the preservation of our State: but if any Minister hath
passed the boundes of his Ma{tie} intentions, we have bene
informed y it was not the purpose of his Catholique Ma{tie}:
and yet for all that, in differences arysings betwene us and
the State of Millan we have shewed bothe courage & love,
aswell in deedes as in wordes; But your Commonwealth with
threats & violence hath made shew of greater bravado against
the Church, then we did against those Ministers of his
Catholique Ma{tie}; in the controversie betwene us and the State

Our republique lyves vnder the protection of the kinge Ca =
tholique, wthout payinge him any tribute or donative secrett   30
or manifest; But youres dependeth vpon a barbarous kinge,
vnto whom, and to whose Ministers we know, that vnder
the name of a donative you disbursse a Tribute of great
quantitie of Golde; and yet for all that ⟨wth⟩ when the –
humoure takes him, he makes Warr vpon you and ill   35
intreateth your Ambassadores, wch his Catholique Maiestie
dothe not to ours./ Your Commonwealth thinkes it an
honor not to yeild one Iott vnto the Pope, yea even in –
matters due vnto him; And we Iudge it a greater repu =
tation for vs to yeild to the Successour of St Peter not   40
onlie his owne, but ours also; not havinge regarde to this
present Pope (although of himself he meriteth muche,
aswell for his holie Intention & the integritie of his life,
as for the admirable meanes whereby he was advaunced
to this degree) but onlie to the dignitie & person of him,   45
to whom he is *Lieutenant*./ The kinge Catholique –
hathe alwayes had a good inclination to the peace of Italie, and
the preservation of our State: but if any Minister hathe
passed the boundes of his Maiesties intentions, we have bene
informed yt it was not the purpose of his Catholique Maiestie   50
and yet for all that, in differences arysinge betwene vs and
the State of *Millan* we have shewed bothe courage & teeth,
aswell in deedes as in wordes; But your Commonwelth wth
threates & violence hathe made shewe of greater braverie against
the Churche, then we dyd against those Ministers of his   55
Catholique Maiestie in the controversie betwene vs and the State

of *Millan*./ That wch your Republique esteemes an honor, to
contend wth the Pope: We holde as a disgrace; and contrariwise
we thinke our selues to be the true Successores and Imitatours
of our Auncestores, when we defend his holines wth our bodies   60
and wth our goodes;/ Your Commonwelth makes profession of
resistinge his holines: and we have resolved to offer against them
that goe about to smoother &·deface his authoritie, bothe our money
and our lyves./   Your State makes great reckoninge of
peace and frendship wth the Turke: and wee doe more esteeme   65
the Amitie of the Vicar of Christ./ The letter wrytten
by your highnes reprehendeth vs of basenes in havinge so easelye
consented to the Pope: And wee esteeme it an indignitie in
your commonwelth to resist the Sea Apostolike in matters so
Iust./   Our Republique dothe muche reverence Ecclesi =   70
asticall excommunications and Interdictes, bicause that Catholique
Faithe wch was sowen amonge our Auncestores, the same have we
always conserved in her puritie: wch we wolde also might be –
observed in your State, not forgettinge the great preiudice bothe
⟨ter.⟩ temporall & Spirituall wch at other tymes you have sustained   75
by means of Papall excommunications and Interdictes./ Wee
in difficulties yt concerne Iurisdiction Ecclesiasticall, vse not to
aske the advise of wicked men and Apostataes who counsell
accordinge to our sence; but of divines, to be reverenced bothe
for the puritie of their doctrine, & integritie of their conversation,   80
Nor will we arrogate to our Selves Superioritie over the
Ecclesiasticall Bushoppes of the Citties by vs possessed; –
bycause we do not acknowledge yt any Secular Prince may
Iustlie clayme any suche prehominence, but yt it is rather vsurped./

of Millan. | That wch your Republique esteemes an hon[or], to
contend wth the Pope: Wee holde as a disgrace; and contrariwise
wee thinke our selves to be the true Successors and Imitatours
of our Auncestors, when we defend his Holines wth our bodies
and wth our goodes; | yor Comonwealth makes profession of
resistinge his Holines: and wee have resolved to oppose against them
that goe about to smoother & deface his authoritie, bothe wth money
and our lyves. | yor State makes great workeinge of
peace and friendshipp wth the Turke: and wee doe more esteeme
the Amitie of the Vicar of Christ. | The letter written
by yor Highnes representeth us as Rashnes in havinge so rashlye
consented to the Pope: And wee esteeme it an indignitie in
yor Comonwealth to resist the Sea Apostolike in matters so
just. | Our Republique dothe muche reverence Ecclesi=
asticall excommunications and Interdictes, because that Catholique
faithe, wch was sowen amongst our Auncestors, the same have we
alwayes conserved in her puritie: wch we would also mought be
observed in yor State, not forgettinge the great miseries bothe
temporall & Spirituall wch at other tymes we have sustained
by meanes of Papall excommunications and Interdictes. | Wee
in difficulties & concerne jurisdiction Ecclesiasticall, use not to
aske the advise of wicked men and Apostates who counsell
accordinge to our sence; but of Bishops, to be reverenced bothe
for the puritie of their doctrine, & integritie of their conversation,
Nor will we arrogate to our selves Superioritie over the
Ecclesiasticall Bisshoppe of the Citties by us possessed; —
because we do not acknowledge that any Secular Prince may
justlie clayme any suche preheminence, but y^t it is rather to usurpe. |

And when their is an Apostolicall priviledge, we say not that the Pope hath no power to revoke it, when it is abusd, wch is an argument y no Seculer Prince hath any such authoritie of himselfe, but by deputacion; and must depend on him y first graunted it, if at least he have any graunt, and will not arrogate that as proper & personall to himselfe, wch is but of courtesie any doubtall. |

We know that in your present necessities, Popes have protected yor State against the violence of Infidells, and if Popes had not bene, other Princes had abandoned you; but their authoritie hath concluded leagues in yor State against yor enemyes; and yet you Ingratefull for suche benefytts, would make the worlde beleve, y you have no need of the Pope, but rather y he is in Italie an Opposite to yor State; And we on the other syde doe acknowledge as a singular benefitt, y our Italie alone hath wthin it the Papacie, being so muche greater then other Princes, by how muche the Soule is more excellent then the bodie, and the spirituall good then the Temporall. |

Our men goe traffickings all the worlde over, wch worlde consisteth not onlie in yor Dominions, and therefore whẽ yor territories are wantings unto them, they are not presently in London. |

It is a lesser ill to Venice and not to type ill rome well to others, then to Venice and to bringe others into the same errour. |

And therefore yor Highnes might have shoared the very tinges of y letter, since we doe not a whitt repent us to have rebuked our deawes against y Ambassador. | But we are iust greved to see yor Comonwealth so stiffe as not to condiscend to y iust desyre of his Beatitude, puttings in hazard for light cause to kindle in Italie a fyre unquenchable, & so dangerous & hurtfull as yor State must of necessitie call into yor service people of false religion and corrupt Consciences. |

And when their is an Apostolicall privilege, we say not   85
that the Pope hathe no power to revoke it, when it is abused,
wch is an argument yt no secular Prince hathe any such authoritie
of himself, but by deputacion; and must depend on him yt first
graunted it, if at least he have any graunt and will not arro =
gate that as proper & personall to himself, wch is but of curtesie   90
accydentall./ Wee know that in your vrgent Necessities,
Popes have protected your State against the Violence of
Infidells, and if Popes had not bene, other Princes had
abandoned you; but their authoritie hathe concluded leagues in
your Favour against your enemyes; and yet you Ingratefull for –   95
suche benefyttes wolde make the worlde beleve, yt you have no neede
of the Pope, but rather yt he is in Italie an Opposite to your
State; And wee ⟨the⟩ on the other syde doe acknowledge as a
singular benefitt, yt our Italie alone hathe wthin it the Papacie,
beinge so muche greater then other Princes, by how muche the Soule   100
is more excellent then the bodie, and the Spirituall good then the
Temporall./ Our men goe traffickinge all the worlde over,
wch worlde consisteth not onlie in your dominions, and therfore when
your territories are wantinge vnto them, they are not presently –
vndone./ It is a lesser evill to Erre and not to gyve ill   105
counsell to others, then to Erre and to bringe others into the same
errour./ And therfore your highnes might have spared the
wrytinge of yt letter, since we doe not a whitt repent vs to have
revoked our decrees against ye Ambassadores./ But we are Iustly
greeved to see your Commonwelth so stiffe as not to condiscend to ye   110
Iust desyer of his Beatitude, puttinge in hazard for light causes
to kindle in Italie a fyre vnquenchable, & so daungerous & hurtfull,
as your State must of necessitie call into your service people of
falce religion and corrupt Conscience./

[73   *c*. March – June 1608   see Commentary]

Sir I have not deserv'd what I suffer by your Austeritie, yf   1
the two or three lynes you crost, were spoken; My vttermost to sup =
presse them was enough for my discharge; To more then wch, no
promysse can be rackt by reason; I see not myne owne Plaies; Nor
carrie the Actors Tongues in my Mouthe; The action of ye mynde   5
is performance sufficient of any dewtie, before the greatest Authoritie
wherein I have quitted all your former favoures, And made them more
worthie then any you bestowe on outward observers; Yf the thrice
allowance of ye Counsaile for ye Presentment; have not weight –
enoughe to drawe youres after for the Presse; My Breath is a hope: 10
les Adition; Yf you say (for your Reason) you know not if more
then was spoken be now written no No; Nor can you know that,
if you had bothe the Copies; Not seeing the first at all: Or if
you had seene it presented, your Memorie could hardly confer wth
it so strictly in the Revisall, to descerne the Adition; My short   15
Reason therefore can not sounde your Severitie; Whosoever it were
yt first plaied the bitter Informer before the frenche Ambassador
for a matter so far from offence; And of so muche honor for his
Maister, as those two partes containe; performd it wth the Gall
of a Wulff, and not of a Man; And theise hartie, & secrett   20
vengeances taken for Crost, & Officious humers, are more Politiq
then Christian; Wch he that hates, will one day discover in ye op
Ruyne of their Auctores; And thoughe they be trifles: he yet laie
them in Ballance, (as they concerne Iustice, and bewray Appetites
to the greatest Tyrannye) wth the greatest; But how easely   25
soever Illiterate Aucthoritie settes vp his Bristles against Pover
Me thinkes youres (beinge accompanied wth learninge) should rebate ye
pointes of them: And soften the fiercenes of those rude Manners;
You know Sir, They are sparkes of the lowest Fier in Nature, that
flye out vppon weakenes, wth everie pufft of Power; I desier not,   30
you should drenche your hand in the least daunger for mee; And
therefore (wth entreatie of my Papers returne) I cease ever to
trooble you./.   By the poore subiect of your
                                       office for the present./

Sr, I haue not deserued, what I suffer by yor Austeritie; if
those two or three lynes you crost, were spoken; My vttermost to sup=
presse them was enough, for my dischardge; To more then soe, no
promyse can be racht by reason; I see not mynt owne Plaints; Nor
renew the Actors Tongues in my Mouth; The action of i mynde
is performance sufficient of any doutes, before the greatest Authorities;
wherwth I haue quitted all yor former fauor, And made them more
worthie then any you bestowe on outward obseruers; If the thirst
allowance of i Counsails for i Presentment; haue not weight
enough to drawe yor cares for the Prayse; My Breath is a fee=
ble Addition; If you say (for yor reason) (you know not if more
then was spoken be now rewritten no No; How can you know that,
if you had bothe the Copies; Not seeing the first at all; Or if
you had seene it presented, yor Memorie could hardly confer wth
it so strictly in the Retifall, to discerne the Addition; My short
Reason therefore can not sound yor Austeritie; Whosoeuer it was
i first placed the bitter Informer before the sweete Ambassador,
for a matter so farr from Offence, And of so much Honor for his
Maister, as those two partes containes; performd it wth the Gall
of a Wulfe, and not wth a Man; And these hastie, & somwhat
vngeniall taken for Zwrest, & Officious humors, are more Politiq
then Christian; wth He that hates, will one day discouer in i of
Anger of their Authors; And thoughe they be christes; he yet laies
them in Ballance, (as they concerne Justice, and bewray Hypocrites)
to the greatest Tyrannye wth the greatest; But how easely
soeuer Illiterate Authoritie settes vp his Bristles against Power,
Me thinke yor (being accompanied wth Learnings) should rebate i
pointes of them; And soften the fiercenes of those rude Manners;
you know Sr, They are sparkes of the lowest Fiers in Nature; that
flye out vppon weaknes, wth there puffe of Power; I desire not
you should droncke yor hand in the least danger for mee; And
therefore (wth outwatie of my Papers returne) I cease euer to
trouble you. /

By the poore subiect of yor
offent for the present. /

My lord:

You have fedd me so longe wth Hope, & emptie promisse,
that they have emptied in me all the portions yt belonge
to a gentleman, or a free man; To rassinye any more
Coles of yor Complement, wthout some fytt expression of
the spiritt borne wth me; were servile and Asinine; If
wth brothers iff yor Lo: intend to vtter yor greatnes, you
must chuse other shandors then myne to ffvstaine them;
I know his right vertuous & sacred Maiestie, made you
not greate, to so lyttle purpose; I have fytted yor Lo: wth
a Smyle, & have brought you many rither Smyles a farre off;
since the tyme is my poore, one, so more hand, hath bene
delayed by you; Though Charitie begins at a Mans
solff, it must yet extend to others: or els, it is no more
Charitie, but Solfelove; In wth fashionable fountains,
lett not yor hono drowne wth yor Person; Delayes that
racke and delusions, for wth you may more fustlye
degrade me, then looke I sold endure them; I hope
therfore yor Lo: will not that loosely vppe my longe
expectations the slipp, but wth some fytt observation
of yor words and Noblesse, present my dewtie to my
solff, And desorve it to yor sorties; wch (makinge
good what you have often assurde) shall more hono
you in me, and others; then all the dishonorable flatterie
you can vse to yor solff; And these intreatings of yor
Lo: to consider; I rest, at the Consideration
worked.

f. 49v

[74   after 24 March 1603   see Commentary]

My lord: 1
You have fedd me so longe wth Ayre, & emptie promises,
that they have emptied in me all the patience yt belonges
to a gentleman, or a free Man; To carrye any more –
Coles of your Complement, wthout some fytt expression of   5
the spiritt borne wth me; were servile and Asinine; In
wch burthens if your lordshippe intend to vtter your greatnes, you
must chuse other shoulders then myne to ⟨st⟩ sustaine them;
I know his right vertuouse & sacred Maiestie, made you
not greate, to so lyttle purpose; I have fytted your Lordshippe wth   10
a suyte, yt hathe brought you many riche suytes a farre of;
since the tyme yt my poore, one, (so nere hand) hathe bene
delayed by you; Though Charitie begins at a Mans
self, it must yet extend to others: or els, it is no more
Charitie, but selflove; In wch fashionable fountaine,   15
let not your honor drowne wth your Person; delayes thus
rackt, are delusions, for wch you may more Iustlye
degrade me, then looke I should endure them; I hope
therefore your Lordshippe will not thus losely gyve my longe
expectations the slipp, but wth some fytt observation   20
of your worde and Noblesse, prevent my dewtie to my
self, And deserue it to your service; wch (makinge
good what you have often assur'de) shall more honor
you in me, and others; then all the dishonorable flatteries
you can vse to your self; And thys intreatinge your   25
Lordshippe to consider; I rest, as the Consideration –
workes./.

[75   after 24 March 1603   see Commentary]

My Lord: 1
Your delayes have bene so longe vppon the racke, that
they now confesse them selues to be mere delusions;
and to Mocke me for +all+ my seriouse observance, is no –
requitall worthie +of+ your Noblesse; Nor can I be blam'de   5
if it enforce me to open my Mouthe so farre against
my hart, that your honor, wch I chusde above all
others to be the obiect of my love and service, be
now the turnd subiect of my Iust Imputations; Your
Lordshippe (by your Grace and greatnes wth our soveraigne)   10
hathe good meanes to settle your dignities, in the loves
of many Englishe knightes and gentlemen; wch I take
it was one of the endes for wch his highnes advanc't
you, But in steade of your deserved hartie favoures,
to gyve vs all (in your delusions) politique defiance,   15
were a contempt to greate for your greatnes; and a
defect too muche vnfytt for your Fortunes; And
be your Lordshippe assur'de, the observation of your worde,
and vse of your Eminence out of vertue, in the
deserved benefitt of others; will be a greater   20
good to you, then all the Imitated selflove you
can learne out of the fashion; wch intreatinge youre
good Lordshippe to consider:/ I rest as ye Consideration
workes./

My Lord:

Yo{u}r delayes haue bene so longe vppon the worke, that
they now confesse themselues to be meere Delusions;
and to Mocke me for my serious obseruance, is no
requitall worthie yo{u}r Nobleness. Now can I be blamed
iff it enforces me to open my mouthe so farre against
my forte, that yo{u}r honor, w{ch} I thinke aboue all
others to be the obiect off my loue and seruice, be
now the turned subiect off my Iust Imputations; yo{u}r
Lo: (by yo{u}r Grace and greatnes of our soueraigne)
hathe good meanes to settle yo{u}r Deputeis, in the loues
off many Englishe knightes and gentlemen; w{ch} I take
it was one off the endes for w{ch} H{is} Highnes advanc't
you, But insteade off yo{u}r deserued fauxte fauours,
to gyue toe all (in yo{u}r Delusions) politique distance,
were a contempt too great for yo{u}r Greatnes; and a
Defect too muche vnfytt for yo{u}r Statelines; And
be yo{u}r Lo: assurede, the obseruation off yo{u}r woorde,
and Deste off yo{u}r Eminence out off vertue, in the
Deserued benifitt off others; will be a greater
good to you, then all the Imitated selfloue you
can learne out off the fashion; w{ch} wishinge yo{u}r
good Lo: to consider:/ I wss ab{y} Consideration
worked. /

Brother, wheeras ith no lyttle griph, I see yor vnkindones,
and how you contend even ageinst nature to forgett him wch
bothe religion & reason comaundes you to love, I thought
good beinges free from either intreaties or perswasion,
to disburden my selfe of that, wch iff you were as you
should bee, might bee sufficient to make you pittie mee
though not helpe mee, The groundes of this difference
betweene you / and mee are onlie suggestions annext to
a willingnes to make any thinge knowe that tendes to my
disgrace, although I confesse I have highlie offended
God in abusinge his gratious provisions many and
sundrie wayes, sayinge me helpe even from strangers,
by whom I have had maintenaunce sins the death off my
father, whose goddes: God and yor owne conscience
knowes how they were disposed, but iff you can in glori=
fyinge yor selfe make relations how barely I have spent
my tyme, and what great fortunes I have neglected,
(though never any meanes or helpe proffred by you)
you thinke yor love is sufficiently showne; I can
truely avouche, I have taken far greater paines then ever
you did, first lyvinge in exile the space off .14.
yeares, in all wch tyme I was no whett chargeable
to my frinds, then after in Hungaria were I
served against the Turke, & then in Poland I
served .4. yeares: wch are testimonies off my no
vnwillingnes iff it had pleased God to advaunce mee,
when you remayninge at home wth lesse paines have
raysed yor selfe; But their is nothing makethe mee
faultie but my pouertie, nor any thinge sweetethe you

[76]

Brother, whereas wth no lyttle griefe, I see your vnkindenes,   1
and how you contend even wth nature to forgett him wch
bothe religion & reason commaundes you to love, I thought
good beeinge free from either intreatie or perswasion,
to disburden my self of that, wch if you were as you   5
should bee, might bee sufficient to make you pittie mee
though not help mee, The groundes of this difference
betweene you and mee are onlie suggestions annext to
a willingenes to make any thinge true that tendes to my
disgrace, although I confesse I have highlie offended   10
God in abusinge his gratious provisions many and
sundrie wayes raysinge me help even from straungers,
by whom I have had maintenaunce since the death of my
Father, whose goodes: God and your owne conscience –
knowes how they were disposed, but if you can in glori =   15
fyinge your self make relations how barely I have spent
my tyme, and what great fortunes I have neglected,
(though never any meanes or help proffred by you)
You thinke your love is sufficiently showne; I can
truely avouche, I have taken far greater paines then ever   20
you dyd, First lyvinge in exile the space of .i4.
yeeres, in all wch tyme I was no whytt chargeable
to my Frendes, then after in *Hungaria* where I
served against the Turkes, Then in Ireland I
served .4. yeeres: wch are testimonies of my no   25
vnwillingnes if it had pleased God to advaunce mee,
when you remayninge at home wth lesse paines have
raysed your self; But their is nothing maketh mee
faultie but my povertie, nor any thinge serveth you

better to finde fault then your prosperitie, but I pray you   30
tell mee, what were frendship if not shown in adversitie,
and how should brotherlie love shew it self better then
in affliction. God knowes what shadowes you blinde
the worlde wthall to cover your vnnaturall & vnworthie
disposition, Shewing your self more like Iacobb then   35
Ioseph, For the one did but hurt his brother wthout offence,
and the other did help his brethren having had cause
to the contrarie, but now it is no more *Homo Homini*,
but it is *frater fratri damon*, your high prysinge that
lyttle help I have receyved from you, hathe made me   40
a lyttle to vndervalue it, & puttes me in feare to come
further in your debt, wch no miserie shall ever compell me
to, and yet no crosse or adverse fortune shall ever
poyson my true and naturall love to you, but I will
be glad & reioyce to see you flourishe, wherfore thus   45
muche have I wrytten though to lyttle purpose, onlie
to satisfie my mynde, wch still perswades mee you are
my brother, wch name, although now a discreditt to you,
yet it may please God to bestow some vnexpected fortune
vpon me, And then I shall become it well Ionghe, till   50
wch tyme, I pray God to blesse bothe you and youres,
and blesse me once wth wealth, and then I shall be
sure of your love And so I rest./ .

better to finde fault then yo{r} prosperitie, but I pray you
tell mee, what newe frendshipp is not shewen in adversitie,
and how should brotherlie love shew it self better then
in afflictio. God knowes what shadowes you blinde
the worlde withall to color your vnnaturall & vnworthie
disposition, Esteeming yo{r} self more like Jacobb then
Josepp, for the one did hate his brother without offence
and the other did love his brethren having had cause
to the contrarie, but now it is no more Homo Homini,
but it is frater fratri damon, yo{r} high praysings that
lyttle Josepp I have received from you, have made me
a lyttle to vnderbalne it, & putte me in feare to come
further in yo{r} debt, w{ch} no miserie shall ever compell me
to, and yet no crosse or adverse fortune shall ever
poyson my true and naturall love to you, but I will
be glad & desyres to see you florissh, w{ch} before this
tymes have I written though to lyttle purpose, onlie
to satisfie my mynde, w{ch} still perswades mee you are
my brother, w{ch} name, although now a discredit to you,
yet it may please God to bestow some Vndeserved fortune
vpon me, And then I shall esteeme it worth honor, till
w{ch} tyme, I pray God to blesse bothe you and yours,
and blesse me once w{th} wealth, and then I shall be
sure of yo{r} love And so I rest ./

S, habing vnderstood through the relation of my frende
how muche you are displeased, and y neither submission
nor interception off frende can any way move you from
yo settled (I will not say) cruell resolution; But
being restrayned to speake, I have ventured once more
to write vnto you, not going about any intreatie or
excuse, having so lyttle hope off eyther, but onlie to
answere yo exportation as touchings the eyther you
promise, or otherwyse to performe my journey; w
to deale plainly, I can do neither; for the one, I
was not borne so fortunate, and for the other, tyme
permytts not. but How soeuer, my poore Carkasse you
may yf shall have at yo pleasure, for the difference
is not muche, eyther to sterve at home or in prison
And you can but thrust him downe that is alreadye
fallinge. But it may be that Religion ioyned w reason
may so temper yo wrothis disposition, knowinge that
Mercie is more Aamons then Sobernes, that you may
be brought to a charitable consideration off my ouersighte.
I know no outward punishment can so muche torment
me, as my inward discontent, especially, for the losse
off so worthie a frend, yet iff my cause off offence
might be indifferently argued, I have wronged my selfe
more then you, for say twentie pownds were lost, the
benefitt off my journey might have satisfied a far greater
somme, besydes the gayinge off yo love & euerlasting
good opinion, but iff it were not too late to lose the

[77]

Sir, having vnderstood through the relation of my frendes   1
how muche you are displeased, and yt neither submission
nor intercession of frendes can any way move you from
your setled (I will not say) cruell resolution; Yet
beeing restrayned to speake, I have ventured once more   5
to wryte vnto you, not goinge about any intreatie or
excuse, havinge so lyttle hope of either, but onlie to
answere your expectation as touchinge the gyving you
securitie, or Otherwyse to performe my Iourney; wch
to deale plainlye, I can doe neither; for the one, I   10
was not borne so fortunate, and for the other, tyme
permyttes not: but how soever, my poore Carkasse you
may & shall have at your pleasure, for the difference
is not muche, either to Sterve at home or in prison
And you can but thrust him downe that is alreadye   15
fallinge, But it may be that Religion ioyned wth reason
may so temper your worthie disposition, knowinge that
Mercie is more Famous then Revenge, that you may
be brought to a charitable consideration of my oversightes,
I know no outward punyshment can so muche touche   20
me, as my inward discontent, especially for the losse
of so worthie a Frend, yet if my cause of offence
might be indifferently argued, I have wrongd my self
more then you, for say twentie pounde were lost, the
benefitt of my Iourney might have satisfied a far greater   25
Somme, besydes the gayninge of your love & everlasting
good opinion, but if it were not too late to vse these

poore reasons in myne owne defence, I were a happie man
Wherefore I appeale onlie to your Mercie, either iustly
to punyshe me, or wth an vnlooktfor Clemencie, voide   30
of any doubt of honest satisfaction to pardon mee,
And thus fearefull to offend you with so distastinge
a Circumstance, referringe all to youre owne will
and pleasure, I humblie take my leave./.

[78]

Mr Sares, I did not thinke to finde a man   1
of your fashion, so vncertain in your proceedinges,
I doe but ascribe it to my lacke of Iudgement
to gyve credytt to everie idle protestation, where
fore as at your request I sent my lute, So I   5
pray you at my request send it backe againe,
For I see youre wares and your woordes are not
of one price, and my wantes can hardlie be
satisfied wth winde; But yet I wolde wishe
you not to play to muche on him that is already   10
to farr out of tune, for therin you will make
but a Messe of sower Musicke, and hereafter
promysse no more rashely, then you will per =
forme advisedlye, So shall you neither wrong
others nor youre self. And so I rest   15

poore was out in myne owne defence, I were a happie man

wherefore I appeale onlie to yor Mercie, either iustly

to punishe me, or wth an vnlookt for Clemencie, voide

off any doubt off honest satisfaction to redeem mee,

And thus fearefull to offend you wth so distastinge

a Circumstance, referringe all to youre owne will

and pleasure, I humblie take my leaue. /

Mr Dawe, I did not thinke to finde a man

off yor fashion, so vncertain in yor proceedinge,

I doe but ascribe it to my lacke off Judgement

to giue weight to viewe idle protestation, where

fore as at yor request I sent my lute, So I

pray you at my request send it backe againe,

flor I see youre wares and yor woordes are not

off one price, and my wantz can hardlie be

satisfied wth windes; But yet I would wishe

you not to play to much on him that is alredy

to farr out off tune, for therin you will make

but a Messe off sower Musicke, and hereafter

promise no more wrongs, then you will per-

forme advisedly, So shall you neither wrong

others nor your selff. And so I rest

To Mr John dowland at the
Lantgraves Courte by your hoste

John dowland. I take well yor kinde remembrance
to me by letters wch ere this tyme I would have
answered, but for the uncertaintie of yor abydinge.
Now I understand y^t you remain in the Lantgraves
Courte: A Prince whom I hono^r for his high
renowmed vertues, being therby desyrous to see
him, and have determyned (god willinge) as I
passe those partes, wch his favo^r to kisse his
hand, if it be not presumption: I wish he knew
my desyre to do him service, and wheresoe^r er
I become, I will wth hono^r and reverence speake
& thinke of him. It is reported here, of his
purpose to see the Queene, I wish it for
the good of either, here, to be a Prince wthout
Peere, his, to be a Queene wthout Comparison.

You shall not neede to doubt of satisfaction here,
for her Matie hath wished divers tymes yor returne:
fferdinando hath told me her pleasure twise, wch being
now certified you, you may thereby answer all objections.
Therefore feare not longer then other occasions (then
yor doubte here) do detain you. I have heard of yor
estimation every where, whereof I am glad, & take y^t
wth other parte of yor service once to me, for w^{ch}

f. 52v

[79   1 December 1595 or 1596   see Commentary]

        To Sir Iohn Dowland at the   1
        Lantgraves Courte Yeue these
Iohn Dowland. I take well your seuerall remembraunces
to me by letters wch ere this tyme I wolde have
answer'de, but for the vncertaintie of your abydinge.   5
Now I vnderstand yt you remain in the Lantgraves
Courte: A Prince whom I honor for his high
renowmed vertues, being therby desyrous to see
him, and have determyned (god willinge) as I
passe those partes, wth his favoures to kisse his   10
hand, if it be not presumption: I wishe he knew
my desyer to do him service, and whereso ere
I become, I will wth honor and reverence speake
& thinke of him./ It is reported here, of his
purpose to see the Queene, I wishe it for   15
the good of eyther, hers, to see a Prince wthout
Peere, his, to see a Queene wthout Comparison.

You shall not neede to doubt of satisfaction here,
for her Maiestie hath wished divers tymes your return:
Ferdinando hathe told me her pleasure twise, wch being   20
now certified you, you may therwth answer all obiections.
Therfore forbeare not longer then other occasions (then
your doubtes here) do detain you./ I have heard of your
estimation every where, whereof I am glad, & take yt
wth other partes of your service once to me, for wch   25

f. 53r

I will do you all the pleasures I can, I wishe you –
health and soone return and Commytt you to god. London:
j December ./.

your olde Mr and Frend:
H noel: 30

[80   9 February 1598   see Commentary]

To my Loving Frend Mr Iohn   1
Dowland. Bacheler in Musicke: London:/
Mr Dowland, I Imagyn'd your departure from me had
bene either to serue her Maiestie or at the least for some
other preferment fytt for a man of your worthe: the   5
letter importinge lyttle lesse wch cald you home. the
wch I vnderstand Since hathe tooke no place, either for
want of good Frendes to prefer you, or by some particuler
ill hap that many tymes followes men of vertue, but
to the purpose, Yf you do thinke yt the acceptaunce of   10
my service may any way better your estate, I will assure
you yt entertainment, yt every way, you shall hold youre
self content; Thus referring you to youre best
consideration, together wth the counsell of your Frendes:
I rest: expectinge your aunswere.   15

Dated at *Zieghaine* the .9.
off Februarij. 1598./.   *Maurice* the
                                    Landgrave off
                                    hessen./.

J will do you all the pleasures J can, J wishe you
health, and soone returne and Comytt you to god. London:
j December./.
                            yo͞r olde M͞r and ffreind:
                                  H noel:

    To my Loving ffreind M͞r John
      Dowland. Batcheler in Musick: London:/
M͞r Dowland, J Jmagyned yo͞r departure from me had
bene either to Court her Ma: or at the least for some
other preferment fytt for a man of yo͞r worthe. the
letters importinge lyttle lesse u͞s cald you home. the
wͨh J vnderstand since hathe tooke no place, either for
want of good fortude to preferr you, or by some particuler
ill happ that many tymes followed men of desarte, but
to the purpose, yͨf you do thinke the acceptance of
my service may any way better yo͞r estate, J will assure
you yͭ entertainment, yͭ euerie way, you shall hold your
self content; & thus referringe you to your best
consideration, togethͤr wͭh the counsell of yo͞r ffreinde:
J rest: expectinge yo͞r aunswere.

Dated at Sieghaine the 9.
of ffebruarij. 1598./.
                              Mauriee the
                              Landgrave of
                              Hessen./.

The feruent Regard Right honorable that I haue
alwayes born to Soldiers & Martiall affaires: hathe
bothe drawne my pen to wryte this discourse, and
emboldned me to dedicate the same vnto your Lo: /
Accompting the matter, & the man, of whom I
make protection. So fytt th'one for th'other, & either
of bothe so fytt for the best, as without some simile
they could not well be seperard. ffor who knowes
not (that knowes any thinge) how worthelie in
all ages Soldiers haue bene honowrd, wth speciall
stabo dignities, & prefermentes. / Or who so
ignorant that is to seeke, what dewe right and
interest your Lo: hathe to honor: being as worldly yor
owne, bothe by birthright, & powers art. Naturally
discending from the Nobilitie of so many famous
ancestors, and worthelie atchyeinge the same by
your Lo: owne honorable desartes; And for a fur=
ther increase of happines, God hathe blest you
wth many other good graces; Nature hath enrich
you wth especiall fauor: And ffortune (yf theire
be any ffortune) hathe wonderfully furthered you
wth happie begynnynge. / Go forward there in hap=
pie tyme, & defere not the perfectinge of so great
towardnes wth dangerous delayes; slip not in suche
sort th'aduantage of Oportunitie as might any kinde
of wayes eclipse the brightnes of your springinge honor,
but wth a full & setled resolution, Marche on even
to the foremost ranck of trewe Nobilitie. A place
reserued for suche as more esteeme of honor then
of ease, of credit, then comoditie. And accordinge

[81   see Commentary]

The Reverent Regard Right honorable that I have   1
alwayes born to Soldiers & Martiall affaires: hathe
bothe drawn my pen to wryte this discourse, and
emboldned me to dedicate the same vnto your Lordshippe/
Accompting the matter, & the man, of whom I   5
crave protection. so fytt th'one for th'other, & either
of bothe so fytt for the best, as wthout some Iniurie
they could not well be severed. For who knowes
not (that knowes any thinge) how worthelie in
all Ages soldiers have bene honored, wth speciall   10
Favoures, dignities, & prefermentes./ Or who so
ignorant that is to seeke, what dewe right and
interest your Lordshippe hathe to honor: being assuredly your
owne, bothe by birthright, & purchase. Naturally
discending from the Nobilitie of so many famous   15
ancestores, and worthelie atchyvinge the same by
your Lordshippes owne honorable desartes; And for a fur =
ther increase of happines, God hathe blest you
wth many other good graces: Nature hath enricht
you wth especiall favoures: And Fortune (yf their   20
be any Fortune) hathe wonderfully furthered you
wth happie begynnynges./ Go forward then in hap =
pie tyme, & defer not the perfectinge of so great
towardnes wth Daungerous delayes, slip not in such
sort th'advantage of Oportunitie as might any kinde   25
of wayes Eclipes the brightnes of your shyninge honor,
but wth a full & setled resolution, Marche on even
to the formost ranck of trewe Nobilitie. A place
reseru'd for suche as more esteeme of honor then
of ease, of creditt, then commoditie. And accordinge   30

to your Lordshippes good Example, as will not sticke, voluntarilie
to offer them selues to all honorable paines & perills
(vnder the Ensignes of Martiall discipline) for the
benefite of their Countries; but not for those that
Imbase the Nobilitie of their birthes wth the continu =   35
all entertainment of vaine home pleasures, & Idle
delicasie, those poysoned Serpentes, & professed enimies
to Manhood & Magnanimytie./ For as none can –
attaine to honor wthout vertue, nor to vertue wthout paines,
so dishonor dothe alwayes follow vyce, & vyce Idlenes. –   40
But of this your Lordshippe may be most assured, yt you have already
made so many steppes towardes yt place, wherevnto I seeme to
to hasten you, yt your equalls (I meane in ordinarie accompt)
wth a kinde of Ielous admiration, do watche to see what
fruytes shall be gathered of this your forward Bloominge   45
springe, Your faithfull frendes & followers, do greedely attend
for farther proceedinges, & generally your whole Countrie,
hathe laide suche an expectacion vpon you? as is not
lookt for of others; It is their dewe, & your dett: they –
demaund it, & you must performe it, for none are born onlie   50
to them selues./ But pardon me my lord I humblie crave it,
for I feare me a fervent zeale grounded vpon a faithfull
good will, bothe vnto your Lordshippe and to the cause, hath caried
me to farr./ I had thought but lightly to have touched
this point, and I doubt it will heavely burthen my self. for   55
I vainlye goinge about to sett an Edge vpon yt wch is already
perfectlye sharpe, groslye bewray myne owne blunt imperfecti =
ons./ But I trust your Lordshippe will not take yt for presumption,
wch comes of affection; nor way how I geve, but what I
gyve, as one yt is careles of ye shell: yet priseth the kernell./   60

to yoᵉ Loᵖ good example, as will not sticke, voluntarilie
to offer them selues to all honourable paines & perills
(vnder the ensigne off Martiall discipline) for the
benefitts off their Countries; but not for those that
imbase the Nobilitie off their birthes wⁱᵗ the continu=
all entertainement off wanton & vaine pleasures, & Idle
delicacie, those personed & corporall, & professed inimies
to Manheod & Magnanimitie; ffor as none can
attaine to Honor without trauail, nor to vertue without paine,
so dishonor doth always follow vice, & vppon Idlenes. —
But off this yoᵉ Lo: may be most assured, yᵗ you haue already
made so many steppes towarde yᵉ place, whervnto I seeme to
perswade you, as yᵗ equalls (I meane in ordinarie accompt)
wⁱᵗ a kinde off Ielous admiration, do watche to see wᵗ at
frendes shall be gathered off this yoᵉ forwarde Blessings
springes, yoᵉ faithfull frendes & followers, do greedely attend
for farther proceedinge, & generally yoᵉ whole Countrie,
hathe laide suche an expectacion vppon you? as it not
lookt for off others; It is their dewe, & yoᵉ dett: they
demand it, & you must performe it, for none are borne onlie
to them selues. But vpon me my lord I humblie craue it,
for I feare me a feruent zeale grounded vppon a faithfull
good will, bothe vnto yoᵉ Lo: and to the cause, hath caried
me to farre. I had thought but lightly to haue touched
this point, and I doubt it will greatly burthen my selfe. for
I thinke goinge about to sett an edge vpon yᵗ wᶜʰ is already
perfectlye sharpe, grosslye bewray myne owne blunt imperfecti=
ons. But I trust yoᵉ Lo: will not take yⁱˢ for presumption,
wᶜʰ comes off affection; now way how I speke, but what I
speke, as one yᵗ is carelesse off yᵉ shell: yet precisethe yᵉ kernell.

And although this my worke may seeme but a gleanynge
after other mens harveste, my selfe not plowing the grounds,
yet I truste yo[r] Lo: wille to allow off it, as my labo[r] shall
not be altogether fruytles, nor it vnperformed: iff yo[r] Lo:
vouchsafe to afforde me your honorable protection and
favorable acceptance, The one I doubt not off in respect
off the matter, the other I hope well off for that I know
it is agreable w[i]th the Nobilitie off yo[r] mynde, as well to
accepte off small thinges thankfully, as to yelde great thinge
bountifully! Leavinge therfore as well all doubtfull readinge
w[i]th some thinke hard to deny, as also all curious circum=
stances off filed phrase & refyned sentence, fytt
Ornamentes for Oratores, and moste matter to cloake vacnid
rowe symnes: I will thus comely like a soldier (yet
most humblie) take my leave off yo[r] Lo: beseechynge
th[e] mightie Lord off hostes, the only ruler off Armys, and
geber off all victories: so to defend you from yo[r] foes,
and enable yen you for yo[r] frende, that to the confusion
off the one, and comfort off the other: yo[r] Tenantine
may longe enioye the fruyt off their expectacion.
And yo[r] Lo: still encrease in all honorable Creditt
& desyred felicitie./

                                        yo[r] Lo: most humbly
                                        & ready at all com[m]and./

f. 54v

And although this my worke may seeme but a gleanynge
after other mens harvestes, my self not plowing the grounde,
Yet I trust your Lordshippe will so allow of it, as my labores shall
not be altogether fruytles, wch is performed: yf your Lordshippe
vouchsafes to afforde me youre honorable protection and   65
favorable acceptance; The one I doubt not of in respect
of the matter, the other I hope well of for yt I know
it is agreable wth the Nobilitie of your mynde, aswell to
accept of small thinges thankfully, as to gyve great thinges
bountifully./ Leaving therfore aswell all doubtfull cravinges   70
wch some thinke teache to denye, as also all curious Cir =
cumstances of fyled phrases & refyned sentences, fytt
Ornamentes for Orators, and meete matter to cloake craftie
conveyaunces./ I will thus homely like a soldier (yet
most humblie) take my leave of your Lordshippe beseechinge   75
yt mightie Lord of hostes, th'only ruler of Armyes, and
gyver of all victories; so to defend you from your foes,
and enable ⟨your⟩ you for your frendes, that to the confusion
of the one, and comfort of the other: Your Countrie
may longe enioye the fruytes of there expectacion.   80
And your Lordshippe still encrease in all honorable Creditt
& desyred felicitie./

                                    Your Lordshippe Most humbly
                                    & ready at all commaunds./

[82   23 May 1610   see Commentary]

To the kinges most excellent Maiestie./   1
Most gratious Soveraigne: Whereas wee your Maiesties most
humble subiectes, the Commons assembled in parliament:
have receyved first by message, and since by speache from
your Maiestie A commaundement of restraint from debatinge   5
in parliament your Maiesties right of imposinge vpon your subiectes
goodes exported or imported out of or into this Realme;
Yet allowinge vs to examyne the greevance of those impositi =
ons, in regard of quantitie, tyme, & other circumstances of
disproporcion therto incident, wee your said humble subiectes   10
nothinge doubtinge, but yt your Maiestie had no intent by that
commaundement to infringe the auncient & fundamentall right
of the libertie of parliament in pointe of exact discussing
of all matters concerninge them & their possessions, goodes –
& rightes whatsoever: wch yet we can not but conceive to   15
be done in effect by this commaundement; doe wth all humble
dutie make this Remonstraunce to your Maiestie: First we hold
it an ancient, generall, & vndoubted right of parliament, to
debate freely all matters wch doe properly concern ye subect
and his right or state, wch freedome of debate. beinge once   20
foreclosed, the Essence of the libertie of parliament is wth =
all dissolved. And whereas in this case the subiectes on
the one syde, & your Maiesties Prerogatyve on th'other, can not
possibly be severed in debate of either: we alledge yt your
Maiesties prerogatives of yt kinde (concerninge directly the   25
subiectes right & interest) are dailye handled & discussed
in all Courtes at Westmynster; and have ever bene freely
debated vpon all fytt occasions bothe in this & all former
Parliamentes wthout restraint, wch being forbydden: it is
impossible for the subiect either to know or maintain his   30
right & proprietie to his owne landes & goodes, though never

To the kings most excellent Ma[jes]tie.

Most gratious Soveraigne. Wee your Ma[jes]tie most humble subiects, the Commons assembled in parliament: Have receyved first by message, and since by speeche from your Ma[jes]tie: A comaundement of restraint from debatinge in parliament your Ma[jes]tie right of imposinge upon our subiects goods exported or imported out of or into this Realme; That allwayes to be amongst the greevances of that imposition, in regard of quantities, tymes, & other circumstances of disproportion theirto incident, nott your said humble subiects nothinge doubtinge, but that your Ma[jes]tie had no intent by that comaundement to infringe the auncient & fundamentall right of the liberties of parliament in points of speech disponinge of all matters concerninge them & theirs possessions, goode & rights whatsoever: wch yet wee can not but conceive to be done in effect by this comaundement, doe wth all humble dutie make this Remonstrance to your Ma[jes]tie: first wee hold it an auncient, generall, & undoubted right of parliament, to debate freely all matters wch doe properly concern the subiect and his right or state, wch freedome of debate, beings ours sewed soe, the if the reason of the liberties of parliament is wth all dissolved. And wee reputes in this case the subiect on the one syde, & your Ma[jes]tie Prerogatyve on the other can not possibly be seuered in debate of either: wee alledge that your Ma[jes]tie prerogatives of wch kind concerninges directly the subiect right & interest are daily handled & discussed in all Courts at Westminster; and have ever been freely debated upon all fitt occasions bothe in this & all former parliaments wthout restraint, wch being forbidden: it is impossible for the subiect either to know or maintain his right & proprieties to his owne lande & goode, thoughe neuer

things, never so just & manifest. It may further please
yo[r] Ma[jes]tie. to understand, y[t] wee have no mynde to meddle
but a desire to informe our selves of yo[r] Highnes pre=
rogative in that point, w[ch] his dark, is now most necessa=
rie to be knowen: and though it were to no o[ther] purpose,
y[et] to satisfie the generaltie of yo[r] Ma[jes]ties subiects:
wee finding them selves much greived by these newe
impositions, do languishe in much sorrow & discomfort.
& these wee our dread Soveraigne, being the proper
cause of Parliament, doe pleade for the upholdings
of these our ancient right & liberties; & where it seings
that it hath pleased yo[r] Ma[jes]tie. to insist upon the Iudgment
in the Exchequer, as being direction sufficient for us
without further examynation; upon great desyre of
leavinge yo[r] Ma[jes]tie. unsatisfied in no one point of o[ur] intent
& proceedinges, wee professe something to Iudgment, y[t] wee
neither doe nor will take upon us to referre it, but
our desyre is to know how wee our selves upon y[e] same
was grounded, and the rather for y[t] a generall conceit
is had, that the wee our selves of that Iudgment may be
extended much further, even to the utter unmaking of
the ancient liberties of this kingdom, & of yo[r] subiects
right & propertie to their lands & goods. Even for y[t]
Iudgment it selfe, being the first & last y[t] ever was given
in y[t] kinde, for ought appearing unto us, and being onlie
in one case, & against one man: it can binde in law no
other then y[t] man in y[t] person, & is also reversable by writt of
error granted heretofore by Act of Parliament. And
neither hee nor any other subiect is debarred by it from
tryinge his right in the same or like case in any of
yo[r] Ma[jes]ties courts of records in Westminster. Lastly we

though never so iust & manifest. / It may further please
your Maiestie to vnderstand, yt we have no mynde to impugne
but a desire to enforme our selues of your hignes pre =
rogative in that point, wch if ever, is now most necessa =   35
rie to be knowne: and though it were to no oyer purpose,
yet to satisfie the generaltie of your Maiesties subiectes: –
Who findinge them selues muche grieved by these newe
impositions, do languish in muche sorow & discomfort.
Those reasons dread Soveraigne, beinge the proper   40
reasons of Parliament, doe plead for the vpholdinge
of this our auncient right & libertie; howbeit, seeinge
it hathe pleased your Maiestie to insist vpon yt Iudgment
in th'exchequer, as being direction sufficient for vs
wthout further examynation; vpon great desyre of   45
leavinge your Maiestie vnsatisfied in no one point of our intent
& proceedinges, we professe touching yt Iudgment, yt wee
neither doe nor will take vpon vs to reverse it, but
our desyre is to know the reasons wherevpon ye same
was grounded, and the rather for yt a generall conceit   50
is had, that the reasons of that Iudgment may be
extended muche further, even to the vtter ⟨ry⟩ ruyne of
the auncient libertie of this kingdome, & of your subiectes
right & proprietie to their landes & goodes. Then for ye
Iudgment it self, being the first & last yt ever was given   55
in yt kinde, for ought appearinge vnto vs, and being onlie
in one case, & against one man: it can binde in law no
other then yt person, & is also reversable by wrytt of
Error graunted hertofore by Act of parliament, And
neither hee nor any other subbiect is debarred by it from   60
tryinge his right in the same or like case in any of
your Maiesties courtes of recorde in Westmynster. Lastly we

nothing doubt but our intended proceeding in a full examination
of the right nature & measure of these new impositions (yf
this restraint had not come betwene) should have bene so 65
orderly & moderately caried, & so applyed to the manifold
necessitie of these tymes, And gyven your Maiestie so true a
view of the state & right of your subiectes, that it wold have
bene muche to your Maiesties content & satisfaction, wch we most
desyre: and removed all cause of feares & Ielosies from the 70
Loyall hartes of your subiectes, wch is (as it ought to bee)
our carefull endevour, where as contrariewise in that other
way directed by your Maiestie we can not safely proceede wthout
concludinge for ever the right of the subiectes, wch wthout due
examination thereof we may not doe; Wee therefore youre 75
highnes Loyall and dutifull Commons, not swerving from
the approved steppes of our auncestores, most humblie and
instantly beseech your gratious Maiestie that wthout offence to
the same, we may accordinge to the vndoubted right & libertie
of parliament, proceede in one intended course of a full examy = 80
nation of new impositions, that so we may chearefully passe
on to your Maiesties businesses, From wch this stop hathe by diver =
sion so longe wthhelde vs. And we your Maiesties most
humble, faithfull, & loyall Subiectes, shall ever accordinge
to our bounden duties, pray for your Maiesties longe and 85
happie raigne over vs./.

Nothing doubt but our intended proceeding in a full examinaton
of the right nature & measure of these new impositions (if
this restraint had not come between) should have bene so
orderly & moderably carried, & so applyed to the manifold
necessitie of these tymes, And upon your Matie so true a
view of the state & right of your subiectes, that it would have
bene answers to your Maties content & satisfaction, wch wee most
desyre: and removed all cause of feares & Ielousie from the
Loyall heartes of your subiectes, wch is (as it ought to bee)
our carefull indevour, that yet as contrariwise in that if our
way diverted by your Matie wee can not safely proceede without
conclusinge for ever the right of the subiecte, wch without due
examination thereof we may not doe; Wee therefore youre
highnes Loyall and dutifull Commons, not swearving from
the approved stoppe of our auncestors, most humblie and
instantly besecch your gracious Matie this that without offence to
the same, wee may according to the undoubted right & liberties
of parliament, proceede in our intended course of a full examination of new impositions, that so wee may gracefully passe
on to your Maties businesses, from wch this stop hath no diver-
sion so longe wth held doo. And wee your Maiesties most
humble, faithfull, & loyall subiectes, & all other according
to our bounden duties, pray for your Maiesties longe and
happie raigne ober us, &c. /

Sonne Robart, the vertuous inclinatiõs of thy matchles
mother, by whose tender & godly care thy Infancye
was gouerned, together wth thy education vnder so
zealous and excellent a Tutor, putte me rather in
assurance of the hope that thou art not ignorant
of that Summarie band, wch is onlie able to make
the happie aswell in thy death as lyfe, I meane
thy true knowledge and worship of thy Creator &
Redeemer, whout wch, all other thinges are vaine &
miserable, So that thy youth, being guided by so
all sufficient a Teacher, I make no doubt but he
will furnishe thy lyfe bothe wth divine & Morall
documentes, yet that I may not cast of the care be=
semings a parent towarde his childe, or yt thou
shouldest have cause to deeme thy whole felicitie
& welfare, rather frome other then frome vs whome
thou reueredst thy birthe & beinge, I thinke it fytt
and agreeable to thy affection & loue, to helpe thee
wth suche adurtisments and rules for ye gouernmt
of thy lyfe, as are gayned rather by muche experi=
ences then longe readinges, to thend that thou entringe
into this expenditant age, maist be the better pre=
pared to shun those cautulous courses, whereinto
this worlde and thy lacke of experience may
easely drawe thee. And becaus I will not con=
found thy memorie, I have reduced them into ten
preceptes, and next vnto Moses tables iff thou dost
Imprint them in thy mynde, thou shalt reape the
benefitt & I ye contentment, and these are they./

[83   before 31 August 1589; *c*. 1584 (?)   see Commentary]

Sonne Robert, the vertuous Inclinations of thy matchles   1
mother, by whose tender & godly care thy Infancye
was governed, together wth thy education vnder so
zealous and excellent a Tutor, puttes me rather in
assurance of the hope that thou art not ignorant   5
of that Summarie band, wch is onlie able to make
the happie aswell in thy death as lyfe, I meane
the true knowledge and worship of thy Creator &
Redeemer, wthout wch, all other thinges are vaine &
miserable; So that thy youthe being guided by so   10
alsufficient a Teacher, I make no doubt but he
will furnishe thy lyfe bothe wth divine & Morall
documentes, yet yt I may not cast of the Care be =
seeminge a parent towardes his childe, or yt thou
shouldest have cause to deryve thy whole felicitie   15
& Welfare, rather from others then from whence
thou receyvedst thy birthe & beinge, I thinke it fytt
and agreeable to the affection I beare, to help the
wth suche advertisementes and rules for ye squaringe
of thy lyfe, as are gayned rather by muche experi =   20
ence then longe readinge, to th'end that thou entringe
into this exorbitant age, maist be the better pre =
pared to shun those Cautulous Courses, whereinto
this worlde and thy lacke of experience may
easely drawe thee./ And bycause I will not Con =   25
found thy memorie, I have reduced them into ten
preceptes, and next vnto *Moses* tables if thou doe
Imprint them in thy mynde, thou shalt reape the
benefitt & I ye contentment, and these are they./.

·1·   When it shall please God to bringe the to mans estate,   30
vse greate providence and circumspection in the choyse
of thy wyfe, for from thence may springe all thy future
good or yll; And it is an accion like a *Stragagem* in
Warre, where a man can erre but once./ If thy estate be
good, matche neere home and at leysure, yf weake, then   35
Far of and quickly; Enquier diligently of her disposi =
tion, and how her parentes have bene enclyned in their
Youthe; Let her not be poore how generous soever, for
a man can buy nothinge in the Markett wth gentilitie, –
neither chuse a base & vncomely Creature altogether for   40
wealthe, for it will cause contempt in others and loathing
in thee; make not choyse of a dwarff or a foole, for from
the one thou maist begett a race of *Pigmees*, the other may
be thy daily disgrace; For it will yrke thee to have her
talke, for then thou shalt finde to thy great griefe, that their   45
is nothinge more fulsome then a *Shee foole*./ Touchinge the
Government of thy howse, let thy hospitalitie be moderate,
and accordinge to the measure of thine owne estate, rather
plentifull then sparinge (but not to costly) for I never –
knew any grow poore by keepinge an orderly table./ But   50
some consume themselues through secrett vices, and their
hospitalitie must beare the blame./ Banishe swynishe –
dronckardes out of thy howse, wch is a vice that impaires
health, consumes muche, and makes no shewe, for I never –
knew any prayse ascribed to a dronckard, but the well   55
bearinge of drinke, wch is a better commendation for a brew =
ers horsse or a drayman, then for either gentleman or
servingman./ Beware that thou spend not above three of
the Fower partes of thy revenue, nor above one third part

1. When it shall please God to bring thee to mans estate,
use great providence and circumspection in the choyse
of thy wyfe, for from thence may springe all thy future
good or ill; And it is an action like a Stragagem in
warre, wheare a man can erre but once. If thy estate be
good, match neere home and at leysure, if weake, then
farre off and quickly; Enquire diligently of her disposi=
tion, and how her parents have bene inclyned in their
youthe; Let her not be poore how generous soever, for
a man can buy nothinge in the Markett wth gentilitie, ~
neither chuse a base & uncomely Creature altogether for
wealthe, for it will cause contempt in others and loathing
in thee; make not choyse of a dwarfe or a foole, for from
the one thou maist begett a race of Pigmees, the other may
be thy daily disgrace; for it will yrke thee to have her
talke, for then thou shalt finde to thy great greife, that their
is nothinge more fulsome then a Shee foole. Concerninge thy
Goverment of thy howse, let thy Hospitalitie be moderate,
and accordinge to the measure of thine owne estate, rather
plentifull then sparinge (but not to costly) for I never ~
knew any grow poore by keepinge an orderly table. But
some consume themselves through secrett vices, and their
Hospitalitie must beare the blame. Banishe swynishe ~
drunckardes out of thy howse, wch is a vice that impaires
healthe, consumes much, and makes no shewe, for I never ~
knew any prayse ascribed to a Drunckard, but the well
bearinge of drincke, wch is a better commendation for a brew=
ers howse or a drayman, then for either gentleman or
servingman. Beware that thou spend not above thre of
the fower partes of thy revenue, nor above one third part

off that in the most, for thy other two partes will doe no
more then defray thy extraordinaries which will alwayes
surmount thy ordinaries by mutche: for otherwise shalt thou
live like a rich begger in a continuall want; and the
needy man can never live happely nor contented; for
then every least disaster maketh him ready either to
Mortgage or to sell, and that gentleman which then selleth
an acre off land looseth an ounce off Creditt, for gentilitie
is nothinge but ancient riches. So that iff the foundations
sinke, the buildings must needes consequently faile. /

2. Bringe thy children up in learninge and obedience, yet
without austeritie, prayse them openly, reprehend them
secretly: give them good countenaunce, & convenient
maynteaunce, accordinge to thy abilitie, for otherwise thy
life will seeme their bondage, and then what portion
thou shalt leave them at thy death, they may thanke
death for it and not thee; And I am truly perswaded,
that the foolish workinges off some parentes, & the over
strowne carriage off others, causeth more men & women to
take ill courses, then naturally their owne vitious
inclinations; Marrie thy daughters in tyme, least they
Marry them selves; Suffer not thy sonnes to passe the
Alpes, for they shall learn nothinge but pryde, blasphemy,
and Atheisme; And iff by travell they attayne to some few
broken languages, they will profit them no more, then to
have our meates served in divers dishes, neither by my advice
shalt thou trayne them up to warres, for he that setteth up his
rest onlie to live by that profession, can hardly be an honest
man or good Christian, for every warre is off it selfe uniust,
unlesse the good cause may make it iust, besides it is a
science no longer in request, then use; for Soldiers in
peace, are like Chymneis in sommer. /

of that in thy+ne+ howse, for the other two partes will doe no   60
more then defray thy extraordinaries wch will alwayes
surmount thy ordinaries by muche: for otherwise shalt thou
⟨like⟩ live like a rich begger in a continuall want, and the
needy man can never lyve happely nor contented; For
then every least disaster makes him ready either to   65
Morgage or to sell, and that gentleman wch then sells
an acre of land looses an ounce of Creditt, for gentilitie
is nothinge but ancient riches. So that if ye foundations
sincke, the buyldinge must needes consequently faile./.

·2·   Bringe thy Children vp in learninge and obedience, yet   70
wthout austeritie, prayse them openly, reprehend them
secretly; gyve them good countenance, & convenient –
mayntenance, accordinge to thy abilitie, for otherwise thy
lyfe will seeme their bondage, and then what portion
thou shalt leave them at thy death, they may thanke   75
death for it and not thee; And I am verely perswaded,
that the foolish Cockeringe of some parentes, & the over –
stern Cariage of others, cawseth more men & women to
take evill courses, then naturally their owne vitious –
inclinations; Marie thy daughters in tyme, least they   80
Marry them selues; Suffer not thy Sonnes to passe the
Alpes, for they shall learn nothinge but pryde, blasphemy,
and Athisme, And if by travell they attayne to some fewe
broken languages, they will profytt them no more, then to
have one meate served in divers dishes, neither by my advise   85
shalt thou trayne them vp to warres, for he yt settes vp his
rest onlie to lyve by yt profession, can hardly be an honest
man or good Christian, for every warre is of it self vniust
vnlesse the good cause may make it iust, besydes it is a
science no longer in request, then vse: for *Soldiers in –*   90
peace, are like Chymneis in sommer ./.

·3·   Lyve not in the Country wthout corne & cattell about thee,
      for he yt muste present his hand to the pursse for every
      expence of howsholde, may be likened to him that keepes
      water in a Sive, And for that provision thou shalt neede   95
      lay for to buy it at the best hand, for there may be a
      peny in fower saved betwixt buyinge at thy neede, or
      when the Markett & seasons serves fyttest for it. And
      be not willingly attended or served by kinsmen, Frendes,
      or men intreated to stay, for they will expect muche,   100
      & doe lyttle, neither by suche as are amorous, for there
      heades are commonly intoxicated, keepe rather twoo to
      fewe, then one to manie, feede them well and pay them
      wth the most, and then maist thou boldly require service
      at there handes ./.   105

·4·   Let thy kindred and allies be welcome to thy table,
      grace them wth thy countenance, and ever further them
      in all honest accions, for by that meanes thou shalt
      so double the band of nature, as thou shalt fynde them
      so many advocates to plead an Apologie for thee behinde   110
      thy backe. But shake of these *Glowormes*, I meane *Para =
      sites* and *Sycophantes*, who will feede and fawne vpon thee
      in thy Sommer of prosperitie, but in any adverse storme,
      they will shelter thee no more then an arbour in winter./

·5·   Beware of Suretishippe for thy best Frend, for he wch   115
      payeth another mans debtes seekes his owne decay, but yf
      thou canst not otherwise chuse, then rather lend yt money
      from thy self vpon good bond though thou borow it, so maist
      thou pleasure thy Frend, and happely also secure thy self,

3: Lyve not in the Countrey without corne & cattell about thee,
for he that must present his hand to the purse for every
expence of householde, may be likened to him that keepest
water in a Sibe, And for that provision thou shalt neede
lay for to buy it at the best hand, for there may be a
peny in fower saved betwixt buyinge at thy neede, or
when in the Markett & seasons serve fyttest for it. And
be not willingly attended or served by kinsmen, ffreindes,
or men intreated to stay, for they will expect muche,
& doe lyttle, with no by such as are answerd, for their
heades are commonly inappropriated, keepe rather twoo to
fower, then one to manie, feede them well and pay them
with the most, and then maist thou boldly require service
at theire hande.

4: Let thy kindred and allies be welcome to thy table,
grace them with thy countenance, and ever further them
in all honest actions, for by that meanes thou shalt
so double the band of nature, as thou shalt finde them
so many advocates to pleade an Apologie for thee behinde
thy backe. But shake off these Glowormes, I meane Para=
sites and Sycophants, who will feede and fawne upon thee
in the somner of prosperitie, but in any adverse storme,
they will shelter thee no more then an arbour in winter.

5: Beware of suretishipps for thy best freind, for he that
payeth another mans debts seeketh his owne decay, but if
thou canst not otherwise chuse, then rather lend thy money
from thy selfe upon good bond though thou borrowe it, so maist
thou pleasure thy freind, and happoly also secure thy selfe,

Neither borrow money off a Neighbour or friend, but rather ~~of a meere~~ from a meere stranger, where paying for it thou maist heare no more off it, for otherwise thou shalt relinquish thy Creditt, loose thy freedome, and yet pay to him as deare as to the other. In borrowinge off money be more precious off thy worde, for he that hath care to keepe day off payment is lord Commaunder many tymes in another mans goodes.

6. Undertake no suite against a poore man w[i]thout wearying much & wronge for theire makinge him thy Competitor, besydes: it is a base conquest to triumphe w[he]re there is small resistaunce, neither attempt lawe against any man before thou be fully resolved y[a]t thou haste the right on thy syde, and then spare not for money nor paines, for a chaunce or two so thinges will followe & obteyned, may after free thee from suites a great part off thy life.

7. Be sure ever to keepe some great man thy frend, but trouble him not for trifles, Complement him often, p[rese]nt h[i]m w[i]th many, yet smale guiftes & off little charge, and iff thou have cause to bestow any great gratuitie, let it then be some such thinge as may be daily in sight, for otherwise in this ambitious age, thou maist remaine like a hoppe w[i]thout a pole, live in obscuritie, & be made a footeball for every insultinge Companion to spurne at.

8. Towardes thy superiours be humble yet generous, w[i]th thy equalls familiar yet respectyve, towarde inferiours she we

f. 58v

Neither borow money of a Neighbour or frend, but rayer 120
⟨of a meere⟩ from a meere straunger, where payinge for
it thou maist heare no more of it, for otherwise thou
shalt eclipse thy Creditt, loose thy freedome, and yet
pay to hym as deare as to the other, In borrowinge of
money be ever pretious of thy worde, for he that cares 125
to keepe day of payment is lord Commaunder many
tymes in another mans goodes ./.

·6· Vndertake no suyte against a poore man wthout receyving
muche wronge for therein makinge him thy Competitor,
besydes: it is a base conquest to tryvmph where there 130
is small resistaunce, neither attempt lawe against any
man before thou be fully resolved yt thou haste the
right on thy syde, and then spare not for money
nor paines, for a Cause or two so beinge well followed
& obteyned, may after free thee from suytes a great 135
part of thy lyfe ./.

·7· Be sure ever to keepe some great man thy frend, but
trouble him not for tryfles, Complement him often,
present wth many, yet small guyftes & of lyttle charge,
and if thou have cause to bestow any great gratuitie, 140
let it then be some such thinge as may be daily in sight,
for otherwise in this ambitious age, thou maist remaine
like a hoppe wthout a pole, lyve in obscuritie, & be made
a footeball for every insultinge Companion to spurn at./.

·8· Towardes thy superiours be humble yet generous, wth thy 145
equalls familier yet respectyve, towardes inferiores shew

muche humilitie & some familiaritie, as to bowe thy bodie,
stretch forth thy hand, & to vncover thy head, & suche like
popular Complementes, the first prepares a way to advaun
cement, the second makes the knowne for a man well bredd,   150
the third gaines a good report, wch once gotten, may be easely
kept; for high humilities take such roote in the myndes
of the multitude, as they are easelier wonne by vnprofi =
table Curtesies, then Churlishe benefittes, Yet do I advise
thee, not to affect nor neglect popularitie too muche, Seke   155
not to be .E. and shun to be .R. / .

·9·   Trust not any man too farr wth thy Creditt or estate, for
it is a meere follie for a man to enthrall himself to his
Frend further then if iust cause be offred he should not
dare to become otherwise his enemye./ .   160

·10· Be not scurrulous in conversation, nor stoycall in thy ieastes,
the one may make the vnwelcome to all companies, the other
pull on quarrells & get the hatred of thy best frendes, Ieastes
when they savour too muche of truth, leave a ⟨hatred⟩ bitter =
nes in the mynde of those yt are touched, And although   165
I have alreadie pointed all this Inclusive, yet I thinke it
necessarie to leave it thee as a *Caution*, bicause I have
seene many so prone to quippe & gird, as they wolde rather
loose there frend then their Ieaste; And if by Chaunce
there boylinge brain yeild a quaint scoff: they will tra =   170
vell to be delyvered of it, as a woman wth childe. Those
nimble apprehensions are but the froath of witt./ .

mixe humilitie & some familiaritie, as to bowe thy bodie,
stretche forthe thy hand, & to vncover thy head, & suche like
popular complementes; the first prepares a way to advancement; the second makes thee knowne for a man well bredd,
the third gained a good reporte, wch once gotten, may be easily
kept; for these humilities take suche roote in the myndes
of the multitude, as they are easilier wonne by vnprofitable curtesies, then churlishe benefittes, yet do I advise
thee, not to affect nor neglect popularitie too muche, seeke
not to be &c. and shun to be R. /

/ Trust not any man too farre wth thy creditt or estate, for
it is a mere follie for a man to enthrall himselfe to his
frend further then iff iust cause be offred he should not
sticke to become otherwise his enemye. /

/ Be not scurrulous in conversation, nor stoyrgull in thy iaste
the one may make thee contemptuous to all companies, the other
pull on quarrells & get thee hatred of thy best frends; iaste
wch on thy labour too muche off truth, leaue a kind off bitter-
nes in the myndes off those it are touched, And althoughe
I haue alreadie pointed all this heerefore, yet I thinke it
necessarie to leaue it heere as a Caution, because I haue
sene many so prone to quippe & gird, as they would rather
loose theyr frend then theyr iaste; And iff by missanure
theyr boyling braine yield a quaint scoff: they will trau-
aille to be delyvered off it, as a woman wth childe. Those
nimble apprehensions are but the froath off witt. /

Good S.r I am bold to put you in mynde off my late request
comending it & my selfe to yo.r best loue, promysyng also
to acknowledge it, though I neuer be able to requite it. /
Please you to make it short, though I be long in wayeting
y.e good off hym. / & in plaine woordes bycause I woulde
ingraue it vpon his graue stone for all men to see and
vnderstand. /

My ffather was ever truly religious from his youth vp=
warde, / louing to y.e Ministery & to all men, / & exceeding
full off mercy & compassion to the poore. / And in the
towne where he liued he alwayes sought after peace, not
only for hym selfe, but for all the towne, / making many
one freinde after their falling out. / He was wonderfull
louing & naturall to his wyfe & children, his house was
for all straungers as also for freinds. / And notwithstanding
his bountie towarde y.e poore, both at home & abroade,
And his liberalitie in house keeping, yet such was y.e great
mercy off God, as he liued & dyed in very riche estate,
& more & c. as I coulde gladly gaue you take notice off. /

If I coulde speake as much good off hym as he deserued
& as I woulde I coulde not contein it in this paper: but all
this I leaue & comend to yo.r fauour w.ch I will alwaies
studie to be made worthie off. /

                                      Ambrose Bedell. /

f. 59v

[84   see Commentary]

Good Sir. I am bold to put you in mynde of my late request,   1
commending it & my self to your best love, promyssing ever
to acknowledg it, though I never be able to requite it./
Please you to make it short, though I be long in repeating
ye good of him ./ & in plaine wordes bycause I wolde   5
engrave it vpon his grave stone for all men to see and
vnderstand./

My Father was ever truly religious from his youth vp =
ward./ Loving to ye Ministery & to all men./ & exceeding
full of mercy & compassion to the poore./ And in the   10
towne where he lived, he alwayes sought after peace, not
only for him self, but for all the towne./ making every
one frendes after there falling out./ he was wonderfull
loving & naturall to his wyfe & children, his house was
for all straungers as also for frendes./ And Notwthstanding   15
his bountie towardes ye poore, bothe at home & abroade,
And his liberalitie in housekeeping, Yet such was ye great
mercy of God, as he lyved & dyed in great richesse & estate,
A point Sir wch I wold gladly have you take notice of./
Yf I should speake as muche good of him as he deserved,   20
I professe I could not contain it in this paper; but all
this I leave & commend to your favour wch I will alwaies
studie to be made worthie of./
                              Frauncis Bedell./

f. 60r

[85　　　　　　　　*c.* February 1613 (?)　　　　　see Commentary]

Sir./　　　　　　　　　　　　　　　　　　　　　　　　　　　　1
Necessitie, not my will, sendes me vnto you a borrower of 20s.
if you may: this last dismall arrest, hath taken from all
my Frendes something, & from me all I hd: & to day I am
to meete wth some Frendes at dinner returned from Virginia,　　5
& God is witnes wth me I have not to pay for my dinner,
All my thinges be at Pawne, & I yet indebted to Ro: wife,
Love me you still (if you please) I will give you no other
cause; & let not .N. know of my name, or beeing in any
place hereafter, I am Ielious of him: if I were assured　　　10
of +what+ is very likely, I wold not be so evill intreated, and have
patience: looke well vnto your self: & looke well vpon your
self, & you shall finde he is no companion for you; but it
may be I sound herein harshly to your love; yet know it
comes from a true love to you; Vale:/ youres ever .W.*S*.　　15

[86　after 15 February 1612/13; before Autumn 1614 (?)　see Commentary]

Sir/　　　　　　　　　　　　　　　　　　　　　　　　　　　　1
For Godes love let me trouble you no more wth wordes nor pistles,
My offer is faire & satisfactorie; A suretie, bothe for the
Principall & interest. Your mere Citiner will be so answerd./
Of wch sort, many have forborn me fyve & twentie yeares　　5
for fyve & twentie tymes so much: And parted satisfied wth =
out one peny interest./ Be but secur'de: your scrivener askes
no more; Iust dealing men are free though nere so poore./
Here's Poetrie for you./ Let me be free then; do not insult,
Tys vulgare; you are Noble, and a lover of vertue: I have　　10
labor'd for you, when others neglected you;　For Mr doctor:
I have bene a Factor; of myne Owne mere motion, wthout
his desire, +or+ desert./ Let this be my purgatorie:/ In good faith
Sir I am busie even for life: let me but live and I will pay
you all: resting all youres. Geo: *Ch*:/　After Christmas　　15
(god willing) I will infallibly attend you. vouchsafe free dispen =
sation till then, and live happiest of men./

Necessitie, not my will, bids me vnto you a borrower off 20.
iff you may: this last dismall arrest, & ath taken from all
my frends somethinge, & from me all I had: & to day I am
to meete with some frends at dinner returned from Virginia,
& God is witnes with me I have not to pay for my dinner,
All my things be at Pawne, & I grow indebted to mo: wise,
love me you still (iff you please) I will give you no other
cause; & let not M. know off my wants, or beinge in any
plate heereafter, I am iealious off him: iff I were assured
off it: is very likely, I would not be so evill intreated, and have
patience: looke well vnto yor selfe: & looke neuer vpon yor
selfe, & you shall finde yt is no companion for you; but it
may be I send heerein harshly to yor love; yet know it
comes from a true love to you; Dale: / yor eu^r M. S.

ffor Gods love let me trouble you no more with wordes nor wisshes
My offer is faire & satisfactorie; A smarte, both for thy
principall & interest: yor mere Citizen will be so answerd:
Off my sort, many have forborne me five & twentie yeares:
for five & twentie tymes so much: and parted satisfied with=
out one peny interest: / Be but seconde: yor cred^rs aske
no more; Iust dealing men are not thence now so poore:
Gods Pockie for you: / Let me be free then; do not insult,
& by vulgars; you are Noble, and a lover off vertue: I have
labor^d you, when others neglected you; / ffor M^r doctor:
I have bene a factor; off myne owne mind motion, to sent
his desire, do it: / Let this be my purgatorie: / In good faith
E^r I am bound, & too soone for life: let me but live and I will pay
you all: wishing all yor. Geo: Ch: /   After Christmas
God willing I will infallibly attend you, have safe free dispen=
sation till then, and live happiest off men: /

To the Kinges Ma:tie /

Humblie showeth, y[a]t, hauinge aboue Nine yeares i[n] late Prince
Henry in place off a Sewer in ordinarie, And in all y[a]t tyme
consuminge, hid whole meanes, neuer wrong[i]ng any subie or
seruice, And now put from hid place vnder Prince Charles;
It would please y[o]r most excellent Ma:tie to take into y[o]r Royall
compassion, vppon hid highnes Princely Intention (being so sod=
dainly preuented) could not bee accomplished; And to refer y[e]
poore shippwrack[t] estate, & willing industrie, to y[e] examinac[i]on and
iudgment off some one or two off y[e] y[o]r Ma:ties most honorable Counsell;
by whose consideringe y[e] highnes dueful trouell in so meane a
fortunac[i]on, may take time information shall by me redouned
by my enforced suyle, & accordingly informinge y[o]r Ma: y[o]r fauor
my nought suite may redue you, And for all y[o]r highest sacred
commiseration off mee so miserablie lost, I shall ever be most
zealously bound to all gratitude, and pray as bounessarth[?] for
y[o]r Ma:ties wished and endles felicitie /

To the highst honoraule, the Earle off Northampton:
Lord Priuie Seale, & one off his Ma:ties most
Honorable priuie Counsaile.

The humble Petic[i]on off Geo: Chapman:

Beseecheth y[o]r good Lo[rd]: to vouchsafe y[e] reading off this annexst
petic[i]on, and to take notice off my deseruid suite herein contay=
ned; The ground thereof being a due dett (the promisse off a
Princes bounty on hid deathbed) growing from a serious and
valuable cause (two yeares studie & writinges imposd by his
highnes vppon a poore orphan, whose Pen is his Plough), & the
sole meanes off his maintenance; That y[o]r Lo[rd]: being a most
competent Iudge off my paines in this kind; may please out off
y[o]r Noble inclination to learning, to countenance my constrained
motions, made for no mony; But yt the same goe over Copyhold
off the Princes Land, off y[e] 4[e] rent, yff any such I can finde.

f. 60v

[87   after 6 November 1612   see Commentary]

   To the Kinges Maiestie /   1
Humblie sheweth, yt serving above Nine yeares ye late Prince
Henry in place of a sewer in ordinarie, And in all yt tyme
consumynge his whole meanes, never receyving any suyte or
benifite; And now put from his place vnder Prince *Charles*;   5
It wold please your most excellent Maiestie to take into your Royall
compassion, whom his highnes Princely Intention (being so soo =
dainely prevented) could not see recompenc'd; And to refer your
poore suppliantes estate, & willing meritt, to ye examination and
wysdome of some one or two of your Maiesties most honorable privie Counsell;
yt (for avoyding your highnes vnfitt trooble wth so meane a   11
suppliance) may take true instruction of all thinges convenient
for my enforced suyte, & accordingly informe your Maiestie how farr
my necessitie may move you; And for all your right sacred
comisseration of one so miserablie left, I shall ever be most   15
zealously bound to all gratitude; and pray as vncessantly for
your Maiesties wished and endles Felicitie./

[88   after 6 November 1612   see Commentary]

   To the Right honorable: the Earle of Northhamton: 1
   Lord Privie Seale, & one of his Maiesties most
    honord⟨lbe⟩ privie Counsaile./
   The humble Peticion of Geo: Chapman:
Besecheth your good lordshippe to vouchsafe ye reading of this annext   5
Petition, and to take notice of my enforced suite therin contay =
ned; The ground thereof being a due debt (the promisse of a
Prince voucht on his deathbed) growing from a serious and
valuable cause (two yeares studie & writinge imposd by his
highnes vpon a poore man, whose Pen is his Ploughe, & the   10
Sole meane of his maintenance) That your Lordshippe being a most
competent Iudge of my paines in this kinde; may please out of
your Noble inclination to learning, to countenance my constraind
motion, made for no money; but onely some poore Coppiehold
of the Princes land, of 40s Rent, if any such I can finde.   15

Nor needes your Lordshippe doubt giving President to any, no one being –
able, of this Nature, to alledge ye like service; None but my self
having done homer; wch will sufficiently distinguish it from any
other. For if what Virgile divinely affirmes be true, yt easier it
is to gaine ye Club from *Hercules*, then a verse from *Homer* (inten =   20
ding so to gaine & mannadge it, yt we make it our owne) I hope fewe
els can plead to ye Prince so difficult a service? wch if your Lordshippe please
the rather to consider; I shall be enabled to proceede in ye further worke
commaunded by his highnes, and pay to your most worthie Name and
memorie, the tribute of my best paines; and daily prayers for youre   25
honores longe continewed eminence in all honor & happines./

[89   after 15 February 1612/13   see Commentary]

Sir as I hold my self once fortunate in your love & good opinion, so   1
nothing hath of late so much affected me, as ye discontinuance of your
woonted kindenes & affection. For had I not at this tyme some reasons
more pressing then ordinarie to esteeme your frendship in perticulare,
yet such hath ever bene my generall care wth all due respect and   5
observance to give contentment to my frendes, as I desire to lyve no
longer, then I may be thought worthie of their love & kinde estimation,
When I call to mynde how in ye late Princis tyme, you were not wan =
ting to me in all fytt offices wch might procure my good wth his
highnes; and besydes, how woorthy a frend I then had of you to   10
resort vnto in my private wantes, I can not but be much greeved to
finde so great an alteration as now I doe: you then being ready
to pleasure me out of your owne; whereas now you show your self most
vnwilling to gyve way to other mens bountie in ye due rewarde of my
paines, wch I ye rather wonder at, in yt the ground of this chaunge is   15
so obscure, & insensible, as wth no studie nor examination of my self,
it can fall wthin my apprehension; vnlesse yt be turnd to my hurt,
wch ought to have bene construed for my benefite, my too much paines in
yt busines, by me wth others vndertaken; Concerning wch my paines, if

Nor neede yo.r Lo.p: doubt giving President to any, no one being ~
able, oft this Nature, to alledge y.e like service; None but my self
haveing donne Honor; w.ch will sufficiently distinguish it from any
other. ffor if it weare Hercule ditimely asfirmed betrue, y.t easier it
is to gaine y.e Club from Hercules, then a verst from Homer (inten=
ding so to graue a damadge it, to no make it our owne) I hope sure
All men pleade to y.e Prince so difficult a subiect? w.ch if yo.r Lo.p pleast
to vouchsafe to consider; so shall be enabled to proceede in y.e service
commaunded by his Highnes, and pay to yo.r most worthy Name and
memorie, the tribute oft my best paines; and daily prayeis for yo.ur
Honor's longe continued eminence in all good & happines.

S.r. as I held my self once fortunate in yo.r late & good opinion, so
noth ing hath oft late so much afflicted me, as y.e discontinuance oft yo.r
wonted kindones & affection. ffor had I not at this tyme some reasons
now pressing then ordinarie to esteeme yo.r freindship in perticulear,
yet surely hate deere bene my generall regard & all due respect and
observance to giue contentment to my freinds, as I desire to liue no
longer, then I may be thought worthie oft their loue & kinde estimation,
vppon I call to my selfe how in y.e late Princes tyme, you weare not wan=
ting to me in all full office wch might procure my good wth his
highnes; and besyde, how worthy a freind I then had oft you to
resent vnto in my priuate wante, I can not but be much greeued to
finde so great an alteration as now I doe: you then being ready
to pleasure me out oft yo.r owne; whereas now you shew yo.r selfe most
vnwilling to gyve way to other mens benefits in y.e due rewardes of my
paines, w.ch I y.e rather wonder at, in y.t the ground oft this yt seeme it
so obscure, & insensible, as wth no studie nor examination oft my self,
it can fall wthin my apprehension; vnless the be turned to my hurt,
wch ought to haue bene reserued for my benifits, my too much paines in
y.e busines, by me wth other consideracion; Concerning wch my paines, it

yo[r] so great dislike tharof did negatiō ariſe out off yo[r] selues;
I may not contest wth thoſe [y]t weare my appointed Judges; or
Justifie my Labours, iff you in yo[r] owne Judgements thought them
worthie of reprehension. but iff by the inspiration off my
malicious detractors (who approue nothing but what they
either haue done, or take on them to haue done them selues)
ye were drawen to a dislike; let it I pray you suffice
to enterteyne theire pardonable conceipt, [y]t in that thoughle
aſwellie, for all it was ordayned [y]t to say [y]t leaſt it did
not diſpleaſe. But howsoever I cannot yet boaſt [y]t my
paines were to be eſteemd as paines; my tymes & diligent
attendances employed thearin, might claime a due conſidera=
tion. And though valuinge my Labours, ex condigno; they
might be thought already to haue receyved sufficient re=
warde; yet conſidering y[e] object of myne employment was
moſt liberally dealt w[th]; I may ex congruos of all my aparts
in yo[r] equall distribution; And thinge so playnlie, damned, and
penaltie were rewarded out off yo[r] full bountie; I thinke it
hard, [y]t I (the reviser, and in part Inventor) ſhould be put
off wth England & Scoamabout, & such ſingopenndos, to be payd
by a few of particulars, what such or such a peece might
be priſed at; or whether the whole & ſomme might amount
to allow ten pounds or no.

Some of my familie; who had not [y]e beſt ſucceſſe, were yet
thought worthie a hundred Markes; the leaſt in ould fiftie
pounds: and what valuation ſoever it pleaſd my detractors
to ſett on my Labours, yet I am aſſured [y]t in myne owne conceſſ,
I haue as well employd [y]t tyme & paines to [y]e benefite off
no leſſe a ſomme. Not to inſiſt upon theſe particularons,
my conclud: [y]t iff you were not then ſatisfied w[th] [y]t I had
done; you will yet at [y]e laſt be ſatisfied w[th] w[a]t I haue

your so great dislike therof did wholie arise out of your selues;   20
I may not contest wth those yt were my appointed Iudges; or
Iustifie my labours, if you in your owne Iudgmentes thought them
worthie of reprehension. but if by the instigation of my
malicious depravers (who approve nothing but what they
either have done, or take on them to have done them selues)   25
ye were drawn to yt distaste; let it I pray you suffice
to answere their preiudicate censures; yt in that Royall
assemblie, for wch it was ordayned (to say ye least) it did
not displease./ But howsoever ye successe had bene: yet my
paines were to be esteemd as paines; & my tyme & diligent   30
attendance employed therein, might claime a due considera =
tion. And though valuinge my labours, *ex condigno*; they
might be thought already to have receyved sufficient re =
warde; yet considering yt others of meaner employment were
most liberally dealt wth; I may *ex congruo*: challeng a parte   35
in your equall distribution; And seeing players, dauncers, and
painters, wre rewarded out of your full bountie; I thinke it
hard, yt I (the wryter, and in part Inventor) should be put
wth Taylors & Shoomakers, & such snipperados, to be paid
by a bill of perticulars, what such or such a peece might   40
be pris'd at; or whether the whole Somme might amount
to above ten poundes or no.
Some of my facultie, who had not ye best successe, were yet
thought worthie a hundred Markes; the least in others fiftie
poundes: and what valuation soever it pleased my detractors   45
to sett on my labours, yet I am assured yt in myne owne course,
I could have employed so much tyme & paines to ye benifite of
no lesse a Summe./ Not to insist vpon these capitulacions,
my suyte is: yt if you were not then satisfied wth yt I had
done; you will yet at ye last be satisfied wth what I have   50

suffred; yt is: losse of reputation, want, and imprisonment:
the daunger whereof still pressing me, will not give me leave
to rest wth such ⟨an⟩ answere as *Habet mercedem suam*, let
my vrgent want I pray you excuse this my shamefull –
importunitie, being otherwise lothe to give you offence, to   55
whom I have bene so much formerly beholden. And so
in expectation of your kinde & speedy answere I rest.

        Youres to be disposed.
        Of desart:
        By equitie   60
        he hath his rewarde

[90   14 December 1610   see Commentary]

Sir/   1
 Although length of the voyage, & distance of ye place
where you are, wold require a long letter, and the busines
that we have in hand touching your plantacion a large discourse,
(yet must I crave pardon of you, if considering many pre =   5
sent Impedimentes) I wrap vp a great desyre of advertise =
ment and of good affection in fewe wordes, my desire is cheefe =
ly to let you vnderstand how well your travell in that place
where you are, is interpreted amongst all good & wise men,
wch having bene still in love wth long & hazardous voyages,   10
more to profytt your knowledge then for any other profytt,
shewes yt you have a mynde much in love wth vertue, and are
a fytt *Achates* for such an *Æneas*, as is our Noble & worthie
Generall the lord *Delawarre*. Yf you knew good Mr Strachey,
the care yt I have of this Plantacion, ye travell yt I have ta =   15
ken therein, (bothe before & since it pleased them to call me

suffred; +hɨ ibɨ: lossɨ ofɨ reputation, want, and imprisonment:
the daunger vigorous still pressing me, will not giue me leaue
to rest the surre _____ answere, as Habet mercedem suam, let
my rigorous want I pray you excuse this my vnmanerly ~
importunitie, being otherwise loth to giue you offence, to
whom I haue bene so much formerly beholden. And so
in expectation ofɨ your kinde & speedy answere I rest.

                              yorɨ to be disposed of

                         ofɨ desart.

                         By equitie

                              he hath his reward

Ωɨ 1.

Although length ofɨ the voyage, & distance ofɨ the place
where you are will require a long letter and the besines
that we haue in hand throughout yorɨ plantacon a large discourse;
yet must I craue pardon ofɨ you, (ifɨ considering many present impedimentes) I render you a great quʒantitie of aduertise-
ment and ofɨ good affection in fewe wordes, my desire is chieifɨ-
ly to let you vnderstand how well yorɨ trauell in that place
where you are, is interpreted amongst all good & graue men,
we hauing bene still inrolled vp long & hazardous voyages,
more to manifest yorɨ knowledge then for any other profitt,
Reaued ifɨ you haue a mynde more in loue wth vertue and are
a fytt Achates for such one Eneas, as is our Noble & worthie
Generall the lord Delawarre. Ifɨ you knew good mr _____
the care yt I haue ofɨ this Plantacon, ye trauell I haue ta=
ken therein, & both before & since it pleased them to call me

into that councell) and y⁻ officer that y⁻ doth not onlie bearin in
mea, but stand out to their divers offshare owe, for y⁻ fur=
therance & advancement of this, & so instante, you
would thinke y⁻ my passage & say, with or farther was prinse of
of or complement & y⁻ of the noblest men y⁻ don speake
or wryte (except y⁻ in y⁻ word litle God, & more honored
we all the workinges of worldly felicitie in these two words,
Latari et benefacere, implying a peaceful Minde accompaied
with well doinge, (from which cannot be shaved,) we gate
more cause to be expressfully inly glad then you, y⁻ gate y⁻
comfort of so great a well doing, to which no other may be
compared, for what welldoing can be greater, then to be y⁻
stocke & authore of a people, and of a people y⁻ shall serve
to glorifie God, which is y⁻ ende of all our Creation, and to
redeeme them from Ignorance & infidelitie, to y⁻ true
knowledge & worshippe of God, whereby you are made
partakers of this promisse, y⁻ thereof. But other vnto
Vertuousell, shall shine as y⁻ starres in y⁻ firmament,
wherein I rabie so of happines, y⁻ I cannot (by reason of
my infirmitie) have a perfecte y⁻ Comfort by my travaile
bye: if I ease by my suddaine sparat home I shall not neede
to aduertize you, goe to travis we of self, for y⁻ opperations
these shall make y⁻ out gon & vse of my admonition, w⁻
my affectionpoole willingly afford you, if y⁻ were caus:
and I know, y⁻ y⁻ difficulties & straibons of the place, and
y⁻ sundnet of these people w⁻ whom you gate to doe, w⁻
these other difficulties (of which we are sore sensible y⁻
for y⁻ y⁻ selb) will make you carefull to pleasure God, w⁻
may blesse all y⁻ you vndatak, and walke in a Noble

into the counsell) and ye Fire yt doth not onlie burn in
mee, but flames out to the view of every one, for ye fur =
therance & advauncement of this ⟨holye⟩ honorable enterprice, you
wold thinke yt my speeche hath neither fashion nor purpose   20
of a complement./ Yf the wysest man yt ever spake
or wrytt (except him yt was both God & man) summed
vp all the reckeninge of worldly felicitie in these two wordes,
Lætari et benefacere, implying a cheerefull Mirthe accompanied
wth well doinge, (from wch it can not be severed,) who hath   25
more cause to be cheerefull & inly glad then you, yt hath ye
comfort of so great a well doing, to wch no other may be
compared, for what welldoing can be greater, then to be ye
stockes & authors of a people, and of a people yt shall serue
& glorifie God, wch is ye ende of all our Creation, and to   30
redeeme them from Ignorance & ⟨infe⟩ infidelitie, to ye true
knowledg & worshippe of God, whereby you are made
partakers of this promisse, yt they wch lead others vnto
Righteousnes, shall shine as ye Starres in ye firmament,
wherein I envie your happines, yt I cannot (by reason of   35
my profession) be a partaker of yt Comfort by my travell
their, as I am by my endevour here at home, I shall not need
to advise you how to carie your self, for your experience –
there hath made you outgone all vse of my admonition, wch
my affection wold willingly afforde you, if there were cause: 40
and I know, yt ye difficulties & straitenes of the place, and
ye hardnes of those people wth whom you have to doe, wth
those other difficulties (of wch we are even sensible here
for your sake) will make you carefull to please God, who
must blesse all yt you vndertake, and walke in a Noble –   45

example of Iustice & truthe, wch onely doth enforce a reputa =
tion & respect from other men./ And in vaine it is in such
a place to pretend to be vertuous, except a man be ⟨b⟩ vertuous
indeede, and yt vertue extend it self vnto example.
Therefore, since I assure my self, yt of this advise you have no   50
neede, I will conclude wth an earnest request, yt you wold be
pleased by the return of this shippe to let me vnderstand–
from you the nature & qualitie of ye soyle, & how it is like
to serue you wthout helpe from hence, the manners of ye people,
how ye Barbarians⟨e⟩ are content wth your being there, but   55
especially how our owne people doe brooke their obedience, how
they endure labor, whether willingly or vpon constraint, how
they lyve in ye exercise of Religion, whether out of conscience
or for fashion, And generally what ease you have in the
government there, & what hope of ye successe, wherein I desire   60
you & coniure you, by our auncient acquaintance & good inten =
tions, to deale Clearely wth me, as I wold do wth you in ye like
case, yt thereby I may be truly able to satisfie others, & to direct
my counsells & endevores for prevention of evill, if there be any;
In requitall whereof, you shall commaund me both there, & els –   65
where, wheresoever it shall please God to direct our fortunes
to meete, to assiste you in any course for your good, And so recom =
mending my service & affection to your self & ye +right+ honorable Lord, I recom =
mend you & your endevores in my prayers to ye direction & protection of
Godes divine providence. Resting./   70
                                        Your ever loving frend
M. *temple*. 14⁰. Decembrer.   to command
1610./   *Rich Martin*
                    To ye worthy my very loving frend.
                    william Strachey Esquier in   75
                              Virginia
                 By ye hercules whom god preserue ./.

an example of justice & truthe, which onely dothe enforce a recognition & respect from other men. And in vaine it is in suche a place to pretend to be vertuous, except a man be vertuous indeed, and his vertue extend it selfe whole example.

Therefore, since I assure my self, that of this advise you have no neede, I will conclude with an earnest request, that you would be pleased by the returne of this shipp to let me understand, ... you the meanes to qualifie the of Eagle, & would be like to serve you without glorie from hence, the manners of the people, how the Barbarians are content with your beinge there, but especially how our owne people doe brooke their obedience, whether they indure toile, whether not willingly or upon constraint, how they be in the exercise of Religion, whether out of conscience or for fashion, And generallye what you thincke ... to governe them, & what hope of the Country, requesting you ... you & conivre you, by our auncient acquaintance and ... inten-tion, to deale obscurely of me as friend do of friend in the like case, ... I may be truely able to satisfie those ... divert my conseil ... induce for prevention of will, either to any in ... any particular negoce, you doe commaund me ... may ... request that it pleaseth God to direct ... fortunes to make, to assist your ... events for your good, And so recommending my ... & affection to your ... Lord, I recommend you & your endevors in my prayers to the direction & protection of Gods divine providence. Resting.

M. temple. 14° Decembr.
1610.

your ever lovinge frend
to command
Rich Martin

To ... wh. my deare lovinge frend
willm Strachy ... in

Virginia

By ye ... upon God preserve.

To the right honourable: the Governors of the
Hospitall of King James.

The humble petition of Peter Florentine that

Most humbly sheweth. etc.

That your petitioner well knowing of the honourable
charitable act of the said honourable hospitall etc.

And he well knowing he is able through by the great favour
persons qualified to be approved wounded surgeon of the
foundation of this same honourable hospitall etc.

He being a good in birth and education, he first at the fountain
... honourable doctrine our late Soveraigne tyme, of
the said honourable doctrine a good under the Collours of
... William ... for many years, and re-
...

And spent many years ... into ... parts of
Christendom and other ... as by ... Certificate
and otherwise may appeare.

Humbly truelie shewing his life and ... was what questioned, being otherwise qualified in ... matters, that he may
be a those wounded to further such doctrine service, as your
honours wisdomes shall in the hospitall thinke etc.

[91   *c.* mid–1613; before 13 November 1613   see Commentary]

      To the Right honorable: ye Governores of ye   1
        hospitall of king Iames./.
    The humble peticion of Peter Feryman gentleman
Most humbly sheweth :/

That your peticioner well knowing of this Memorable &   5
Charitable Act of ye late deceassed Tho. Sutton Esquier /

And wthall knowing he is as he trusteth by your honores favours,
a person quallified wth in ye expresse woordes & intent of the
Foundation of this ever Memorable hospitall./.

As being a gentleman in birth and education, As first at ye Inner   10
Temple, then at Court in our late Soveraignes tyme, of
blessed Memorie; A Souldier & gentleman vnder ye Collours of
yt woorthie Sir Phillip Sydney for many yeeres, and re =
spected by him, and so farr yt he was Imployed from that
warre into England to his honorable Father in lawe Sir Frauncis   15
Walsingham, and his service recommended to other of the
honorable Privie Counsell of yt tyme; as many lyving of place
can testifie. having also bene at Sea in her late Maiesties
Services, and her highnes Shippes wth honorable persons./
And spent many yeeres in Travaile, into divers partes of   20
Christendome and els where, As by Authentike Certificate
and otherwise may appeare./

humbly trulie shewing his life and Manners was never questio =
ned, being otherwise quallified in Song & Musick, that he may
be a chiefe meanes to further such devine Service, as your   25
honors Wisdomes shall in yt hospitall Erect./

And therefore being very Aged, nor hath many yeeres to lyve:
having spent his meanes in these forraigne Imploymentes and
travailes: & desyring a short quiet & retyred lyfe./

In all true humblenes he submittes himself in all thinges to   30
your honores, most humbly praying and Imploring all your right
Noble favoures, to make him a member in this Memorable worke,
So and in such sort as your honores thinke fytt. And he will dayly
vnfaynedly pray for the happines of his Soveraigne Maiestie
& Royall Issue; wth your honores & posterities long to continue,   35
And will wth Psalmes & Hymns, daily praise & magnifie ye
blessed Trinitie in vnitie, And sing sweete peace to all his honorable
Patrons and Benefactores./.

[92   see Commentary]

Whereas there is a Peticion preferred by Peter Feryman gentleman   1
entituled, To the Right honorable, the Governores of kinge
Iames his hospitall, and herevnto Annext./ Wee whose names
are here vnder subscribed, do certifie to all honorable personages
and others whosoever. That ye contentes of the said Peticion –   5
many of vs know to be true, and all of vs beleue to be true;
And thus farre we all expressely certifie of our owne certaine
knowledge, yt he is a gentleman of much integritie & honestie,
& well esteemed of wth parsons of good ranck & quallitie, his
lyfe & Manners hath bene alwayes sound & even, nor so much as   10
in the least degree questioned. And surely thus much for trut =
hes sake, wth our well wishinges to him, wee witnes wth subscrip
sion of our handes./

And therefore being very of god, now hath many years to labo:
... spirit his meanes in theise ... imploymente and
... professing a ... quiet to ... his ...

For all ... submitte him selfe in all things ... the
... ... for ever ... all ...
Noble ... to make ... ...
... ... shall and he will ...
... ... of his ... ...
Royall ... ... to ... ...
And will ... ... magnifie ...
... ... honoure, And sing sweete peace to all his ...
Patrons and Benefactors. /

Whereas there is a Petition preferred by Peter ... gent:
entituled, To the right honourable, the Governors of Kings
... his ... ...
... ... subscribed, do testifie to all ... ...
and ... ... of the said Petition
... of ... ... to be true and all of his ... to be true;
And ... knowe we all ... testifie of our owne ...
knowledge, ... he is a gentleman of ... integritie honestie,
... ... present ... good ... qualities, his
life & Manners ... beene alwayes sounde ... nor so much ...
in the least degree questioned. And ... this much for ...
his sake, we ... well wishinge to him, have ... ... subscription of our handes. /

I do not offend vsually this way; and therefore one Importunacye may be the better suffred. I pray you to be carefull of this Gent: necessitie, and further it willingly, and in thynne you shall make me the bolder to you; who holpe in a busines of far greater spurrtie as this, doth not now require the meditor much, then to mindeful of his owne good name. I shall goe to visite them effectually, and so I lender to thanke you. Least I should be turnous to you, Madame in sollicitinge you to that, to which by ye selfe, you are so prompt and willing.

yr true lover & frend

Ben: Jonson.

To my worthy & Honord
frend: Mr Leech /

Sr
I am confident of your trust in my frendshipp to importune your helpe to the furdering this Gentlemans suite, the bearer, whose name is Saker, vize (of my knowledge) is a most honest man, and worthie of a most better fortune to her selfe then so: how so it is, he himselfe will best acquaint you withe, and the circumstances which should perswade to it, or to which I pray you giue credit in all, for I know that Madame will not allow any thing subiect to suspition. You binde me to you to be euer thankfull: And they are not the least curtesies, that make more then one beholden. Let him finde I pray you that I haue credit with you by your vndoubtinge what you can for him chearfully: And I will take care you

f. 64v

[93   *c.* mid–1613; before 13 November 1613 (?)   see Commentary]

Mr Leech/   1
I do not offend vsually this way: and therefore one Impor =
tunacye may be the better sufferd. I pray you to be carefull
of this Gentlemans necessitie, and succoure it willingly, and in
tyme. you shall make me ever beholden to you; he yt helpes   5
in a busines of so great charitie as this, doth not more
succor the Needers want, then he increaseth his own good
name: I pray you Sir to write very effectually, and so
I leave to troble you: least I should do Iniurie to your
Nature in solliciting you to that, to wch of your self, you are   10
so prompt and willing.
            Your true lover & frend
To my worthy & Honord   *Ben*: *Ionson*.
frend: *Mr. Leech* ./ .

[94   *c.* mid–1613; before 13 November 1613 (?)   see Commentary]

Sir   1
I am bold, out of my trust in your frendship, to requeste your
help to the furdering this Gentlemans suite, the bearers,
wth my lordes favour: who (of my knowledg) is a most honest
man, and worthie of a much better fortune, then yt he sues   5
for: what it is, he himself will best acquaint you wth, and
the circumstances yt should perswade to it, To wch I pray
you give credit in all, for I know his Modestie will not
vtter any thing subiect to suspition. You binde me to you
to be ever thankfull: And they are not the least curtesies,   10
that make more then one beholden. Let him finde I pray –
you that I have credit wth you by your vndertaking what
you can for him chearfully: And I will take care you

shall not repent you: If it be any thing to hold./

                            Your poore vnprofitable   15
                            ⟨Frend⟩ lover./
To my honord & vertuous   *Ben Ionson.*/
Frend. *Mr Tho*: Bond
Secret. to my honored Lord
the Lord Chauncellor   20
of England./.

[95   3 May 1596]

              The Testimoniall of Hierusalem   1
                    in English

To all and singuler to whom these presents shall come, greeting
in our Lord God everlasting./ Be it knowne in what Manner – –
Frauncis Maddison, a discreete and deuout gentleman of the Citie   5
of London Englishman (accompanied with one Peter Feryman
Gentleman: and one other Companion Englishmen) who for Chri =
stianitie and devotion sake: came to this Holie Citie of Ierusalem
the first day of May being Saturday: 1596: And to the Holie Se =
pulcher of our Lord Iesus Christ, from whence (death being sub =   10
dued) Hee arose againe the third day most Gloriously: And to the
holy Mount Caluarie, where (for our Redemption) he suffred a
most bitter death: And to Mount Oliuet from whence (in the
sight of his Disciples) by his owne vertue hee ascended into heaven:/
And to the place where the Virgin Mary in the Vale of Iesaphat   15
was buried, and from whence she was taken vp into Heaven;

ſhall not repent you : If it be any thing to gould. |

Yo.r poore vnprofitable

~~ffrind~~ ſer. |

To my honord & beloued
ffrind : M.r Tho: Bond
Seruant to my Lo. Lord
the Lord Chancellor
of England :|.

Ben Jonson. |

The Testimoniall of Hierusalem
in English

To all and ſingulars to vvhom theſe preſents ſhall come, greeting
in our Lord God euerlaſting. Be it knowen in what Manner
ffrauncis Maddiſon, a vertuous and deuout gentleman of the Citie
of London Engliſhman (accompanied vvith one Peter ffreyman
Gentleman : and one other Companion Engliſhmen) vvho for Chri=
ſtianitie and deuotion ſake, came to this Holie Citie of Ieruſalem
the firſt day of May being Satturday : 1596 : And to the Holie Se=
pulchre of our Lord Ieſus Chriſt, from vvhence (Death being ſub=
dued) Hee aroſe againe the third day moſt Gloriouſly : And to the
Holy Mount Caluarie, vvhere (for our Redemption) hee ſuffred a
moſt bitter death : And to Mount Oliuet from vvhence (in the
ſight of his Diſciples) by his owne vertue Hee aſcended into Heauen : |
And to the place vvhere the Virgin Mary in the Vale of Ioſaphat
vvas buried, and from vvhence ſhe vvas taken vp into Heauen ;

And vvhere the holy Supper of our Lord vvas instituted, vvhich
is the pledge of our Saluation: And vvhere many other Sacramentes
vvere performed; And to Bethany also, vvhere Lazarus being foure
dayes dead and buried: vvas raised by our Lord from death to life.
And Mount Jury, vvhere our blessed Lady saluted Elizabeth; And
to Bethlem also the Citie of Dauid, vvhere Christ the sonne of God
douchsafed to be laid in a Maunger; And there vvas reueiled of the
Sheepheardes: and vvorshipped of the Wise Men: And to many other
places, in vvhere our Sauiour himselfe, (of his vnspeakable cle-
mency,) douchsafed to vvorke our Saluation; And cheifely
in these places, vvhere Christians at this day are vvont to
visit vvith his said Companions; And he the said Francis of
a godly affection and vvhole hart did vvorship: And because
many in this spacious vvorld are named Francis: This is the
foresaid Francis, vvhich for his outward appearaunce hath, on
the out side of his right arme a vvhite marke or Scarre
like to the hurt of a Goomes shott. In vvitnesse vvhereof I
Frier Iohn Francis Salandra, Warden of Hierusalem,
Commissarie Apostolick of the Holy Land: haue caused these
to be sealed vvith the great Seale of our Office, and haue
signed the same vvith my hand. Dated at Ierusalem, in our
Sacred Couent, of our holy Sauiour, the third day of
May, in the yeere from the Childe birth of the Virgin,
1596. as aforesaid.

Fr: Io: Francis Salandra: vvritten vvith
myne owne hand.

And where the holy Supper of our Lord was instituted, which
is the pledge of our Saluation: And where many other Sacraments
were performed; And to Bethany also, where Lazarus being fouer
dayes dead and buried: was raised by our Lord from death to life./   20
And Mount Iury, where our blessed Lady saluted Elizabeth; And
to Bethlem also the Citie of David, where Christ the sonne of God
vouchsafed to be laid in a Maunger; And there was visited of the
Shepheards: and worshipped of the Wise Men: And to many other
places, in which our Sauiour himselfe, (of his vnspeakable cle =   25
mency,) vouchsafed to worke our Saluation; And chieflye
in those places, which Christians at this day are wont to
visit with his said Companions; And he the said Francis of
a godlye affection and whole hart did worship: And because
many in this spacious World are named Francis: This is that   30
foresaid Francis, which (for his outward apparance) hath on
the but side of his right arme a white Marke or Starre
like to the hurt of a Goonne shott./. In witnesse whereof I
Frier Iohn Francis Salandra, Warden of Hierasalem,
Commissarie Apostolicke of the Holy Land: haue caused these   35
to be sealed with the great Seale of our Office, and haue
signed the same with my hand./   Dated at Ierusalem, in our
Sacred Covent, of our holy Sauiour, the third day of
May, in the Yeere From the Childe birth of the Virgin,
1596. as aforesaid./   40
     Fr: Io: Francis Salandra:/ written with
       myne owne hand./.

[96   October 1591   see Commentary]

A note of the true discourse of ye fight   1
wch ye Revenge had wth the Spaniardes.
The last of August we all Ryding at Flower, we then
discried ye Spanish fleete, wherevpon ye Revenge wayed, &
bare wth them, so dyd ye rest of all oure fleet. The   5
Revendge got the winde of Nyne of ye Spaniardes, & Nyne
more came to ye windeward of her againe. Then .3. Arma =
does presently clapt aborde ye Revendge, about .4. of the
clocke in ye afternoone, & contynued fight vntill three of
the clock in ye morninge, in wch tyme there were aboard the   10
Revendge one after an other of great shippes .19. not one
of ye smaller sort durst come nigh her, of wch .19. wee
of ye Revenge sunck .3. & spoyled .13. wch went to the
Terceres ye next day. One hulk wch we sunk had in
her .450. men, ye second a great Armatho, had in her   15
300. men, ye third a galleon had in her .250. men, so at
3. of ye clocke in ye morninge they fell of from vs, & for =
sooke vs all. Our Mastes of ye Revendge were all spoyld,
not one standing: & when we saw yt we could not go from
them, & our owne fleete being all from vs, Our Captaine   20
thought good to come to parley wth them, to see what –
mercy they wolde graunt vs, otherwise we were determined
to fight so long as we could, & so at ye last to fyer our shipp.
wherevpon they graunted vs our lyves, & yt no man should
be hurt: & so the shipp was dd. being so beaten downe, yt   25
she was not almost able to stand vpon ye water, nor service
able. So our men were divided amonge ye Spanish fleete,
.10. to one ship, 10. to an other & so of ye rest. Our Captain

66

A note off the true discourse off ye fight
wch ye Robucke had wth the Spaniarde:

The last off August wee all ryding at Flores, wee then
discried ye Spanish flecte, wherupon ye Robucke wayed, &
stere wee knowe, to kepe ye wethr off vs all owr flecte. The
Robucke got the windwd off Nyne off ye Spaniarde, & Nyne
more came to ye windward off ye Robucke, & yet we 3. Armada
dyd prsently clap aboard ye Robucke, about 4. off ye
clocke in ye afternoone, & continued fight vntill 4. wer off
the clock in ye mornings, in wch tyme ther wer aboard the
Robucke one after an other off ye greate shipes, 19. not one
off ye smaller sort durst come me ner vs, off wch 19. wer
off ye Robucke sunck. 3. & spoyled. 13. wch went to the
leward ye next day. One Gult wch was sunck had in
her. 450. men, ye second a greate Armada, had in her
300. men, ye third a gallion had in her. 250. men, so at
3. off ye clocke in ye morninge they fell off from vs, & for-
sooke vs all. Owr Maste off ye Robucke wer all spoyled,
not one standing: & when wee saw we wee could not go from
them, & owr owne flecte being all from vs, Owr Captaine
thought good to come to parley wth them, to see what
mercy they woolde grannte vs, otherwise wee were determined
to fight so long as wee could, & so at ye last to fyre ye shipp,
wherupon they grannted vs owr lyves, & yt no man shuld
be hurt: & so ye shipp was lost, being so beaten downe, yt
he was not almost able to stand vpon ye water, nor service-
able. So owr men wer devided amonge ye Spanish flecte,
10. to one shipp, 10. to an other & so wth. Owr Captaine

Sr Ri: Grinfild being deadly woundid wth a shott, was ca-
ried abord the Spanyard, wher he dyed two days after. / When we began our fight, we
were in ye Revenge 250. men, & when the fight was done,
we were 120. / The Revenge was broughte wth a greate
Armado to the Tercers, wher at a point she was
lost wth foule weather wth 300. spaniards in her, & 13.
spanish ship wer lost the same tyme. / We were 15
men sent abord a spaniard, a man of warre, wch shipp
was lost, & an Indian man took robin a lindsey too
at St Myghaelles. and we lost ther 3. of our men & 6
6. spaniards. /

Whereas John Rogers gent. is my servant, for whom I have
speciall employment. Theese are to require you & every
of you to forbeare to molest, arest, or imprison my
said servant, during this present Parliament, and 15.
dayes after, as you will answere to the contrary at
your uttmost perill. Geven under my hand & signet
at   the   day of december. 1610. /

To all Maiors, Sherifes, Bailifes
and other his Mat officers, to whom
it shall appartaine. /

Sir R. Grinfield being deadly wounded wth a shott, was –
caried aboord the Admyrall of ye Spaniardes, where he   30
lyved two dayes after./ When we began our fight, we
were in ye Revendg .250. men, & when the fight was done,
we were .120./ The Revendg was towed wth a greate
Armatho to the Terceres, where at ye point she was
lost wth fowle weather wth .300. spaniardes in her, & .13.   35
spanish ships more lost the same tyme./ We were .12.
men put aboord a spaniard, a man of warre, wch shippe
was lost, So an Indian man tooke vs in & landed vs
at St Mychaells. and we lost there .3. of our men, &
60. spaniardes./   40

[97   December 1610   see Commentary]

Whereas Iohn Rogers gentleman is my servant, for whom I have   1
speciall employment. These are to requier you & every
of you to forbeare to molest, Arest, or imprison my
said servant, during this present Parliament, and .15.
dayes after, as you will answere to the contrary at   5
your vttmost perills. Gyven vnder my hand & signet
at   the   day of december. 1610./

To all Maiores, Sheriffes, Bailiffes
and other his Maiesties officers, to whom
it shall appertaine./.   10

f. 67r

[98   see Commentary]

Sacer scholarum Genius (Illustissime vir) qui Iam   1
diu imminentes suas ruinas, et semesos lapides ingenijs
æternis honestauit noluit diutius iniurias temporis, aut
inopinatum forte casum pertinescere, sed precipitium sibi
landanda temeritate apparauit. Ad euius rudera, et Sacrum   5
puluerem te etiam inter ceteros solenni dolore inuitasset, ni
satius duxisset secundos Natalium Fastos, quam vltimi
choragium funeris celebrare,

[99   11 May [1615 – 1619]   see Commentary]

Good Mr. Bagley./.   1
The booke I promised was from day to day promised mee by the
next neighbour./ It shall be whites falt: if it be not brought you
wellbound this weeke, which I haue giuen him charge to see done./
But to the matter: I vsually once a day examine my sonnes, and this   5
can well say out of myne owne knowledge: Neuer since my eldest came
to schoole, he could not at any one tyme either conster his lesson perfectly
or say it without booke or perse it./ its miraculous to mee, and a thinge
in tyme will be a great dishonor to the schoole, and is direct betraying
of youth:/ for myne owne part, that day shall not passe but I will   10
and must take an account of my sonnes studies. And this day I finde he
neither said lesson, part, or did so much as looke of a booke; I lay it
not as a falt to you, for he is not your charge; These are things in =
excusable, if my pen be to tart, know it concerns a very carefull father
to a sonne of whom I know their is inough to proffitt./ Thus commit =   15
ting him with his brother to your care in his Masters absence, with my
harty commendations in hast I rest./.   Your loving Frend Rafe .W./.
My house Aldersgate streete .11. of May./.
     Good Mr Bagley take some care of them, & heare them your selfe./.
To my very loving Frend Mr Bagley at Charterhouse, these./.   20

Sacer scholarum Genius (Illustissime vir) qui iam
diu imminentes suas ruinas, et semesos lapides ingenijs
æternis honestauit noluit diutius iniurias temporis, aut
inopinatum forte casum pertinescere, sed precipitium sibi
landanda temeritate apparauit. Ad euius rudera, et Sacrum
puluerem te etiam inter ceteros solenni dolore inuitasset, ni
satius duxisset secundos Natalium Fastos, quam vltimi
choragium funeris celebrare,

Good Mr Bagley

Tey books I promised voab from day to day promised not by ther
next neigebo.r It shall be vorilds fall: if it be not brought you
voill bound this vooks, voring I haue giuen him charge to se donn.
But to ther matter: I vsually once a day examine my sonnes, and this
ran voill say out of myne owne knowledge: Neuer since my first came
to schools, he could not at any one tyme either conster his lesson perfectly
or say it without books or papers it is miraculous to me, and a thinge
in tyme will be a great dishonor to ther schools, and it directe betraying
of youth: for myne owne part, that day shall not passe but I will
and must take an account of my sonnes studies. And this day I finde he
neither said lesson, part, or did so much as looke of a booke: I lay it
not as a fault to you, for es it not your charge: These are thinges in=
excusable, if my pen be to tart, know it concernes a very carefull fation
to a sonne of his vacom I know he gir is inough to processill. Thus commit=
ting him voith his brother to your care in his Master absens, voith my
hearty commendations in east Frost. yor louing friend Vabs vo.
my gould Schoole gate shistill. 11. of May.
Good Mr Bagley take some care of them, es hauer they your salt.
To my very loving friend Mr Bagley at Chaderus ouse, th ese.

I am sorie you are so much offended hauing so little cause:
how much your eldest sonne hath profited since he came to this
schoole, or at least how well he hath bene taught, I doubt not
but Mr Grey will sufficiently make knowne vnto you at his
returne. In the meane tyme in his absence, as he himselfe hath
apointed, I giue his schollers no newe Lectures, but make them
repeat their old: vnlesse your sonne hath done among they wote
euery day sithence, you doe therfore most vniustly charge me with
his neglect that for a day he did not not so much as looke vpon
a booke. Be aduised what you write for your owne credit sake:
for, vt quisqz contentissimus est ita salutissimo a lingua est, And
we haue approued our selues to those that haue knowne vs longer
then you, and can iudge of vs as well. Neuer any yet gaue vs such
sound language, forbeare such speeches vnlesse you gaue the patience
to heare them returned backe againe, vnlesse we can more sasily do,
then you can suffer. We betray not our youth, we sell not theirs
vnto them, but our paines, vnlesse are profitable to euery scholler
according to his capacitie. what extraordinary matter is in your
sonne hauing but so little experience of him I cannot tell & do
assure my selfe you can as little iudge. Some are blinded with
ignorance, others with affection, some with hate. How easie a
thing is it for a father to be deceiued in his childe, when many a
man is deceiued in him selfe. The diligence of the Masters
is not alwaies to be measured by the proficiencie of the schollers:
Some cannot learne, some can and will not, though they be taught
with neuer so much mildnes or seueritie. Did you know how often

f. 67v

[100   shortly after item 99]

Sir   1
  I am sorie you are so much offended having so little cause;
how much your eldest sonne hath profited since he came to this
schoole, or at least how well he hath bene taught, I doubt not
but Mr Gray will sufficiently make knowne vnto you at his   5
returne./ In the meane tyme in his absence, as hee himselfe hath
apointed: I giue his schollers no newe Lectures, but make them
repeat their old: which your sonne hath done among the rest
euery day hitherto, you doe therefore most vniustly charge me with
this neglect that for a day he did not <u>not</u> so much as looke vpon   10
a booke./. Sir be aduised what you write for your owne credit sake:
p. for, vt quisque contemtissimus est ita salutissimæ linguæ est,/ And
we haue approued our selues to those that haue known vs longer
then you, and can iudge of vs as well./ Neuer any yet gaue vs such
hard language, forbeare such speeches vnlesse you haue the patience   15
to heare them returned backe againe, which we can more easely doe,
then you can suffer./ We betray not our youth, we sell not Wordes
vnto them, but our paines, which are profitable to euery scholler
according to his capacitie./ What extraordinary matter is in your
sonne having but so little experience of him I cannot tell, I doe   20
assure my selfe you can as little iudge./ Some are blinded with
ignorance, others with affection, Some with both./ How easie a
thing is it for a father to be deceyued in his Childe, when many a
man is deceyued in him selfe? The diligence of the Master
is not alwaies to be measured by the proficiencie of the scholer: 25
Some cannot learne, some can and will not, though they be taught
with neuer so much mildenes or seueritie./ did you know how often

we are tormented with teaching of such that learnes nothinge
at all, you would thinke this I write no paradox; if you be
offended that sometimes being absent, or otherwise busi⟨ . ⟩ed, we   30
apoint the greater to heare the lesser, we do but as your selfe
and other men of much imployment, we doe something by others
as well as by our selues, partly I confesse for our owne ease, and
partly for the better profiting our schollers./.

f. 68v, f. 69r, f. 69v

BLANK

yow are tormented with hearing off sute that beareth nothing
at all, yow would thinke this I write no paradoxe; if you be
offended that sometimes being absent, or otherwise busied, we
apoint the greater to heare the lesser, we do but as your selfs
and other men off much imployment, we do something by others
as well as by our selues, partly I confesse for our owne ease, and
partly for the better profiting our schollers. /.

[101　　　　late 1614 (?); before 16 March 1615　　　see Commentary]

Paul Tomsom his letter　　　　　　　　　　1
vnto the Kinge./.
Most Mightie Prince and gratious Soueraigne, that by myne
owne follye in one Action: I haue plucked the Towre of Si =
loah vpon my head, to myne owne shame: and drawne the blacke　　5
Mantell of infamie and disgrace ouer the face of this famous ,,
vniuersitie and Churche; And to conclude, haue prouoked
Gods wrathe, and your highnes indignation against me./
Yf I should denye it, My sighes, my teares, my groanes, my
outward passions, would sufficiently make knowne to the　　　　10
worlde: that it was not Paul; but I? which am *Primus*
peccatorum in +me+ ⟨ne⟩ vno totus scandelizatus Israell: I am the man
that haue worthely deserued the effect of Gods wrathe, and the
rod of your indignation: I doe therefore in all humilitie prostrate
my selfe at your Maiesties feete, humbly craving pittie, & pardon:　15
with teares, and prayers; and if there be any place for the first
and last request, of a poore soule forsaken of God & Man,
I humbly pray that lyving I may haue: *Lucem solis, calorem*
ignis, et solitudinem; as fitt meanes to make vp my accounts
with God & the Colledge; and dyinge, *Aiax* his wish to　　　20
be found of *Teucer,* ⟨..⟩

f. 70v, f. 71r, f. 71v, f. 72r, f. 72v, f. 73r, f. 73v, f. 74r, f. 74v, f. 75r,
f. 75v, f. 76r, f. 76v

BLANK

Paul Tomson his letter
vnto the kinge.

Most Mightie Prince and gratious Soueraigne, that by myne
owne follye in our station: I haue plucked the tower of shin=
loage vpon my head, to myne owne shame: and drawen the blacke
Mantell of infamie and disgrace ouer the face of this famous
Vniuersitie and Colledge; And to conclude, haue prouoked
Gods vengeaunce, and your higenes indignation against me.
If I should denye it, My sighes, my teares, my groanes, my
outward passions, would sufficiently make knowne to the
worlde: that it was not Paul; but I, vor ipse, am Primus
peccatorum in vno totus scandelizatus Israell; I am the man
that haue vvretchedly deserued the wrath of Gods vengeaunce, and the
rod of your indignation: I doe therefore in all humilitie prostrate
my selfe at your Maiesties feete, humbly crauing pitie, & pardon:
vvith teares, and prayers; and if there be any place for the first
and last request, of a poore soule forsaken of God & Men,
I humbly pray that liuing I may haue: Lucem solis, calorem
ignis, et solitudinem; as fitt meanes to make vpp my accounts
vvith God & the Colledge; and dying, fiat his will to
be found of fewer, &c.

f. 77r

[102   May–June 1603; May 1603 – August 1604   see Commentary]

Advertisementes of a Loyall Subiect to   1
his gracious Soveraigne: drawne from the
observations of the peoples speeches :/

.1.   It is said yt your Maiestie will not continue protection of the lowe
Countries: They be the onlie Yokefellowes (as it were) of your   5
Religion. And althouth (I doubt not) Your Maiesties high wisdome
will foresee all inconveniences. Yet these simple Gospellers mourne
for your resolution. And god graunt your Maiestie repent not their –
defection, *alias* distruction. For if the Spaniard prevaile
against those poore forsaken men, his forces by Sea, are more   10
then treble: peace will quicklie enriche him, Wealth will add
to his pryde, his pryde will encrease his hatred to your Religion
and people, and the Pope the firebrand of dissention, even
when you are disapointed of your Aidsman by Sea in the
worlde, will discover his wonted malice against vs, ye pretended   15
tytle of his *Infanta* is not vnknowne to your Maiestie. It shall not
want the Antichristian furtheraunce: The Spaniard is
his dearest childe, Your kingdome will be short for them to
warr vpon ./.
            Principijs obsta, fere medicina paratur ./   20

.2.   It is said, if your Maiestie discontinue the league wth the States, the
Frenchmen are ready to entertaine the bargaine, there is a certain
Antipathy betwene them and vs, and it is hard to Iudge, whether
the Spaniard or the Frenchmen will prove worst neighbours
vnto you: Your trewe subiectes therfore pray you to keepe   25
them bothe at the staves ende./.

.3.   It is said yt your Maiestie receyves Infinite nomber of peticions: and
the poore foolish people thinke the kinge hathe leasure to
entend every pryvate mans busynes; Ryd your handes betymes of
suche importunities, and (except your Maiestie see great cause to   30
the contrarie) referr them to the ordynarie Courtes of Iustice

Advertisemente of a Loyall Subiect to
his gracious Soueraigne: drawne from the
observations of the peoples speeches:

1. It is said yͭ yoᵉ Maᵗⁱᵉ will not continue protection of the lowe
Countries: They be the onlie yokefellowes (as it were) of yoᵉ
religion. And althougͭ (I doubt not) yoᵉ Maᵗⁱᵉˢ highe wisdome
will forsee all inconueniences. Yet these simple Gospellers mourne
for yoᵉ resolution. And god grannt yoᵉ Maᵗⁱᵉ repent not their
desertion, alias distraction. ffor if the Spaniard preuaile
against those poore forsaken men, his forces by Sea, are more
then treble: peace will quicklie enriche him, wealth will add
to his pryde, his pryde will encrease his hatred to yoᵉ religion
and people, and the Pope the firebrand of dissention, even
when you are disapointed of yoᵉ aidsman by Sea in the
worlde, will discover his wonted malice against vs, yᵉ pretended
tytle of his Infanta is not vnknowne to yoᵉ Maᵗⁱᵉ. It shall not
want the Antichristian furtherance. The Spaniard is
his deareist childe, yoᵉ kingdome will be short for them to
walke vpon.

Principijs obsta, sere medicina paratur.

2. It is said, if yoᵉ Maᵗⁱᵉ discontinue the league wͭ the States, the
frenchmen are ready to entertaine the bargaine, there is a certaine
Antipathy betwene them and vs, and it is hard to iudge, whether
the Spaniard or the frenchmen will proue worst neighboures
vnto you: yoᵉ trewe subiecte therfore pray you to keepe
them bothe at the States ende.

3. It is said yͭ yoᵉ Maᵗⁱᵉ wearyes Infinite number of peticions: and
the poore foolish people thinke the kings hathe leasure to
attend every priuate mans busynes; And yoᵉ hande betymes of
these importunities, and (except yoᵉ Maᵗⁱᵉ see great cause to
the contrarie) referr them to the ordynarie Courtes of Iustice

ordeyned for the ending of all differences, But yf any
complain truelie against the cheefe officers, of what place
or dignitie soever they bee: Here then yo⁵ selfe (Gracious
Soveraigne) make but one or two examples of Iustice, and
we shall see a golden chainge suddenlye. But yf: Lex
rationis, must be pent in lawe, and the iniust censor must
be severely punished, least the Magistrate be brought in
contempt. ¶

·4· It is said, yᵗ yoʳ Maᵗⁱᵉ giveth mercy: Liberalitie in a prince
is a necessarie vertue, but yoʳ Coffers are said not to
be so full as they neede emptyinges, nor yoʳ estate in so
great securitie, yᵗ it may endure a Leane Treasurye, ¶
after two or three yeares tryall of yoʳ Neighbors and
Confederates affections, and better vnderstanding of youre
owne fortunes and occasions, yoʳ Maᵗⁱᵉ shall better discerne
out of what plentie, in what manner, & to whom to gyve:
yoʳ subiectes have bene of late yeres charged wᵗʰ subsidies,
and wᵗʰout doubt the Commons are poore, needy, & in debt.
They desyre some ease, they wonder that youre Highnes
doeth not remytte the remainder of the taxes & subsidies
yet beginde; they say it hath bene the custome of kinges
at theire first entrance to the Crowne so to doe, and theire
hope in that is deceyved. ¶

·5· They pray you, not to followe the opinion of Rehoboams yor
chancellors, nor to suffer the long vse of taxes & subsidies
to turne to an habitt, for they woulde (in defence of youre
Maᵗⁱᵉ, the Gospell, & the State) that they will be prodigal
of theire lyves and lyvinge. ¶

·6· They say that some are advanced vnto places of Iustice

f. 77v

ordeyned for the ending of all differences, But yf any
complain trulie against the Cheefe officers, of what place
or dignitie soever they bee: here them your self (gracious
Soveraigne) make but one or two examples of Iustice, and   35
we shall see a golden chainge suddenlye. But yet: *Lex*
rationis, must be put in vre, and the vniust accuser must
be severely punyshed, least the Magistrate be brought in
contempt. /.

.4.   It is said, yt your Maiestie giveth muche: Liberalitie in a prince   40
      is a necessarie vertue, but your Coffers are said not to
      be so full as they neede emptyinge, nor your estate in so
      great securitie, yt it may endure a Lean Treasurye, /
      after two or three yeeres tryall of your Neighboures and
      Confederates affections, and better vnderstanding of youre   45
      owne fortunes and occasions, Your Maiestie shall better discerne
      out of what plentie, in what manner, & to whom to gyve:
      Your Subiectes haue bene of late yeres charged wth subsidies,
      and wthout doubt the Commons are poore, needy, & in debt.
      They desyer some ease, they wonder that youre highnes   50
      dothe not remytt the remainder of the taxes & subsidies
      yet behinde; they say it hathe bene the custome of kinges
      at their first entraunce to the Crowne so to doe, and their
      hope in that is deceyved./.

.5.   They pray you, not to followe the opinion of *Rehoboams* yong   55
      Councellores, nor to suffer the long vse of Taxes & subsidies
      to turne to an habitt, for they vowe (in defence of youre
      Maiestie, the Gospell, & the state.) that they will be prodigall
      of their lyves and lyvinges./

.6.   They say that some are advaunced vnto places of Iustice   60

altogether vnfytt for them, for that they are vtterly ignorant
of our lawes and customes: our advauncement to those of the
Governors, was wont to be, as to those of the feild: from an
olde soldier to a lieftenaunte, from a lieftenaunte to a Captaine,
and so ordinarily to every place of the Campe./ Now indeede   65
in the daunger their is some difference; for an vnskyllfull
Generall can seldome offend, moree then once: and then his
lyfe and all payes for it; But suche a Magistrate may
by a thowsand ignorances peradventure enriche him self,
and wronge an infinite nomber of poore people./.   70

.7. They say that the office of mrshipp of the Rolles shall be
     executed by a deputie, The patentee is held for a wyse and
     honorable gentleman but the deputy now spoken of is not of
     honest fame, And god forbyd yt so good a king, should make
     so badd a president, as to suffer a Cheife place of Iustice,   75
     to be executed (or rather abused) by a deputy; or that the
     patentee should make sale of your Maiesties fayre guift./ The place
     was in a manner executed by a deputy before, suche were the
     Iudges wch *Pro tempore* were Commyssioners, but the due vse of
     the afternoone, wch the Mr of the Rolles did vsually spend to   80
     heare and ende many cawses, was a cheife want, whereof the
     Clyaunt Complayned./ wch Course (it is said) the Mr nowe
     can not follow, by reason of his ⟨owne⟩ more nere & necessarie
     employmentes about your Maiestie./.

.8. It is said, that the respect at the Courte of the Scott (by all   85
     attendant officers there) is so partiall, as the English fynde
     them selues muche disgraced; The meanest of that Countrie
     may enter the presence, and where not wthout Controule: but
     the English verie vnreasonablye (Iwis) are kept out, the fault
     is not said to be your Maiesties: it is the foolish grosse Clayming of 90

altogether vnfytt for them, for that they are vtterly ignorant
of our lawes and customes: our advancement to those of the
Gobernors, was wont to be, as to those of the feild: from an
olde soldior to a lieftenute, from a lieftenute to a Captaine,
and so ordinarily to every place of the Campe. / Now indeede
in the danger there is some difference; for an vnskyllfull
Generall can seldome offend, more then once: and then his
lyfe and all payes for it. / But suche a Magistrate may
by a thowsand ignorances peradventure enriche him selfe,
and wronge an infinite nomber of poore people. /

They say that the office of m'ship of the Rolls shall be
executed by a deputie, The patentee is helde for a wyse and
honourable gent: but the deputy now spoken of is not of
honest fame, And god forbyd y' so good a King, sholde make
so badd a president, as to suffer a cheife place of Iustice,
to be executed (or rather abused) by a deputy; or that the
patentee sholde make sale of yo' Ma'tie favour guift. / The place
was in a manner executed by a deputy before, suche were the
iudges w' Pro tempore were Commissioners, but the one rest of
the afternoons, w' the M' of the Rolls did vsually spend to
heare and ende many causes, was a cheife want, wherwof the
Obiect complayned. / w' Course (it is said) the M' nowe
can not follow, by reason of his more newe & necessarie
employments about yo' Ma'tie. /

It is said, that the respect at the Courts of the Civill (by all
attendant officers there) is so partiall, as the English fynde
them selves muche disgraced. / The meanest of that Countrie
may enter the presence, and wyew not w'owt Controwle: but
the English (more vnreasonablye (fwis) are kept out, the fault
is not said to be yo' Ma'tie: it is the foolish grosse Clayming of

some of the English. But yo[r] Ma[tie] must provide least such
indiscretion breede a disswete emulation betwene vs, who ough[t]
as we now professe but one god, & one kinge, so to have but
one hart: and yo[r] English subiects not to be disgraced,
for it must be confessed (right noble king) that the kingdom
& people of England made you great; Many offices have
bene taken away from the English, & gyven to the Scott,
and some y[t] have served the State wth good comendations
Ch-- now yo[r] Ma[tie] must esteeme deere to yo[r] self
remaine vnthought of and vnrewarded.

9. It is said, y[t] yo[r] Ma[tie] purposed to alter the manners of
our government, & y[t] fault is founde at our common lawes:
Philiplimyus did iudicially comend our lawes of England
and especyally our tryall by the Oathes of .12. men, w[ch]
is w[th]out doubt the best & equallest Course, and in it self
least Culpable of Corruption; & verie alteration even
in private families (much more in a kingdome) breedeth vnst-
bilely: doubtlesse their be abuses in the Comon-weale vsed,
& cheifly in the Arbitrarie Courts; But of yo[u]r Ma[tie]
owne experience gyve the highest allowance to our common
Lawes and Statutes, w[ch] be even suting to the cvrrente
and natures of the people and kingdome.

10. It is said, y[t] yo[r] Ma[tie] of an ingenious and Royall nature,
not delighting in popular salutations, dothe passe by great
troopes of yo[r] Commons wth a kynde of kingly negligence,
neither speaking nor loking vpon them; The poore sorte
of people are bolde wth yo[r] Ma[tie], they prvaise of the manners
of their late Queene: who when she was publiquely

some of the English. But your Maiestie must provide least such
indiscretion breede a discreete emulation betwene vs, who ought
as we now professe but one god, & one kinge, so to have but
one hart: and your English Subiectes not to be disgraced;
for it must be confessed (Right noble king) that the kingdome   95
& people of England made you great; Many offices haue
bene taken away from the English, & gyven to the Scott,
and some yt have served the State wth good commendations,
⟨a long⟩ (wch now your Maiestie must esteeme dewe to your self)
remaine vnthought of and vnrewarded./.   100

.9.   It is said, yt your Maiestie purposed to alter the manner of
our government, & yt fault is founde at our common lawes:
Philiplimycus did Iudicially Commend our lawes of England,
and especyally our tryall by the Oathes of .12. men, wch
is wthout doubt the best & equallest Course, and in it self   105
least Culpable of Corruption; Everie alteration even
in pryvate famelies, (muche more in a kingdome) breedeth hurly
burly: doubtlesse their be abuses in the Courtes at westminster;
& cheifly in the Arbitrarie Courtes; But yf youre Maiesties
owne experience gyve the highest allowances to our common   110
Lawes and Statutes, wch be even senting to the occurrentes
and natures of the people and kingdome./.

.10. It is said, yt your Maiestie of an Ingenious and Royall Nature,
not delighting in popular salutacions, dothe passe by great
troupes of your Commons wth a kynde of kingly negligence,   115
neither speaking nor loking vpon them; The poore sorte
of people are bolde wth your Maiestie, they prate of the manner
of their late Queene: who when she was Pupliquely

seene abroade, wolde often say and speake kyndly to ye multitude,
discovering her Royall acceptance of their acclamations, many –   120
tymes also stayinge, yt her subiectes hungrie eyes might haue their
fyll in beholding their soveraigne, Your Maiestie must needes therfore
in some sorte satisfie their zealous affections, or els the poore
Raskalls so farr as they dare will be angrie wth you./.

.11. It is said, yt your Maiesties followers, as well English as Scottish,   125
doe proclayme open sayle of the most noble & auncyent –
order of knighthoode, whereby some (Contrary to youre
highnes intent) of vnworthie Condition, for bribes have bene
vnworthely made knightes, to the dishonor of your Royall palace,
and the disgrace of other noble & vertuous knightes./.   130

.12. (*Vox Plebes*) I wot not what to call them, but some there be
that most vnnaturally and vnreverently by egregious lyes,
wounde the honor and good fame of our deceased Soveraigne,
not onlie taxing her governement, but her person wth sundrye
manifest vntruthes, and the *Indigesta molis*, your Commons of   135
London (I should say some of them, for doubtlesse all are
not lewde) haue put out her name where it was engraven,
vnder the Armes of the kyngdomes, And it is said, that they
are aboute to alter Certaine Monumentes once dedicated to her;
as being loath (belike) to be at any newe cost wth your Maiestie: 140
Surelye these slaunders be the devyses of the Papistes,
aymynge thereby at the defamation of the Gospell: yt wyll
therefore be a parte truely Magnanimyous in your Maiestie to provide
for the preservacion of her famous memorye, by all good meanes.

.13. It is said, yt many auncyent and poore officers at Courte be   145
displaced, & the places gyven to your Countrymen the Scottes;

beene abroade, wolde often say and speake kyndly to ye multitude
discoveringe her Royall acceptance oß their acclamations, many ~
tymes also sayinge, yt her subiectes eyesighte mighte haue theire
fill in beholdinge their soveraigne, yor Matie must needes therfore
in some sorte satisfie their zealous affections, or els the poore
rascalls so farre as they dare will be angrie wth you. /

2. It is said, yt yor Maties followers, as well Englishe as Scottishe,
doe proclayme open sayle oß the most noble & auncyent ~
orders oß knighthoode, wherby some (contrary to your
highnes intent) oß vnworthie condition, for bribes haue bene
vnworthely made knightes, to the dishonor oß yor Royall palace,
and the disgrace oß other noble & vertuous knightes. /

2. (Vox Plebes) I wot not what to call them, but some there be
that most vnnaturally and irreverently by egregious lyes,
wounde the honor and good fame oß our deceassed Soveraigne,
not onlie taxing her governement, but her person wth sundrye
manifest vntruthes, and the Indigesta molis, yor Commons oß
London (I shoulde say some oß them, for doubtlesse all are
not lewde) haue put out her name where it was ingraven,
vnder the Armes oß the kyngdomes, And it is said, that they
are aboute to alter Certaine Momments once dedicated to her,
as being loath (belike) to be at any newe cost wth yor Matie:
Surely these slanders be the devyses oß the Papistes,
aymynge therby at the defamation oß the Gospell: yt wyll
therfore be a parte truely Magnanimyous in yor Matie: to provide
for the preservacion oß her famous memorye, by all good meanes

3. It is said, yt many auncyent and poore officers at courte be
displaced, & the places gyven to yor Countrymen the Scotte:

In deede to say the truthe, it is meete y[t] yor Matie knowne for=
dambe should be for yor Matie wearest imployments; nor
is it any dishono[r] to the English nation, that the good
Scottishmen be preferred, so y[t] you leave not the well
diservinge disgraced; The people are well termed a
beast of many heades, so many men so many myndes; yet
(w[ch] is the worke of God) I heare that every man loveth
& reverenceth yo[r] Ma[tie]; Let therfore the admirable
manner of yo[r] Ma[tie] commynge to so opulent a kingdome,
be ever before yo[r] eyes; God is cheeflye to be honored,
True Religion more and more to be advanced, and y[e] common
wealth cherished, w[ch] consisteth cheifly of homeborne
men; It were good we could forgett all differences of
Nations, and repayre y[e] almost decayed name of Brittish
doubtlesse unto so wyse a Prince a word is enoughe,
And therfore poore I, who have alwayes in my pryvate
Conference mainteyned yo[r] Ma[tie] just title so far as I
durst will here ende./ blessings my god y[t] I see this
happie day, wherein the kingdomes so long dissevered,
be now unyted in one royall person; whose posteritie
I hope will so serve god, as they shall Continewe
kinge of this land, untill the dissolution of the
universall ./. Amen ./.

f. 79v

In deede to say the truthe, it is meete yt your Maiesties knowne ser =
vauntes should be for your Maiesties nearest imploymentes; nor
is it any dishonor to the English nation, that the good
servytours be preferred, so yt you leave not the well   150
diservinge disgraced; The people are well termed a
beast of many heades, so many men so many myndes; yet
(wch is the Worke of God) I here that every man loveth
& reverenceth your Maiestie; Let therfore the admirable –
manner of your Maiesties Commynge to so Opulent a kingdome,   155
be ever before your eyes; God is cheeflye to be honored,
True Religion more and more to be advaunced, and ye Common
wealth Cherished, wch consisteth cheifly of homeborne
men; It were good we could forgett all dyfferences of
Nations, and repayre yt almost decayed name of Brittein.   160
Doubtlesse vnto so wyse a Prince a worde is Inoughe,
And therfore poore I, who haue alwayes in my pryvate
Conference maintayned your Maiesties Iust title so far as I
durst: will here ende./ blessinge my god yt I see this
happie day, wherein the kingdomes so long dissevered,   165
be now vnyted in one Royall person; whose posteritie
I hope will so serve god, as they shall Continewe
kinges of this Land, vntill the dissolution of the
vniversall./.   Amen./.

[103   before 30 June 1592   see Commentary]
Most honorable and ever my good Lorde. Where of your great goodnes   1
& favour towardes me, I was once admytted & taken to the nomber of
them yt be of your honores service and clothe: the countenaunce whereof,
as it ever was an inwarde comforte to my self: so your Lordship
standing my good Lorde & Mr: I have the more safely passed and   5
overbroken many troubles and Iniuries intended or offred by any my
adversaries; And though neither my hap by any your Lordshippes
occasions to vse me in the little I coulde: neither my abilitie to do
your Lordshippe any pleasinge service, haue ever bene suche as might any
thinge deserue: Yet the trust I take to me of your honores forewoon =   10
ted bountie dothe embolden me, and the extremities of my present dist =
resses doe enforce me, thus humblie to beseche the continuance
of your honorable favour at this my hardest tyme; One only cause
most honorable lorde dothe cheefely presse me. (the matter
betwixte my sister & me) In the well or evill ending whereof   15
the weale or woe, of me and myne swayeth for ever; And yt
wth the rest, I referr to this bearer, as one well acquainted wth
all yt concerns me, if it please your good Lordship to vouchsafe
him the hearinge./ My Sister and Nephewe have extended
my landes (and all yt I have) bothe in kent & Essex, at xxv s   20
by yere./ so yt I have neither sufficient maintenance to relieve
my necessitie, nor can I compounde +wth+ my other creditores, or have
any meane to enlarge my self: but by all likelihoode they have
determyned yt here I shall ende the poore remainder of my aged
yeres./ Yf by equitie, or the good favour of your honor towardes me,   25
my said Sister & Nephewe be not brought to better reason.
Who have of themselues to my Lord Chauncelor, Sir henry
Cobham and others, made semblant & attested, yt they ment
all for the good of me & my poore children./ But through
their default I continue in pryson, to the enlarging of my   30
expences, & the shorteninge of my dayes./ I shall be content

Most honorable and other my good Lordes. Where of yo[r] great goodnes
& favor towardes me, I was once admytted & taken to the nomber of
them y[t] be of yo[r] honor[s] s[er]vice and clothe: the comforte wherof
as it ever was an inwarde comforte to my self: so yo[r] Lordships
standing my good Lordes & m[rs]. I have the more safely passed and
overbroken many troubles and iniuries intended or offred by any my
adversaries; And thonge neither my hap by any yo[r] Lordshippes
occasions to use me in that little I could: neither my abilitie to do
yo[r] Lo: any pleasinge service, have ever bene suche as might any
thinge deserve: Yet the trust I take to me of yo[r] honor[s] foresworn=
ted bounties dothe embolden me, and the extremities of my present dist=
resses doe enforce me, thus humblie to beseche the contynuance
of yo[r] honorable favor at this my hardest tyme; One only cause
most honorable lordes dothe chesely presse me. (the matter
betwixte my sister & me) in the troble or still ending whereof
the weale or woe, of me and myne swayeth for ever; And t[he]
w[ch] the rest, I referre to this bearer, as one well acquainted w[th]
all y[t] concern me, if it please yo[r] good Lordship to vouchsafe
him the hearinge. / My Sister and Nephewes have extended
my londe (and all y[t] I have) bothe in Kent & Essex, at p[ro]cess
by yow. / so y[t] I have neither sufficient maintenance to relieve
my necessitie, nor can I compounde w[ith] my other creditor[s], or have
any means to enlarge my self: but by all liklyhode they have
determyned y[t] here I shall ende the poore remainder of my aged
yeres. / If by equitie, or the good favor of yo[r] honor towardes me,
my said Sister & Nephewes be not brought to better reason.
who have of themselves to my Lord Chancelor, S[r] Henry
Cobham and other, made semblant & attested, y[t] they ment
all for the good of me & my poore children. / But thronge
their default I contynue in prysson, to the enlarging of my
sorrowes, & the shorteninge of my dayes. / I shall be content

(being set at libertie) duringe my lyfe to take onlie so much
yerely, as my ordinarie charges be nowe here in pryson, yea
iff it were lesse: and let my Sister & Nephewe take all in
rest till my creditors be paide, & them selues fully satisfied,
so yt the inheritance may come to my sonnes after my death;
wherinto not doubtinge but they will be ordered by yor honor
letters, here humbly crauinge the same: wth the remembrance
off my bounden dutie to yor honor, and my good Ladie. I
take my leaue. /

My good ffrende, I am greatly importuned by my olde servant
Robert Sidley, as well to moue an order and ende off the matters
& causes twixt you and him hanginge vndetermined: As also
to require from you for him some supplie off suche somes, as
for the defrayinge off the charges off his diett, lodginges, &
other necessaries off lyfe, he hathe partlie borrowed off his
derest frendes; who therby hindred, now daily burden him
for repayment: And themselues indebted in the house, are
therby in danger to be put to harder wardes. The particulers
off wch somes this bearer may shewe you. Wch first good Mr
Sidley and Mrs Sidley, I pray you let be at my request
supplied to the olde man; And then for other cause So Robert
Sidley sayth, where nowe his charge in pryson is fiftie
poundes and aboue yerely: wch is wasted together wth his diuse,
wthout satisfying my debte, and wch iff he were out off pryson
myght be set forthe to the payment off his debte; he saith
iff he may haue vi.C.li. wch will ridd him forthe off pryson,
he will be content yt you still holde all his landes at some
conuenient rate, till as well yt vi.C.li. as all other somes
wch in reason and equitie should be by you demaunded (some
due fauour alwayes shewed) shall be leuied & to you fully
answered & satisfied. / Off wch his offer I hartely pray
you to consider in suche frendshippe & kindnes, as may giue

(being set at libertie) duringe my lyfe to take onlie so muche,
yerely, as my ordinarie charges be nowe here in pryson, yea
if it were lesse: and let my Sister & Nephew take all ye
rest till my creditores be paide, & them selues fully satisfied,   35
so yt the inheritance may come to my sonnes after my deathe;
whereto not doubtinge but they will be ordered by Your honores
letters, here humbly craving the same: wth the remembraunce
of my bounden dutie to your honor, and my good Ladie. I
take my leave./.   40

[104   30 June 1592]

My good Frendes, I am greatly importuned by my olde servaunt   1
Robert Sidley, aswell to move an order and ende of the matters
& causes twixt you and him hanging vndetermined: As also
to require from you for him some supplie of suche sommes, as
for the defrayinge of the chardge of his dyett, lodginge, &   5
other necessaries of lyfe, he hathe partlie borrowed of his
derest frendes; who thereby hindred, now daily burden him
for repayment: And themselues indebted in the house, are
thereby in daunger to be put to harder Warde. The perticulers
of wch sommes this bearer may showe you./ Wch first good Mr   10
Sidley and Mrs Sidley, I pray you let be at my request
supplied to the olde man; And then for other cawses Robert
Sidley sayeth, where nowe his charge +in+ ⟨is⟩ prison is fiftie
poundes and above yerely: wch is wasted together wth his daies,
wthout satisfying any debte, and wch if he were out of prison   15
might be set forthe to the payment of his debtes; he saith
if he may have vj xxli: wch will ridd him forthe of prison,
he will be content yt you still holde all his landes at some
convenient rate, till aswell yt vj xxli: as all other sommes
wch in reason and equitie should be by you demaunded (some   20
due favour alwayes showed) shall be levied & to you fully
answered & satisfied./ Of wch his offer I hartely wish
you to consider in such frendship & kindnes, as may give

me occasion more willinglie to travell the ending of those
causes, and the stablishinge of firme frendship betwixt   25
you; wch in my opinion concerneth no lesse the credit,
then the commoditie of bothe parties./ I am informed
your selues have said, and I am sure the worlde dothe
thinke: that your extent at xxv s yerely, shoulde be to the
good of Robert Sidley; I pray you now let it be so   30
seene. And so I bid you hartely farewell, ye Blacke
Fryers this Last of Iune. 1592./.

[105   3 January 1603/4]

A warrant from the Counsell   1
These are to will, and in his Maiesties name straightlie to
charge & commaunde you: vpon the receipt hereof to repaire
to the dwelling or abiding places of Will: Iones of Lynne:
gentleman and Tho: Fitche of Lockin in the Countie of Midds: 5
or to any other place or places where you shall vnder =
stand of there being; and to charge & cause them by vertue
hereof, all excuses set aparte: to come in your companie
before me to the Courte, or where I shall be; to answere
to suche matters as at there commynge on his Maiesties behalfe   10
they are to be charged wthall: Whereof fayle you not
at your perills. At the Courte at Whitehall: the
thirde of Ianuarij. 1603.
                              To Ro: Tilney. one of ye Messin =
                              gers his Maiesties Chamber./.   15

[106]

Bedfellow: my longe absence and scilence together may st+r+ongly   1
importe my neglectinge of you; were my occasions knowne my
excuse were made; I have bene beleue me so toyled wth myne
owne busynes: & so tyed to a continuall prosecuting, as I
coulde not slacke the following of them one hower./ Let me   5
now knowe what is to be done in your causes, & they shall want
no handling yt I can give them. And vpon this resolution I rest
                         Youres in sorte as you knowe:

me occasion more willinglie to travell the ending off those
transes, and the stablishinge off firme frendship betwixt
you; wch in my opinion concerneth no lesse the credit,
then the comoditie off bothe parties. I am informed
yor selues have said, and I am sure the worlde dothe
thinke: that yor extent at most yearly, shonlde be to the
good off Robert Dudley; I praye you now let it be so
seene. And so I bid you hartely farewell, from Blacke
fryers this Last off June. 1591.

A warrant from the connsell

These are to will, and in his Maties name straightlie to
charge & commaunde you: vpon the receipt hereof to repaire
to the dwelling or abiding places off will: Jones off hymes
gate: and Tho: ffiskes off Lockin in the Countie off Midd:
or to any other place or places where you shall vnder=
stand off them being; and to charge & cause them by vertue
hereof, all excuses set aparte: to come in yor companie
before me to the Courte, or where I shall be; to answere
to suche matters as at their comynge on his Maties behalfe
they are to be charged withall: whereof fayle you not
at yor perills. At the Courte at whitehall: the
thirde off January. 1603.

                         To Tho: Tilney, one off the Mess in=
                         gers his Maties litle Chamber.

Bedfellow: my longe absence and silence together may strongly
impute my neglectinge off you; were my occasions knowen my
excuse were made I have bene before me so toyled wth myne
owne busynes: & so tyed to a continuall prosecuting, as I
conlde not slacke the following off them one hower. Let me
now knowe what is to be done in yor transes, & they shall want
no handling that I can give them. And vpon this resolution I rest
                                             yor in sowle as you knowe.

The answere of a peticion: written in the
bottome of ye same peticion; as his honour
commanded.

So many untruethes, so boldly avouched; & delyvered to yor
honor under his hand, may shew this plantiffe to be notablye
impudent. It is true yt he complayned to my Lo: of Cant
in like sorte as now he dothe to yor honor, presuminge
therby to have wronngst my disgrace; but it is most
untrue, yt his grace either ordered the matter, or dismist
me his service. It is likewise untrue yt by yor honors
service I obtayned an Iniunction of peviledge to stay his
proceedinge; I had my Iniunction of course in ye Chauncerie,
by priviledge of sute, as all her maties subiectes have.

The delay of his sute hath bene his desyre, and not
my slacknes: in hope therby to bring it to compromise.
he caused me to be sent for to the Mr of the Rolles:
& there Mr Doncke wisht me to order it, wch so
well liked, as I was contented to put it to those, whom
this plantiffe himselfe had named & chosen. and am yet
most willing to have it ended, either by them, or els any
other yt shall be thoght honest & sufficient persons.
I humblye crave, yt yor honor would be pleased to take ye
hearing of the matter yor selfe. He complaines of the
damage of iij or iiij. and I of an hundred. He upon
subtletie, I upon equitie. I will pawne my poore credit
& lief to yor honor, to prove the untruethes of this plan-
tiffs peticion; wth many other indirect circumstances.
as breache of oathe for sealing of bonde & performaunce
of covenaunt. All wch I referr &c.

[107]

The answere of a peticion: written in the
bottome of ye same peticion; as his honor
commaunded./.

So many vntruthes, so boldlye avouched: & delyvered to your
honor vnder his hand, may shew this plantife to be notablye
impudent./ It is true yt he complayned to my Lord of Canterbury
in like sorte as now he dothe to your honor, presumynge
thereby to haue wrought my disgrace; but it is most
vntrue, yt his grace either ordered the matter, or dismist
me his service./ it is likewise vntrue yt by your honores
service I obtayned an Iniunction of privilege to stay his
procedinges;/ I had my Iniunction of course in ye Chauncerie,
by prioritie of sute, as all her Maiesties subiectes have./.
The delay of his sute hathe bene his desyer, and not
my slacknes: in hope therby to bring it to compremise./
he caused me to be sent for to the Mr of the Rolles:
& there Mr Sonckye wisht vs to order it, wch I so
well liked, as I was contented to put it to those, whom
this plantife himself had named & chosen./ and am yet
most willing to have it ended, either by them, or els any
others yt shall be thought honest & sufficient persons./
I humblye crave, yt your honor wolde be pleased to take ye
hearing of the matter your self./ He complaines of the
damage of .iij.li or iiij li ./ and I of an hundred./ he vpon
suttletie, I vpon equitie./ I will pawne my poore credit
& lyfe to your honor, to prove the vntruthes of this plan =
tifes peticion; wth many other indirect circumstances./
as breache of Oathe for sealing of bondes & performance
of covenantes./ All wch I referr &c./.

1

5

10

15

20

25

[108   6 October 1603   see Commentary]

Right trustie and welbeloved we greete you well. Whereas we   1
are gyven to vnderstand, yt their are sondrie Colemeaters roomes
or places belonging to our Cittie of London lately falne voide
& now in your guyfte. And being crediblye informed also of the
sufficiencie & meetenes every way of the bearer hereof our   5
subiect William Huxley, a freeman of ye said Cittie, for ye
executing of one of ye foresaid places. These are therefore
earnestly to require you, yt (wthout difficultie) you will
forthwth vpon the receipt of these our letters: graunt & bestow
one of ye said places wth all the rightes & fees therto belonginge 10
vppon ye said Wm huxley, wch we shall take verie acceptablye.
And so we byd you farewell. From our Courte at

[109   after 1 November 1603 (?)   see Commentary]

Right trustie and welbeloved we greete you well. Whereas   1
we directed our former letteres to Sir Robert Lee knight, late Lord
Maior of our Cittie of London, in ye behalf of William huxley
being a freeman of our said Cittie: For a Colemeaters roome
or place in our Cittie of London aforesaid. of wch roomes or   5
places we are ⟨w⟩ verie well assured their be .4. of them voide
and (now in your guyfte) are onlie executed by some of your officers
to your owne – behoofe: being also crediblie informed, yt the said Wm.
huxley is a verie honest man, & every way meete to execute ye
same. Of wch our letteres directed as aforesaid, we receyved not   10
answere to our good lykinge: as though our letteres had bene but of course,
or els had bene sent from some ordinarie person, & not from our
self. Wch slender regarde of our said former letteres, we take not
in good parte./ These are therefore once again to require you, that
(wthout more difficultie) you will forthwth vppon ye receipte of these 15
our letters, graunt & bestow one of ye said places, wth all ye rightes & fees
thervnto belonging vpon ye said Wm huxley, wch we shall take in good
parte, & be occasioned to remember. And so we byd you fare =
well From our Courte at Whitehall./.

To our Trustie & welbeloved, the Maior and
Aldermen his brethren of our Cittie of London

82

Right trustie and wellbeloved we greete you well. Whereas we
are gyven to vnderstand, yt there are sondrie Colemakers roomes
or places belonging to our Cittie of London latelie falne voide
& now in yor guyfte. And being crediblye informed also of the
sufficiencie & meetenes every way of the bearer hereof, our
subiect william Gupley, a freeman of ye said Cittie, for ye
executing of one of ye forsaid places. These are therefore
earnestlie to require you, yt (wthout difficultie) you will
forthwth vpon the receipt of these our lettres: graunt & bestow
one of ye said places wth all the rightes & fees therto belonginge
vpon ye said wm Gupley, wch we shall take verie acceptablye.
And so we byd you farewell. From our Courte at

Right trustie and wellbeloved we greete you well. Whereas
we directed our former lres to Sr Robert Lee knight, late Lord
Maior of our Cittie of London, in ye behalf of william Gupley
being a freeman of our said Cittie. for a Colemakers roome
or place in our Cittie of London aforesaid. of wch roomes or
places we are verie well assured there be 4. of them voide
and (now in yor guyfte) are onelie executed by some of yor officers
to yr owne behoofe: being also crediblie informed, yt the said wm
Gupley is a verie honest man, & every way meete to execute ye
same. Of wch our lres directed as aforesaid, we receyved not
answere to oor good lykinge: as though oor lres had bene but of course
or els had bene sent from some ordinarie person, & not from our
self. wch slender regarde of oor said former lres, we take not
in good parte. These are therefore once again to require you, yt
(wthout more difficultie) you will forthwth vpon ye receipt of these
oor lettres, graunt & bestow one of ye said places, wth all ye rightes & fees
therevnto belonging vpon ye said wm Gupley, wch we shall take in good
parte, & be occasioned to remember. And so we byd you farewell From our Courte at Whitehall. /.

To our Trustie & wellbeloved, the Maior and
Aldermen his bretheren of our Cittie of London

Mr Doctor Griffin, for the good reporte is comonly bruted
of you amongst the poore captyves in the kinge benche, I have
thought good to comend to your speryall hearing and efforchnall
handlinge, the distressed cause of a poore gent now in durance
there, for the state of whose depending betwixte him & his
peevishe adversaries: whom my self have knowne upon treatie
had wth them, verie maliciously bent towardes him; that I
referre to their delyvry who shall solicit you for him.
Yet this muche for the matter at large you shall receyve
from me; that at the first it may appeare, this gent hath
iust cause to seeke, and is well worthie to fynde her Ma:
gracious favor, wch by her hignes comyssion is in that case
provyded, and be your faithfull travailes to be extended
towarde him. Understand I pray, This gentleman,
A man of qualitie, and honest condition, endewed wth many
verie comendable partes: was receyved into the grace of
Sr Philip Sydney, an honorable gent: as you know
well disposed wth all bountie to recompense the well
deservinge of all men in vew of any merrit: upon the
hope of receyvinge that good, wch by often proofe made
in others, this gentleman had reason to expect in him
self: to his overcharge greatly, as hath falne out
by the sodayne death of yt Noble knight, he followed
him in the best course & manner of expendinges, in the
service of her Ma: in the low countries. Since yt
havinge fayled of his hope in this, he hath in dew course
and honest sorte endevored to make full satisfaction of
all the arrerages he was brought in by the meanes as
hath bene said; And thorough the most iniurious and
inconsiderate handlinges of his adversaries, hath bene

f. 82v

[110   after 17 October 1586; before 24 March 1603   see Commentary]

Mr docter Griffin, for the good reporte is commonly bruted   1
of you amongst the poore captyves in the kinges benche, I have
thought good to commend to youre specyall hearing and effectuall
handlinge, the distressed case of a poore gentleman now in durance
there, for the state of Causes depending betwixte him & his   5
peevishe adversaries: whom my self have knowne vpon treatie
had wth them, verie maliciously bent towardes him; that I
referr to their delyuerye who shall solicit you for hym./
Yet thus muche for the matter at large you shall receyve
from me; that at the first it may appeare, this gentleman hathe   10
iust cause to seeke, and is well worthie to fynde her Maiesties
gracious favour, wch by her highnes Commyssion is in that case
provyded, and by youre faithfull travailes to be extended
towardes him./ Vnderstand I pray, ⟨   ⟩ This gentleman,
⟨A.⟩ A man of qualitie, and honest condition, endowed wth many   15
verie commendable partes: was receyved into high grace by
Sir Philip Sydney, an honorable gentleman as you knowe
well disposed wth all bountie to recompence the well
deservinges of all men yt were of any meritt: vpon the
hope of receyvinge that good, wch by often proofe made   20
in others, this gentleman had reason to expect in him
self: to his overcharge greatly, as hathe falne out
(by the sodayne death of yt Noble knight) he followed
him in the best course & manner of expendinges, in the
service of her Maiestie in the lowe Countries./ Since yt,   25
having fayled of his hope in this, he hathe in due course
and honest sorte endevored to make full satisfaction of
all the arrerages he was brought in by the meanes as
hathe bene said; And thorough the most iniurious and
inconsiderate handlinge of his adversaries, hathe bene   30

debard from his good proceedinges by a long imprysonment.
In redresse whereof, whatsoever paines you shall take, I
will take it for a greate pleasure done to my self (so tender
a regarde have I of him) And besydes, you shall binde
vnto you suche a one for his libertie, as by the meanes   35
therof I make no doubte shall be enabled to deserve it,
and will ever thankfully requite it. Thus for ye present
I byd you hartely farewell./

Good docter, do not thinke at the intreatie of some frend,
I wryte to you of course: I assure you I haue an earnest   40
care and an hartie desyer to do the gentleman good: of whom
you shall here more by this bearer ./.

[111]

My very good Lord: I am to recommend vnto you ye cause   1
of this my frend Mr Thomas Lownde: who hathe a matter
triable this next Terme in the common pleas before you
against one Browne for a Tythe in Leicestershyre: the
cause is greatlye borne by the said Browne, and in respect   5
of hys greate favour wth the Iurors, and some other –
extraordinarie meanes wrought by him; Mr Lownde
is like to receyve some hard measure in his Tryall, except
it please your Lordship at my earnest request to extend
your lawfull favour vnto him: wch I will gladly requite   10
in any thinge I may towardes your Lordshippe: and so
wth my hartie Commendations I byd you farewell ./.

debard from his good proceedings by a long imprisonment.
In redresse whereof, what soever paines you shall take, I
will take it for a greate pleasure done to my selfe (so tender
a regarde have I of him) And besydes, you shall bynde
unto you suche a one for his libertie, as by the meanes
thereof I make no doubte shall be enabled to desserve it,
and will ober thankfully requite it. And thus for the present
I byd you hartely farewell.

Good doctor, do not thinke at the intreatie of some frend,
I wryte to you of course: I assure you I have an earnest
care and an hartie desyre to do the gent good: of whom
you shall heare more by this bearer.

My very good Lord: I am to recommend unto you the cause
of this my frend Mr Thomas Lowndes: who hathe a matter
triable this next terme in the Common pleas before you
against one Browne for a Tythe in Leicestershyre: the
cause is greatlye borne by the said Browne, and in respect
of his greate favour with the Jurors, and some other
extraordinarie meanes wrought by him; Mr Lownde
is like to receyve some hard measure in his Tryall, except
it please your Lordshipp at my earnest request to extend
your lawfull favour unto him: wich I will gladly requite
in any thinge I may towarde your Lordshippe: and so
wich my hartie commendations I byd you farewell.

Sweete Love, vppon w[hi]ch all good seasons, plaine dealings,
true meanings, entire love and affection, I seeke & serue for.
I comend you as an honest man, farr from all dissimulation,
before God and heaven I protest it. I am neither
Androwes, nor any of his sect: my soule shall answeare
it. My love is yours, and I am yours: and all shall be
at yo[ur] dispose: to rule and governe as you list, w[i]thout
controll or contradiction. yo[ur] frinds shall be myne,
and I will indevor to love all y[a]t like you. Farr be it
from me to see you revenged or discontented. I have
often intreated to know yo[ur] doubtes, y[a]t I might bettre
answeare and fully resolve you; there must needes be some,
and those in all kyndnes I beseche you discover.
I have not bene earnest to hasten to swyftly yo[ur]
determynation, to th'end you might fully w[i]th dew regarde
resolve w[i]th yo[ur] selfe, and make all tryalls for yo[ur] best
satisfaction. I refer my selfe generally to the whole
worlde, to God and to you, to censure my life: I make
you Judge, and attend yo[ur] pleasure. My love is not
slowe, though for these reasons before expressed, I have
gyven respit to yo[ur] resolution. eyth[er] I shall be
yours, or you will be myne: delay me not still, but
gyve me some hope, and let my love fynde some requitall.
You love yo[ur] frinds, and Childrens children: and so to doe
is iust & naturall: and yet these loves are not the
nearest: but a kinde loving husband is another yo[ur] selfe,
and halfe of yo[ur] selfe: exceedinge all loves in the highest
degree: the kyndest comforts y[a]t ever you had, much
more then yet you have ever conceyued. Now farewel

[112]

Sweete Love, whom wth all good tearmes, plaine dealinge,   1
true meaninge, entier love and affection, I seeke & sewe for./
I courte you as an honest man, far from all dissimulation,
before God and heaven I protest it./ I am neither
Androwes, nor any of his sect: my soule shall answere   5
it./ My love is youres, and I am youres: and all shall be
at your dispose: to rule and governe as you list, wthout
controll or contradiction./ Your Frendes shall be myne,
and I will sweare to love all yt like you./ Far be it
from me to see you wrong'd or discontented./ I have   10
often intreated to knowe your doubtes, yt I might bothe –
answere and fully resolve you; There must needes be some,
and those in all kyndnes I beseche you discover./
I have not bene earnest to hasten to swyftely youre
determynation, to thend you might fully wth due regarde   15
resolve wth your self, and make all tryalls for your best
satisfaction./ I refer my self generally to the whole
worlde, to God and to you, to Censure my lyfe: I make
you Iudge, and attend your pleasure./ My love is not
slowe, though for these reasons before recyted, I have   20
gyven respitt to your resolution./   Yf I shall be
youres, or you will be myne: delay me not still, but
gyve me some hope, and let my love fynde some requitall.
You love your frendes, and Childers children: and so to doe
is Iust & Naturall: and yet these loves are not the   25
nearest: but a kinde lovinge husband is another your self,
and parte of your self: exceedinge all loves in the highest
degree: the kyndest comforte yt ever you had, muche
more then yet you have ever conceyved./ Nor takes

it away these former loves, but rather confyrmes them in   30
the best condition./   Pardon these lynes yf
they be to tedious, I coulde wryte wthout ceasinge, tho
loath to leave, yet here an ende./
Farewell sweete love, and doe me right: I crave but
Iustice, love him yt loves you: or els &c :/   35
I haue no name, I have lately lost it: looke in your hart
and there you shall fynde it: So will I rest
and ever Youres ./.
                                    To my Sweete Love
                                    Fayre Mistresse .B.   40

[113]

Save him (Sweete wydowe) yt lyves at youre mercie,   1
and seekes no favoure but onlie youres; that holdes you deare,
and loves you muche, yea ten tymes more then he or they who
soever they be that love you most: and if you doubt it, make
but the proofe, & rest indifferent: So shall you best knowe   5
who best deserues you, and who is most worthie to holde and
enioye you./ When first my frendes did move me to see you,
I was but slowe to give them the hearinge: and so I lost
tyme sixe weekes at the least, wch nowe I repent me syxe
thousand tymes; For after I hearde by many reportes, your   10
modest behavior, discretion, & goodnes; I then was verie
desyrous to see you; and havinge seene you at sundrie tymes,
myne eyes coulde tell me, your person, your presence, and all
thinges els, did farr exceede all yt wch before I had hearde
reported: But most of all, your kynde enterteynment, & fayre   15
condition, your exceeding curteous & sweete behavior that day
in your howse, (where I holde my self happie and ten tymes
blessed by your good companie) encreast my affection athousand

it away these former lines, but rather confirmed them in
the best condition.| Pardon these lines yf
they be to tedious, I could write without ceasinge, tho
loath, to leave, yet heer an ende.|
farewell sweete love, and doe me right: I make but
Justice, love him yt loves you: or els yt.|
I have no name, I have lately lost it: looke in yor hart
and there you shall fynde it: So will I rest.
and ever yor.|

        To my Sweete love
        faire Mistress B-

I love him (Sweete Maydens) yt lyves at your mercie,
and seekes no favours but onlie yours; that loveth you deare,
and loves you muche, yea ten tymes more then els or they whoe
forbes they be that love you most: and if you doubt it, make
but the proofe, & rest indifferent: So shall you best knowe
whoe best deserves you, and whoe is most woorthie to holde and
inioye you!| When you first my frinde did move me to see you
I was but slowe to give them the hearinge: and so I let
tyme slip wasted at the least, noe newes I spent me uppon
them and tymes; Now after I hearde by many reportes, yor
modest behavior, discretion, & goodnes; I then was more
desyrous to see you; and havinge seene you at sundrie tymes,
myne eyes could tell me, yor person, yor presence, and all
thinges els, did farr exceede all yt noe before I had hearde
reported: But most of all, yor kynde interteynment, & fayre
condition, yor exceedinge curtesie & sweete behavior that day
in yor howse, (where I felte my selfe happie and ten tymes
blessed by yor good companie) increast my affection a thousand

tymes more, and makes me to lyve perpetually y pwrsl. If I knowe
in this case I shall want no counnysel, now twinst repputed to
findes my love; but let me entreate this quate at yor handes
to vowchsafe me the hearing before you condempne me, and if
I can not prosserve my credit from staine and tounge of the
wicked and enuious, kill me, condemne me, and cast me away
from yor sweete presence and faus for euer,
I coulde pearehapse commend my selfe to desserve as woll as
the best yt courted you: but thisdome, discreation, humanitie,
& modestie: dothe all denye it, and byde me be silent:
he neuer was borne yt neuer was wronged, and there was
neuer Louer yt was not attended wt enuie, hatred, malice,
and all thinges ells yt mighst worke him a mischiefe:
the theefe, the traytor, the cruell murtherer, are neuer
hang'd before they be heard: let me not finde lesse iustice in
you, or harder measure then these malefactors: Condempne
me not then before you heare me. If love offend you,
pardon the first fault, or punysh at yor pleasure but not
to sharpely: O that I might be bolde wt yor fauour, or yt
you woulde promysse me not to be angrie: My tuns shall be
alwayes to make you merie: and yor musike to mee shalbe
good musike: Make me yor man I will serue and attend you,
I will loue you alwayes and euer defend you; what is yours
leave? or what my like you. I will doe you credit amongst
the best, I will please you bothe at bed and at borde: and
all the dayes and howres of my lyfe, and you can not possible
euer offend me; Make me but yor man, and you shall be euer
my Mistresse, my love, my lyfe, and my hartte: and all good
thinge that I can imagine. Doo you but Commande, and
loe, if I be not most ready at all tymes to please and content
you to yor hartte desire: Binde me yor prentice for
teame of yeares; nay for terme of my lyfe; yt bondage

f. 84v

tymes more, and makes me to lyve perpetually youres./ I knowe
in this case I shall want no enimyes, nor vniust reportes to   20
hinder my love; but let me entreate this grace at your handes
to vouchsafe me the hearing before you condempne me, and if
I can not preserve my credit from staine or touche of the
wicked and envious, kill me, condemne me, and cast me away
from your sweete presence and favour for ever./   25
I coulde perhapes commend my self to deserue as well as
the best yt courtes you: but Wisdome, discretion, humanitie,
& modestie: dothe all denye it, and bydes me be scilent:
He never was borne yt never was wrongd, and there was
never Lover yt was not attended wth envie, hatred, malice,
and all thinges els yt might worke him a mischiefe:/   30
The theefe, the Traytor, the cruell murtherer, are never
hang'd before they be heard: Let me not finde lesse iustice in
you, or harder measure then these malefactores: Condempne
me not then before you heare me. Yf love offend you,
pardon the first fault, or punysh at your pleasure but not   35
to sharply: O that I might be bolde wth your favour, or yt
you wolde promysse me not to be angrie: My case shall be
alwayes to make you merie: and your mirthe to mee shalbe verie
good musicke: Make me your man I will serue and attend you,
I will love you alwayes and ever defend you; What is youre   40
feare? or what ⟨w.⟩ myslike you. I will doe you creditt amongst
the best, I will please you bothe at bed and at borde: and
all the dayes and howres of my lyfe, and you can not possiblie
ever offend me; Make me but your man, and you shall be ever
my Mistresse, my love, my lyfe, and my harte: and all good   45
thinges that I can Imagine: Doe you but Commaunde, and
see if I be not most ready at all tymes to please & content
you to your hartes desire: Binde me your Prentice for
tearme of yeares; nay for terme of my lyfe; yt bondage

shall be my everlastinge freedome, pleasure, ioye, & exceedinge 50
happines. That departure of youres, that sodeyne departure,
was more greevous to me: then my pen can wryte, or you will
beleeue: but your returne, your most happie returne (as well I
hope) shall returne my content, my pleasure, my ioye, and my
hartes delight. Yf my letter be longe, it is longe of you: 55
for you are the cause I can fynde no ende. / I coulde wryte
a whole volume in prayse of your self, and your sweete perfec =
tions. / Perhapes for your pleasure you will tell me
I flatter; I answere you no, and you may beleue me; For
all those that know me can verie well tell, I never enter = 60
teyned so foule a Monster: I speake as I thinke, I can
not dissemble: I never taught this tongue to lye: let him
doe so that can not be his owne, but baselye must lyve at
anothers devotion. / Thus Sweetest Wydowe
that lyves to mee: my lyfe; before my love shall end: I 65
cease to wryte, but never shall cease to Love and serve you.
   Youres; and none in the worlde but Youres.

[114 21 February 1589/90 – 9 February 1603/4 see Commentary]

   To the Right honorable the Countesse 1
    of warwicke: /.
Madam, Your self a Ladie: A widdowe: and of either
estate (as report sayeth) the verie Honor & trew president:
can not I assure me want in you that honorable pittie, 5
the wofull estate of a gentlewoman, a Widdowe, and excee =
dinglye wronged: may iustlie clayme in any worthie mynde./
To your honor therfore have I (as one exceedingly wanting it)
at this tyme addressed my self; I was once the wyfe
of Mr Williams your Honors poore countryman; and sometymes 10
neither meanly loved, respected, nor imployed by the Earle
Your most honored Father. / I have bene nowe this twentie

shall be my everlastinge freedome, pleasure, ioye, & exceedinge
happines. That departure of yo⁵, that sodayne departure,
was more greebous to me: then my pen can wryte, or you will
beleeve: but yo⁵ returne, yo⁵ most happie returne (as well I
hope) shall returne my content, my pleasure, my ioye, and my
hartes delight.   If my letter be longe, it is longe of you:
for you are the cause I can fynde no ende. /   I could wryte
a whole volume in prayse of yo⁵ selfe, and yo⁵ sweete perfec=
tions. /   Perhappe for yo⁵ pleasure you will tell me
I flatter; I answere you no, and you may beleeve me; ffor
all those that know me can verie well tell, I never enter=
toyned so foule a Monster: I speake as I thinke, I can
not dissemble: I never taught this tongue to lye: let him
doe so that can not be his owne, but basely must lyve at
anothers devotion. /   This wretched wydowe
that lyved to mee: my lyfe; before my love shall end: I
ceasse to wryte, but never shall ceasse to Love and serve you.
                    yo⁵; and none in the worlde but yo⁵

To the Right honorable the Countesse
of warwicke: /.

Madam, yo⁵ selfe a Ladie: A widdowe: and of either
estate (as report sayeth) the verie Hono⁵ & true president:
can not I assure me want in you that honorable pittie,
the woefull estate of a gentlewoman, a widdowe, and excee=
dinglye wronged: may in this clayme in any worthie mynde.
To yo⁵ Honor therefore have I (as one exceedingly wanting it)
at this tyme addressed my selfe;   I was once the wyfe
of M⁵ williams yo⁵ ho: poore countryman; and somtymes
either meanly loved, respected, now imployed by the Earle
yo⁵ most ho: Father. / I have bene nowe this twentie

fyve yeares in trouble for my dower and lyvinge, all my endebto=
res above one thousand poundes apoynted (whether by the ministers
of the Judges, the subtelties off myne owne counsell, or by what
meanes its god best knowes) remayninge yet fruictleslye imployed:
my yeares are many, my estate (onlie raised by these delayes
and apoyntes) worse then I am willinge to publishe: my sole hope
(yf at the least this barren age may beare any) restethe onlie
in her Ma(tie) mercye and supreme Justice: whi that I may the
better obtaine, vouchsafe gratious Lady to acquainte her Ma(tie)
wth this my straunge and most Lamentable estate: or yf my
poore merit may not seeme worthie so muche; (yet at the least
to assist me by meanes off that highe place yor vertues have
in honor procured you, to delyver my selfe to her highenes
my distressed case and petiton for just remedie thereof:) Assure
yor selff the cause is most just, and the action on yor parte
so honorable, as will remaine even rewarded to yor honor in the
performance; Wherein as you shall shewe yor self a true
inheriter off the charitie and bountie off mynde sometyme
enrichinge yor most worthie father; So shall you binde me
duringe the small remnant off my life, to publishe yor goodnes
and pray for yor all and other well thinges. 1.

I finde doctor Hudson colde and dull: and yet I thinke
for himself he will be fast and sure: this familiare was
out off the towne: otherwise he will not intreate; But I will
procure; I dare assure you off a full Number: I wolde
be glad off a solemne presence. 1 At two off the Clocke
I will visitt you wth a Trinitie off doctors at the least.
I pray let me be comended as before, and to Mr Linacres
whom I shame to have forgotten. 1 Happie successe wth
a gentle farewell. 1

yor etcet: etc:
J. B.

fyve yeares in troble for my dower and lyving, all my endevoures
wth above one thowsand poundes expences (whether by the iniustice
of the Iudges, the trecherie of myne owne counsell, or by what   15
meanes els god best knowes) remayninge yet succesleslye imployed:
my yeares are many, my estate (onlie cawsed by these delayes
and expences) worsse then I am willinge to publishe: my sole hope
(yf at the least this barren age may beare any) resteth onlie
in her Maiesties mercye and supreme Iustice: wch that I may the   20
better obtaine, Vouchsafe gratious Lady to acquainte her Maiestie
wth this my straunge and most Lamentable estate: or yf my
poore meritt may not seeme worthie so muche; Yet at the least
to assist me by meanes of that high place your vertues have
in Courte procured you, to delyver my self to her highnes   25
my distressed case and peticion for iust remedie therof./ Assure
your honor the cause is most iust, and the action on your parte
so honorable, as will remaine even rewarded to your Honor in the
performance; Wherein as you shall shewe your self A true
inheriter of the Charitie and bountie of mynde sometyme   30
enrichinge your most worthie Father; So shall you binde me
duringe the small remnant of my lyfe, to publishe your goodnes
and pray for your all and ever well beinge./.

[115]

I finde Doctor hudson colde and dull: and yet I thinke   1
for himself he will be fast and sure: His familiars are
out of the towne: others he will not intreate; But I will
procure; I dare assure you of a full Number: I wolde
be glad of a solempne presence./ At two of the Clocke   5
I will visitt you wth a Trinitie of doctars at the least:
I pray let me be commended as before, and to Mr Linnacker
whom I shame to have forgotten./ Happie successe wth
a hartie farewell./
                                    Youres: ever Youres: 10
                                        I B.

[116]

Now of honestie Mr Feriman touchinge the matter of your iust   1
chalenge: I am as vnapt to make an excuse, as the cause it self
is vnable to beare a defence. That I be no whit partiall to
my self in my censure, I haue greevouslye trespast against you,
in honestie, in frendshippe, in all good manner: The confession   5
of a / heavy fault hathe made me ready for a hard sentence.
Howsoever any hope by a stronge expected meanes of satisfying
you hathe hitherto beguyled me, and bene some occasion to move me
defer my commyng to you for this day & yt day; And further
howsoever also a fearfull distrust of your harde conceyte, and a   10
self accusing shame you shoulde have cause to thinke me either
vnable or vnmyndefull to performe that, wch in severall regardes
I stoode so neerely bounde vnto, hathe ⟨made me⟩ wthhelde me from
you even when my foote hathe bene over the thresholde of your
lodginge; Yet I will well manifest vnto you and sufficiently   15
witnesse my desier & care to deserve well of you: and of that
good gentleman Mr Sidley: of whom I will now neither
vtter my conceyt, nor expresse my affection./ Mr Feryman, I
will yet make three dayes furder delay for commynge to you: tyll
then thincke well and Commaunde still./.   20
                        Youres as he prayes you esteeme
                        him:/. I.B./

[117]

Sir I had yesterday the entertainment I expected at *Hiegate*.   1
where I wished you: and where I vsed good commendations of your
self./ I have promised to hasten my retorne to London, and to
accompanie my Cosen of the hill mostely./ my desyer is to have
your direction at my commynge backe./ Wherefore if it shall like   5
you to leave woorde at your Lodginge if you have cause to be
absent when you will return: And thus wishinge all happines
to attend you, I leave never leavinge to love you./.
                        Your kinde vnfayned frend.
                        H.G./ .   10

86

Now off honestie Mr Sherman touchinge the matter off yor iust
chalenge: I am as vnapt to make an expense, as the cause it selfe
is vnable to beare a defence. That I be no whit partiall to
my selfe in my censure, I haue greedously trespast against you,
in honestie, in frendshippe, in all good manner: The confession
off a hearty fault hathe made me ready for a hard sentence.
Howsoeuer any hope by a stronge expected meanes off satisfying
you hathe hitherto beguyled me, and bene some occasion to moue me
deferr my comynge to you for this day & yt day; And further
howsoeuer also a fearefull distrust off yor harde conceyte, and a
selfe accusing that you sholde haue cause to thinke me either
vnable or vnmyndefull to performe that, wch in seuerall regardes
I stoode so neerely bounde vnto, hathe —————— withelde me from
you when my foote hathe bene ouer the thresholde off yor
lodginge; yet I will well manifest vnto you and sufficiently
witnesse my desire & care to deserue well off you: and off that
good gentleman Mr Sidley: off whom I will now neither
vtter my conceyt, nor expresse my affection. Mr Sherman, I
then thinke well and Commaund still.

Yor as he prayses you esteeme
him. I. B.

Ps. I had yesterday the entertainment I expected at Hiegate
whear I wished you: and whear I tolde good comendations off yor
selfe. I haue promised to hasten my retourne to London, and to
yor direction at my comynge back. my desyer is to haue
you to leaue woordes at yor lodginge iff you haue cause to be
absent when you will retourne: And thus wishinge all happines
to attend you, I leaue neuer leauinge to loue you.

Yor kinde vnfayned frend.
H. G.

Good Mr Harrington; the late losses I have had at play together
with the disappointe of some worships I looked for, forceth me
somewhat against good manners to send unto you for so little
I lent you: otherwise I wolde have willingly (as I hope
you so conceyve) stayed yor owne leysure. And so with the
thankfull returne of yor bookes by this my man, I commend
you to the God of all goodnes. from my lodging this. 17.
of January. 1588.
                            Yor well affected poore frend.
                            N. Coote.

Mr Harrington: I assure my self yt you have now utterly
forgotten mee: in yt I have not in all this tyme bene satisfied
that little ye owe mee.   Surely I can not thinke that
gentleman either much carefull of his owne reputation, or
of doing me right, yt shall borrow my money in such sorte
as you dyd, and not to repaye the same within the Moneth.
And therefore after so many Monethes you must pardon
me for putting you in remembrance: for though it be but
a meere tryfle, yet it will even now doo me muche
pleasure:
                            Yor well wishinge poore frend
                            N. Coote.

As I sayd afore so againe, that it is not possible to persuade
me, yt the loosing of my whole debt can approve yor libertie.
wch yf it were once apparent I wolde answer otherwyse
for me to play the prologue, & in conclusion the foole, I shold
but make my self yt wch I purpose not. The name yt you
offer may perhappe serve my turne, but then I must accept it,
uppon it may worke yor discharge & not afore. wch yf I shall
have nothing in hand, I think nothing at all I shall have.
I will enquire of the man, and such I will take as may
be founde, though the tyme be long. Yor frend
                            R F.

[118   17 January 1588 (1589?)   see Commentary]

Good Mr harrington; the late losses I have had at play togey   1
wth the disapointes of some receiptes I looked for, forceth me
somewhat against good manners to send vnto you for yt lyttle
I lent you: otherwyse I wolde have willinglye (as I hope
you so conceyve) stayed your owne leysure. And so wth the   5
thankfull returne of your bookes by this my man, I commend
you to the God of all goodnes. from my lodging this .17.
of Ianuarij. 1588.
                    Your well affected poore frend:
                         N. Coote./   10

[119   after 17 January 1588 (1589?)   see Commentary]

Mr harrington: I assure my self yt ye have now vtterly –   1
forgotten mee: in yt I haue not in all this tyme bene satisfied
that lyttle ye owe mee. Surely I can not thinke that
gentleman either muche carefull of his owne reputation, or
of doinge me right, yt shall borrow my money in such sorte   5
as you dyd, and not to repaye the same wthin the moneth /
And therefore after so many Monethes you must pardon
me for putting you in remembraunce: for though it be but
a meere tryfle, yet it will even now doo me muche
pleasure:/   Your well wishinge poore frend   10
                         N. Coote./

[120   see Commentary]

As I sayd afore so againe, that it is not possible to perswade   1
me, yt the leesing of my whole debt can afforde your libertie./
wch yf it were once apparaunt I wolde answere otherwyse /
for me to play the prologue, & in conclusion the foole, I should
but make my self yt wch I purpose not./ The name yt you   5
offer may perhapes serue my turn, but then I must accept it,
when it may worke your discharge & not afore./ Yf I shall
have nothing in hand, I think nothing at all I shall have,/
I will enquire of the man, and such I will take as may
be secure, though the tyme be longe./   Your Frend   10
                         R I.

f. 87r

[121   after 26 February 1602   see Commentary]

The humble Peticion of the Sisters   1
and Coheirs of Robert Lord Burgh.
is./
That vntill your Maiestie in your Princely wisdome shall thinke
meete to place & settle the honour of the Said Barony   5
either vpon the eldest daughter as the Custome hath bene, or vpon
any other of the abovenamed Coheirs (wherein they all submytt
themselues: and do most humbly attend your gratious pleasure
in that behalfe) Your Maiestie wolde not so muche disgrace the
said Coheirs, as to gyve eare to the ambitious Suyte of   10
one yt importuneth your Maiestie for the said honor, havinge neither
Tytle to demaunde it, nor meanes to maintaine it./

[122   July 1603 – 5 December 1603   see Commentary]

Cosen. I am sorie you have cause to try my good will,   1
where I haue no power to shew yt; your husbandes case
excludeth respectes of pryvate frendship, bycause my
publick dutye forbyddeth any such affection./ Yf
your request had stood wth reason of State, it should   5
haue bene furthered; So shall any other curtesie
wch I can do you be readely performed when I know
your desyres. In the meane tyme I wishe you comforte
and end
                              Your loving kynsman   10
                              and Frend.
I thank you for your sweete meates,   *Ro: Ceccyll*
the rather bycause I +thinke+ they were of
your owne hand./.
                     To my very loving Cosen and   15
                     Syster in law, Mrs Elizabeth Brooke

The humble Petition of the Sisters
and Cosins of Robert Lord Burgh.

16.

That untill yo[r] Ma[tie] in yo[r] Princely wisdome shall thinke
meete to place & settle the honour of the said Barony
either upon the eldest daughter as the Custome hath bene, or upon
any other of the abovenamed Cosins (wherein they all submitt
themselves; and do most humbly attend yo[r] gratious pleasure
in that behalfe) yo[r] Ma[tie] woold not so much disgrace the
said Cosins, as to gyve eare to the ambitious suyte of
some & importunitye yo[r] Ma[tie] for the said honor, havinge neither
tytle to demaunde it, nor meanes to maintaine it.

Cosen, I am sorie you have cause to try my good will,
where I have no power to pleasure it; yo[r] husbande cast
excludeth respecte of private frendship, because my
publick dutye forbiddeth any such affection. If
yo[r] request had stood with reason of state, it shoold
have bene furthered; So shall any other curtesie
wh[ich] I can do you be readely performed when I know
yo[r] desires. In the meane tyme I wishe you comforte
and end
                              yo[r] loving kynsman
                              and frend.

I thank you for yo[r] sweete meates,
the rather because I thinke I have
yo[r] owne hand.   Ro: Cecyll

              To my very loving Cosin and
              Syster in law, M[rs] Elizabeth Brooke

Bess: Because I heare well of you, & beleeue no less; I will vse an vnwoonted kindness, and so as you increase in yeares, yf you proceede in vertuous condicons, I will enlarge my loue & multiplie the affections of a father towards you. Know this: it is now time for you to distinguish betwene good and bad: and as you see those that doe well haue honor of it, and the worser sorte haue shame of euill conditions, so learne to embrace that which hath glorie in it selfe, and to shun that which bringeth skorne & contempt. Your Mother is carefull in your breedinge: you must be as obedient in your behauio\r. alwaies remember that neither father, mother, beautie, nor personage, can giue grace to a maide, if she become not those ornamentc with modestie. Your eyes are giuen you to beholde them yt may be patterns to you of sober conuersation: Tourne them away from vncomely spectacles. Your eares can not denye audience to ciuill speakers: but remoue your whole bodie from entisinge tongues. This is my first admonition. God imprinte his graces in youre harte and euer bless you. Brill: No: 16.

Youre louinge father
Thomas Burgh.

[123   16 November 1587 – 16 November 1595   see Commentary]

Bess: Because I heare well of you, & belieue no less; I will vse an   1
vnwoonted kindness, and so as you increase in yeares, yf you proceede in
vertuous condicions, I will enlarge my loue & multiplie the affections of
a father towards you. Know this: it is now time for you to distinguish
betwene good and bad: and as you see those that doe well haue honor of it,
and the worser sorte haue shame of euill conditions, so learne to embrace   6
that which hath glorie in it selfe, and to shun that which bringeth skorne
& contempt. Your Mother is carefull in your breedinge: you must be
as obedient in your behaviour. alwaies remember that neither father, mother,
beautie, nor personage, can giue grace to a maide, if she become not those
ornamentes with modestie. Your eyes are giuen you to beholde them yt   11
may be patterns to you of sober conuersation: Tourne them away from
vncomely spectacles. Your eares can not denye audience to ciuill speakers:
but remoue your whole bodie from entisinge tongues. This is my
first admonition. God imprinte his graces in youre harte and euer   15
bless you. Brill: No: 16·

                              Youre louinge father
                              Thomas Burgh. / .

f. 88r

[124   after 4 May 1605; *c*. mid–1605 (?)   see Commentary]

                    To his Most Gratious Maiestie./.   1
Vouchsafe most Excellent Soueraigne to take mercifull notice, of
the submissiue and amendsfull sorrowes, of your two most humble and
prostrated subiects for your highnes displeasure: Geo: Chapman and Ben:
Ihonson; whose chiefe offences are but two Clawses, and both of them   5
not our owne; Muche lesse the vnnaturall Issue of our offenceles intentes:
I hope youre Maiesties vniuersall knowledge will daigne to remember: That
all Authoritie in execution of Iustice, especiallie respectes the manners & liues
of men commaunded before it; And accordinge to their generall actions, cen =
sures any thinge that hath scap't them in perticuler; which can not be so   10
disproportionable: yt one beinge actuallie good, the other should be intentionally
ill; if not intentionallie (howsoeuer it may lie subiect to construction)
where the whole founte of our actions may be iustified from beinge in
this kinde offensiue; I hope the integrall partes will taste of the same –
loyall and most dutifull order: which to aspire, from your most Cesar =   15
like Bountie (who Conquerd still to spare the Conquerd: and was glad
of offences that he might forgiue) In all diiection neuer = inough
itterated sorrowe for youre high displeasure, and vowe of as muche
future delight, as of youre present anger; we cast our best partes at
youre highnes feete, and our worse to hell./.   20

                    George Chapman./.

To his Most Gratious Maiestie.

Vouchsafe most Excellent Soueraigne to take mercifull notice, of
the submissiue and amendsfull sorrowes, of your two most humble and
prostrated subiects for yo{}r highnes displeasure: Geo: Chapman and Ben:
Ihonson; whose chiefe offences are but two Clawses, and both of them
not our owne; Much lesse the vnnaturall Issue of our offenceles intents:
I hope youre Maiesties vniuersall knowledg will daigne to remember: That
all Authoritie in execution of Iustice, especiallie respects the manners & liues
of men commaunded before it; And accordinge to their generall actions, cen=
sures any thinge that hath scapt them in perticuler; which can not be so
disproportionable: y{}t one beinge actuallie good, the other should be intentionally
ill; if not intentionallie (howsoeuer it may lie subiect to construction)
where the whole founte of our actions may be iustified from beinge in
this kinde offensiue; I hope the integrall partes will taste of the same
loyall and most dutifull order: which to aspire, from your most Cesar=
like Bountie (who Conquerd still to spare the Conquerd: and was glad
of offences that he might forgiue) In all direction of neuer=inough
itterated sorrowe for youre high displeasure, and vowe of as muchs
future delight, as of youre present anger; we cast our best partz at
youre highnes feete, and our worst to hell. /.

George Chapman.

Most worthely honord. /.

Off all the ouersights for which I suffer, none repents me so much
as that our vnhappie booke was presented without your Lordshippe:
allowance, for which we can plead nothinge by way of perdon: but
your Person so farr remou'd from our requir'de attendance; Our Play
so much importunde, And our cleere opinions, y nothinge it contain'd could
worthely be held offensiue; And had your good Lordshippe: vouchsafte
this addition of grace to your late free bounties, to haue heard our
reasons for our well way'd Opinions; And the wordes trulye related,
on which both they and our enemies Complaints were grounded;
I make no question but your Impartiall Justice, wolde haue stoode
much further from their Clamor, then from our acquitall; which
indifferent fauour, if yet, your no lesse then Princelye respect
of vertue, shall pleass to bestowe on her poore obseruant, and
Commaunde my Appearaunce; I doubt not but the Tempest that
hath dryuen me into this wrackfull harber, will cleere with my
Innocence; And withall, the most sorrowe inflictinge wrath of
his Excellent Maiestie; which to my most humble and zealous
affection is so much the more stormye, by how much some of my
obscured laboures haue striu'd to aspire in stead therof his &
Illustrate fauoure. And shall not be the least honor to his
most Royall vertues. /.

                              To the most worthy and honorable
                              Protector of vertue: The lord
                              Chamberlaine :/

                         George Chapman. /.

[125   after 4 May 1605; *c.* mid–1605 (?)   see Commentary]

Most worthely honord ./.   1

Off all the ouersightes for which I suffer, none repentes me so much,
as that our vnhappie booke was presented without your Lordshippes
allowance, for which we can plead nothinge by way of perdon: but
your Person so farr remou'd from our requir'de attendance: Our Play   5
so much importun'de, And our cleere opinions, yt nothinge it contain'd could
worthely be held offensiue; And had your good Lordshippe: vouchsafte
this addition of grace to your late free bounties, to haue heard our
reasons for our well wayd Opinions; And the wordes trulye related,
on which both they and our enemies Complaintes were grounded;   10
I make no question but your Impartiall Iustice, wolde haue stoode
much further from their Clamor, then from our acquitall; which
indifferent fauour, if yet, your no lesse then Princelye respect
of vertue, shall please to bestowe on her poore obseruant, and
Commaunde my Appearaunce; I doubt not but the Tempest that   15
hath dryuen me into this wrackfull harber, will cleere with my
Innocence; And withall, the most sorrowe inflictinge wrath of
his Excellent Maiestie; which to my most humble and zealous
affection is so much the more stormye, by how much some of my
obscured laboures haue striu'd to aspire in stead therof his –   20
Illustrate fauoure. And shall not be the least honor to his
most Royall vertues ./.
                    To the most worthy and honorable
                    Protector of vertue: The lord
                    Chamberlaine:/   25
              George Chapman./.

f. 89r

[126   after 4 May 1605; *c.* mid-1605   see Commentary]

Notwithstandinge youre lordshipps infinite free bountie hath perdon'd &   1
grac't, when it might iustlie haue punisht; and rememberd our poore
reputations, when our acknowledgd dewties to your lordshippe, might
worthely seeme forgotten; yet since true honor delightes to encrease wth
encrease of goodnes; and yt our habilities and healths fainte vnder our –   5
yrcksome burthens; we are wth all humilitie enforc't to solicite the pro
pagation of youre most noble fauours to our present freedome; And the
rather since we heare from the Lorde Dawbuey, that his highnes hath –
remitted one of vs wholie to youre Lordshippes fauoure; And that the other –
had still youre Lordshippes passinge noble remembraunce for his Iointe libertie; wch
his highnes selfe would not be displeasd to allowe; And thus wth all   11
gratitude admyringe youre no lesse then sacred respect to the poore
estate of vertue,/ neuer were our soules more appropriate to the
powers of our liues, then our ⟨vtt⟩ vttmost liues are consecrate
to youre Noblest seruice./.   15
                    George Chapman.

f. 89v

BLANK

Notwithstandinge youre lordshipps infinite free bountie hath perdon'd &
grac't, when it might iustlie haue punisht; and rememberd our poore
reputations, when our acknowledgd dewties to your lordshipps, might
worthely seeme forgotten; yet since true honor delightes to encrease w^th
encrease of goodnes; and y^t our habilities and healths fainte vnder our
yrcksome burthens; we are wth all humilitie enforc't to solicite the pro
pagation of youre most noble fauours to our present freedome; And the
rather since we heare from the Lorde Dawbuey, that his highnes hath
remitted one of vs wholie to youre Lo: fauoure; And that the other
had still youre Lo: passinge noble remembrance for his ioynte libertie; w^ch
his highnes selfe would not be displeas'd to allowe; And thus wth all
gratitude admyringe youre no lesse then sacred respect to the poore
estate of vertue, neuer were our soules more appropriate to the
powers of our liues, then our ~~all~~ vttmost liues are consecrate
to youre Noblest seruice. |.

George Chapman.

[127   after 4 May 1605; *c*. mid–1605 (?)   see Commentary]

Most honorable Lord: 1
Although I can not but know your Lordshippe to be busied wth far greater and
higher affaires, then to haue leysure to discend sodainlye on an estate
so lowe, and remou'd as myne; yet, since the cause is in vs wholie mista =
ken (at least misconstrued) and yt euerie noble and Iust man, is bounde to
defend the Innocent, I doubt not but to finde your Lordshipp full of yt woonted
vertue, & fauoure; wherwith you haue euer abounded toward the truth./   7
And though the Imprisonment it selfe can not but grieue mee (in respect
of his Maiesties high displeasure, from whence it proceedes) Yet the
Manner of it afflictes me more, beinge commytted hether, vnexamyned,   10
nay vnheard (a Rite, not commonlie denyed to the greatest Offenders)
and I. made a guiltie man, longe before I am one, or euer thought to bee:
God, I call to testimonye what my thoughtes are, and euer haue bene of
his Maiestie; and so may I thryue when he comes to be my Iudge &
my Kinges, as they are most sinceere: And I appeale to posteritie   15
that will hearafter read and Iudge my writings (though now neglected)
whether it be possible, I should speake of his Maiestie as I haue done,
without the affection of a most zealous and good subiect. It hath euer
bene my destenye to be misreported, and condemn'd on the first tale; but
I hope there is an Eare left for mee, and by youre honor I hope it,   20
who haue alwaies bene frend to Iustice; a vertue that Crownes
youre Nobilitie./ So with my most humble prayer of your Pardon,
and all aduanced wishes for your honor, I begin to know my dutie,
which is to forbeare to trouble your Lordshippe till ⟨.⟩ my languishinge estate
may drawe free breath from youre Comfortable worde./.   25
                                   Ben: Iohnson./

Most honorable Lord:

Although I can not but know yo:r Lo: to be busied wth far greater and
higher affaires, then to haue leysure to discend sodainlye on an estate
so lowe, and remou'd as myne; yet, since the cause is in vs wholie mista=
ken (at least misconstrued) and yt euerie noble and Iust man, is bounde to
defend the Innocent, I doubt not but to finde yo:r Lordshipp full of yt woonted
vertue, & fauoure; wherwith you haue euer abounded toward the truth.
And though the Imprisonment it selfe cannot but grieue mee (in respect
of his Maiesties high displeasure, from whence it proceedes) Yet the
manner of it afflicts me more, beinge commytted hether, vnexamyned,
nay vnheard (a Rite, not commonlie denyed to the greatest Offenders)
and I made a quiltie man, longe before I am one, or euer thought to bee:
God, I call to testimonye what my thoughts are, and euer haue bene of
his Maiestie; and so may I thryue when he comes to be my Iudge &
my Kinges, as they are most sinceere :   And I appeale to posteritie
that will hearafter read and Iudge my writings (though now neglected)
whether it be possible, I should speake of his Maiestie as I haue done,
without the affection of a most zealous and good subiect. It hath euer
bene my destenye to be misreported, and condemn'd on the first tale; but
I hope there is an Eare left for mee, and by youre honor I hope it,
who haue alwaies bene frend to Iustice; a vertue that Crownes
youre Nobilitie./ So with my most humble prayer of your Pardon,
and all aduaunced wishes for yo:r honor, I begin to know my dutie,
which is to forbeare to trouble yo:r Lo: till : my languishinge estate
may drawe free breath from youre Comfortable worde./

                                   Ben: Iohnson./

My honorable lord.

It hath still bene the Tyrannye of my fortune so to oppress my endeuours,
that before I can shew my selfe gratefull in the least, for former &
benefites, I am enforc't to prouoke youre bounties for more. May it
not seeme grieuous to yo̅ Lordshipp, that now, my Innocence calles vpon
you (next a Deitie) to her defence. God him selfe is not auerted at
Iust mens Cries; And you y̅ approche that diuine goodnes, and supplie
it here on earth in your place and honors, cannot employ yo̅ aydes
more worthely, then to the common succour of honestie, & vertue,
how humbly so euer it be plac'd. I am here (my most ho: Lord)
vnexamyned or vnheard, commytted to a vile prison, and w̅ me
a Gent: whose name may perhaps haue come to youre Lo: one M̅r
George Chapman, an honest, and learned Man; The cause (
wolde I could name some worthier, though I wish we had knowne
none worthy of our imprisonment) is (the worde irkes me that our
fortune hath enforst vs to such a despisde course) a Play my Lorde:
whereof we hope, there is no man can iustly complaine, that hath
the vertue to thinke but fauourably of him selfe; if our Iudge bringe
an equall Eare; Mary if w̅ preiudice we be made guiltie afore our
Tyme, we must embrace the Asinine vertue, Patience.

My noble Lord: they deale not charitably that are to wittie in another
mans workes, and vtter sometymes their owne malicious meaninges
vnder our woordes; I protest to your honor: and call God for
testimonye, (since my first Error, w̅ch yet is punished in me, more
w̅th my shame,   then it was then with my bondage) I haue so attem=
pred my stile, that I haue giuen no cause to any good man of griefe;
and if to any ill, by touchinge at his vice, it hath alwaies bene with a
regarde, & sparinge of his person; I may be otherwise reported, but
if all y̅t be accusd should be presently guiltie, there are fewe men
wolde stand in the state of Innocence; I beseech your Lordshipp,
suffer not other mens Errors or faults past to be made my Crymes,

[128   after 4 May 1605; *c.* mid–1605 (?)   see Commentary]

My honorable lord./   1
It hath still bene the Tyrannye of my fortune so to oppress my endeuours,
that before I can shew my selfe gratefull in the least, for former –
benefites, I am enforc't to prouoke youre bounties for more./ May it
not seeme grieuous to your Lordshipp, that now, my Innocence calles vpon   5
you (next a Deitie) to her defence. God him selfe is not auerted at
Iust mens Cries; And you yt approche that diuine goodnes, and supplie
it here on earth in your place and honors, can not employ your aydes
more worthely, then to the common succour of honestie, & vertue,
how humbly so euer it be plac'd. I am here (my most honored Lord)   10
vnexamyned or vnheard, commytted to a vile prison, and wth me
a Gentleman whose name may perhaps haue come to youre Lordshippe one Mr
George Chapman, an honest, and learned Man; The cause (I
wolde I could name some worthier, though I wish we had knowne
none worthy of our imprisonment) is (the worde irkes me that our   15
fortune hath enforst vs to such a despisde course) a Play my Lorde:
whereof we hope, there is no man can iustly complaine, that hath
the vertue to thinke but favourably of himselfe; if our Iudge bringe
an equall Eare; Mary if wth preiudice we be made guiltie afore our
Tyme, we must embrace the Asinine vertue, Patience./   20
My noble Lord: they deale not charitably that are to wittie in another
mans workes, and vtter sometymes their owne malicious meaninges
vnder our woordes; I protest to your honor: and call God for
testimonye, (since my first Error, wch yet is punished in me, more
wth my shame, then it was then +with+ my bondage) I haue so attem =   25
pred my stile, that I haue giuen no cause to any good man of griefe;
and if to any ill, by touchinge at his vice, it hath alwaies bene with a
regarde, & sparinge of his person; I may be otherwise reported, but
if all yt be accusd should be presently guiltie, there are fewe men
wolde stand in the state of Innocence; I besech your lordshipp,   30
suffer not other mens Errors or faults past to be made my Crymes,

but let me be examin'd both by all my workes past, and this present:
whether I haue euer hetherto ⟨hetherto⟩ giuen offence in any thinge I
haue written to a Nation, to a publicke order, or state, to any person
of honor, or Authoritie, but haue labor'd to keepe their dignitie as myne   35
owne person safe. But least in beinge to diligent for my excuse, I
may incurre the suspition of beinge guiltie. I become a most humble
sutor to youre Lordshippe that you will be the meanes wth the honorable Earle
of Suffolke, we may come to our aunswere, or if in your wisdomes
it shall be thought vnnecessary: yt you will be the most honord   40
Cause of our libertie, where freeinge vs from one Pryson, you shall
remoue vs to another: wch is eternally to binde vs and our Muses,
to the gratefull honoringe of you and yours to Posteritie, as your owne
vertues haue by many Discents of Auncestors Enobled you to Tyme.
                                   Ben: Iohnson ./.

but let me be examin'd both by all my workes past, and this present :
whether I haue euer hetherto ~~hetherto~~ giuen offence in any thinge I
haue written to a Nation, to a publicke order, or state, to any person
of honor, or Authoritie, but haue labor'd to keepe their dignitie as myne
owne person safe. But least in beinge to diligent for my excuse, I
may incurre the suspition of beinge guiltie. I become a most humble
sutor to youre Lo: that you will be the meanes wth the ho: Earle
of Suffolke, we may come to our aunswere, or if in yor wisdomes
it shall be thought vnnecessary: y^t you will be the most honord
Cause of our libertie, where freeinge vs from one Pryson, you shall
remoue vs to another: wch is eternally to binde vs and our Muses,
to the gratefull honoringe of you and yours to Posteritie, as yor owne
vertues haue by many Discents of Auncestors Enobled you to Tyme.

Ben: Johnson : 1.

Noble Lord.

I haue so confirm'd Opinion of yo.r vertue, And am so fortified in myne owne Innocence, as I dare (without blushinge at any thinge saue youre Trouble) put my Fame into youre hands: (which I prefer to my lyfe.) The cause of my commytment I understand is his Maiesties high displeasure conceyued against me; ffor w.ch I am most Inwardlie sorie; but how I should deserue it, I haue yet I thanke God so much integritie as to dowbt. If I haue bene misreported to his Maiestie, the punishment I now suffer may I hope merite more of his Princelye — fauoure, when he shall know me trulie: Euerie Accusation doth not condemne, And there must goe much more to the makinge of a guiltie man, then Rumor. I therfore craue of yo.r Lo: this Noble Benefitt, rightly to informe his Maiestie, y.t I neuer in thought, worde, or Act, had purpose to offend or grioue him, but w.th all my powers haue studied to shew my selfe most loyall and zealous to his whole disseignes, y.t in priuate & publique, by speech and writinge, I haue euer profest it, And if there be one man, or deuill to be produc'd y.t can affirm the contrarie; let me suffer vnder all extremitie, y.t Iustice, nay Tyrannye can inflict; I speake not this w.th any spiritt of Contumacie, for I know there is no subiect hath so safe an Innocence, but may reioyce to stand iustified in sight of his Soueraignes mercie. To which we most — humblie submytt our selues, or lyues and fortunes.

Ben: Johnson.

f. 91v

[129   after 4 May 1605 (?); *c.* mid–1605 (?)   see Commentary]

Noble Lord./.   1

I haue so confirm'd Opinion of your vertue, And am so fortified in myne
owne Innocence, as I dare (without blushinge at any thinge saue youre
Trouble) put my Fame into youre hands: which I prefer to my lyfe./.
The cause of my commyttment I vnderstand is his Maiesties high   5
displeasure conceyued against me; For wch I am most Inwardlie
sorie; but how I should deserue it, I haue yet I thanke God so much
integritie as to dowbt./ If I haue bene misreported to his Maiestie, the
punishment I now suffer may I hope merite more of his Princelye –
fauoure, when he shall know me trulie: Euerie Accusation doth not   10
condemne, And there must goe much more to the makinge of a guiltie
man, then Rumor./ I therfore craue of your Lordshippe this Noble Benefitt, –
rightly to informe his Maiestie, yt I neuer in thought, worde, or Act,
had purpose to offend or grieue him, but wth all my powers haue –
studied to shew my selfe most loyall and zealous to his whole disseignes, 15
yt in priuate & publique, by speech and writinge, I haue euer profest it.
And if there be one man, or deuill to be produc'd yt can affirm the contrarie;
let me suffer vnder all extremitie, yt Iustice, nay Tyrannye can –
inflict; I speake not this wth any spiritt of Contumacie, for I know
there is no subiect hath so safe an Innocence, but may reioyce to stand   20
iustified in sight of his Soueraignes mercie./ To which we most –
humblie submytt our selues, our lyues and fortunes./.

                                             Ben: Iohnson./.

f. 92r

[130   after 4 May 1605 (?); *c*. mid–1605 (?)   see Commentary]

Excellentest of Ladies. /   1
And most honor'd of the Graces, Muses, and mee; if it be not a sinne
to prophane your free hand with prison polluted Paper, I wolde intreate
some little of youre Ayde, to the defence of my Innocence, wch is as cleare
as this leafe was (before I staind it) of any thinge halfe=worthye   5
this violent infliction; I am commytted, and wth mee, a worthy Friend,
one Mr Chapman, a man, I can not say how knowne to your Ladishipp, but
I am sure knowne to mee to honor you; And our offence a Play, so
mistaken, so misconstrued, so misapplied, as I do wonder whether their
Ignorance, or Impudence be most, who are our aduersaries. / It is now   10
not disputable, for we stand on vneuenbases, and our cause so vnequal =
ly carried, as we are without examyninge, without hearinge, or with
out any proofe, but malicious Rumor, horried, to bondage and fetters;
The cause we vnderstand to be the Kinges indignation, for which we
are hartelye sorie, and the more, by how much the less we haue deseru'd   15
it. / What our sute is, the worthy employde soliciter, and equall –
Adorer of youre vertues, can best enforme you. /.
                                                        Ben: Ihonson. /.

[131   after 4 May 1605 (?); *c*. mid–1605 (?)   see Commentary]

The Noble fauoures you haue done vs, Most worthy Lord: can not be so   1
conceald, or remou'd: but that they haue broke in vpon vs, euen where
we lye double bound to their Comfortes; Nor can we doubt, but he who
hath so farre, and freelie aduentur'd to the reliefe of our vertue, will
goe on to the vtmost release of it; And though I know your Lordshippe hath   5
bene far from doinge any thinge herin to youre owne Ambition; Yet be
pleas'd to take this protestation, that (Next his Maiesties fauoure)
I shall not couet that thinge more in the worlde, then to expresse the
lastinge Gratitude, I haue conceiu'd in soule towards your Lordshipp. /
                                                        Ben: Iohnson. /.   10

Excellentest of Ladies.

And most honor'd of the Graces, Muses, and mee; if it be not a sinne
to prophane yo free hand with prison polluted Paper, I wolde intreate
some little of youre Ayde, to the defence of my Innocence, wch is as cleare
as this leafe was (before I staind it) of any thinge halfe=worthye
this violent infliction; I am committed, and wth mee, a worthy Friend,
one Mr Chapman, a man, I cannot say how knowne to yo Ladishipp, but
I am sure knowne to mee to honor you; And our offence a Play, so
mistaken, so misconstrued, so misapplied, as I do wonder whether their
Ignorance, or Impudence be most, who are our aduersaries. It is now
not disputable, for we stand on vneuenbases, and our cause so vnequal=
ly carried, as we are without examyninge, without hearinge, or with
out any proofe, but malicious Rumor, horried, to bondage and fetters;
The cause we vnderstand to be the Kinges indignation, for which we
are hartelye sorie, and the more, by how much the less we haue deseru'd
it. What our sute is, the worthy employde soliciter, and equall
Adorer of youre vertues, can best enforme you.

Ben: Jhonson.

The Noble fauoures you haue done vs, Most worthy Lord: cannot be so
conceald, or remou'd: but that they haue broke in vpon vs, euen where
we lye double bound to their Comforts; Nor can we doubt, but he who
hath so farre, and freelie aduentur'd to the reliefe of our vertue, will
goe on to the vtmost releafe of it; And though I know yor Lo: hath
bene far from doinge any thinge herin to youre owne Ambition; yet be
pleas'd to take this protestation, that (Next his Maiesties fauoure)
I shall not couet that thinge more in the worlde, then to expresse the
lastinge Gratitude, I haue conceiu'd in soule towards yo Lordshipp.

Ben: Johnson.

Most worthely honor'd.

for mee not to solicite or call you to succoure in a tyme of such neede, were
no lesse a sinne of dispaire, then a neglect of youre honor; Yo^r Power,
youre Place, and readinesse to do good inuite mee; and myne owne cause
(which shall neuer discreditt the least of yor fauours) is a mayne encou=
ragement; If I lay here on my   desert, I should be the more back=
ward to importune you; But as it is (most worthy Earle) our
offence beinge our misfortune, not our maliee: I challenge yor ayde, as
to the common defence of vertue; But more peculiarlye to mee, who
haue alwayes in hart so perticularly honor'd you. I know it is now no
Tyme to boast affections, least while I sue for fauours I should be
thought to buy them; But if the future seruices of a man so remou'd to
you, and low in Meritt, may aspire any place in yor Thoughts, let it
lye vpon the forfayture of my humanitie, if I omitt the least occasion to
expresse them. And so not doubtinge of youre Noble endeuors, to reflect
his Maiesties most ~~repentante~~ repented on oure partes, & sorrow'd
for displeasure. I committ my fortune, Reputation, and Innocence,
into youre most happie handes, with reiterated protestation of being
euer most gratefull./.

                                        Ben: Johnson./.

[132   after 4 May 1605 (?); *c*. mid–1605 (?)   see Commentary]

Most worthely honor'd ./.   Mongomerie.   1

For mee not to solicite or call you to succoure in a tyme of such neede, were
no lesse a sinne of dispaire, then a neglect of youre honor; Your Power,
youre Place, and readinesse to do good inuite mee; and myne owne cause
(which shall neuer discreditt the least of your fauours) is a mayne encou =   5
ragement; If I lay here on my desert, I should be the more back =
ward to importune you; But as it is (Most worthy Earle) our
offence beinge our misfortune, not our malice: I challenge your ayde, as
to the common defence of Vertue; But more peculiarlye to mee, who
haue alwayes in hart so perticularly honor'd you. I know it is now no –   10
Tyme to boast affections, least while I sue for fauours I should be
thought to buy them; But if the future seruices of a man so remou'd to
you, and low in Meritt, may aspire any place in your Thoughtes, let it
lye vpon the forfayture of my humanitie, if I omitt the least occasion to
expresse them. And so not doubtinge of your Noble endeuors, to reflect   15
his Maiesties most ⟨repentante⟩ repented on oure partes, & sorrow'd
for displeasure. I commytt my fortune, Reputation, and Innocence,
into youre most happie handes, with reiterated protestation of being
euer most gratefull./.
                              Ben: Iohnson ./   20

f. 93r

[133   after 4 May 1605 (?); *c*. mid–1604 (?)   see Commentary]

Most Noble Earle:/   Pembrooke./.   1

Neither am I or my cause so much vnknowne to youre Lordshipp, as
it should driue me to seeke a second meanes, or dispaire of this to your
fauoure. You haue euer bene free and Noble to mee, and I doubt not
the same proportion of youre Bounties, if I can but answer it with   5
preseruation of my vertue, and Innocence; when I faile of those,
let me not onlye be abandon'd of you, but of Men./ The Anger of
the Kinge is death (saith the wise man) and in truth it is little
lesse with mee and my frend, for it hath buried vs quick. And
though we know it onlie the propertie of Men guiltie, and worthy of   10
punishment to inuoke Mercye; Yet now it might relieue vs, who
haue onlie our Fortunes made our fault: and are indeede vexed
for other mens licence. Most honor'd Earle, be hastie to our
succoure, And, it shall be our care and studye, not to haue you repent
the tymely benefit you do vs; which we will euer gratefullye   15
receyue and Multiplye in our ⟨ackow⟩ acknowledgment./.
                              Ben: Iohnson./.

Most Noble   Earle:/   Pembrooke./   13

Neither am I or my cause so much vnknowne to youre Lordshipp, as
it should driue me to seeke a second meanes, or dispaire of this to your
fauoure . You haue euer bene free and Noble to mee, and I doubt not
the same proportion of youre Bounties, if I can but answere it with
preseruation of my vertue, and Innocence; when I faile of those,
let me not onlye be abandon'd of you, but of Men ./ The Anger of
the Kinge is death (saith the wise man) and in truth it is little
lesse with mee and my frend, for it hath buried vs quick. And
though we know it onlie the propertie of men guiltie, and worthy of
punishment to inuoke Mercye; Yet now it might relieue vs, who
haue onlie our Fortunes made our fault: and are indeede vexed
for other mens licence . Most honor'd Earle, be hastie to our
succoure, And, it shall be our care and studye, not to haue you repent
the tymely benefit you do vs; which we will euer gratefullye
receyue and Multiplye in our ~~ackno~~ acknowledgment ./

                                        Ben: Johnson:/.

You demaunde what you ~~should~~ shall doe, the woman on the banke syde can better resolue you. I am no fortunteller. / Liue vnder youre owne starres. Some happie influence no doubt attends you: If you prosper, I will neuer dispaire. Onlie thus much, I think that all that loue w[ch] is built on your beautie, will ruine when the foundation fayles; for my selfe, I speake it to the face of heauen, that I once loued youe more then it. I held you worthie to be good bicause I thought you willinge; I should haue esteemde my selfe happie, if I might haue made you so: Blessed if I might haue enioyed you so. / But I finde a Page, or a gentlemanvsher may wth a good face, and omnipotent golde, make an honest woman a whoore, but to make a whoore an honest woman, is beyonde the laboures of Hercules. / but let experience teach you youre error. / I enuie not him that shall possesse you. if you haue wrongd me, let youre owne inconstancye punish it selfe; for I can not wish you worsse then to be what you are.

Ex epistola. 58. ad Martinum Lidium Concionatorem. /

Definitum a deo [mala] quicquid euenit, non tamen peccatum cuius fons à sola voluntate nostra. Exempli causa: In Tarquinij adulterio in — caedibus. ab Herode Innocentum duo spectanda: factum ipsum et crimen — factum a deo definitum et comprehenditur sub fatali illa lege. Crimen quod soli voluntati inhaeret, fateri qui possimus sine iniuria dei: Causa omnium rerum diuina voluntas, omniumq; euentuum etiamsi mali sint: at non causa causae mediae quoties ea mala. alias quomodo effugimus vt non auctor ille sit mali, vt non adprobator? Itaq; ea que ex Act. u adducuntur, huc accommodo. mortem xpi destinatam ab aeterno, — proditionem Iudae ab aeterno, mediaq; omnia quae ad salutare illud opus ferrent: sed non crimina adnexa ipsis factis. quibus — fundamentum in impia tantum voluntate. /

[134]

You demaunde what you ⟨should⟩ shall doe, the woman on the banke syde can
better resolue you. I am no fortunteller./ Liue vnder youre owne starres.　　　2
Some happie influence no doubt attends you; If you prosper, I will neuer
dispaire. Onlie thus much, I think that all that loue wch is built on your
beautie, will ruine when the foundation fayles; for my selfe, I speake it　　　5
to the face of heauen, that I once loued youe more then it. I held you
worthie to be good bicause I thought you willinge; I should haue esteemde
my selfe happie, if I might haue made you so: Blessed if I might haue
enioyed you so./ But I finde a Page, or a gentlemanvsher may wth a
good face, and omnipotent golde, make an honest woman a whoore, but to　　10
make a whoore an honest woman, is beyonde the laboures of Hercules./
but let experience teach you youre error./ I enuie not him that shall
possesse you. if you haue wrongd me, let youre owne inconstancye
punish it selfe; For I can not wish you worsse then to be what you are.

[135　　　　　　　　28 November 1583　　　　see Commentary]

　　　　　Ex epistola .58. ad Martinum Lidium　　　　　　1
　　　　　　　Concionatorem ./.
Definitum a deo quicquid euenit, non tamen peccatum cuius fons à
sola +mala+ voluntate nostra. Exempli causa: In Tarquinij adulterio in –
cædibus. ab Herode Innocentum duo spectanda: factum ipsum et crimen.　　5
factum a deo definitum et comprehenditur sub fatali illa lege. Crimen,
quod soli voluntati inhæret, faterî qui possimus sine iniuria dei: Causa
omnium rerum diuina voluntas, omniumque euentuum etiamsi mali sint:
at non causa causæ mediæ quoties ea mala. alias quômodo effugimus
vt non auctor ille sit mali, vt non adprobator? Itaque ea que ex Act .ıı.　　10
adducuntur, huc accommodo. mortem christi destinatam ab æterno, –
proditionem Iudæ ab æterno, mediaque omnia quæ ad salutare illud
opus ferrent: sed non crimina adnexa ipsis factis. quibus –
fundamentum in impia tantum voluntate./.

[136]

Sir Not wearie of my Shelter, but vncertaine, why the Forme   1
of the Clowde, still hovers over me, when the Matter is disperst,
I write to intreat your Resolution; And all this tyme have not
in this sort visited you, for feare I should seeme to giue spurrs
to your free disposition; But now, (least Imagininge me hotter   5
of my libertie then I am, you should thinke me vnhowsd, and not
to have presented you wth my first thankefull Apparaunce) I
thought good to send out this dove; And thoughe I am put, by
the Austeritie of the offended tyme to this little pacience, Yet
can I not be so thankleslye Ielouse of the knowinge Iudgment –   10
from whence your actions proceede, to retaine any thought of youre
Favoures Repentaunce; or neglect of their extension in the safe Retreat;
when your daungerous charge for me, was so Resolute & worthie./
    I am the same I was, when you thought me worthie of youre
vertuous kindenes; and will ever remaine (whatsoever I may be)   15
                              Wholy Youres in all Affectionate
For his right worthie and   Requitall./
exceedinge good Frend *Mr.*
Crane: Secretorie to my Lord
Duke of Lennox. :/   20

[137]

I am sorie yt I should put you to this Exygent, & muche more yt you 1
will be put to it so vnnecessarilie; *Da Natis operam Diuûm Conuiuia*
linguens; You must return this note by this bearer, for this yt comes after;
Mr. E: is as willinge as Necessarie for all your affayres; And since
the discharge of them, is not to be done by one in no showe; The   5
request I made to you, is turnd to this; That you wolde let him have
your blacke stuffe Suyte to be made fytt for him; And wth yt, will he
make meanes to travayle in your affayres wthout Bondes, woordes, or
any other cost to you; Yf ⟨w⟩ you will doe any thinge, you can not
refuse this, Therefore let it be as speedely, as you wolde have   10
youre turne serv'd by him; and in any case send this fragment back.
By God (my best George:

O: Not wearie off my Scholler, but somtimes, when the stormes
off the clowdes, still hovers over me, when the Matter is disperst,
I write to intreat yo: Resolution; And all this tyme have not
in this sort visited you, for feare I should seme to give bounes
to yo: free disposition; But now, (least Imaginings me hotter
off my libertie then I am, you should thinke me Unhowl'd, and not
to have presented you w:th my first thankfull Apparance) I
thought good to send out this debt; And though I am gone, by
the Austeritie off the offended tyme to this little paynures, yet
can I not be so thanklesshy Jelouse off the knowinge Judgment —
from whence yo: actions proceeds, to retaine any thought off your
slothe Repentances; or neglect off their restoration in the safe retreat,
as in yo: Dangerous charge for me, was so Resolute & worthie;
I am the same I was, when you thought me worthie off your
vertuous kindnes; and will ever remaine (wretch'dar I may be)

                    Wholy yours in all Affectionate
                          Regardall.

for his right worthie and
especiall my good frend Mr
Crane: Secretarie to my Lord
Duke off Lennox. :/

I am sorie y:t I should put you to this Expense, & muche more y:t you
will be put to it so unnecessarilie; Da Natis operam Divûm Convivia
linquens; You must returne this note by this bearer, for this y:t I send afore:
Mr E: is as willinge as Necessarie for all yo: affayres; And sinse
the discharge off them, is not to be done by one in no howr; The
request I made to you, is turned to this; That you would let him have
yo: blacke stuffe sute to be made fitt for him; And w:th w:ch will he
make meanes to travayse in yo: affayres w:thout Bandes, woorsted, or
any other cost to you; Iff so you will doe any thinge, you can not
refuse this, Therfore let it be as speedoly, as you would have
yo:r owne turne serv'd by him; and in any case send this fragment back.

By God (my best George:

To the right ho: the lo: Ellesmere: Lo:
Chauncelo.r of England

The humble Peticion of George Chapman

Whereas abouts. 25. yeares past, the Peticon became bounde to save
one John woollfall of London Broker harmlesse from a Bonde
made by them bothe to one Richard Adams of London Lynnendraper,
The said bond being. 24. yeares since discharged by the Peticon.r
wch he is able to prove by sufficient wytnes, and the said
woollfall no way damnified; Notwthstanding the Bonde was
wch he delyvered vncancelled; and by him lefte to one Jo: woollfall his
sonne; who (havinge them now to shew) proceedeth wth his
fathers Cossenage; ———————— that, against the Petic.r
wth all extremitie of lawe;

The Petic.r humblie besecheth yo.r Lo: that (havinge exhibited
his bill in Chauncerie for the Redresse hereof, ——————
—————————————————— against ———————— now; &
(for ———— the like detencion of Bonde (& Cossenage) ———
stood on the Pillorie; by Censure of the honorable Court of
Starre Chamber; Against the Justice hereof: his Crime
now defend: hathe lately comytted most punisheable Scandall,
It wolde please yo.r good Lo: to graunt an Iniunction for the
stayinge of the said Jo: woollfall the Comon proceedinges vppon
the aforesaid Bonde at the Common lawe; And ————————— tha.
to ———— suche consionable Order; as yo.r Lo: (vpon y.e equall
heavinge of bothe: in yo.r approved wysdome and Relligious
respect to that temperate Iustice; wch is fustlie superior to
the Lawes in.st extremitie) shall impartially practise; for wch
————————— shall pray for yo.r Lo: wcorthie health, hono.r & happines

f. 94v

[138   17–27 April 1608   see Commentary]

To the right honorable the lord Ellesmere: lord   1
Chauncelor of England
The humble Peticion of George Chapman
Whereas aboute .25. yeares past, the Peticioner became bounde to save
one *Iohn woollfall* of london Broker harmlesse from a Bonde   5
made by them bothe to one Richard Adams of London lynnendraper,
The said bond beeing .24. yeares since discharged by the Peticioner
wch he is able to prove by sufficient wytnesse, and the said
woollfall no way dampnified; Notwthstandinge the Bondes was –
reserv'd vncancelld; and by him lefte to one Io: woollfall his   10
Sonne; who (havinge them now to showe) proceedes wth his
Fathers Cosenages; ⟨and enforceth them, in this⟩, against the Petic
wth all extremitie of lawe;
The Peticioner humblie beseecheth your Lordshippe that (havinge exhibited
his bill in Chauncerie for the Redresse hereof, ⟨And his affir   15
mations at first sight gyvinge some hope to prepare your Lordshippes good
Opinion; since they are vrgd⟩ against ⟨the dishonestie of⟩ one; yt
(for ⟨this, or⟩ the like detention of Bondes & Cossenages) ⟨twice⟩
stood +twice+ on the Pillorie; by Censure of the honorable Court of
Starr Chamber; Against the Iustice whereof: his Sonne   20
now defend : hathe lately commytted most punysheable Scandall)
It wolde please your good Lordshippe to graunt an Iniunction for the
stayinge of the said Io: woollfall the Sonns proceedinges vpon
the aforesaid Bondes at the Common lawe; And ⟨enforcinge⟩ +enioyninge+ him
to ⟨abyde⟩ suche conscionable Order; as your Lordshippe (vpon ye equall 25
hearinge of bothe: in your approved wysdome and Religious
respect to that temperate Right; wch is Iustlye Superior to
the Lawes iust extremitie) shall impertially prefixe; For wch
the Peticioner shall (as he hathe longe bene bound ⟨to⟩) ⟨most Affec =
tionately⟩ pray for your Lordshippes woorthie health, honor, & happine   30

[139 after 6 November 1612 – before 17 November 1615 see Commentary]

        To the Right honorable, the Lordes of   1
           his Maiesties privie Counsell :
        The humble Petition of Geo:
           Chapman gentleman /

Vouchsafe (most honord Lordes) your free consideration of   5
my enforc't suyte; That attending, fower yeares our late lost
Prince; in a service commaunded by his highnes (being the
translation of Homers Iliads out of the Greeke) And
being promist, wth his often Princely protestation of likinge,
(bothe out of his owne rare towardnes, and confirmation of   10
the best in the Homericall language) three hundred poundes;
And vppon his deathbed a good Pension during my life; –
Commaunding me to go on wth the Odysses; All wch Sir
Tho: Challenor can truly wittnesse; yet never receyvinge
pennye; but incurringe seaven score poundes debt, by my tyme   15
spent in that service, wch all know I could have employde to
the profitt of as great a Summ; The want whereof, wthout
your charitable Prevention must ende in my endles imprisonment;
It may please your most equall Lordshippes, not to value such
a worke, at a lesse Rate, then any Mechanicall service; Nor   20
his extraordinarie Princely promisse, lighter then a customarie
debt; But to this my first suyte and last Refuge, stand iust
& conscionable Sanctuaries; For wch: the little Rest of my
poore ould life, shall ever pray knowinglie and faithfullie
for yow   25

To the Right honorable, the Lordes of
His Ma:ties privie Counsell:

The humble Petition of Geo:
Chapman gent.

Vouchsafe (most honord Lordes) yor free consideration of
my enforct suyte; That attending, fower yeares our late lost
Prince; in a service comaunded by his Highnes (being the
translation of Homers Iliads out of the Greeke) And
being promist, wth his often Princely protestation of likings,
(broke out of his owne rare towardnes, and confirmation of
the best in the Homericall language) three hundred poundes;
And vppon his death bed a good Pension during my life; —
Commaunding me to go on wth the Odysses; All wth &c.
Sr Tho: Challoner can truly wittnesse; yet never receyuinge
penny; but incurringe shaben score poundes debt, by my tyme
spent in that service, wch all know I could have employd to
the profitt of as great a Summ; The want whereof, wthout
yor charitable Prevention must ende in my endles imprisonment;
It may please yor most equall Lordshippe, not to value such
a worke, at a lesse rate, then any Mechanicall service; Now
his extraordinarie Princely promiss, lighter then a customarie
debt; But to this my first suyte and last Refuge, stand iust
consionable Sanctuaries; After wch: the little Rest of my
poore ould life, shall ever pray knowinglie and faithfullie
for you

Good Mr Payton

The want of a little money lies neere heavie on me vpon the
cariage of a great deale venture, I am readie to sinke vnder it,
if your kindnes support me not. Small things are sometimes great
impediments to bee: A moate or atom in the eye, makes as great an
eclipse as the whole earth abrode, and farther off especially brought
bee. Such an hindring is the want of poore fiue shillings to myne
already loose disiointed estate. If your owne necessitie will abate
it, pray spare it to me for a while, you can not en purchase your
selfe more thankefulnes, nor me aduantage so good cheape.

                                yor assured frend
                                Tho: Spelman,

f. 95v

[140   see Commentary]

Good Mr Royden   1

The want of a little money lies more heavie on me, then the
carriage of a great deale would, I am readie to sink vnder it,
if your kindnes support me not. Small things are sometimes great
impediments to vs: A moate or acom in the eye, makes as great an   5
eclips as the whole earth abrode, and farther of, & equally benights
vs. Such an vndoing is the want of poore fiue shillings to myne
already loose disiointed estate. Yf your owne necessitie will abate
it, pray spare it to me for a while, you can never purchase your
self more thankfulnes, nor me advantage so good cheape ./   10
                 Your assured Frend
                 Tho: Spelman.

8
Annotations

(f. 1r)
1 *Lord keepers*] i.e., Sir Thomas Egerton, baron Ellesmere (1540?–1617) who became Lord Keeper 6 May 1596; see *DNB*
2 *Earle of Essex*] Robert Devereux, second earl of Essex (1566–1601); see *DNB*
6 *shoold*] conj.; poss. "showld"
20 *hold*] conj.
27 *youre*] conj. terminal *e*

(f. 1v)
57 Bene ... tempore] cf. Cicero, *Ep. ad Fam.*, IV, ix, 2: "tempori cedere, id est, necessitati parere, semper sapientis est habitum."

(f. 2r)
58–59 Lex ... fortunæ] Seneca perhaps, but untraced
73–74 *conquer ... fortitude*] cf. Seneca, *Ep.* 113: "imperare sibi maximum imperium est"

(f. 3v)
58 *Carase*] qy. i.e., "Carcase" (*r* and *c* have merged)
66–67 *Earle Marshall of England*] honorary office given Essex in 1597 to restore his precedence before Charles Howard, Lord Admiral and newly created earl of Nottingham; see Cheyney, *Hist. England*, II, 445–47

(f. 4r)
75 *yeelde*] see Introduction, section I
81–82 Phymbria: Phyneas: *his complaintes*] see Cicero, *Pro Sexto Roscio Amerino*, XII, 33
85 *vylest of all indignities*] perhaps the famous ear-boxing; see Commentary on item 1

(f. 4v)
3 *.29. November. 1599*] see Commentary
4 *dilapentions*] not in *OED*, but see *s.v.*, depilation, 2: "the action of spoiling or pillage."

(f. 5r)
10 *talkinge wth Tyrone*] Essex met Hugh O'Neill, second earl of Tyrone (1550?–1616) at Ballachuch on 7 September 1599; see Cheyney, *Hist. England*, II, 504–511
13 *Wormewood*] qy. Thomas Butler, tenth earl of Ormonde (1532–1614); see *DNB*
16–18 *leavinge his charge ... contrarie*] Elizabeth withdrew Essex's original permission to return; see Cheyney, *Hist. England*, II, 484 and 491

(f. 5v)
3 *overaymed*] another text (see Commentary) reads "overweighed"; not in *OED*
4 *perticuler*] cf. f. 6v, line 23 for expansion
16 *preserue*] cf. below, line 28
19 *discontynuance from Courte*] Essex was banished shortly after his return from Ireland in September 1599, but not for the first time

(f. 6r)
49 *Esawes ... voyce*] see Genesis 27:15–22; Rebekah disguised the "smooth" Jacob as the "hairy" Esau (cf. "rowgh malice ... smooth-simplicite" in ll. 50–51)

(f. 6v)
1 *Ladie Rich*] Essex's sister, Penelope (1562?–1607) married Robert, third baron Rich of Leighs
c. 1581; see *DNB*
26 *ambitious*] conj.; poss. "ambitions"; cf. f. 10r, line 43

(f. 7r)
32 *they will seeme shall be easie*] sic
35 *downe*]   and   41 *taken*] qy. underlining in different ink
50–51 *two of them ... Countrie*] Walter Devereux, first earl of Essex (1541?–1576) died in
Ireland; see *DNB*

(f. 8r)
1 *Frauncis Bacon*] (1561–1626), at this time counsel to the Queen; see *DNB*
2 *henrie howarde*] first earl of Northampton (1540–1614), close friend of Essex and James VI
and I; see *DNB*
9 *better water*] qy. i.e., Essex's friendship
11 *my*] qy. underlining in different (later) ink
13 *Premunire*] writ charging accused with creating *imperium in imperio*
14–15 *lord Chiefe Iustices ... Attarney generall*] Sir John Popham (1531?–1607) and Sir Edward Coke (1552–1634), respectively; see *DNB*
27 *greater man*] Birch, *Mem. Eliz.*, II, 460, says Bacon means Cecil
29 *personn*] cf. f. 2v, line 88 "personne"; *OED* also cites "persoun(e)"

(f. 8v)
31 *superiour*] note expansion
35–36 Nulla remedia ... salutaria] untraced, but cf. Cicero, *Pro Cluentio*, 67 and *Tusc. Disp.*,
V, 26.74

[item 7]
6 *Richmond*] a palace
10 *that worthie gentleman*] Essex

(f. 9r)
29 *war-*] qy. orig. "war = "
32 *doe*] conj. terminal *e*
33 *fruites*] conj. terminal *es*
38–39 *wise and honest dothe*] sic; copy printed in *HMC Salisbury*, IX, 406–407 reads "wise
and honest letter doth ...."

(f. 9v)
1 *Mr Secretarie*] Robert Cecil, later first earl of Salisbury (1563–1612); see *DNB* and *Complete
Peerage*
8 *Traytor*] for spelling, see below, line 18
11 Richard the .2·] Elizabeth often compared herself with Richard II; see Commentary on item
81 for the crisis over Sir John Hayward's book on Henry IV
19 *Blunt*] Sir Christopher Blunt, Essex's step-father, accompanied him to Ireland; see
Cheyney, *Hist. England*, II, 477

(f. 10r)
30 *advauncement*] poss. "advanncement"
45 *Temple*] "one *William Temple* his [Essex's] *Secretary*" appears in [Francis Bacon?] *A
Declaration of the Practices & Treasons ... Robert late Earle of Essex ...* (1601; STC 1133), E4v
and "Mr. Temple" was held with other rebels in the Gatehouse (*HMC Salisbury*, XIV, 170)

(f. 10v)
66 *Davis*] Sir Charles Davis, another of Essex's officers in Ireland
68 *to keepe the Lord Keeper*] during the abortive rebellion; see Cheyney, *Hist. England*, II,
529
78 *seditious booke*] i.e., Sir John Hayward, *The ... life ... of ... Henrie IIII* (1599; STC
12997); see Commentary on item 81

79–80 *Celsitudine ... trecherous bosome*] see the translation of this passage in Commentary on item 81 and the articles cited there

88 *Cobham, Rawley, & Cicill*] i.e., Henry Brooke, eleventh lord Cobham (1564–1619); Sir Walter Ralegh (1552?–1618); Robert Cecil (1563–1612); see *DNB* and, for Cobham, *Complete Peerage*, III, 349–350

(f. 11r)

96 *advauncementes*] note abbrev.

(f. 11v)

1 *Docter Asheton*] Abdias Ashton (1563–1633), Essex's personal chaplain

4 *Articles whervnto I set my hand*] see *Cal SP Dom*, 1598–1601, pp. 594–595 for text

8 *Lord Constable of the Tower*] Thomas Howard, first earl of Suffolk (1561–1626); see *DNB*

9–10 *afternoone ... dyed*] Essex died 25 march 1601

12–13 *Dr. Barlow preached*] sermon printed as STC 1454; see Commentary

17 *Lords*] conj. possessive

18 *two Drs. handes*] Thomas Montford also attended Essex; for Barlow, see *DNB* and for both Barlow and Montford, see Birch's biographical notes in *Mem. Eliz.*, II, 479

28–29 *private enimyes*] see above, f. 10v, ll. 87–88

(f. 12r)

40–41 *discontented ... true religion*] see above, f. 10r, ll. 34–41

47 *land,*] conj. punc.

49 *·3.*] for this and the next articles' specifically religious significance, see the Langston essay cited in the Commentary

(f. 13r)

99 *lords*] conj. possessive

100 *meaninge,*] conj. punc.

(f. 14v)

31 *b⟨..⟩de*] another text reads "breede"; see Commentary

35 *another*] note abbrev. of terminal -*er*

37 *thie*] orig. "this"

41 *Offices ... of the Wardes*] the Court of Wards

48 *shipwracke*] poss. "shipwrakke"

(f. 15r)

71 *Subditorum ... formidolosæ*] Sallust, *Catiline*, VII, 2–3

(f. 15v)

5 *Marie Candish*] i.e., Mary Cavendish; see Commentary

6 *Lord Wentworth*] see Commentary

(f. 16r)

1 *Chidiock Tichborne*] (1558?–1586), member of the Babington conspiracy to free Mary Stuart; see *DNB*

13 *done*] an unusual *d* for this hand

(f. 16v)

6 *Southampton*] Henry Wriostheley, third earl of Southampton (1573–1624); see *DNB*; note abbrev.

20 *Lieftenaunt of the Tower*] Sir John Peyton (see *Cal SP Dom*, 1603–1610, pp. 25–26)

25 *at wch*] erasure of *w*.. between these words; hole in paper

32 *Lord of kynlos*] Edward Bruce (1549?–1611), controversial appointee to the Mastership of the Rolls; see *DNB* and below, item 102 and Commentary

(f. 17r)

36 *Henry Nevill*] (1564?–1615); see *DNB*

[item 14]
9 *weedes*] conj. terminal *s*
18 *Crouches*] i.e., "crutches"

(f. 17v)
[item 16]
12 *Lord Buckhurst*] Thomas Sackville, first earl of Dorset (1536–1608), became Lord Keeper 19
May 1599; see *DNB*

(f. 18r)
1–2 *Therle of Northumberland*] Henry Percy, ninth earl of Northumberland (1564–1632); see
DNB
2 *Sir Frauncis Vere*] (1560–1609); see *DNB*
3 *Captain Whitlocke*] Edmund Whitelock (10 February 1564 – *c.* 23 August 1608); see Commentary
6 *the Brill*] Dutch cautionary town, held for the English by Burgh and then Vere
7 *the States*] i.e., the native Dutch (largely North Holland) government
17 *satisfac* =] conj. punc.

[item 18]
2 *Northumberlands*] note abbrev.; conj. possessive

(f. 19r)
12 *Lordshippes*] conj. possessive
28 *a Grandfather*] i.e., John de Vere, fifteenth earl of Oxford (14??–1540); see *Complete Peerage*

[item 20]
7 *Frauncis*] note expansion

(f. 19v)
15 *Maiesties*] note unusual abbrev.

[item 21]
7–8 *doctor lodge & Mr Field*] perhaps Thomas Lodge (1558?– 1625) and Nathan Field (1587 –
1633); see *DNB* and Commentary
17 Hitchin] see Commentary
18 *thinke*] conj. terminal *e*

(f. 20r)
18 *reioyc*] qy. "reioyce"

(f. 20v)
[item 24]
3 *poore Ladies*] i.e., Mary Wingfield, daughter of James Harington of Exton; see Commentary
4 *her Sonne*] probably James Wingfield, the eldest
12 *late Offendors*] probably a reference to several survivors of Essex's rebellion
13 *Sir Edwarde Winckfield*] or "Wingfield" (d. 1603; see Commentary); not to be confused
with two others: the unmarried colonist, Edward Wingfield (fl. 1600), noticed in *DNB* and
perhaps the son of the man mentioned here, or Sir Edward Wingfield (d. 1638) who accompanied Essex against Tyrone and succeeded his cousin Sir Richard (d. 1631) to a large estate in
Ireland

(f. 21r)
27 *Lord Admyrall and Mr Secretarie*] Charles Howard, first earl of Nottingham (*c.* 1536 –
1624) and Robert Cecil; see *DNB*

[item 25]
1 *Mr* Cooke] Edward Coke (1552 – 1634); see *DNB*
3 *dartfoord*] a town in Kent between London and Gravesend

(f. 21v)
18 *late Lord Treasurer*] William Cecil, lord Burghley (1520 – 1598) became Lord Treasurer 15 July 1572; see *DNB*

[item 26]
1 G.N.] unidentified
   Lord chiefe Iustice] probably Sir John Popham (1531? – 1607); see *DNB*

(f. 22r)
9 *Imposed*] conj. *m*

(f. 23r)
1 *Worshipful*] conj.; perhaps "Worthie"
28 *Worships*] conj. expansion and possessive

(f. 23v)
1 *Sonne* Micah] unidentified, but see Commentary

(f. 24r)
[item 29]
38 Danburie] a town in Essex, near Maldon
40 Marie Wither] unidentified, but see Commentary
41 *Robert Barnard*] unidentified

[item 30]
1 *Sonne* Abell] unidentified, but see Commentary

(f. 24v)
14 and 27 *Lordshippes*] conj. possessive
29 Anto: Hoborne] Antonio, or Anthony, Holborne (*c.* 1548 – *c.* 29 November 1602): see *DNB* and Commentary

(f. 25r)
[item 32]
8 *Mr Morrison*] see Commentary
13 *li.*] note abbrev. for "librae" (i.e., pounds)
18 *Caisho*] the Morrison country mansion, Cashiobury, Herts.
20 Dorothie Moryson] see Commentary

[item 33]
3 *the* .P.] i.e., the pox
   the .G.] i.e., the gout
8 *aboutes.*] conj. punc.
12 *And*] conj. capital; note unusual form and cf. "Althoughe" at beginning of letter
   henry Catlain] unidentified
13 *Margate*] coastal town in Kent

(f. 25v)
[item 34]
2 *commend*] note error in margin width
3 *Ladyship*] conj. expansion
13 *yerfore*] i.e., "therefore"

(f. 26r)
5 *Ladyships*] conj. expansion and possessive
20 *you*] note unique superscript; qy. to avoid confusion with flourish of *I* (line 19)

(f. 26v)
20 *woodstreete counter*] a prison

(f. 27r)
[item 38]
40 *continuall*] conj.; note evidence of mending *u*/*n*

[item 39]
14 *youres whose*] qy. punc. between these words
20 *Mistresse*] conj. expansion; see below, line 25

(f. 27v)
1-2 *where . . . Maladie*] a couplet
16 *Mistresse Trentam*] unidentified

(f. 28v)
[item 42]
1 *Iosias Kirton*] see Commentary
2 *the Fleete*] a prison
6 ⟨*..st*⟩] qy. "most"
8 *vices*] qy. *V*
10 *honors*] conj. plural

(f. 29r)
[item 43]
4, 19, 25 *Lordshippes*] conj. possessive
6 *lordshippes*] conj. possessive

[item 44]
1 *Mr Feryman*] probably Peter Ferryman; see Introduction, section III
6 A.G.] unidentified

(f. 30r)
[item 47]
4 *vntruthe*] qy. "vntrathe"

(f. 30v)
2 *Grayes*] the town of Grays, west of Tilbury
3 *Mr durainges*] unidentified
20 *lycence*] orig. "lycens"

(f. 31r)
2-3 *Mr Chapman*] George Chapman (1559?–1634), poet; see Commentary

(f. 31v)
[item 51]
1 *Mr Ferryman*] probably Peter Ferryman, see Introduction, section III
    I am] otiose mark between these words
4 *Mr Royden*] poss. "Roydon": Matthew Roydon (fl. 1580–1622), poet and Chapman's
friend; see *DNB*
10 *exer*] inner margin extensively mended, poss. obscuring punc.
18-19 I Letany ... deliuer us] *OED* does not record "litany" as a verb, though it may be a
nonce-formation here; "Letany" and "english" may have been reversed by the copyist—if so,
the sentence would refer to the Roman Catholic litany of the saints in which the response is
"Libera nos, domine": cf. the Litany in the *Book of Common Prayer*
21 William Strachey] traveller and colonist (1572–1621); see Commentary and items 86 and 90

(f. 32r)
5 *Iohn Puckeringe*] (1544–1596), Lord Keeper, 1592–1596; see *DNB*
20 *Walter Leveson*] see Commentary and *DNB sub* Richard Leveson, his son

(f. 32v)
59 *Exchequer*] for expansion, see above, line 10

(f. 33v)

2 *Cham,*] Mohammed III (reigned 1595–1603); qy. punc.

23–24 *Lawrence Oliphant . . . Robert Douglas*] both men died in March 1584/5; see *Complete Peerage*, IX, 294 and X, 54; for the later rumor, see *Cal Scottish Papers*, 1597–1603, p. 555 (a letter of 17 September 1599)

(f. 34r)

37 ⟨.⟩] either cancel or unusual ampersand

51 *obligue*] i.e., "oblige"; form not recorded in *OED*

53 *our ... Ambassador*] Henry Lello, acting from December 1597 and officially appointed 25 September 1599 (see *Cal SP Ven*, 1592–1603, pp. 371–72 and 375); for his embassy, see A.C. Wood, *A History of the Levant Company* (1935), p. 82.

(f. 34v)

4 Ta+i+cosama] i.e., Toyotomi Hideyoshi (1536–1598), *de facto* ruler of Japan; for precisely the same confusion and titles in documents of 1596, see *Cal SP Colonial, East Indies, China and Japan,* 1513–1616, p. 98

12 Vuight] i.e., "Wight"

21 Occidentali ci] qy. comma between these words

22 riceu⟨e⟩r] qy. modern ink blot

26 sudditi] otiose mark above word

(f. 35r)

35 Beniamino Vuod] i.e., "Benjamin Wood"; see Commentary

(f. 35v)

2 *Polands Ambassador*] Paulus de Ialines (see G.P. Rice, *The Public Speaking of Queen Elizabeth* [New York: Columbia University Press, 1951], p. 103; ibid., pp. 104–105 prints a slightly different text derived from *HMC Salisbury*, VII, 315–316)

10 *nouiter*] paper damage follows this word

(f. 36v)

5 *christian*] note common abbrev.

(f. 38v)

1 *Archbushop of Yorke*] Matthew Hutton (1529–1606); see *DNB*

2 *Salisburie*] Robert Cecil (1563–1612) created first earl of Salisbury 4 May 1605

(f. 39r)

36 Cranborne] at the time of Hutton's original letter, Cecil would properly be addressed as Viscount Cranborne; see this item, line 2 and Commentary

37 *Father*] William Cecil, baron Burghley (1520–1598); see *DNB*

43 *hun =*] the tittle must be otiose, since expansion would produce "hunntinge," a form not recorded in *OED*

46 *Ecclesiasticall Commyssion*] see Commentary

49 *Sir Iohn* Bennett] member of Council for the North (d. 1627); see *DNB*

51 *Maiestie as*] otiose mark between these words

53 *Thorpe*] official residence of the Archbishops of York

(f. 39v)

1 *Sir Fraunces drake*] circumnavigator and admiral (1540?–1596); see *DNB*

2 *Mr Iohn Foxe*] martyrologist (1516–1587); see *DNB* and Commentary

8 Cales] Cadiz, Spain

23 Don Pedro] apparently, Don Pedro de Acuña or Acugna; see J.S. Corbett, *Drake and the Tudor Navy*, rev. ed., 2 vols. (1899), II, 84nl

(f. 41v)

1 *Mildemay*] (1520?–1589); see *DNB*

20 *presente*] conj. R.S. Sylvester

(f. 42r)
3 *william*] note expansion
23 *yereof*] i.e., "thereof": an unusual abbrev., but see item 34, line 13 and f. 55v, line 36
26 cum] usual stroke for omitted nasal after vowel

(f. 42v)
1 Chuetes … Pinchback] neither identified
9 *commest*] *OED* does not record a double *m* spelling of the 2nd person singular
15 *brother, (wth)*] note rearrangement of punc.
18 *Oddes,*] poss. "Oddes."

(f. 43r)
14 *runnes*] conj.; cf. *OED, s.v., sb.,* 10, but poss. "ruines"

(f. 43v)
2 *last Lord Cobham*] probably Henry Brooke, eleventh lord Cobham (1564–1618), see *Complete Peerage*, III, 349–350 and Commentary
3 *fatherlesse infantes*] children of George and Elizabeth (Burgh) Brooke
4 *Noble Graundfather*] William Brooke, tenth lord Cobham (1527–1597)
21 *I may*] otiose mark between these words; see item 51, line 1

(f. 45r)
1 *Mr T*] unidentified
2 *straunge*] conj.
28 *bobde*] cf. *OED, s.v., v*1, 1, or poss. late example of *v*2, 2

(f. 45v)
31 *knewe*] poss. "knowe" but see *o/w* ligature in "how" later in the line

(f. 46r)
1 *Great Turkes*] i.e., Ahmed I (reigned 1603–1617), but see Commentary
14 *Rodulphus*] Rudolf II (reigned 1576–1612), Holy Roman Emperor

(f. 46v)
39 *Raigne. 2.*] poss. "Raigne, 2."

[item 71]
5 *hath*] some letter (*o*?) obscured by terminal *h*

(f. 47r)
25 *Churche.*] the second *h* has the scribe's characteristic terminal form

(f. 47v)
29 *republique*] note abbrev. from Latin
29–30 *kinge Catholique*] Phillip III of Spain
31 *barbarous kinge*] i.e., the Turkish Sultan, Ahmed I

(f. 48r)
57 *honor*] conj.
71 *excommunications*] note tittle

(f. 49r)
10 *hope:*] probably "hope = " orig.
21 *humers*] poss. "humors"   *Politiq*] qy. "Politique" orig.
22 *op*] qy. "open" orig.
23 *laie*] qy. "laies" orig.
26 *Pover*] qy. "Povertie" orig.
27 *rebate*] i.e., "to make dull, blunt" (*OED, s.v., v*1, 4, citing Chapman's *Iliad*), perhaps mixed with figurative use from falconry, "to settle down" (*OED, s.v., v*1, 1). Cf. *The Revenge*

of Bussy D'Ambois, 3.2.17–19 and "To . . . Robert Earle of Somerset" before *Andromeda Liberata*, 11. 180–84 (*Poems*, p. 309).

(f. 49v)
15 *fashionable fountaine*] poss. alluding to *The Fount of New Fashions*, for which George Chapman received £4 from Philip Henslowe in September and October 1598; cf. item 75, ll. 21–22 and Ben Jonson's *Cynthia's Revels or The Fountain of Self-Love* (1600–1601)

(f. 51r)
38 *more*] poss. "mere"
38–39 Homo ... damon] poss. alluding to Plautus, *Asinaria*, II, 88: "homo homini lupus"
42 *compell me*] words linked in text

(f. 52r)
30 *vnlooktfor*] plausibly considered a single word

[item 78]
1 *Mr Sares*] qy. William Seres (junior), the stationer; see R.B. McKerrow, *Dictionary of Printers and Booksellers ... 1557–1640* (Bibliographical Soc., 1910), p. 239 and C.J. Sisson, *Lost Plays of Shakespeare's Age* (Cambridge: Cambridge University Press, 1936), p. 118n
11 *farr*] very clear correction from "far"

(f. 52v)
1 *Sir Iohn Dowland*] i.e., the musician, never knighted; see *DNB* and Poulton, *John Dowland*
20 *Ferdinando*] Poulton, *John Dowland*, p. 47n suggests "Ferdinando Heybourne or Richardson (*c.* 1559–1618)," but Chamberlain (*Letters*, I, 326 and n14) makes it almost certain that it is Heybourne here referred to

(f. 53r)
30 H noel] (Sir) Henry Noel; see Poulton, *John Dowland*, pp. 420–421

[item 80]
5–6 *the letter*] i.e., item 79
8 *want of good Frendes*] poss. alluding to Henry Noel who died shortly after Dowland's return to England
8–11 *particuler ... will assure*] for mending, see Commentary
16 Zieghaine] Ziegenhaine, a town between Marburg and Bad Hersfeld
17 Maurice] or Moritz (1572–1632); see Poulton, *John Dowland*, p. 415
18 *Landgrave*] changed from "Lantgrave"

(f. 53v)
17 *Lordshippes*] conj. possessive

(f. 54r)
42–43 *to to*] *sic*
48 *you?*] unusual punc.

(f. 54v)
83 *Lordshippe*] perhaps "Lordshippes"
84 *commaunds*] conj. expansion

(f. 55r)
4 *first by message*] 12 and 14 May 1610; see *Proc. Parliament 1610*, II, 85–92
  since by speache] 21 May 1610; see ibid., II, 100–107
19 *subect*] *sic*

(f. 55v)
32 *though never*] repeated from last line, f. 55r
36 *oyer*] i.e., "other"; cf. item 34, line 13 and f. 42r, line 23
43–44 *yt Iudgment in th'exchequer*] 4. Jac. I, Mich., a judgment against John Bate who refused to pay the imposition on currants; see Commentary

(f. 56v)
1 *Sonne Robert*] i.e., Robert Cecil (1563–1612)
2 *mother*] Mildred Cooke (1524/26–1589); see *Complete Peerage*, II, 429
6 *Summarie band*] other texts (see Commentary) read, "Summum bonum," but this reading makes good sense

(f. 57v)
88 *vniust*] mark beneath *t* may be comma displaced by crowding (i.e., quire stabbed or sewn before writing)

(f. 58v)
120 *rayer*] i.e., "rather": cf. item 34, line 13, f. 42r, line 23 and f. 55v, line 36

(f. 59r)
156 .E. ... .R.] usually expanded as "Essex" and "Ralegh," respectively; the anachronism indicates a sophisticated source
161 *stoycall*] *c* mended

(f. 59v)
1 *request,*] for punc., see above, f. 57v, line 88
13 *there*] scribe undecided between "there" and "their[e]"
18 *estate,*] for punc., see above, line 1 and f. 57v, line 88
24 *Frauncis Bedell*] unidentified; in this part of the MS, "signatures" often appear in secretary hand

(f. 60r)
[item 85]
7 *Ro: wife*] qy. "Robert's wife"; "Roydon's wife"
9 *.N.*] unidentified
15 *.W. S.*] probably William Strachey (1572–1621); see Commentary

[item 86]
4 *Citiner*] i.e., citizen
15 *Geo: Ch:*] i.e., George Chapman (1559?–1634)

(f. 60v)
8 *dainely*] poss. "dainly"
   your] note unusual abbrev.

[item 88]
1 *honorable:*] note rare duplication of punc.
   Northhamton] Henry Howard, first earl of Northampton (1540–1614); see *DNB*
3 *honord*] orig. "honorable"
5 *lordshippe*] note unusual abbrev. and cf. ll. 11, 16, 22
5–6 *annext Petition*] perhaps item 139; see Commentary

(f. 61r)
[item 88 continued]
18 *homer*] a reference to Chapman's translation of Homer; see Commentary
19–20 *what Virgile ... from* Homer] see *Vita Donati*, ll. 194–195 in *Vitæ Vergilianæ Antiquæ* (Oxford: Clarendon, 1954)

(f. 61v)
20 *selues*] conj.
27–28 *Royall assemblie*] 15 February 1613/14, when Chapman's masque was presented to celebrate Princess Elizabeth's marriage

(f. 62r)
[item 89 continued]
53 Habet mercedem suam] perhaps not a quotation, but cf. Isaiah 40:10 (Vulgate)

[item 90]
14 *lord* Delawarre] Thomas West, twelfth baron De la Warre (1577–1618), Governor and Captain General of Virginia; see *DNB*
    Mr Strachey] William Strachey, traveller and colonist (1572–1621); see Commentary

(f. 62v)
17 *counsell*] of the Virginia Company
24 Lætari et benefacere] Ecclesiasticus 3:12 (Vulgate)
36 *profession*] lawyer and M.P.
39 *outgone*] *sic*

f. 63r)
73 Rich Martin] (1570–1618), at this time secretary of the Virginia Company; see *DNB*
    Decembrer] conj. expansion
75 *william Strachey*] note expansion; for Strachey, see above, line 14
77 *hercules*] a ship's name

(f. 63v)
6 *Tho. Sutton*] merchant and philanthropist (1532–1611); see *DNB*
15–16 *Frauncis Walsingham*] statesman (1530?–1590); see *DNB*

(f. 64v)
1 Mr Leech] see Commentary
4 *Gentlemans*] conj. possessive

(f. 65r)
[item 94]
18 Tho: *Bond*] John Donne's successor as secretary to Thomas Egerton; some writers repeat Coryate's error, "John" Bond (cf. Herford and Simpson, I, 201 and R.C. Bald, *John Donne: A Life* [Oxford: Oxford University Press, 1970], p. 194 and note)
20 *the Lord Chauncellor*] Thomas Egerton, first baron Ellesmere (1540?–1617); see *DNB*

[item 95]
5 *Frauncis Maddison*] unidentified

(f. 65v)
21 *Iury*] conj.; see Luke 1:38ff. The Biblical account refers to the hills of Judah (called "Judaea" in Greco-Roman times) also known as "Mount Judah" (see George Adam Smith, *Historical Geography of the Holy Land*, 25th rev. ed. [1931], p. 325); Elizabethans often referred to Judaea as "Jewry" or "Jury," hence the spelling here (see Richard Hakluyt, *Principal Navigations* ... 12 vols. [Glasgow: MacLehose, 1903–1905], V, 250: " . . . the provinces of Syria, Palestina, and Jurie" and E.H. Sugden, *A Topographical Dictionary to the Works of Shakespeare* ... [Manchester: Manchester University Press, 1925], p. 287).
34 *Iohn Francis Salandra*] unidentified

(f. 66r)
3 *Flower*] Flores
5 *bare*] conj.
14 *Terceres*] Terceira
    sunk] perhaps "sonnk"
25 *dd.*] i.e., "delivered"; an unusual abbrev. in this context

(f. 66v)
29 *R. Grinfield*] Richard Grenville (1541?–1591); see *DNB*
39 *St Mychaells*] i.e., São Miquel, largest of the Azores

[item 97]
1 *Iohn Rogers*] unidentified; see Commentary
9 *Maiesties*] note unusual abbrev.

(f. 67r)
[item 99]
1 *Mr Bagley*] Henry Bagley, usher of Charterhouse school; see Commentary
3 *whites*] not identified; perhaps among those listed in R.B. McKerrow, *Dictionary of Printers and Booksellers ... 1557-1640* (Bibliographical Soc., 1910), pp. 288-89
17 *Rafe .W.*] not identified; see Commentary

(f. 67v)
10 *not not*] sic
12 *vt quisque ... est*] untraced, perhaps not a quotation, although the marginal *p* seems to call attention to this line; Chapman's printed texts occasionally have technical signs in the margin ("Simi." for "simile," for example: see *Poems*, p. 181)

(f. 70r)
1 *Thomsom*] see Commentary
11 *but I?*] qy. punc.
11-12 Primus peccatorum ... Israell] conflation of I Timothy 1:15 and Matthew 5:30 (Vulgate)

(f. 77r)
7 *mourne*] qy. "mornne"
15-16 *pretended tytle of his* Infanta] to the throne of England
20 Principijs ... paratur] Horace, *Remedia Amoris*, 91
22 *certain*] qy. orig. "certaine"
27 *peticions*] note otiose tittle
28 *kinge*] qy. "Kinge"

(f. 77v)
37 *vre*] i.e., use
51 *remainder*] note expansion
51-52 *subsidies yet behinde*] payment dates following Elizabeth's death were: 31 October 1603; 31 March 1604; 31 October 1604; see C.T. Clay, "A Document Relating to ... a Subsidy under the Act of 1601," *Yorks. Archaeological Journal*, 33 (1936-38), 309-313
55-56 Rehoboams *yong Councellores*] see I Kings 11:4-11 and James's speech to Parliament, 19 March 1603 (in *Workes* [1616; STC 14344], p. 491)

(f. 78r)
71 *mrshipp*] i.e., "mastershipp"

(f. 78v)
99 ⟨*a long*⟩] cancelled through some form of erasure
102 *fault ... at our common lawes*] see James's speech to Parliament, 21 March 1609 (in *Workes* [1616; STC 14344], pp. 532-533)
103 *Philiplimycus*] probably Philip de Comines (*c.* 1447-*c.* 1511), French diplomat
108 *westminster;*] note contraction; qy. punc.

(f. 79r)
119 *say*] sic; qy. "stay"

(f. 80r)
23 *enlarge my self*] from prison
27 *Lord Chauncelor*] Sir Christopher Hatton held the office from 29 April 1587 until his death 21 November 1591; Puckering then succeeded as Lord Keeper; see *DNB*
27-28 *Sir henry Cobham*] qy. English diplomat (d. 1605?), uncle of Henry Brooke, eleventh lord Cobham (*HMC Salisbury*, XVII, 582)

(f. 80v)
2 *Robert Sidley*] unidentified; see next item
17 *xxli*] i.e., twenty pounds (cf. item 32, line 15); the total is presumably "six score pounds"

(f. 81r)
[item 105]
4 *Will: Iones*] unidentified   *Lynne*] qy. King's Lynn, Norfolk
5 *Tho: Fitche*] unidentified   *Lockin*] untraced; not a modern place
14 *Ro: Tilney*] unidentified

(f. 81v)
5 *notablye*] orig. "notable"
6 *Canterbury*] note expansion
17 *Sonckye*] poss. "Senckye"; unidentified

(f. 82r)
[item 108]
6 *William Huxley*] unidentified

[item 109]
2 *Robert Lee*] see Commentary

(f. 82v)
1 *docter Griffin*] unidentified; poss. a divine
2 *kinges benche*] a prison
14 *pray,*] paper damaged and poss. erased after this word

(f. 83r)
2 *Thomas Lownde*] unidentified
4 *Browne*] unidentified

(f. 83v)
5 *Androwes*] unidentified

(f. 84r)
40 *Mistresse .B.*] unidentified; see Introduction, section III

(f. 84v)
47 *see if*] otiose mark between these words

(f. 85r)
[item 114]
1-2 *Countesse of warwicke*] presumably Anne Russell (1548–1604), wife of Ambrose Dudley
who held the title from 26 December 1561 until his death, 21 February 1590
3 *A widdowe*] Anne survived her husband by fourteen years; she died 9 February 1603/4
6 *gentlewoman*] flourish at end poss. indicates abbrev.
10 *Mr Williams*] unidentified   *Honors*] conj. possessive
12 *honored*] conj. expansion; perhaps "honorable"
   Father] Francis Russell, second earl of Bedford (1527–85)

(f. 85v)
[item 115]
1 *Doctor hudson*] unidentified; probably a divine
7 *Mr Linnacker*] unidentified
11 *I B.*] qy. Sir John Burgh (1562–94); see *DNB*

(f. 86r)
[item 116]
1 *Mr Feriman*] Peter Ferryman; see Introduction, section III and Commentary, *passim*
17 *Mr Sidley*] unidentified, but see above, letters 103 and 104; this Sidley may be the nephew
of 103's writer
22 *I.B.*] qy. Sir John Burgh; see *DNB*

[item 117]
1 Hiegate] still an independent village north of London
4 *Cosen of the hill*] unidentified; presumably a jesting reference to some resident of Highgate, which took its name from the toll barrier erected at the top of the steep hill on which the village was built
10 H.G.] unidentified; qy. Henry Goodyere

(f. 86v)
[item 118]
1 *Mr harrington*] unidentified
  togey] i.e., "together"; final flourish very faint
7-8 *17. of Ianuarij. 1588*] probably 1589, new style
10 N. Coote] qy. Sir Nicholas Coote; see Commentary

[item 119]
2 *all this tyme*] this letter appears to be a further dun, written some time after item 118

[item 120]
8 *think*] poss. "thinke"
11 R *I.*] unidentified

(f. 87r)
1-2 *Sisters and Coheirs*] these four women, all daughters of Thomas, fifth baron Burgh (d. 14 October 1597) were: Elizabeth Brooke, Anne Drury, Frances Coppinger, and Katherine Knyvett
2 *Coheirs*] the initial capital here and elsewhere on this folio closely resembles this hand's italic *C*
  Robert Lord Burgh] sixth and last lord Burgh, inherited the title at the age of three (in 1597) and died 26 February 1601/2, whereupon the title fell into abeyance
6 *eldest daughter*] Elizabeth Burgh Brooke

[item 122]
2 *your husbandes case*] George Brooke (fourth son of William, Lord Cobham); the reference is to his attainder for treason in the "Bye Plot" (July 1603)
12 Ro: Ceccyll] Robert Cecil (1563-1612), principal secretary of state; see *DNB*
16 *Syster in law*] Cecil married Elizabeth, eldest daughter of Lord Cobham, in August 1589
  Elizabeth Brooke] Elizabeth, eldest daughter of Thomas Burgh married George Brooke (see line 2, above) in 1599 and thus became Cecil's sister-in-law

(f. 87v)
1 *Bess*] Elizabeth Burgh (Brooke); see petition, 121 and letter, 122
8 *Your Mother*] Frances Vaughan, married to Thomas Burgh before the Yorkshire Visitation of 1584
16 *Brill*] or "Brielle," just west of Rotterdam, captured by the Sea Beggars in 1572 and garrisoned by the English from 1585
18 *Thomas Burgh*] Thomas, fifth baron Burgh (before 1558 – 14 October 1597): see Introduction, section III; he was nominally governor of Brill from 1586/7 to 1597, ambassador to Scotland in 1593, and died as Lord Deputy of Ireland

(f. 88r)
4 *highnes displeasure*] at the performance or printing of *Eastward Ho!* (by Chapman, Jonson, and Marston); the play remarks satirically on James and his Scots
6 *not our owne*] the two prisoners may allude to their (absent?) fellow-author, John Marston

(f. 88v)
3-4 *Lordshippes allowance*] the Lord Chamberlain's permission had been required for any public dramatic performance since 1581 (see Chambers, *Eliz. Stage*, I, 288–99; IV, 263–64 and 285–87)
5 *your Person so farr remou'd*] Suffolk accompanied James on progress during the summer of 1605; see Commentary on letter, 124

24–25 *lord Chamberlaine*] Thomas Howard, first earl of Suffolk (1561–1626), who held the office from 4 May 1603 until Carr received it in 1614

(f. 89r)
1 *youre lordshipps ... bountie*] presumably Suffolk's pardon, or efforts to secure the King's pardon
6 *yrcksome*] otiose mark over *m*
6–7 *propagation of ... fauours*] Chapman and Jonson (see ''our'' in ll. 2,3,5) apparently seek some further aid; perhaps they have already been pardoned or refer here to benefits antedating the *Eastward Ho!* imprisonment
8 *Lorde Dawbuey*] should read ''Dawbney'' for ''D'Aubigny,'' i.e., Esmé Stuart, Sieur D'Aubigny (1579–1624); see *Complete Peerage*, VII, 607–608
9 *one of vs*] probably Jonson, apparently living with D'Aubigny in this period (but see Herford and Simpson, XI, 576–577)
    Lordshippes] conj. possessive
10 *Lordshippes*] conj. possessive

(f. 90v)
10 *honored*] note expansion
13 *I*] conj.
24 *testimonye*] note dagger in margin
    my first Error] Jonson was imprisoned, August 1597, for his part in *The Isle of Dogs*; see Herford and Simpson, I, 217–218
25 *then*] paper damage before this word

(f. 91r)
39 *Suffolke*] Thomas Howard, Lord Chamberlain; see *DNB* and above, item 125

(f. 91v)
21–22 *most-humblie*] Herford and Simpson, I, 197 read ''must humblie,'' one of several errors

(f. 92r)
[item 130]
11 *vneuenbases*] *sic*
13 *horried*] *sic*; Herford and Simpson, I, 198 print ''hurried''

[item 131]
9 *Gratitude*] qy. mended from ''Gratitide''

(f. 92v)
1 *Mongomerie*] Philip Herbert (1584–1650) became earl of Montgomery on 4 May 1605 and succeeded his brother as earl of Pembroke in 1630; see *DNB*
6 *desert*] qy. erasure before this word

(f. 93r)
1 *Pembrooke*] William Herbert, third earl of Pembroke (1580–1630); see *DNB*
7–8 *The Anger ... death*] cf. Seneca, *Medea*, 494

(f. 94r)
18–19 Mr. Crane] not further identified
20 *Duke of Lennox*] Ludovic Stuart (1574–1624); see *DNB*

[item 137]
1 *Exygent*] qy. orig. ''Exigent''
2–3 Da ... linguens] an unidentified hexameter
4 Mr. E:] unidentified

(f. 94v)

4 *aboute .25. yeares past*] Chapman's opponent gives the date 12 July, 27 Elizabeth (i.e., 1585); see article cited in Commentary

5 Iohn Woollfall] see Commentary

16 *good*] conj. terminal *d*

19 *stood* + *twice* + *on the Pillorie*] in late 1594; see article cited in Commentary

21 *defend*] qy. flourish for "defends"

23 *vpon*] conj.

30 *Lordshippes*] conj. possessive

(f. 95r)

8 *Homers*] note form of *H* here and in line 11

14 *Tho: Challenor*] (1561–1615), appointed Prince Henry's governor in 1603; see *DNB*

18 *endles imprisonment*] perhaps a general fear or a reference to Jones's suit against Chapman (see Commentary on item 120 and article cited there)

(f. 95v)

1 *Mr Royden*] qy. Matthew Roydon (fl. 1580–1622), poet and Chapman's friend; see *DNB*

5 *acom*] qy. orig. "atom"; some flaw in pen or paper may have obscured part of a *t*'s ascender, or "acorn" has been mis-copied

12 *Tho: Spelman*] unidentified, but see Commentary

9

Commentary on Selected Letters

1/15 July(?) 1598

Date: This letter and the following reply are traditionally dated 15 and 18 October, respectively (Birch, *Mem. Eliz.*, 2:384 and 386); these dates must, however, be incorrect. Chamberlain (*Letters*, 1:46) writes on 3 October 1598 that Essex "is at court in as goode terms (they say) as ever he was." *Cal SP Dom*, 1587–1601, p. 89 notes that Essex was back at court before 15 September, attending a Privy Council meeting on 10 September, and Thomas Lake mentions his participation in court business in a letter of 28 September (Collins, *Letters*, 2:102–3). John Speed in *The History of Great Britaine* (1611; STC 23045) prints both letters and dates Egerton's "Iulie 18. An. 1598" (p. 877). Speed need not be trusted implicitly, but either July or August would be more likely months for the exchange, unless some quarrel subsequent to the queen's boxing of Essex's ear and his reply by putting hand to sword occurred. No record of such a second, violent altercation exists, though it may be remembered that only Camden recounts the ear-boxing incident. Huntington MS. HM 102, ff. 6r–9v and MS. Harl. 677, ff. 109v–114r have versions of these letters headed, "A letter of the L. Keepres to the E. of Essex beinge committed after his returne from Ierland" and "A lettere of the L. Keeper to ye E of Essex being committed at his returne from Ireland," respectively. Essex rushed back from Ireland on 24 September and arrived at Nonesuch 28 September 1599. Since he had been committed to Egerton's guard on 1 October 1599, it seems unlikely that the Lord Keeper should write a letter (even one intended for publication) to a man staying in his own house, under his constant guard, without any reference to those facts (cf. ll. 85–87). The extraordinary date in Folger MS. V.a. 164—". . . the ix^th of Ianuary: An°: Dm 1601" (f. 104r)—is certainly wrong. Essex's reference to "the Scandall . . . gyven me" and his surprising but not especially tactful reference to Fimbria make the mid-1598 date plausible. E. M. Tenison, *Elizabethan England*, 12 vols. (Royal Leamington Spa, England: Privately printed, 1930–60), 10:475 n.1, lists several manuscripts of the letters and many more exist; the originals have not been found. Tenison also cites a letter of 13 October placing Essex at court (from *HMC Salisbury*, 8:387).

2/18 July(?) 1598

Date: See above under Commentary on letter 1.

This letter formed one of Bacon's accusations against Essex at his first trial (5 June 1600); Bacon objected especially to the phrase "passionate indignation of a prince" and the question "can not princes Erre?" (see Birch, *Mem. Eliz.*, 2:388 and 450). Essex's modern apologists and others attempting to salvage Birch's dating have suggested that Egerton wrote his letter when the whole matter had been settled, simply to provoke an intemperate response from the earl.

3/29 November 1599

See Birch, *Mem. Eliz.*, 2:440 and Collins, *Letters*, 2:146–48 for descriptions of this accusation and trial.

4/mid-1598—before 5 June 1600(?)

Date: Folger MS. X.c. 11, a contemporary copy of this letter, has the scribe's marginal note, "An°: 1600," the only dated copy I have seen. The letter also appears in *Scrinia Sacra . . . A Supplement of the Cabala* (1654; Wing S2110), pp. 25–26 where it seems to introduce a group of letters (including copies of items 1 and 2) associated with Essex's actions in 1598. The catalogue entry for MS. Harl. 677, ff. 114v–115r, another copy, has the heading, "By the Earle Marshall to her Maiestie"; Essex lost that title on 5 June 1600, having gained it 28 December 1597. The letter also appears in Folger MS. V.b. 214, ff. 106r-v.

5/late February(?) 1600

Date: Birch (*Mem. Eliz.*, 2:442–43) dates this letter "towards the end of February," and many versions exist (e.g., Add. MS. 4130, ff. 58r–61r, Birch's source, "M.K.'s Collection"; Huntington MS. HM 102, ff. 15r-v; Folger MS. V.b. 214, ff. 205r-v).

6/3 December 1599

Date: Within a few days, Bacon wrote two very similar letters, one to Henry Howard, the other to Robert Cecil, answering charges of hypocrisy (or worse) in his attitude toward Essex. Birch dates this letter 3 December 1599 (*Mem. Eliz.*, 2:459), as does the copy in the Cecil papers (*HMC Salisbury*, 9:405–6). The Cecil collection also includes an undated copy of Howard's answer (ibid., pp. 406–7;

see letter 7 below). James Spedding, *Life and Letters of Francis Bacon*, 7 vols. (Longman, 1868), 2:161–62, prints both letters from the mutilated and undated version in *Resvscitatio . . . several . . . works . . . of . . . Francis Bacon . . .* Third Edition . . . 1671 [Wing B321], L2r–L3v. Huntington MS. HM 102, f. 9v has Bacon's letter to Cecil, dated "from Grays Inn the first of December." With two such verbally similar letters, however, confusion over which came first might easily arise; nonetheless, it seems best to accept the joint testimony of the Cecil papers and Birch's mysterious "copy in the Bodleian library." Thus, letter 7 would presumably follow 3 December quite shortly.

7/shortly after 3 December 1599

Date: See Commentary on letter 6 above.

8/after 13 February and before 19 February 1601

Date: Although most of the material in this speech appears in accounts of Essex's trial, this item does not come from that trial itself. Cecil spoke very little at the trial (in Westminster Hall, 19 February 1601), although it seems likely he coached some of those who did. Thus, this speech must have been made, perhaps ex tempore as Cecil says (ll. 15–18), after the examination of Sir Christopher Blunt (l. 61; dated 13 February in *HMC Salisbury*, 11:49) and before the trial. In any case, this item is not the same as a speech attributed to Cecil and dated "xj of Februarij 1601" by Folger MS. V.a. 164, ff. 96v–99r.

9/shortly after 25 March 1601

Date: Ashton refers to "my Lords [i.e., Essex's] Confession" written "in the ende of the booke" (l. 17) by which he means either (a) William Barlow's sermon of 1 March 1601 (STC 1454), which concludes with "The true copy, in substance, of the late Earle of Essex, his behauiour, speach, and prayer, at the time of his execution" (E3r–E7r) or (b) *A Declaration of the Practices & Treasons . . . committed by Robert late Earle of Essex* (1601; STC 1133—attributed to Francis Bacon), which concludes with "The Earle of Essex his Confession to three Ministers, whose names are vnder written, the 25. of Februarie 1600" (Q4r-v). The sermon was entered in the S. R. on 18 March and must have been published shortly after the date changed; although there is no entry for *A Declaration*, it too must have come shortly after Essex's execution and the new year's beginning. On balance, Ashton probably means the second "confession," which appears over Barlow's and Thomas Montfort's names; it includes a simplified version of Essex's last conversation, which has many verbal similarities to this text.

Ashton's presence in the tower evidently comforted Essex a great deal, but also led to suggestions that Ashton had abused a conscience-stricken prisoner at the behest of politically motivated members of the Privy Council. For details of Essex's last weeks, see Beach Langston, "Essex and the Art of Dying," *Huntington Library Quarterly* 13 (1949–50): passim, esp. pp. 122–23. This letter, apparently hitherto unknown, offers support for Langston's (and James Spedding's) defense of Ashton from anonymous charges of political manipulation; yet Ashton received £40 from the Privy Council on 24 March (see *APC*, 1600–1601, p. 180). Another copy appears in Folger MS. V.b. 214, ff. 266r–268r (without "signature").

10 / before 25 October 1600

Date: Writing from "*Gressenhall* the 25 of October 1600," John fferreur (or Ferrour) sent a copy of this item headed "Certayne newe Conclusions" to (Sir) Henry Spelman. Ferrour's letter and text is now Add. MS. 34599, ff. 7r–8v. He writes, "I beseech you impute not the profanenesse of the vnknowne Author as a blemish to the guiltlesse ⟨readers⟩ Writers reputation." His text differs very slightly from the Folger version: for "compassion" (l. 12), Ferrour has "vnkyndnesse"; for "man" (l. 15), "Ladye"; for "quite hym" (l. 34), "make them quite forsaken." Ferrour's text omits two phrases from ll. 44–46: "worthie & famous men" and "and broken their neckes." He also omits the translation of the Sallust quotation.

This cynical document's brutal exposition of courtly *Realpolitik* suggests it bears a satirical or libelous relation to the "advice to a son" literature represented in its traditional and sincere form by item 83. The formula could be used to frame a general satire through scandalously and exaggeratedly pragmatic counsel: see Nicholas Breton's *The Vncasing of Machivils Instructions to his Sonne* (1613; STC 17170 and 3704.3), which appeared in another edition in 1615. "Certein Principles, or Instructions" follows the manuscript's opening section of Essex material and may be related in fact or in the compiler's mind to Essex. Certainly, the partisans of Ralegh and of Essex attacked one another's favorites in such hypothetical and fictional forms (see, e.g., Pierre Lefranc, *Sir Walter Ralegh, écrivain, l'oeuvre et les idées* [Paris: Colin, 1968], App. N, pp. 665–75), and they might have chosen this type for their attacks.

On the other hand, assuming that the manuscript's quasi organization here begins to collapse, the obvious alternative satiric targets would be Burghley and Robert Cecil, both violently attacked in the mid- and late-1590s. (*Cal SP Dom* and *HMC Salisbury* show that libels of Cecil continued to the end of his life). Burghley's "Advice" was the most famous in the period, and a libelous travesty might find an audience easily capable of making the connection. The specificity of "The Offices . . . of the Wardes" (l. 41) in the midst of generalizations might point to the father and son who successively held the Mastership of that lucrative court. The comments on various "estates" (ll. 52ff.—soldiers, preachers, scholars, merchants) appear in many literary genres, but the attention to universities may narrow the field of possible subjects since Burghley, Essex, and Cecil in turn held the Chancellorship of Cambridge. Whatever its provenance and intent, the document offers a fascinating glimpse of what at least one writer thought true to the political facts of life.

Robert Dent kindly called my attention to a reference to the B.L. copy of this document in A. Hassell Smith, *County and Court: Government and Politics in Norfolk, 1558–1603* (Oxford: Clarendon Press, 1974), pp. 145–46.

11 / ca. mid-1603–1604

Date: Various references suggest a date early in James's reign—e.g., "to redresse our wronges . . . and gyve vs true administration of Iustice" (ll. 16–17); "god hathe nowe gyven vs freshe hopes again by your excellent Maiestie" (ll. 20–21); "we are of this opinion in england" (ll. 22–23). Certainly, James received many such petitions at the very beginning of his reign.

The "fower score yeeres and vpward" (ll. 6–7) is presumably wrong. Marie (or Mary) Wentworth married William Cavendish of Grimston Hall, Trimley St. Martin, Suffolk (see W. L. Rutton, *Three Branches of the Family of Wentworth* [Privately printed, 1891]) and thus joined a family including the famous circumnavigator Thomas Cavendish, her husband's uncle (see W. A. Coppinger, *County of Suffolk*, 5 vols. [Sotheram, 1905], 5:225). Although *Complete Peerage* says Mary's father, Thomas, first baron Wentworth, married "about 1520," Rutton's pedigree puts Mary late among that worthy's seventeen children, so that eighty years of age must be an exaggeration. Her nephew, William, married Elizabeth Burghley (see Burghley's holograph pedigree of Wentworth in PRO SP 12/246/98).

13 / 5 April 1603

Date: Just before starting south for London and the English throne, James signed a warrant for Southampton's release and addressed a circular letter to his new subjects informing them of his action. Southampton and Neville were released 10 April. For another copy, see Add. MS. 33051, f. 53.

14 / 7 May 1603 or 15 March 1604

Date: Plague and a consequent fear of crowds curtailed celebration of James's first arrival in London; on 7 May 1603 he left Theobalds and rode to the Charterhouse, being greeted on the way by the sheriff and lord mayor of

London. From the Charterhouse he went to the Tower where he observed martial festivities, accepted the Tower's keys, and looked at the Mint and the lions (11–12 May). For these and further details, see T. M., *The True Narration of the Entertainment of his Royall Maiestie . . . with all or the most speciall Occurrences* (1603; STC 17153 and 14433). James then withdrew to the country, returning for a triumphal entry on 15 March 1604.

This oration, apparently delivered by a child (see ll. 22–24) at a point fairly close to London, does not appear in any of the accounts I have seen. Stephen Harrison, *The Archs of Triumph* (1604; STC 12863) in his "Lectori Candido" reports, "The first *Obiect* that his Maiesties eye encountred (after his entrance into *London*) was part of the children of *Christs Church Hospitall,* to the number of 300. who were placed on a Scaffold, erected for that purpose in *Barking Church-yard* by the *Tower*" (K1r). Despite the topographical discrepancy—"wthin fower myles" (l. 25) versus the roughly two miles separating All Hallow's Barking Church from Temple Bar—this event seems the likeliest occasion for item 14. Many orations and greetings were, however, not presented, though often recorded, so item 14's date must remain tentative. The chief alternative would be 7 May 1603, which may be supported by the item's placement between item 13 of 5 April 1603 and item 16 of 20 July 1603.

15/ca. mid-1603–1604(?)

Date: The petition suggests that James may be unfamiliar with cock-fighting, at least in its English forms, but the petitioner expects the king to follow the sport. The date is conjectural, although item 16 might have been written, as well as copied, after this item.

16/20 July 1603

William Huxley reappears in this manuscript and later in 1603; see items 108 and 109.

17–20/23 or 24 April–ca. 26 April 1602

Date: Add. MS. 25247, ff. 308r–311v gives a variant account of this incident and dates Northumberland's first letter "St. George's Day [Friday 23 April] the last yeare of Queene Eliz. [1602]." Chamberlain reports on 26 April, "I heard but yesternight that my Lord of Northumberland had put him [Vere] a question and that he aunswered yt home" (*Letters,* 1:139; a full description appears on 1:143–44). See also *Cal SP Dom, 1601–3,* pp. 202–5 and the muddled account (similar to Add. MS. 25247) in John Somers et al., comp., *A Collection of Scarce and Valuable Tracts...*, 4 vols. (F. Cogan, 1748), 1:101–4. Arthur Collins, *A Supplement to the ... Peerage of England,* 2 vols. (W. Innys, 1750), 2:727–32 follows the Add. MS. account to which he adds Vere's responses (this manuscript ff. 18v–19r and 19v) and dates Northumberland's first letter *"Saturday* the 24th of *April."* As these references show, many descriptions of the quarrel survive. The example here, the fullest set of materials I have seen, may have reached the compiler through Captain Edmund Whitelocke, a follower of Essex and later a pensioner of Northumberland. See Sir James Whitelocke, *Liber Familicus,* ed. J. Bruce, Camden Society Publications, vol. 70 (1858), pp. 5–11 and G. R. Batho, ed., *Household Papers of Henry Percy, Ninth Earl of Northumberland (1564–1632),* Camden Society Publications, 3d ser., vol. 93 (1962), p. 90. Edmund Whitelocke attended Cambridge and Lincoln's Inn; among his friends were Richard Martin (see item 90) and Inigo Jones (see PRO SP 14/66/28–29).

Many noblemen went to Ostend to pursue martial glory under Elizabeth's greatest commander. Conflicts between soldiership and courtship arose frequently; Vere and Northumberland seem to have been especially bitter opponents. See, e.g., *Cal SP Dom,* 1601–3, p. 70 (an earlier altercation); Edward Grimestone, trans., *A True Historie of the Memorable Siege of Ostend* (1604; STC 18895), pp. 27, 30, 46; Clements R. Markham, *The Fighting Veres* (Sampson and Low, 1888). Vere's own account of the siege appears in Harl. MS. 3638, ff. 172r–176v), later published in another version in *The Commentaries of Sr. Francis Vere* (Cambridge, 1657; Wing V240), pp. 118–131.

21 / mid- to late-1603(?)

Date: This letter almost certainly refers to the plague ("yt evill spirritt yt furiously rageth in the bowels of the desolate cittie") that marked 1603 in one of the most fearsome European epidemics between the Black Death of 1348–49 and the Great Plague of 1665. F. P. Wilson's chapter on the plague of 1603 in *The Plague in Shakespeare's London* (Oxford: At the University Press, 1927) gives the details of this terrible visitation; mortality figures for the city and its environs led Wilson to conclude that "almost a sixth of the inhabitants perished in one year" (p. 115). See also J. F. D. Shrewsbury, *A History of Bubonic Plague in the British Isles* (Cambridge: At the University Press, 1970), pp. 264–85 and chart 50, p. 328.

Among those praised for courageous activities in the stricken city was one Dr. Thomas Lodge, who published a *Treatise of the Plague* (preface dated 19 August 1603; STC 16676); he is almost certainly the man mentioned here since no other Lodge was a doctor in London before 1700 (see William Munk, comp., *The Royal College of Physicians,* 2d rev. ed., 3 vols. [Royal College of Physicians, 1878], vol. 1 [1518–1700], pp. 155–56). Lodge, of course, also wrote plays, poetry, and prose satires; among the latter is *A Fig for Momus*

(1595; STC 16658) in which he mentions members of his circle, including Daniel (on D2v ff.) and, anagramatically, Roydon (as "Donroy" on D2r). The Privy Council had closed the theaters on 19 March, and they did not reopen until 9 April 1604 (Chambers, *Eliz. Stage,* 1:302 and 4:349–50); in the interval, the players—like the court, the lawyers, and much of London's population— took to the provinces. One company, the Children of the Chapel, however, does not appear to have performed anywhere during the period, a fact which makes it possible that one of their most famous actors, Nathan Field (sixteen years old in 1603 and therefore appropriately called "Mr"), might have remained in London and thus received the "letteres" mentioned here.

Since new plays were neither in demand nor possible under the restricted conditions of touring performance, playwrights who were not also actors or shareholders might themselves withdraw to the country. While "Hitchin" is not the name of a well-known Elizabethan playwright, it is the name of Chapman's native Hertfordshire town (cf. "The Tears of Peace," ll. 76–77; Chapman, *Poems,* pp. 174–75). Might the copyist have mistaken place of origin for sender? Chapman was a good friend of Lodge's close friend, Roydon, and a good friend of Field. (He wrote a prefatory poem for *Woman is a Weathercocke.*) Chapman remained in London as late as 30 May 1603 (see C. J. Sisson, *Lost Plays of Shakespeare's Age* [Cambridge: At the University Press, 1936], p. 62). After this section was written, Albert H. Tricomi published "Two Letters Concerning George Chapman," *Modern Language Review* 75 (1980):241–48, making many of the same identifications, but suggesting "at least a strong possibility that it was written by his [George Chapman's] brother" (p. 245).

24 / February 1601–March 1602(?)

Date: Sir Edward Wingfield was about to leave for Ireland 17 January 1599 (see Chamberlain, *Letters,* 1:62) and commanded the fort at Munster as of 1 January 1603 (*Cal SP Ireland,* 1601–3, p. 550). He did, however, return to England in late March 1602 (*HMC Salisbury,* 12:97) and at that time wrote Robert Cecil, "I knowe not wheather my Cominge to the Cowrte maye be offensiue or no, wch makes me bowld to Intreate your honors advise: I haue sent my Eldest sonne to knowe your honors pleasure. . . . My desire . . . is but to see her Maggestie wch by your honorable means I do hoppe to Effect. . . ." (PRO SP 12/283a/78, f. 190r; dated "the 17 daye of Appryll" with a secretarial addition, "1602"). Earlier, Wingfield was not so confident of Cecil's support (see *HMC Salisbury,* 10:292; 25 August 1600), and he did return to Ireland without employment (ibid., 12:208–9). By 14 September, Mary, Lady Wingfield, wrote Cecil begging that her husband be given Sir Francis Vere's command (ibid., 12:372). All this hectic chase of position suggests that the present petition preceded Wingfield's return from Ireland in 1602. The expression "nowe in Your Maiesties service in Ireland" (l. 14) may of course mean merely that Wingfield is so occupied, not that he is physically in Ireland at the instant of writing, though it suggests the latter. Lady Wingfield's phrase, "the fyne worthelie imposed vpon some of the late Offendors" (ll. 11–12) probably refers to the survivors of Essex's rebellion (see Chamberlain's list in *Letters*, 1:123); in any case, this source of reward is not mentioned in either April or September 1602. On balance, the period between the trial of the Essex group (February 1601) and Wingfield's return from Ireland (March 1602) seems most likely.

Sender: The references to poverty and to Sir Edward's presence in Ireland, "Private wthout imployment" (ll. 14–15) make it clear that this petition comes from Mary Wingfield, daughter of James Harington of Exton (see Sir Henry Ellis, ed., *Visitation of . . . Huntingdon, 1613*, Camden Society Publications, vol. 43 [1849], p. 131) and not from Anne, daughter of Edward, Lord Cromwell of Okeham, wife of a much more successful relative also named Sir Edward Wingfield (d. 1638); see M. E. Wingfield, Lord Powerscourt, *Muniments of the . . . Family of Wingfield* (Mitchell and Hughes, 1894), pp. 6 and 39–40.

Evidence for the date (1603) of the death of the Sir Edward Wingfield mentioned here comes from the inquisitions post mortem cited in the *Victoria History of . . . Huntingdon*, 3 vols. (St. Catherine Press, 1926–36), 3:80. Powerscourt's volume is unreliable.

25 / February 1601 (1602?)

This plea, or another, eventually succeeded. The Signet Office docket books have two references to the matter: in July 1604, "an exoneracion . . . unto Alexander Newby late of durtmouth . . . for the killing of one Tho. Dunce" appears with a note "in such sort as the late Queene did discharge . . . by her former letteres" (PRO SO 3/2, sub datum); in June 1607, James renews the pardon and the docket notes that the new pardon "contayneth in effect no more then was formerly graunted unto him, but that in Lawe it is more effectuall" (PRO SO 3/3, sub datum). From the later docket comes further detail: Newby's original indictment was "about eight yeeres since" (i.e., mid-1599), but Mr. Justice, later Sir, Francis Gawdy "perceaving the cause was carried with some mallice acquainted the late Queene therwth and procured a discharge for the said Newby. . . ." See also *Cal SP Dom*, 1603–10, pp. 135 and 476.

29 / 13 February 1601 (1602?)

George Wither (1525–1605) served as rector of Danbury, Essex, for many years; no genealogy gives the names mentioned here (Marie, Micah, Abell), but

George had pronounced Puritan leanings (hence the sons' names?), and it is hard to doubt that some connection exists. See Reginald F. Bigg-Wither, *Materials for a History of the Wither Family* (Winchester, England: Warren, 1907), pp. 12–13 and pedigree facing p. 11.

30/13 February 1601 (1602?)

See Commentary on item 29.

31/late 1597(?)

Date and Addressee: Peter Short published Anthony Holborne's *The Cittharn Schoole* (STC 13562), dedicated to Thomas Burgh, in 1597; this book is the first collection of Holborne's music, although a few pieces had been published earlier. It seems likely that this letter was addressed to Burgh; unfortunately, no S.R. entry survives, although Short entered four other books of music between 10 October and 21 November 1597. The letter probably accompanied a manuscript or presentation copy given to the dedicatee (see ll. 13–18). Burgh, who died on 14 October 1597 in Ireland, may have already arrived there, since Holborne cannot "vysit" his patron (ll. 6–8). It is also possible that the letter accompanied a presentation copy of *Pauans, Galliards, Almains and other short Aeirs* (1599; STC 13563), dedicated to Sir Richard Champernowne; in this latter case, it might be Holborne himself who was out of the country. Although a London resident (and presumably in London ca. 1597, when he wrote a commendatory poem for Thomas Morley's *Plaine and easie Introdvction to Practicall Mvsicke* [1597; S.R. entry 9 October 1596; STC 18133]), Holborne traveled as a government messenger on several occasions, including a trip to the Netherlands in early 1599. For information about Holborne's government service, a full summary of his biography, and a discussion of his other patrons (who included the Countess of Pembroke), see Brian Jeffery, "Anthony Holborne," *Musica Disciplina* 22 (1968):129–206. Jeffery believes that Holborne set some of Edmund Spenser's poetry to music (see pp. 142–43).

In any event, it appears likely that Holborne's connection with Burgh (and perhaps the Low Countries and/or the countess of Pembroke's literary circle) accounts for the letter's presence in this manuscript. Thomas Burgh was regarded, evidently, as a generous patron of music (see above, Introduction, p. 31). This letter appears as Appendix M, pp. 117–18, in J. M. Ward, "A Dowland Miscellany," *Journal of the Lute Society of America* 10 (1977):5–153. Some of Holborne's music from the 1599 collection has recently been recorded on Decca DSLO 569.

32 / 7 April 1599

Sender: Dorothy Moryson was the widow of Sir Charles Moryson, who died in 1599 (see A. C. S. Hall, comp., *Guide to the Reports of the HMC, 1911–1957,* 3 vols. [H.M. Stationery Office, 1966], 2:1187), apparently just before the writing of this letter. He completed the mansion at Cashiobury, Herts., begun by his father (see *DNB*, s.v. "Morison, Sir Richard").

Addressee: The closing, "Your loving Sister," and the reference to "your brother and his" [i.e. Sir Charles' brother? or "your brother's family"?] (l. 16) cause difficulties in narrowing the field of possible recipients. Assuming that the closing indicates some familial relation, one may suggest Dorothy Moryson's sisters-in-law as addressees: Jane, who married first, Lord Edward Russell and second, Lord Grey of Wilton; Elizabeth who married first, Sir William Norris and second, the earl of Lincoln; Mary, who married Bartholomew Hales. Only the last of these three women would seem likely to welcome a gift of £4. The second phrase causes problems because both *DNB* and the Herts. visitations of 1572 and 1634 (see Harl. Soc. Pub., vol. 22 [1886], App. 1, p. 116) show Sir Charles to have been an only male child; in any case, "Mr Morrison" (l. 8) presumably refers, familiarly, to Sir Charles himself. Finally, Dorothy may be writing to her own sister—i.e., a member of the Clark family, of whom nothing is known.

38 / 29 February 1599/1600(?)

Date: If this is a copy of a letter from Chapman and if he were only once imprisoned in the Counter in Wood Street, then the item should be be dated 29 February 1599/1600. PRO C 25/65, in the Answer by John Woolfall to a bill preferred by Chapman, states that Chapman had been imprisoned 9 February 1599/1600 in Wood Street Counter on Woolfall's father's suit (see below, item 138 and Commentary); since the writer states "I remayne in woodstreete counter, and so haue I done these twentie days in execution" (ll. 20–21), that would place the date (under the large assumptions above) as 29 February, since 1600 was a leap year.

42 / before 24 March 1603

Date: Line 10 indicates that this item predates Elizabeth's death. References to Kirton, who became muster master for Wiltshire (30 June 1604; see *Cal SP Dom,* 1603–10, p. 126), are rare before James's accession.

43/

This letter cannot be identified with any certainty. Given the compiler's apparent interest in both the earl of Essex and Chapman, however, two pieces of internal evidence deserve note. The letter-writer uses a common Elizabethan image for artistic creation when he writes that his "first fruytes were graste by your Lordshippes most honorable favoures" (ll. 3–4); Essex first patronized Chapman's published poetry (see Allardyce Nicoll, ed., *Chapman's Homer*, Bollingen Series 41, 2 vols. [1956; reprint ed., Princeton, N.J.: Princeton University Press, 1967], 1:xv–xvi, 503–6, and 543–46). The author writes from somewhere outside Wales ("remember me *their*," l. 18; my italics), and the anonymous lord intends to travel "into wales." At the height of Essex's penultimate conflict with the queen, Londoners frequently mentioned his intention to travel into Wales. Philip Gawdy, for instance, wrote on 13 June 1600:

> The newes of my Lo. of Essex cause hearing wer to no purpose to tell you, bycause euery body knowes it so well . . . but indeade euery body thinkes he sholde be forthewith sett at lybertye, withe theis conditions to forbeare going into Wales, and comming to the courte. (*Letters of Philip Gawdy*, ed. I. H. Jeayes [J. B. Nichols, 1906], p. 99)

Presumably, the danger foreseen by Gawdy and others was of Essex's raising support in a country where his family had long held estates, far from London's authority. These connections are of course very tenuous, but intriguing.

46, 47, 48/

These letters seem to form a sequence in the ruptured affair; an apparent attempt to rectify matters appears in items 49 and 50.

49/

The strange shift in the tone and matter of this letter may best be explained by assuming that "this enclosed letter" actually begins at line 10 with the phrase, "I hope you will not looke I should vse any excusyve terms. . . ."
Addressee: the writer of letter 50?

50/

This anonymous letter, which seems to be the result of the requests made in letter 49, provides the sole evidence for Chapman's courtship of a widow.

Around it other letters on a similar subject probably should be grouped. There is of course only inference to support the identification of "Mr Chapman" (ll. 2–3) with the poet: first because he is the only identifiable "Chapman" in this manuscript and second because he is known to have had an older, more successful brother (ll. 5–8 and 28–34). Although this manuscript's grouping cannot provide a reliable chronology, it may be noted that the dated, or datable, items in this part of the manuscript come from the two or three years on either side of 1600. See Introduction, pp. 29–31.

51 / early 1609(?)

Date: S. G. Culliford transcribes this letter in *William Strachey* and there gives the date as "early in 1609" (p. 94). Culliford has no evidence for this statement other than the facts that Strachey was financially embarrassed at this time and that in Hilary term, 1609, Ferryman lost a suit for debt (ibid., p. 96). The letter must remain without a certain date, though Culliford's remarks on the friendship among Roydon, Bales, and Ferryman should be noted (ibid., p. 95); Culliford's references to MS. V.a. 321 require verification.

52 / 28 May 1594–30 April 1596

Date: Puckering's term as lord keeper gives the limits of this item's original.

Leveson's "protection" eventually ran out; Chamberlain writes on 8 December 1598, ". . . Sir Walter is staide in the Fleet being faln into hucksters handes (I mean his old creditors) who laide a traine for him and caught him at Lambeth" (*Letters,* 1:57), but later reports (with some satisfaction), "Sir Walter Lewson is dead in the Fleet and so his creditors paide in theyre eare" (ibid., 1:169; 4 November 1602).

54 / 1600

If "Beniamino Vuod" is to be identified with the Captain Benjamin Wood, "a man of approved skill in navigation" (Richard Hakluyt, *The Principal Navigations.* . . , 12 vols. [Glasgow: MacLehose, 1903–5], 11:407), who left England after 11 July 1596 with a fleet of three ships bound for China, then this letter is apparently a forgery. Donald Ferguson has shown almost conclusively that the fleet never reached China and that the ships and crews were all lost, probably in late 1598 or 1599. See Ferguson's introduction to *The Travels of Pedro Teixeira,* Hakluyt Society Publications, ser. 2, vol. 9 (1902), pp. xliii–lviii and his letter, "Captain Benjamin Wood's Expedition of 1596," *Geographical Journal* 21 (1903):330–34; for garbled contemporary material, see Samuel Purchas, *Hakluytus Posthumus*. . . , 20 vols. (Glasgow: MacLehose, 1905–7), 2:288–97. Hakluyt prints Queen Elizabeth's letter dispatched with this fleet to the emperor of China (*The Principal Navigations*, 11:417–21).

55, 56 / 25 July 1597

Date: This date, 25 July 1597, appears above the Latin text recorded in Folger MS. V.b. 214, f. 67v; both Latin and English texts are in John Nichols, *Progresses . . . of . . . Elizabeth*, 2d ed., 3 vols. (J. Nichols, 1823), 3:417–18. See also *Cal SP Dom*, 1595–1597, pp. 473–74.

Elizabeth's ex tempore speech on this occasion seemed sufficiently unusual to be remembered by John Evelyn in his *Numismata: A Discourse of Medals, Antient and Modern* (1697; Wing E3505) as one of the reasons to desire her medal (p. 264).

57 / 19 October 1584

Loyalist fears of Roman Catholic plots against Elizabeth, exacerbated by the papal ban against William of Orange and the supposed treasons of various native and foreign agents, came to a focus when Balthazar Gérard assassinated William the Silent on 10 July 1584 (30 June, old style). The Privy Council drew up an oath of "association" and urged that it be distributed as widely as possible. County by county, the great men of the kingdom (including a very young Essex) signed the document, one copy being deposited in London, another being retained by the various lords lieutenant. Thirteen Privy Council members and a group of important lords spiritual signed slightly different documents at Hampton Court, 19 October 1584. For details of relevant religio-political activity in the period 1580 onwards, see esp. J. H. Pollen, *Mary Queen of Scots and the Babington Plot*, Scottish Historical Society Publications, 3d ser., vol. 3 (Edinburgh, 1922), pp. xv–xxx. The wording of item 57 would be more appropriate to secular signers and has many verbal similarities to the précis in *Cal SP Dom*, 1581–90, p. 210; ibid., pp. 211–12 lists "deposit copies" of the oath and pp. 207–8, esp. SP 12/173/87, record the process leading to the oath. Public, or governmental, concern eventually produced "An Act for Provision made for security of the Queen's Most Royal Person" (1585; 27 Eliz. I., c. 1), which received its first reading in the Lords on 10 March 1585. See G. R. Elton, comp., *The Tudor Constitution: Documents and Commentary* (Cambridge: At the University Press, 1965), pp. 76–80. For further details of other copies and the use made of this document by James VI of Scotland, see J. G. McManaway, "Elizabeth, Essex, and James," in *Elizabethan and Jacobean Studies Presented to Frank Percy Wilson*. . . , eds. H. Davis and H. Gardner (Oxford: Clarendon Press, 1959), pp. 219–30, esp. p. 220 n.1.

58 / 18 December 1604

Date: John Strype, *Annals of the Reformation*, 4 vols. (Oxford: Clarendon Press, 1824), 4:545 (Appendix 290), gives this date in a headnote to the text of Cecil's answer. Strype prints Hutton's letter in *The Life . . . of . . . Whitgift*, 4 vols. (Oxford: Clarendon Press, 1822), 3:420–21 (Appendix 50). Ralph Winwood, *Memorials of Affairs of State . . .* , 3 vols. (Ware, 1725), 2:40 and Edmund Lodge, *Illustrations of British History. . .* , 3 vols. (Nicol, 1791), 3:251–52, also print Hutton's letter in slightly variant forms. The implied profusion of surviving manuscripts gives weight to Cecil's complaint "I perceive you have soe undiscreet clarkes, as they are like to make my letters as common as they have made your owne" (Strpye, *Annals,* 4:548).

William P. Haugaard, *Elizabeth and the English Reformation* (Cambridge: At the University Press, 1968) pp. 130–35, describes the Ecclesiastical Commission, founded 19 July 1559 "to ensure that the Acts of Supremacy and Uniformity be 'duly put into execution . . .' " and discusses its varying success. James, as might have been predicted, reacted sharply not to Hutton's religious advice but to his admonitions about hunting: "you [Cecil] have answered it according to my heart's desire, for a scornful answerless answer became best such a senseless proposition" (*HMC Salisbury,* 17:76; see also ibid., p. 121).

59 / April 1587

Date: Since Drake mentions none of his subsequent exploits, he presumably wrote shortly after the Cadiz attack. Although John Foxe died 18 April 1587, poor communications—so eloquently testified by the queen's inability to recall Drake himself—would explain the writer's ignorance of either Foxe's last illness or his death.

Addressee: Nothing in this version of Drake's letter, barring perhaps the closing reference to "your Faithfull remembraunce of vs in your prayers" (ll. 31–32), certainly identifies the recipient as Foxe the martyrologist. Two other early versions of this letter specify as follows: "Mr Jno. Foxe, preacher" (Harl. MS. 167, f. 104r) and "To the right reuerende, godly learned Father, my very good freend, M. Iohn Fox, preacher of the word of GOD" (Thomas Greepe, *The true . . . exploytes, performed . . . by Syr Frauncis Drake . . .* [1587; STC 12343], C3v). These other versions have short paragraphs identifying the secretary who wrote the letter, William Spenser and M. Pynner, respectively, which may suggest that the letter was meant for private or public circulation (i.e., that it was sent in more than one copy). The Harl. MS version describes ll. 42–45 of this item as "An Addition written with Sir Frances owne hande." For Drake's friendship with Foxe, see J. F. Mozley, *John Foxe and His Book* (Society for Promoting Christian Knowledge, 1940), pp. 101–3.

60 / ca. 1585–89(?)

Date: Mildmay succeeded Sackville in 1566 and died in 1589; this item and the next probably come from the period 1585–89, when the Queen's Bench received much attention and an appeal process was introduced. See "An Act for Redress of erroneous Judgments in . . . the King's Bench" (27 Eliz. I. c. 8) and "An Act against Discontinuances of Writs of Error in the . . . King's Bench" (31 Eliz. I. c.1) in A. R. A. Kiralfy, comp., *A Source Book of English Law* (Sweet and Maxwell, 1957), pp. 66–68. In the PRO, SP 12/147/87 (calendared as February 1581) represents a draft of "A Bill for relief of prisoners confined for debt in the Bench. . . ." This bill asks the queen to establish a commission (including various senior clergymen, justices, and aldermen of London and the Home Counties) empowered to investigate individual prisoner's cases, to stipulate methods of repayment, and to free them on those grounds (see esp. ff. 208–10; f. 208 specifically mentions the "Commons in this present parliament assemblyed").

61 / ca. 1585–89(?)

See Commentary on item 60.

Date: If line 20 is literally accurate, then this item would fall into one of the legislative sessions in the probable four-year period: 23 November 1584–27 March 1585; 15 February–23 March 1587; 4 February–29 March 1589. (This list excludes the late 1586 judicial meeting that deliberated Mary Stuart's execution.) See J. E. Neale, *Elizabeth I and Her Parliaments, 1584–1601* (Cape, 1957), p. 190 n. 1.

62 / 9 July 1582

A William Poole, gentleman, received a safe conduct to Poland on 19 September 1590 (*Cal SP Dom*, 1581–90, p. 689); he may be the man banished here.

65 / after 5 December 1603–before 14 June 1610(?)

Date and Sender: This item provides just enough evidence to indicate that it is an appeal by Elizabeth Burgh Brooke (see letter 122 and Commentary) written sometime after her husband's execution on 5 December 1603; more precision is difficult, however, for the word "last" in the phrase "last Lord Cobham" probably refers to the attainder (1603) rather than the death (January 1618/19) of Henry Brooke, eleventh lord Cobham. It seems plausible that Elizabeth Brooke wrote this letter to her brother-in-law, Robert Cecil. By whatever means achieved, some small improvement in the family's fortunes occurred through a private bill of Parliament, 7 Jac. I. c. 18 (14 June 1610), for some details of which see: *Complete Peerage*, 3:350; J. G. Waller, "The Lords of Cobham (Part II)," *Archaeologia Cantiana* 12 (1878):161–63; Foster, *Proc. Parliament 1610*, 1:106–7.

To understand the familial relations mentioned in this letter, one should remember that Henry Brooke's heir was his "lame brother Master George Brooke" (Chamberlain, *Letters*, 1:64) who married Elizabeth Burgh and died a convicted traitor; thus their children (the heirs to the title) were grandchildren of the untainted William, tenth lord Cobham, mentioned in line 4.

66 / after 14 June 1610(?)

Date and Sender: No internal evidence exists to date or identify this item. If its position has any meaning, it may be a further appeal of Elizabeth Brooke, presumably after her son's restitution in blood (14 June 1610; see Commentary on item 65). This petition may, however, owe its position to its similarity of subject to item 65, rather than application to the same family.

69 / 26 October 1605

Date: This date appears in *Cal SP Dom*, 1603–10, p. 237 and is confirmed by contemporary accounts. The letter, sent to William Parker, Lord Monteagle, set in motion the search for the Gunpowder plotters. "A Discovrse of the maner of the Discoverie of the Powder-Treason" appears in *The Workes of the most High and Mightie Prince, Iames.* . . . (1616; STC 14344), pp. 223–46, and reproduces with some small variants this letter on p. 227.

Sender: S. R. Gardiner, in *What Gunpowder Plot Was* (Longmans, Green, 1897), pp. 121–25, discusses this phase of the plot and suggests that Francis Tresham, Monteagle's brother-in-law, was the "author or contriver" (p. 121) of this warning. Thomas Percy has also been suggested as author (see, e.g., James I, *Workes*, p. 229).

For Ben Jonson's involvement, see Herford and Simpson, 1:40–41 and 11:5 and Jonson's epigram (60) to Monteagle.

70 / 1604

Date: This letter confuses Ahmed's age. John Windet printed a similar, though later, letter in *Letters from the great Turke lately sent vnto . . . Rodolphus* (1606; STC 207). Ahmed dates this other letter "The 19. of our Nativitie and the third of our Raigne" (i.e., 1605–6), which is correct; the close of letter

70 should read "Off our Nativitie the .18. yere: and of our Raigne .2." The sultan's threat probably refers to the military offensive that temporarily concluded the long warfare (1593–1606) between Hapsburg and Ottoman.

72/June 1606

Date: Zorzi Giustinian, Venetian ambassador to England, apparently refers to this document in a dispatch dated 20 September 1606: ". . . the Spanish Ambassador has the copy of a certain letter, written, it seems, by the Republic of Genoa to that of Venice, full of impertinent falsehoods. The Ambassador is ashamed to publish it" (*Cal SP Ven,* 1603–7, p. 404). Giustinian's caution over the authorship of the letter appears to have been justified, for Paolo Sarpi, the chief Venetian apologist, reports in *The History of the Qvarrels of Pope Paul .V. with the State of Venice . . .* (1626; STC 21766):

> Whilest these things were treated at *Venice,* at *Rome,* and in the *Courts* of *Princes,* the *Iesuites* did not cease to doe all sorts of euill offices to the *Republique* within and without *Italy* in the Cities where they liued; scattering many calumnies, as well in priuate Discourses, as in their publique Sermons. . . . They forged also false and counterfeit Letters, dispersing them vnder the name of the *Republique* of *Genoa,* to that of *Venice.* . . . (P. 135)

Gambarin, in his edition of Sarpi, *Istoria dell' Interdetto e altri scritti editi e inediti,* 3 vols. (Bari, Italy: Laterza, 1940), 1:71, dates this section of Sarpi's work as referring to events of 14 June–10 August 1606; the forgery would belong, probably, to the earliest part of that period. Gambarin also cites (1:236) the original document of which Sarpi complains: *Copia della lettera scritta della serenissima republica di Genoa, in risposta d'una scrittale dal doge e republica di Venetia.* Stampata in Milano et in Parma, MDCVI. I have not seen this work, but *Dve Lettere vna pvblicata sotto nome della Republica di Genova alla Repvblica di Venetia. . . . La Prima Stampata in Milano, & in Parma, & ristampata poi In Venetia, Con la Risposta. MDCVI.* (B.L. shelfmark 175.f.15[15]) includes the Italian text (pp. 3–5) of the letter translated here. It is described as "Vna Lettera, che si finge esser stata scritta dalla Republica di Genoua alla Repvblica di Venetia." These details all support Sarpi's contention that the "original" is a forgery.

English sentiments were for the most part with the Venetians in this controversy; Sarpi's work found an eager audience and was often translated and published within a few months of its publication in Italy. A typical piece of pro-Venetian writing is *A Declaration of the Variance betweene the Pope, and the Segniory of Venice* (1606; STC 19482), and the youthful Prince Henry was pleased to side with the Venetians (see *Cal SP Ven,* 1603–7, p. 495 and *Cal SP Ven,* 1607–10, pp. 2, 10, 11). English Catholics of course tended to support the

Pope, and the presence of this item may indicate the compiler's Roman Catholic sympathies. For the political background and the broad European significance of the Venetian defiance of the Pope's interdict, see W. J. Bouwsma, *Venice and the Defence of Republican Liberty* (Berkeley and Los Angeles: University of California Press, 1968), pp. 339–483.

73 / ca. March–June 1608

Date, Sender, and Addressee: It has been assumed since Dobell's time that Chapman wrote this letter to Sir George Buck in defense of his ten-act play, *The Conspiracie, and Tragedie of Charles Duke of Byron* (1608; STC 4968) around mid-1608, following a protest by Antoine de la Boderie, the French Ambassador (see, e.g., Chambers, *Eliz. Stage*, 3:257–58). John Gabel, "The Original Version of Chapman's *Tragedy of Byron*," *Journal of English and Germanic Philology* 63 (1964): 433–40, however, suggests that the letter may have been written slightly earlier (p. 435). Granting that the references to the "frenche Ambassador" (l. 17) and "those two partes" (l. 19) make it almost certain that these assumptions are largely correct, the date remains arguable as does the addressee. Edmund Tilney still held the Mastership of the Revels, though Buck, his deputy, seems to have done the work; the *Byron* plays were entered under his hand in the S.R. on 5 June 1608.

The hypothetical sequence of events is: (1) sometime before 6 March 1608 (Gabel, p. 435) La Boderie has the *Byron* plays prohibited as offensive to French sensibilities; (2) early in March, the court leaves London, and the plays, including a *new* scene of conflict between Henry IV's queen and mistress, are performed; (3) La Boderie makes a second complaint, Cecil closes the play and arrests some individuals though the "compositeur" escapes; (4) Sir Thomas Lake, writing for the king, compliments Cecil's action (letter dated "at Thetford this .11. of March 1607" [i.e., 1608, new style]; see *Malone Society Collections*, vol. 2, pt. 2 [1922], pp. 148–49); (5) on 8 April 1608, La Boderie sends a dispatch, published by J. J. Jusserand in "Ambassador La Boderie and the 'Compositeur' of the Byron Plays," *Modern Language Review* 6 (1911): 203–5, recounting some of these events. Gabel, arguing for rearrangement of act-divisions in the *Tragedy of Byron*, makes clear the fact of La Boderie's *two* complaints, one for an early version of the play(s) and another for the altered version incorporating Madame de Verneuil and the Queen of France, apparently in *Byron's Tragedy*, Act 2 (see Gabel, "The Original Version of Chapman's *Tragedy of Byron*," pp. 435–37). La Boderie specifically complains about the new scene and about plays representing an "histoire moderne" and "des choses du temps" (Jusserand, "Ambassador La Boderie," p. 204).

Chapman's letter makes matters more, not less, difficult. The letter requests permission "for the Presse" (l. 10) and thus probably dates from before or well after the scandal, when the furor did not exist or had subsided. The play(s) had certainly been performed: "yf the two or three lynes you crost, *were spoken*" (ll. 1–2; my italics); "I *see* not myne owne Plaies; Nor carrie the Actors Tongues in my Mouthe" (ll. 4–5; my italics). Apparently, two texts existed— the original and a later censored one; the addressee did not witness the first performed (l. 13), and even if he had, could not detect the slight changes "in the Revisall" (l. 15). In fact, the letter does not preclude the "Presentment" of both texts, original and revised, the latter of which is now offered for printing. The omission of any reference to the offensive scene suggests that Chapman writes about a performance of a version lacking it. Certainly "two or three lynes," even at Chapman's disingenuous height, could hardly include all the material La Boderie describes. Gabel concludes that this letter precedes the disaster and refers solely to La Boderie's first objection (p. 435 n. 9). Still, a late (post-8 April 1608) date cannot be ruled out, since the letter mentions "Whosoever it was yt *first* plaied the bitter Informer" (ll. 16–17; my italics). Many men may have hastened to inform the Ambassador, though Chapman writes mostly in the singular, or Chapman may be distinguishing among several reports and several versions, two over which he had control and another, barely alluded to, for which he takes no responsibility.

The "thrice allowance of ye Counsaile for ye Presentment" (ll. 8–9) still remains a puzzle. Chapman may mean only that three meetings were required to pass the play that nonetheless offended the Ambassador as an "histoire moderne" and had to be withdrawn (i.e., after La Boderie's first objection). "Allowance," though, sounds like a distinct event, and "thrice allowance" most plausibly describes three occasions at least somewhat separated in time. When might the Council have been called upon? Certainly after La Boderie's first complaint—perhaps this meeting resulted in the censorship of two or three lines. An earlier "allowance" might be hypothesized for the period when the whole project of ten acts on contemporary French history came before the Council. Finally, the third occasion might have been after La Boderie's second complaint. In this case, Chapman must have been found innocent and thus feels justified in demanding permission to print the purged "second" version, itself quite distinct from the one containing an interpolated scene. Naturally, this explanation places the letter late in the sequence, after 11 March 1608 at the earliest.

Another explanation would begin the cycle of "allowances" much earlier. Marion Jones and Glynne Wickham, in "The Stage Furnishings of George Chapman's *The Tragedy of Charles, Duke of Biron* [*sic*]," *Theatre Notebook* 16 (1961–62):113–17, have shown that printed sources for Biron's life and death were available before Grimestone's translation of Matthieu's history (1607). They conclude:

> that Henslowe commissioned a play from Chettle and Chapman on the subject of Biron in August 1602, and that since the play supported the Government's policy in respect of rebellion it received a licence for perform-

ance without difficulty. We would suggest further that shortly after James I's accession, when the acting companies were reorganized, the play passed out of the hands of Worcester's Company and into those of the Queen's Revels, when it would again have had to be licensed for performance although unaltered. Late in 1607, Chapman, in acute financial straits and prompted by the publication of Grimeston's *Inventorie*, decided to revise the play on his own account with a view to further revival and subsequent publication. Two further licences would then be required, one to act and one to print it. The former was granted without fuss: but once the French Ambassador had levelled objections to the acted version, the licence to print proved difficult to obtain and was granted only after cuts had been made.

Although this argument does not explain the verbal similarities between the plays as we have them and some materials translated by Grimestone and not in print before ca. 1605 or later, it does mean that Henslowe's reference to props "for the playe of Berowne" (or "burone") in September and October 1602 could refer to an earlier version of the play(s) we have, as Greg suggested in 1908 (see R. A. Foakes and R. T. Rickert, eds., *Henslowe's Diary* [Cambridge: At the University Press, 1961], pp. 216–17 and Chambers, *Eliz. Stage*, 3:258). Extending the plays' controversial lifetime in this way would allow many opportunities, perhaps more than three, for "allowances."

In considering the earlier date of 1602, one might also suggest that Chapman may have once encountered domestic English difficulties over the allusions to Essex and the parallels drawn between the earl's and the marshal's careers. The extant text narrates Byron's visit to England (*Byron's Conspiracy*, 4.1), though T. M. Parrott describes the act as having "been cut to pieces by the censor" and adds, "No doubt in the original Byron's visit . . . was represented, not narrated" (*Plays and Poems of George Chapman: The Tragedies* [Routledge, 1910], p. 607). Chapman might well describe the plays, in his dedication, as "poore dismembered Poems" if in fact both the *Conspiracy* and the *Tragedy* had been censored and if each had been the subject of the Council's investigation and "allowance."

Finally, J. E. Ingeldew, in "The Date of Composition of Chapman's *Caesar and Pompey*," *Review of English Studies*, n.s. 12 (1961):144–59, interprets "the thrice allowance of ye Counsaile for ye Presentment" as meaning "the Privy Council had permitted three performances" (pp. 156–57) of the *Byron* plays. That is, "allowance" should be read as a synonym for "performance": I doubt this equation, but in any case it does not solve the dating problem.

74, 75 / after 24 March 1603

Date: Both letters refer to a male monarch (item 74, l. 9 and item 75, l. 13), so the letters probably follow James's accession.

It is tempting to see some connection between these two letters and item 73,

but the compiler may simply have been collecting examples of indignant epis-
tles (cf. item 76) rather than making a series of letters between the same two
individuals or concerning the same issue.

79 / 1 December 1595 or 1596

Date: Diana Poulton, *John Dowland,* p. 47 says that the date 1 December
1596 "can hardly be doubted" for this item; 1595 is also possible. Dowland did
go home, but his hopes were disappointed (Noel died 24 February 1596/7).

Dowland received 2/10 for playing at the performance of Chapman's
Memorable Masque (see letter, 89 and Commentary). Poulton's transcript of
this and the following letter require correction.

80 / 9 February 1598

Poulton (see Commentary, item 79) discusses the circumstances of this invi-
tation (*John Dowland,* p. 50); it is not known whether Dowland returned to
the Landgrave's court. This and the previous item are important and apparently
unique sources for Dowland's biography.

The original scribe has mended this leaf (ll. 8–11). Close examination of the
edges of the mended area, however, shows that not only has a portion of paper
been removed and replaced, but that the text has been changed slightly. For
example, above the *l* of "particuler," the upper parts of two loops (such as
would occur in words ending in *-ld* or other doubled letters with looped
ascenders, such as *-dd* or *-ll*) remain from the original text and above the
double *s* of "assure" (l. 11), the remains of a curved stroke that does not belong
to "of" may be seen. Finally, some original letters have been incorporated into
the crossed *p* of "particuler." The repair or revision certainly took place before
f. 53v was written; the very neat use of the old page's contours in the double *s*
of "assure" suggests that the paper was changed after the writing of line 10.

81 /

This letter seems similar to letter 31; i.e., it accompanied a presentation copy
of a "discourse" (l. 3) or "worke" (l. 61). Despite the numerous details about
the book and the patron, both remain unidentified. The item's position in the
manuscript offers little help in determining the date, since the last dated item
preceding it comes from late 1598 and the one immediately following it from
1610.

The book apparently has a military or quasi-military subject: the author wrote because of his "Regard" for "Soldiers & Martiall affaires" (ll. 1–3); yet the subject may not be contemporary or even restricted to one historical period, since "in all Ages soldiers have bene honored . . ." (ll. 9–10). To some degree, the work is not original, and the author apologizes for "gleanynge after other mens harvestes, my self not plowing the grounds" (ll. 61–62).

About the patron we learn even more. A noble (ll. 15–16: "discendiñg from the Nobilitie of so many famous ancestores"), though still young and in a "forward Bloominge springe" (ll. 45–46), he leads a "cause" (l. 53) approved by the author. "Worthelie atchyvinge" honor by "honorable desartes" (ll. 16–17), the noble lord has made only "happie begynnynges" (l. 22) and must "Go forward" with a "full & setled resolution" (ll. 22, 27) despite the "paines & perills" (l. 32) of an enterprise made worse by "Dangerous delayes" (l. 24). At least partly military (l. 33), this cause will recruit men of several nations or, more likely, several parts of England ("Countries" in l. 34 probably means "counties").

This description fits the earl of Essex very well; printed dedications from the period variously emphasize his youth, ancestry, early accomplishments, promise, and exemplary status. Certainly Essex matches the pattern better than the other military men identified in this manuscript (Thomas Burgh or Francis Vere, for example). Yet the work's nature and contents, as they may be deduced—a translation or commentary, some historical or contemporary narrative, perhaps—do not clearly indicate any one of the books dedicated to Essex after 1587 (the most likely period since Essex would earlier have been too young and too inexperienced for even the blind eye of flattery to ignore). It may be, of course, that the letter—even if sent to Essex—accompanied a manuscript treatise, or a printed volume with the letter-writer's manuscript commentary. Sir Roger Williams in his dedication of the *Briefe Discourse of Warre* (1590; STC 25732–33) mentions giving Essex some manuscript material in French, for example.

If the letter is to Essex and did accompany a printed work itself dedicated to him, two works seem most likely: John Hayward, *The first part of the life and raigne of King Henrie IIII* (1599; STC 12995) and Matthew Sutcliffe, *The Practice, Proceedings, And Lawes of armes* (1593; STC 23468). The fulsome dedication of the former led to the author's imprisonment (cf. ll, 51–60 and see *APC*, 1599–1601, p. 499 and *Cal SP Dom*, 1598–1601, pp. 539–40), and the episode lives for Bacon's quip that though he might not prove Hayward's treason, he could convict him of felony in stealing other men's work (see Birch, *Mem. Eliz.*, 2:439 and S. L. Goldberg, "Sir John Hayward, 'Politic' Historian," *Review of English Studies*, n.s. 6 [1955]:233–44). The fullest modern discussion of the affair, including Hayward's illuminating answers to the charges brought against him, is Margaret Dowling, "Sir John Hayward's Troubles over *His* [*sic*] *Life of Henry IV*," *Library* 11 (1930–31):212–24. W. W. Greg reproduces the notorious dedication and gives a translation in

"Samuel Harsnett and Hayward's *Henry IV*," rpt. in J. C. Maxwell, ed., *The Collected Papers of Sir Walter Greg* (Oxford: Clarendon Press, 1966), pp. 424–36. I quote the most relevant passage from that translation:

> For indeed you [Essex] are great, both in present estimation and in the expectation of future time, you in whom Fortune, formerly blind, may appear to have recovered sight, inasmuch as she is eager to load with honours one who is distinguished by all the virtues. Therefore if you shall deign to receive him [Henry, i.e., Hayward's book] with a glad countenance, he will shelter in great security under the shadow of your name (like Homer's Teucer under the shield of Ajax). May Almighty God long preserve Your Highness safe for me and the common weal, so that we, defended and avenged by your powerful right hand, both in faith and arms, may enjoy a long continuance alike of security and glory.

Although Hayward's book strikes the modern reader as far from a martial discourse, his contemporaries cited several passages that seemed to deride the quality of the troops Elizabeth had given Essex for the Irish expedition (see Dowling, "Sir John Hayward's Troubles," pp. 213 and 215–16).

Sutcliffe's subject matter, largely reformation of military discipline elaborately festooned with historical citations, more nearly approaches the implied contents of the work mentioned in letter 81. Moreover, his long epistle dedicatory often reproduces the sentiment and nears the wording of this item. He has been encouraged by

> that expectation, which all this nation hath of your heroical actions. God hath placed your Lordship as it were on a high stage in this estate. neuer man had greater fauour of the beholders, nor was more likely to obtaine a singular applause of the people. all mens eyes are fixed vpon you, to see what effectes will follow those vertues, and noble partes, the which already haue made your name honourable. as others choose ease, so your Lordship hath followed the wearisome trauailes of warres. (B2r-v)

The author of item 81 takes his leave "thus homely like a soldier" (l. 74) and Sutcliffe claims to write after "dangerous experience both in France, Italy, Flanders, and Portugall" (B4v). (This last claim makes it difficult to believe that this Sutcliffe is to be identified with the Dean of Exeter, as he is by *DNB* and Frances B. Troup, "Some Biographical Notes on Dr. Matthew Sutcliffe, Dean of Exeter, 1588–1629," *Transactions of the Devonshire Association for the Advancement of Science, Literature, and Art* 23 [1891]:171–96.) Sutcliff concludes his dedication,

> The successe I commit to God, the care to you Lordship, and others whom it concerneth: beseeching the Almightie, that is Lord of armies, and gouernour of all our actions, so to direct the affaires of state vnder the gouernance of

our gracious Soueraigne, & giue that fauour to your endeuours, that the glory of the English nation by your noble deedes may be increased. . . . (C1r-v)

If this letter's original did accompany one of these two printed books, its date would be approximately that of their publication, 1599 and 1593, respectively.

82 / 23 May 1610

Date: Given in the identical account in *Commons Journals* (1772), 1:431–32 and Add. MS. 48119, ff. 86r-v (transcript) and ff. 168r-v (debate). See also Foster, *Proc. Parliament 1610,* 2:107–13 (a transcript of the B. L. MS, omitting ff. 86r-v).

The immediate matter of impositions and the larger principle of Parliament's freedom of debate were central in the fourth session (February–June 1610) of James's first parliament. For a discussion of the legal aspects, see G.D.G. Hall, "Impositions and the Courts, 1554–1606," *Law Quarterly Review* 69 (1953): 200–18, esp. pp. 200–205 and n. 15 on John Bate; for the free speech issue, see Foster, *Proc. Parliament 1610,* 1:xi–xxi and passim.

Petition 82 is a petition of right drawn by Sir Edwin Sandys as chairman of the committee of grievances; presumably it was written late 22 May 1610; it was submitted, amended, and passed by Commons on 23 May 1610. The version here incorporates the amendments.

83 / before 31 August 1589; ca. 1584(?)

Date: Since this "letter" foresees Robert Cecil's marriage as a future prospect, it must have been composed before 31 August 1589, when he married Frances Brooke. Folger MS. X.d.212 (an eighteenth-century copy) implies 1586 as the letter's date, and Louis Wright, ed., *Advice to a Son* (Ithaca, N.Y.: Cornell University Press, for the Folger Library, 1962) gives ca. 1584.

If the title page of *Certaine Precepts . . . mans life* (1617; STC 4897)—basically this letter with various other moral advices appended—may be believed, a number of "pocket Manuscripts" of Burghley's advice were long in circulation. Whether the printed editions (another in 1637 reproduces 1617 closely) do derive from "a more perfect Copy" may be doubted. Aside from common errors of Jacobean printing (e.g., substituting "Chap." for "Precept" in one heading and "Precept VII" for "Precept VIII" in another), the 1617 edition omits one of the manuscript's most striking remarks, the anachronistic allusion to Ralegh and Essex (which must date from later than the body of the text), and adds quasi-redundant padding, e.g., "Precept II" concludes, ". . . for Souldyers in Peace, are like Chimneyes in Summer, like Dogges past Hunting, or Women, when their beautie is done. As a person of quallitie once noted to the like effect, in these Verses following . . . [four doggerel lines]" (A7r-v). Earlier in this same precept, the 1617 edition adds an entire paragraph elaborating upon the necessity for a middle course (between a woman "of . . . absolute perfection" and one "base and deformed") when one chooses a wife. Although most printed and manuscript versions do not have very great substantive differences, the order of Burghley's admonitions does vary.

The literary genre to which this item belongs is discussed in W. Lee Ustick, "Advice to a Son: A Type of Seventeenth Century Conduct Book," *Studies in Philology* 29 (1932):409–41 and Agnes M. C. Latham, "Sir Walter Ralegh's *Instructions to his Son*" in H. Davis and H. Gardner, eds., *Elizabethan and Jacobean Studies Presented to Frank Percy Wilson* (Oxford: Clarendon Press, 1959), pp. 199–218. See item 123.

84 /

Although Bedell has not been traced nor the addressee of this letter discovered, a possibility exists that it was sent to one of the poets represented or mentioned in this manuscript. Such requests for poetical piecework from very humble sources were common enough to shape an episode in Thomas Dekker's and John Webster's *North-ward Hoe* (1607; STC 6539). Doll Hornet hopes to lure Bellamont, a character sometimes thought to be modeled on George Chapman, with this plan: ". . . say such a Lady sends for him, about a sonnet or an epitaph for her child that died at nurse, or for some deuice about a maske or so . . ." (Act 2; C4r). Later, when forced actually to specify a task for Bellamont's talents, Doll requests "12. poesies for a dozen of cheese trenchers" (Act 3; D3v).

85 / ca. February 1613(?)

Date: Suggested by Culliford, *William Strachey*, p. 133, but in fact even the identification of "W.S." for Strachey depends upon the Virginia reference (and Strachey's earlier appearance in this manuscript). Strachey lost a suit for debt at this time (8 February 1613) and was certainly in financial trouble.

86 / after 15 February 1612/13; before autumn 1614(?)

Date: The manuscript's rough concentration on the period 1613–14 in ff. 60–65 suggests the tentative date for this item. Chapman suffered financial difficulties so often and so long that the situation itself cannot provide much aid. C. J. Sisson and Robert Butman, "George Chapman 1612–1622: Some

New Facts," *Modern Language Review* 46 (1951): 185–90, have shown that Chapman was certainly out of London between mid-1615 and mid-1617 and probably left in the autumn of 1614.

87 / after 6 November 1612

Date: Chapman joined Prince Henry's entourage almost as soon as James arrived in England (ll. 1–2; cf. Chapman, *Poems*, p. 480 and E. C. Wilson, *Prince Henry and English Literature* [Ithaca, N.Y.: Cornell University Press, 1946], p. 145 n. 45). This item's date must be shortly after Henry's death on 6 November 1612.

88 / after 6 November 1612

Date: As with item 87, Henry's death forms a *terminus a quo.*

Chapman's "two yeares studie & writinge imposed by his highnes" (ll..9–10) may not be meant literally. If it is, then three periods seem possible: (1) 1609–11, the interval between the publication of *Twelue Bookes* [of the *Iliad*] (STC 13633) and of the complete *Iliad* (STC 13634); (2) 1611–13, the interval between the completed *Iliad* translation and the period following Henry's death, presumably devoted to the *Odyssey* (eventually published, in the same manner as the *Iliad*, in 1614–15); (3) late 1612–late 1614, the interval between Henry's deathbed promise (l. 8) and the flurry of S.R. entries for Chapman's translations (i.e., 2 November 1614). Only the last of these three possibilities would influence the item's conjectural date, and the adjacent material apparently concerning Chapman's masque (item 89) may strengthen the case for mid-1613. For further bibliographical details of the Homeric translations, see Chapman, *Poems*, pp. 479–85 and Allardyce Nicoll, ed., *Chapman's Homer*, Bollingen Series 41, 2 vols. (1956; reprint ed., Princeton, N.J.: Princeton University Press, 1967).

The "annext Peticion" (ll. 5–6) may be item 139 (see Commentary). Certainly Northampton would be a "competent Iudge" (l. 12); even his enemies confessed him learned. Chapman apparently never received compensation or reward from the court.

89 / after 15 February 1612/13

Date: Chambers (*Eliz. Stage*, 3:262) and others agree that in this letter Chapman demands reward, or a larger reward, for his part in *The Memorable Maske of . . . the Middle Temple, and Lyncolns Inne* (1613; STC 4981–82), presented 15 February 1613 and published shortly thereafter (the S.R. entry, 27 January, is assumed to be a mistake for "February"). Certainly the letter has Chapman's stylistic quirks and bears his indignation's imprint. The masque's title page declares, "*Supplied, Aplied, Digested, and written, By* GEO: CHAPMAN" (cf. l. 38: "the wryter, and in part Inventor"). James, who "made the maskers kisse his hand at parting" (Chamberlain, *Letters*, 1:425), especially liked the masque, and Chamberlain describes it in lengthy admiration (cf. ll. 27–29: "yt in that Royall assemblie, for wch it was ordayned . . . it did not displease"). Chapman's bitterness has some documentary justification: just such a list of disbursements appears in Christopher Brooke's balance sheet for the masque (W. P. Baildon, ed., *The Records of . . . Lincoln's Inn: The Black Books*, 4 vols. [Lincoln's Inn, 1897–1902], 2:154–57). Although John Dowland's pay "for playing of lutes" appears (p. 156), Chapman's name does not; Inigo Jones's receipt for £110, dated 20 January 1613 (i.e., before the performance) survives (p. 157 n).

Thus, if Chapman wrote this letter (as all scholars agree since Dobell's first attribution), it must have been written after the masque's performance and probably after Prince Henry's death on 6 November 1612 (cf. "ye late Princis tyme") and probably before Chapman's departure from London (see Commentary on item 86). In "The Case for the Attribution of a Chapman Letter," *Studies in Philology* 72 (1975): 72–84, Tucker Orbison surveys a mass of evidence, including the language of this letter and Chapman's relations with possible recipients, in an attempt to narrow the date further. He links this letter with the *Andromeda Liberata* scandal and thus believes "we can consequently establish spring 1614 as the earliest date for the letter in question" (p. 79). I am not so confident of the connection with *Andromeda Liberata,* but it is possible.

Addressee: Chamberlain (*Letters*, 1:425) correctly describes Sir Edward Phelips, Master of the Rolls, and Richard Martin (see item 92) as "chiefe dooers and undertakers"; Christopher Brooke represented Lincoln's Inn. Any of these men might be plausible recipients, but Phelips, who had patronized Chapman in the past (see *Poems*, p. 445 and the dedications to Petrarch's "Seven Penitential Psalms," the *Maske,* and the 1611 *Iliads*) seems the most likely (cf. ll. 1–3: ". . . once fortunate in your . . . good . . . opinion . . . ye discontinuance of your woonted kindnes & affection"). Chapman stayed on good terms with Brooke, apparently, since he contributed a commendatory sonnet to Brooke's *The Ghost of Richard the Third* in 1614 (see Chapman, *Poems*, pp. 367–68.) Having rejected Sir George Buck and Thomas Howard, earl of Suffolk, Orbison (see above, *Date*) also settles on Phelips (d. 11 September 1614) as the likeliest recipient.

90 / 14 December 1610

Richard Martin, M.P., successful lawyer, and Recorder of London, presumably writes here as secretary of the Virginia Company. See Culliford, *William Strachey,* pp. 123 and 126.

91 / ca. mid-1613; before 13 November 1613

Date: Ferryman writes (ll. 24–26) as if either (a) the formulae for life in the hospital had not yet been announced or (b) he had not heard of them. At the second governors' meeting (30 June 1613), some procedures were discussed and entered in the Charterhouse Minute Book; Thomas Sutton's bequest was not free of legal controversy until the Court of Exchequer decision of 2 June 1613, confirmed by Letters Patent of 22 June. Ferryman appears among the first twelve of seventeen men admitted to the Hospital at the "Assemblie holden at the hospital of Kinge James, founded in Charterhouse . . . at the humble petition and onlie costs and charges of Thomas Sutton . . . thirteenth daye of November Anno Dny one thousand six hundred and thirteene . . ." (*ex* communication of the Registrar, Charterhouse). The Charterhouse Brothers' Book also records, "Peter Ferryman entered S[utton's] H[ospital] 3.1614 and dyed on Wednesday the 28th Sept. 1642." See also G. S. Davies, *Charterhouse in London* (J. Murray, 1921), pp. 198–202 and 213.

92 /

Date: See Commentary on items 91 and 93.

93 / before 13 November 1613(?)

Date and Addressee: This letter's position in the manuscript suggests that Jonson is recommending Ferryman for a place in Sutton's Hospital. Other details make this suggestion probable: a John Leech was secretary to the earl of Pembroke in 1613 (see *HMC Downshire,* 4:193 and 198 and Herford and Simpson, 1:200); Pembroke became a governor of Charterhouse in 1614 (see Davies, *Charterhouse in London,* p. 352); Pembroke and his family long patronized Jonson. See Commentary on items 91 and 94.

94 / before 13 November 1613(?)

Date and Addressee: This item appears to be a more detailed version of item 93, i.e., a request to aid another man (Peter Ferryman?) directed by Jonson to a great man's secretary. Ellesmere had been named a governor of Charterhouse in Sutton's will, and his secretary's name was Thomas Bond (see R. C. Bald, *John Donne: A Life* [Oxford: Clarendon Press, 1970], p. 194 n. 1 and John Davies, *Scourge of Folly* [1611; STC 6341], p. 135). *DNB* is confused about Bond.

96 / ca. October 1591

Date: The famous battle here recounted took place 31 August–1 September 1591; the news was "stale" in London by October's end (*Cal SP Dom*, 1591–94, p. 117). Ralegh, it is thought, wrote an excellent and effective account, *A Report . . . of the fight about the . . . Açores*, published anonymously late in 1591 (S.R. entry 23 November; STC 20651). Ralegh mentions several formal interrogations of survivors—"two of the *Reuenges* owne companie, brought home in a ship of Lime [Regis] from the Ilandes, examined by some of the Lordes, and others. . . . This agreeth also with an examination taken by Syr *Frances Godolphin*, of 4. other Mariners of the same shippe. . ." (B3r). This item may be one such account or merely a newsletter; one writer thought that the defeat was being "disguised" for chauvinistic purposes (*Cal SP Dom*, 1591–94, p. 117).

97 / December 1610

The fifth session of James's first Parliament opened 16 October 1610 and ended 9 February 1611. For mention of this item and a discussion of such form letters, see Foster, *Proc. Parliament 1610*, 2:6 n. 4 and 380.

98 /

This item may be a letter fragment, but it sounds more like a school exercise, perhaps related to the next item.

99 / 11 May 1615–11 May 1619

Date: Nicholas Gray was selected Charterhouse's first headmaster on 19 July 1614 and confirmed 3 December 1614; Henry Bagley was the first usher of the new school, serving until succeeded by Nicholas Gray's brother Robert sometime in 1619 (see William Haig Brown, *Charterhouse, Past and Present* [Godalming, England: Stedman, 1879], pp. 137–42). Item 99 must fall, then, into the period May 1615 (the first May in the school's existence) to May 1619, assuming that Robert Gray did not take up his post as usher before mid-1619. If the manuscript continues the approximate chronological grouping visible in the surrounding items, this letter probably belongs to the earliest part of the possible span.

Sender: B. Marsh and F. A. Crisp, eds., *Alumni Carthusiani: A Record of the Foundation Scholars of Charterhouse, 1614–1872* (Privately printed, 1913) note ". . . of the School outside the Foundation the official records are silent; and a complete School Register could only be formed for some thirty years further back than that known to Carthusians as the work of the Rev. W. D. Parish (i.e., within the nineteenth century)" (p. xvii). *Alumni Carthusiani*, pp. 1–4, includes the following foundation scholars whose surnames begin with *W* in the relevant period:

19 July 1614	Edmund Wyffe [or Edmund Wythe] who later graduated Corpus Christi, Cambridge (B.A. 1624, M.A. 1628) and made a will dated 17 February 1667/8
	Frauncis Wittye who died at Oxford 11 August 1623, leaving John Wittye (his father?) as beneficiary
	Thomas Woodshawe who became an apprentice 11 December 1617 and bound April 1618 to Anthony Porter, a draper
	Thomas Wyllett bound to Edward Heath, girdler
	Erasmus Walkerleye, son of John Walkerleye was bound November 1619 to John Sorocold, apothecary
11 December 1617	John Wade who was apprenticed February 1622/23 to John Sharpe, merchant tailor

Although none of these students' fathers apparently had the Christian name Ralph, the "Rafe" of item 99's signature may be a familiar name of some sort.

101 / late 1614(?); before 16 March 1615

Date: Chamberlain, in a letter of 16 March 1615 describing James's reception in Cambridge on 12 March, reports that Tomson (or Thomson) had been pardoned and allowed to retain his livings (*Letters*, 1:588). John Nichols, *Progresses . . . of . . . James I*, 4 vols. (J. B. Nichols, 1828), 3:59 n., mentions a letter from Tomson to Coke, written from Cambridge Castle (where Tomson was imprisoned) and dated 7 November 1614; C. H. Cooper, *Annals of Cambridge*, 5 vols. (Cambridge: Warwick, 1842–53), 3:72–73 n. prints this letter and three others concerning the episode. This petition may have been written when Tomson learned of James's visit to Cambridge. A complete text also appears in Folger MS. V.a. 402, Brian Cave's Commonplace Book (ca. 1625), ff. 11r-v; the letter continues in the manner begun here.

Tomson had been imprisoned for clipping gold and thus earned the title "auri tonsor."

102 / May–June 1603(?); May 1603–August 1604

Date: J. D. Mackie published a transcript of an inferior version (Bodleian Add. MS. D. 109, ff. 148r–149r) of this item in " 'A Loyall Subiectes Advertisement' as to the Unpopularity of James I.'s Government in England, 1603–4," *Scottish Historical Review* 23 (1925):1–17. Despite the fact that Mackie worked from a text whose corruption sometimes makes it unintelligible, his conclusions concerning the date of its original composition are convincing. Mackie believes the reference to the mastership of the rolls places the document's origin after Edward Bruce's appointment (18 May 1603), while "the references to the diplomatic situation seem to prove that the memorial was presented before August 19–29, 1604, when James definitely came to terms with Spain by the Treaty of Lôndon, and probably before the Treaty of Hampton Court with France (July 20–30, 1603)" (ibid., p. 8). Since the Hampton Court treaty was ambiguous, Mackie argues that the writer may have considered England "unpledged," so the later *terminus ante quem* of 20 October 1604, when James adopted the title "King of Great Britain" (cf. l. 160), should probably be accepted. "Summer 1603" is a strong probability for the original's date, then, and "May 1603–August 1604" a near-certainty.

Sender: Mackie (ibid., pp. 6–8) assigned the authorship to Henry Howard, later first earl of Northampton, on several bases: the anti-Spanish bias (associated with Essex and his supporters); the stature with James to permit such a frank, albeit obsequious, memorandum; the appearance in one of Howard's early letters to James of the Ovidian tag (see l. 20 and Sir David Dalrymple, Lord Hailes, ed., *The Secret Correspondence of Sir Robert Cecil with James VI. . . .* [Edinburgh, 1766], p. 60). Mackie must explain, however, the document's strong Protestant tone, since Howard was almost certainly a practicing Roman Catholic; it is also true that Howard was quite unscrupulous in religious matters, especially when maintaining James's favor and his own cherished advancement at James's court. The Ovidian tag is extremely common, surprisingly unesoteric for the "Asiatic" style—the adjective is James's—usually written by Howard (see ibid., p. 116).

Mackie's knowledge and hypothesis concerning the transmission of his text—from a secretary of Robert Carr, earl of Somerset, to John Packer, secretary to the duke of Buckingham and hence in the Packer family to one van den Bempde and thence to G. M. Fortescue who donated the manuscript with many others to the Bodleian in 1872—may have strengthened his belief that Northampton wrote the original. Even Mackie's text is a copy (and I doubt its putative Scottish origin seriously; see his " 'A Loyall Subiectes Advertisement,' " pp. 5–6), and that copy is now known not to be unique. This Folger version is generally a better text, though it omits (probably as a result of eye-skip) two short passages totaling about thirty words. I have found two other copies: Harl. MS. 35, ff. 460r–462v and Harl. MS. 677, ff. 33r–35v. The first of these has the best text of all four identified versions; it definitely lies behind the Bodleian text and must date from before 1628 when the copyist, Ralph Starkie, died. This text also amplifies the title with "written by an unknown Author in An? *1603.*" The other Harleian copy probably dates from the second half of the seventeenth century and was in Bishop Stillingfleet's collection. For further discussion of these two manuscript collections, see A. G. Watson, *The Library of Sir Simonds D'Ewes* (British Museum, 1966) and C. E. Wright, *Fontes Harleiani* (British Museum, 1972). The more surviving copies (assuming roughly equal textual quality and equally early dates), the less secure the inferences from the hypothetical provenance of any one of them. Mackie's ascription of authorship should be weighed carefully, then, in view of the evidence offered by this manuscript and the two copies of the same document in the Harleian collection.

103/before 30 June 1592

Date: This attribution rests entirely on the date of the next item (104), which is apparently the anonymous lord's response to Sidley's request, dated "this Last of Iune. 1592./."

108/6 October 1603

Date and Addressee: Cal SP Dom, 1603–10, p. 44, lists a docket of this letter giving Winchester as the place from which it was sent and the date as 6 October 1603. The lord mayor of London and the aldermen controlled appointments to the office of coalmeter and even without item 109, one would assume that James's letter had been sent to Sir Robert Lee, the current lord mayor.

The appointment of coalmeters (a lucrative and undemanding post) caused conflict between monarch and city for many years as the *Analytical Index to . . . the Remembrancia,* ed. W. H. and H. C. Overall (E. J. Francis, 1878) makes clear. For details of coal metage and conflicts over appointments, see John U. Nef, *The Rise of the British Coal Industry,* 2 vols. (Routledge, 1932), esp. 2:251–59. For William Huxley, see items 16 and 109.

109/after 1 November 1603(?)

Date: James's phrase, "late Lord Maior," probably places this item after 29 September 1603 when Lee's successor, Sir Thomas Bennet, was elected and (in view of the date known for item 108) probably after 28 October when the new lord mayor took office. Since it appears immediately after an item of 6 October 1603, James's letter does not allude, presumably, to Lee's death (22 December 1605).

Addressee: Probably Sir Thomas Bennet (ca. 1550–16 February 1626), lord mayor of London, 1603–4.

110/

Although many men must have been proud to mention their service with Sidney, the only named individual in this manuscript who does say so is Peter Ferryman (see petition 91). If this letter does seek aid for Ferryman, it means he was imprisoned in the Fleet, and that in turn may explain the documents relating to changes in the appeals procedure associated with the complaints of prisoners in the Queen's Bench (see items 60, 61, and Commentary). Ferryman certainly had financial difficulties in 1609 (see item 51 and Commentary) and had to demonstrate poverty in order to qualify for admission to Sutton's Hospital (the Charterhouse; see item 91).

114/21 February 1589/90–9 February 1603/4

Date: Since the countess is described as a "widdowe," this letter must have been written after the death of her husband, Ambrose Dudley, in February 1590, but before, of course, her own death in February 1604.

Her brother, William Russell, preceded Thomas Burgh as lord deputy of Ireland (see item 123 and Collins, *Letters,* 2:25)

118, 119/

Sender: "N. Coote" cannot be positively identified. If this manuscript or its compiler has some connection with the Inns of Court or of Chancery, N. Coote may be Nicholas Coote, who matriculated at Trinity, Cambridge (1588), entered Lincoln's Inn 12 February 1589/90, received a knighthood from James on 25 July 1603, and died 1 September 1633. This last date, somewhat uncertain, appears in *Visitation of Essex,* pt. 2, Harl. Soc. Pub., 14:565. Abraham de Vlieger, *Historical and Genealogical Record of the Coote Family* (Lausanne, Switz.: Bridel, 1900) provides a fairly full but unreliable pedigree.

The Lincoln's Inn register shows that Coote entered from New Inn, an inn of chancery associated with the Middle Temple. The move from an inn of chancery to an inn of court other than the "parent" inn, while not unknown—

Thomas More, for instance, moved from New Inn to Lincoln's Inn—is unusual, and it may imply that Coote drew his friends from Thavies' or
Furnivall's (attached to Lincoln's Inn), rather than from New Inn. If so, then
he might have known Roydon, who attended Thavies' earlier in the decade and
may have continued his association at least until 1593, for he remained in
London during that period (see G. C. Moore Smith, "Matthew Roydon,"
Modern Language Review 9 [1914]:97–98 and Mark Eccles, "George Chapman's Early Years," *Studies in Philology* 43 [1946]: 176–93). Another figure
fairly common in this manuscript, Richard Martin, entered the Middle Temple
from New Inn on 20 February 1586/7. Though none of the other individuals
in this manuscript can be shown to have attended an inn of court or of chancery
at precisely the date given here by Coote, some at least must have overlapped
Nicholas Coote's stay there.

Addressee: One doubts that this person could be the priest William Harrington, executed in February 1594, although he attended Thavies' and Lincoln's
Inn about this time (see Fr. John Morris, "The Martyrdom of William Harrington," *The Month* 20 [1874]:411–23 and R. C. Bald, *John Donne: A Life*
[Oxford: At the University Press, 1970], pp. 58–59). In 1607, both Sir
Nicholas Coote and a "Lord Harrington" were involved in Lionel Cranfield's
efforts to control the starch market (see *HMC Sackville* [*Knole*], 1:155), but
that Harrington belongs to the family of Harington of Exton, none of whom
would be both untitled and a young man or adult (as Coote's correspondent
must be) at this time.

120/

Date, Addressee, and Sender: It seems most likely that all three items on this
page refer to Harrington and that this third letter responds to an appeal from
the imprisoned man. "R.I." may be, however, Roger Jones (son of the sheriff
of London, 1604–5); he had a number of dealings with Chapman traced by
C. J. Sisson and Robert Butman in "George Chapman 1612–1622: Some New
Facts," *Modern Language Review* 46 (1951):185–90. This second possibility
would push the item's date forward to after 1607, perhaps as late as November
1616 when the Joneses's relations with Chapman dissolved in suit and counter-
suit.

121/after 26 February 1602

Date: This petition must have been written after 26 February 1602, when the
sixth and last Lord Burgh died, still a child. See letter, 122, and Commentary.

The education and charge of Robert Burgh had been given to Thomas Bil-
son, bishop of Winchester, because Thomas Burgh's death left the family in

near-poverty (see *HMC Salisbury*, 11:258–59). For details of young Burgh's illness and death, see *HMC Salisbury*, 12:59–60 and 65–66.

122 / July 1603–5 December 1603

Date: Cecil's references to "publick dutye" and "reason of State" suggest that his sister-in-law, daughter of Thomas Burgh and wife of George Brooke, had written seeking Cecil's help in her husband's trial for his part in the "Bye Plot." Brooke was attainted (with others) in July 1603 and executed for treason on 5 December of the same year. Many letters from Brooke and others concerning his case survive in the Hatfield collection, but the Historical Manuscripts Commission reports no original of this letter.

Not only do Cecil's references to state matters make it unlikely that this letter refers to problems raised by Robert Burgh's death (see petition 121), but Cecil's usual practice suggests that he would have eagerly aided a claim that turned solely upon familial aggrandizement. See item 65 and Commentary.

123 / 16 November 1587–16 November 1595

Date: Since this letter is signed "Thomas Burgh" and dated from Brill, it seems likely that it was written while he was governor there. He received the governorship on 6 February 1586/7 and retained the title until his death. Burgh did not, in fact, actually remain in Brill for this entire period. He served as ambassador to Scotland in 1593 (see *HMC Salisbury*, 4:296), went back to the Low Countries, and finally returned to England around 2 February 1595/6 (see ibid., 6:15), suffering from an old illness (see ibid., 5:406–7). Later he received his commission as lord deputy for Ireland (see ibid., 7:175, 186 and Collins, *Letters*, 2:24 and 25), where he died.

The letter of admonition and "favour" from a parent to a child appears often in manuscript collections of the period and in model letter-books published for edification and guidance. See item 83 and Commentary.

124 / after 4 May 1605; ca. mid-1605(?)

Date: This letter evidently initiates the series that deals with Chapman's and Jonson's imprisonment for referring to King James and his Scottish entourage in *Eastward Ho!* Dating of the imprisonment and the letters must account for certain facts: Jonson addresses Robert Cecil as "Salisbury" in letter 128's original and 4 May 1605, when Cecil received that title, thus becomes a *terminus a quo; Eastward Ho!* was entered in the S.R. on 4 September 1605; Jonson was at liberty by about 9 October 1605, when he ate a celebrated dinner with the future Gunpowder conspirators (Herford and Simpson, 11:578). Bibliographical evidence, most recently studied in R. W. Van Fossen's Revels edition of the play (Manchester: At the University Press, 1979), suggests textual revision during printing. The question thus becomes: which event, the performance of *Eastward Ho!* or the play's printing, caused the playwrights' imprisonment? If a performance, why was the play licensed for printing without the offending passages removed? If printing, how could such an offensive play be received into the S.R., only later to cause such a furor that two authors were imprisoned and the text had to be revised in the course of printing? R. E. Brettle, "*Eastward Ho*, 1605; By Chapman, Jonson, and Marston; Bibliography and Circumstances of Production," *Library* 9 (1928–29):287–302, suggests that an unlicensed production took place during the summer of 1605 and that printing after entry in the S.R. had already begun when full knowledge of the play's contents reached the court sometime during the autumn. James and the court certainly had left the city for some months in the summer, and the Lord Chamberlain is known to have accompanied the king for some portions at least of his progress. Brettle cites Chapman's later reference (letter 125, ll. 3–5) to the Lord Chamberlain's absence and implies that the playwrights were (still?) imprisoned in mid-September. While this outline seems the best solution to date, it does not fully acknowledge that neither Chapman nor Jonson ever explicitly mentions the *printing* of *Eastward Ho!* in these letters. Such an omission might be a cautious preparation for a claim that the actors, with or without John Marston (see this item, ll. 5–6), were wholly responsible for the offense, or it may indicate that printing did not cause the authors' difficulties. Two final points: Chapman refers to false informants rather than a governmental official as the source of the playwrights' troubles (letter, 125, ll. 7–12; cf. Herford and Simpson, 1:140 for Jonson's similar claims); if the storm broke after entry in the S.R., then some official must have passed the play as fit for printing. Probably we should end with W. W. Greg's response to Brettle's argument: "perhaps no certain conclusion is possible on the evidence before us" (*Library* 9 [1928–29]:304). In view of these difficulties, it has seemed best not to be too precise and to interpret "ca. mid-1605" very generously.

125 / after 4 May 1605; ca. mid-1605(?)

Date: Another letter, presumably, in the *Eastward Ho!* series; see letters, 124–133 and Commentary on 124.

126 / after 4 May 1605; ca. mid-1605(?)

Date: See Commentary on item 124. The only question about the date of this item arises from Chapman's allusions (ll. 1–2) to having been freed, an event of uncertain date. The "propagation of . . . fauours" that Chapman seeks may be some permission for *Eastward Ho!* or for another play.

Addressee: Presumably Thomas Howard, earl of Suffolk and Lord Chamberlain. Chambers suggests (*Eliz. Stage,* 3:255) that a passage in Chapman's commendatory poem "In Seianvm," published with the quarto *Sejanus,* may refer directly to the playwrights' difficulties over *Eastward Ho!* Lines 150–58 read:

> Most noble *Suffolke,* who by Nature Noble,
>   And iudgement vertuous, cannot fall by Fortune,
> Who when our Hearde, came not to drinke, but trouble
>   The *Muses* waters, did a Wall importune,
> (Midst of all assaults) about their sacred Riuer;
>   In whose behalfes, my poore Soule, (consecrate
> To poorest Vertue) to the longest Liuer,
>   His Name, in spight of Death shall propagate.
>
> (*Poems,* p. 362)

Dating *Sejanus*'s publication precisely has not proved possible; it was entered 2 November 1604 and the rights transferred to its eventual publisher on 6 August 1605. It is assumed that publication preceded Northumberland's commission to the Tower, 27 November 1605. Chapman may, of course, refer to some earlier favor (as in "propagation of . . . fauours"), but the letter's and the poem's explicit references to defending the poet(s) against hostility and interceding with other authorities (cf. "did a Wall importune") make the connection more likely.

Esmé Stuart ("Lorde Dawbuey," l. 8) was a popular man about court and was interested in dramatists and their work. He participated in the so-called masque of lords on 1 January 1604 (Chambers, *Eliz. Stage,* 3:280 and see the full account by Carleton cited in *Cal SP Dom,* 1603–10, p. 68). Later, he appeared in Jonson's "Hue and Cry After Cupid" (the Haddington masque): see Chambers, *Eliz. Stage,* 3:381–82 and Stephen Orgel, ed., *Complete Masques of Ben Jonson* (New Haven, Conn.: Yale University Press, 1971), pp. 107–21. D'Aubigny may have become involved with the culprits through Jonson, whose patron he was and who dedicated the folio *Sejanus* to him. See *Sejanus,* ed. Jonas Barish (New Haven, Conn.: Yale University Press, 1965), p. 25 n. and p. 182 n. and Herford and Simpson, 1, passim and 9:576–77 for Jonson's other references to and relations with D'Aubigny.

127 / after 4 May 1605; ca. mid-1605(?)

Date: See Commentary on letter, 124. With this letter, Jonson makes his first contribution to the many appeals addressed by the jailed dramatists to the Lord Chamberlain and others. The copyist may have chosen to mark the separation between Chapman's letters and Jonson's with the blank side (f. 89v).

Addressee: Jonson writes, probably, to the Lord Chamberlain (see l. 25, "youre Comfortable worde" and the preceding letter from Chapman), but he may be seeking the help of some other influential nobleman, perhaps Esmé Stuart. A holograph of another letter from Jonson (item 128 in this manuscript), this time to Cecil, mentions that the playwright becomes "a most humble suitor to your lordship . . . with the ho. Lord Chamberlain (to whom I have in like manner petitioned). . . ." (*HMC Salisbury,* 17:605–6). It is possible that Jonson's phrase alludes to the original of item 127. See Herford and Simpson, 1:193–96 for transcripts of both letters.

128 / after 4 May 1605; ca. mid-1605(?)

Addressee: A holograph version of this letter, endorsed "the most noblyvirtuous and thrice-honoured Earl of Salisbury" is at Hatfield (*HMC Salisbury,* 17:605–6) and provides the *terminus a quo* for the entire series of letters concerning *Eastward Ho!* by addressing Cecil as "Salisbury" (see Commentary on letter 124). Herford and Simpson call the Folger text a "first draft" and collate it with the holograph (Herford and Simpson, 1:194–96).

129 / after 4 May 1605(?); ca. mid-1605(?)

Date: This letter's position in the manuscript and Jonson's reference to "my commyttment" (l. 5) strongly suggest that it forms part of the *Eastward Ho!* series.

Addressee: The manuscript has a hint of chronological arrangement here: first a sequence by Chapman, then a parallel (?) sequence by Jonson. Perhaps this letter is Jonson's initial plea to his friend and patron, Esmé Stuart, who certainly did work for the poets' release (see letter, 126, and Commentary and Jonson's letter, 131, again probably to Esmé Stuart).

130 / After 4 May 1605(?); ca. mid-1605(?)

Date and Addressee: Jonson's reference to imprisonment with "a worthy Friend, one Mr Chapman" (ll. 6–7) clearly links this letter to the *Eastward Ho!* group. Identification of the addressee depends upon one's estimate of the noble ladies who had both influence at court and concern for Jonson. Felix Schelling guessed the countess of Rutland; Herford and Simpson—more plausibly—suggest Lucy, countess of Bedford (Herford and Simpson, 1:197–98). She was a member of the Sidney family, as were the two Herbert brothers addressed in letters, 132 and 133.

131 / after 4 May 1605(?); ca. mid-1605(?)

Date and Addressee: References to imprisonment and to two prisoners suggest that Jonson writes on his own and Chapman's behalf concerning *Eastward Ho!* Chapman noted (letter, 126, ll. 7–9) that Esmé Stuart had acted as intermediary in securing the poets' release, and this letter is most probably addressed to that nobleman.

132, 133 / after 4 May 1605(?); ca. mid-1605(?)

Date and Addressees: These are the last two letters in the *Eastward Ho!* group and seem to have been written before the poets' release. Of the two Herbert brothers, William, earl of Pembroke, was the more generous and consistent patron of Jonson (see Herford and Simpson, 1:199–200).

135 / 28 November 1583

Date: 28 November 1583 appears at the end of all published texts of this letter.

This item is a version, perhaps from memory, of a section of Lipsius's letter to Martinus Lydius that appeared in *Iusti Lipsi epistolarvm selectarvm centuria prima* (1586; STC 15697) as letter number 58. The printed text of this passage runs:

> Definitum à Deo omne agnosco, quidquid euenit; trepido tamen dicere, peccata ipsa. quorum fontem à sola mala voluntate nostra esse censeam, suprema illa voluntate permittente. Exempli caussa. In Tarquinij adulterio, in caedibus ab Herode innocentum, duo specto: factum ipsum, & crimen. Factum à Deo definitum fateor, &'comprehendo sub fatali illa lege: crimen, quod soli voluntati inhaeret, non videor fateri posse, sine iniuria Dei. Caussam omnium rerum diuinam voluntatem statuo, omniumque euentuum etiamsi mali sint: at non caussam caussę medię, quoties ea mala. Alias quomodo effugimus, vt non auctor ille sit mali? vt non adprobator? Itaque ea quę ex (a) Actis aptissime adducis huc accommodo. Mortem Christi destinatam ab aeterno, proditionem Iude ab aeterno, mediaque omnia quae ad salutare illud opus ferrent: sed non crimina adnexa ipsis factis, quibus fundamentum in impia tantum voluntate.
>
>   *a* Acta Apostea 11 vide

Iusti Lipsi epistolarvm selectarvm centuria secunda (1590; STC 15698) was dedicated to Thomas Burgh.

138/17–27 April 1608

Date: This petition is discussed at length by Mark Eccles in "Chapman's Early Years," *Studies in Philology* 43 (1946): 176–93, esp. pp. 181–86. PRO C 25/65, Chapman's original bill of complaint, is dated 17 April 1608 (see Eccles, pp. 181–82 for partial transcript), so this informal personal petition presumably followed the formal one. With Eccles, one would assume that the petition was written before Woolfall's answer (27 April 1608), or at least before Chapman knew of it, since some information supplied by Woolfall does not appear here.

I have nothing to add to Eccles's account, except the observation that this item looks like a draft of Chapman's petition with changes and omissions, which, where they may be read, suggest a writer seeking the proper tone and phrase. The changes (or "corrections") do not resemble those usually made by the copyist.

139/after 6 November 1612–before 17 November 1615

Date: The limits are fixed by the dates of Prince Henry's death and Sir Thomas Challenor's; the latter, governor to the prince, is mentioned as a living witness in ll. 13–14.

Chapman may refer to this document in his letter to Northampton (item 88, ll. 5–6). Nothing in this item disturbs the tentative dating of Chapman's several pleas (ca. mid-1613), though the casual invocation of "attending, fower yeares our late lost Prince" (ll. 6–7) does not increase one's confidence in the earlier "two yeares studie & writinge imposed by his highnes" (item 88, ll. 9–10). What remains clear is that Chapman entered Henry's service "above Nine yeares" (item 87, l. 2) before the prince's death and that Henry encouraged Chapman to complete the *Iliad* and begin the *Odyssey* translations.

140/

Sender: This Thomas Spelman may be identical with the Thomas Spelman who was the son of Erasmus Spelman and grandson of Sir John Spelman of Narborough (see Walter Rye, ed., *Visitations of Norfolk, 1563, 1569, and 1613*, Harl. Soc. Pub., vol. 32 [1891], p. 265); another of Sir John's grandsons was the famous antiquarian, Sir Henry Spelman (1564?–1641), whose life span suggests that Thomas Spelman could have been alive in the period (ca. 1610–15) roughly indicated by item 140's position in the manuscript.

Index

Only the Introduction, Notes, and Commentary are fully indexed here; names of persons, places, and literary works appearing in the Annotations are also listed. Unidentified individuals represented only by initials in the manuscript are not indexed. Literary and dramatic works appear under their authors' names, and George Chapman's translations are entered under his name. Details of the manuscript itself are entered under "Folger MS. V.a. 321."